Articles on

Witchcraft, Magic and Demonology

A Twelve Volume Anthology
of Scholarly Articles

Edited with introductions by

Brian P. Levack
University of Texas

A Garland Series

Contents of Series

Volume 12

Witchcraft and Demonology in Art and Literature

edited with introductions by
Brian P. Levack

Garland Publishing, Inc.
New York & London 1992

Library of Congress Cataloging-in-publication Data

Witchcraft and demonology in art and literature / edited by Brian P. Levack
     p.   cm. — (Articles on witchcraft, magic and demonology ; v. 12)
    Reprint of works originally published 1917–1989.
    Includes bibliographical references.
    ISBN 0-8153-1035-8 (alk. paper)
    1. Witchcraft in art—History. 2. Witchcraft in literature—History.
3. Demonology in art—History. 4. Demonology in literature—History.
I. Levack, Brian P. II. Series.
BF1563.A77   1992 vol. 12
133.4'09 s—dc20
[700]   92-22872
                                               CIP

Printed on acid-free, 250-year-life paper
Manufactured in the United States of America

Contents

v

Series Introduction

The main purpose of this collection is to bring together a large number of scholarly articles on the subject of witchcraft, magic and demonology. These articles are drawn from a broad selection of journals in many different disciplines. They reflect the sustained interest of historians, anthropologists, legal scholars, psychologists, sociologists, art historians, and literary scholars on the subject. In one way or another they all deal with man's belief in and fear of supernatural evil.

In early modern Europe a witch was believed to be a person who not only practiced harmful magic but who also made a pact with the Devil and sometimes worshipped him in nocturnal assemblies. The magical powers of the witch were generally the concern of her neighbors, who accused her of causing physical harm or bringing about some kind of misfortune. The witch's commerce with the Devil, however, remained the main concern of the clergy and the educated elite, who believed that she was a heretic and apostate involved in a vast conspiracy to undermine Christianity and destroy the moral order. As a scholarly subject, witchcraft involves an investigation of both aspects of the witch's alleged crime. On the one hand it studies magic, which is the human exercise of some preternatural, supernatural, or occult power to produce empirical effects, and on the other hand it is concerned with demonology, the study of evil spirits and its alleged activities. Most of the articles in this collection are concerned with witchcraft in the full early modern European sense of the word, but some focus exclusively on magic, while others are concerned mainly with demonic spirits and their relations with humans.

The majority of the articles in this collection deal with the historical process of witch-hunting in Europe and America between 1450 and 1750. During these years the prosecution of more than 100,000 persons, mostly women, has led scholars to investigate the development of learned and popular beliefs regarding witchcraft, the social and religious tensions which resulted in accusations, the legal processes that were used to bring witches to trial, and the ultimate end of witchcraft prosecutions. Six of the twelve volumes deal with different aspects of this massive judicial assault on witchcraft. Volume 3 includes a variety of interpretations of the entire process of witch-hunting in Europe, while volumes 5, 6, 7, and 8 deal successively with local and regional witchcraft prosecutions in continental Europe, England, Scotland, and Colonial America. Volume 4 explores the large body of printed treatises on witchcraft that helped to spread learned witch beliefs throughout Europe and thus inspired and reinforced the prosecutions.

Three volumes treat themes that are closely related to the great European witch-hunt. Volume 2 studies the various beliefs regarding magic and the Devil that originated in the classical and medieval periods and eventually came together in the cumulative concept of witchcraft in the fifteenth and sixteenth centuries. Volume 9 is devoted to the subject of demonic possession and exorcism. Possession did not always involve the agency of a witch, but a number of witchcraft trials in the sixteenth and seventeenth centuries resulted from allegations that witches had commanded demons to take physical possession of other persons. Volume 10 addresses the question: why do witches, both in Europe during the early modern period and in other cultures at other periods of time, tend to be women? A further objective of that volume is to examine the social and economic context in which witchcraft accusations and prosecutions arose.

The remaining three volumes deal with topics that are only indirectly related to the witchcraft prosecutions of the early modern period. Volume 1 is devoted to anthropological studies of witchcraft and magic among non-literate peoples. This literature has had a strong influence on historical scholarship during the past twenty-five years, and it has contributed to a deeper understanding of the nature of witchcraft, magic and religion. Because of the theoretical value of this literature, the volume serves as an introduction to the entire collection. Volume 11 discusses the learned magic that was practiced during the Renaissance. Although this magic is not directly connected to witchcraft, it possesses enormous importance to the intellectual history of the early modern period and even made a contribution to the development of modern science. The final volume explores the ways in which witchcraft and demonology have served as themes in both art and literature.

The articles reproduced in these volumes were selected on the basis of many different criteria. Some were chosen because of the wealth of information they provide regarding particular witch-hunts or witch beliefs, while others were included because of the cogency of their arguments or the importance of their approaches to the problem of witchcraft. The great majority of the articles were written in the past thirty years, during which time the most valuable scholarship in the field has been done. A few articles, however, date from the late nineteenth and early twentieth centuries, when some of the pioneering work in this field was undertaken.

Introduction

Witchcraft and demonology have been themes of art and literature ever since the classical period. Woodcuts, engravings and paintings have given us rich representations of witches, demons, night-flight, and Sabbaths, while playwrights, poets and novelists have written about pacts with the Devil, enchantments, cases of possession, and witchcraft trials. This work testifies to the enormous power that witchcraft has exercised on the literary and artistic imagination.

The artistic and literary depictions of witches and demons have instrinsic worth as works of art or literature, but they also have much to offer the historian. Their most valuable function in this regard is to provide insights into the nature of the elite concept of witchcraft. Since witchcraft is to a large extent a mental construction, we must rely to a great extent on literary and visual evidence in order to understand how contemporaries viewed magical and demonic phenomena. We have already seen in Volume 4 how witchcraft treatises written by judges and clerics help to serve that purpose, since they often included detailed descriptions of witches' activities. Many of the visual depictions of the witch in the early modern period were based on these written descriptions. Indeed, some engravings and woodcuts were used to illustrate the printed editions of the treatises. The visual sources, however, provide more direct access to the contemporary imagination, and at times they suggest ideas that are not available in the text of the demonological treatises.

The visual evidence of witchcraft is extraordinarily rich, both in its detail and in its symbolism. There is, for example, no better representation of the witches' Sabbath than the engraving by the Polish artist Jan Ziarnko, a work included in Pierre de Lancre's *Tableau de l'inconstance* (1612). The same can be said of the numerous depictions of witches and their activities in the woodcuts of Hans Baldung Grien and the paintings of David Teniers the Younger. The symbolism of Baldung's work, moreover, gives us insights into contemporary attitudes toward female sexuality, as the articles by Dale Hoak show.

Iconographic evidence is central to our understanding of the way medieval and early modern Europeans viewed the Devil. Not only does it help us to trace the gradual transformation of pagan gods into demons and devils, but it also documents the change in attitudes toward the demonic during the late Middle Ages and the early modern period. One of the most striking developments was the more horrifying representation of both the Devil and Hell just prior to and during the Reformation. The heightened fear of the Devil that these images both reflected and created must be taken into account in any explanation of the great European witch-hunt.

Just as the iconographic sources provide access to the witch beliefs of early modern Europeans, they also provide occasional glimpses of their skepticism. In the case of Francisco Goya, who produced his witchcraft paintings and drawings in the late eighteenth and early nineteenth centuries, after the period of witch-hunting had passed, the skepticism was fully developed, and in his Black Paintings it was suffused with a pessimism rarely equaled in modern art. There was more humor but no less skepticism in Bernard Picart's engraving of a witch rising to the Sabbath on a monster (1732), which was modelled on the earlier work of Francesco Mazzola, and in William Hogarth's engraving "Credulity, Superstition and Fanaticism" (1762). Even in the artwork of the sixteenth and seventeenth centuries we encounter flashes of incredulity, which reflect the ambiguity of many intellectuals regarding the learned concept of witchcraft. In Baldung, Albrecht Dürer and Hieronymous Bosch, as well as in the early seventeenth-century engraver Jacques Callot, there is a strain of disbelief that occasionally borders on satire. Bosch may have intended his depiction of witches going to the Sabbath on a flying fish as a moral lesson, but it has produced more amusement than edification.

Literary sources offer many of the same perspectives found in the visual ones, especially in illuminating changing ideas regarding the Devil, the pacts that humans allegedly make with him, and the figure of the witch. We can, for example, learn a considerable amount about early modern European ideas of the pact from Christopher Marlowe's *Dr. Faustus* (c. 1588) and other literary expressions of the Faust legend. We can also learn a great deal about urban sorcerers and witches in the Mediterranean region by reading Fernando de Rojas's play *Celestina* (1499), which was informed mainly by classical images of the witch but which also accurately depicted a type of sorcerer frequently found in the cities of early modern Spain.

Literary sources have the additional advantage of providing insights into the motivation of the witch and her neighbors. In this regard the judicial records are often not very helpful, unless they include the original depositions of witnesses. The literary sources, while possessing none of the apparent authenticity of judicial records, often allow a more complete, if perhaps more imaginary, reconstruction of the circumstances surrounding witchcraft prosecutions. Sometimes this reconstruction took place shortly after the trial, such as in *The Witch of Edmonton* (1621), which is remarkable for its exploration of the social context of the prosecution of the witch

Elizabeth Sawyer. In other cases the reconstruction was undertaken decades or centuries later, when modern writers set their work in the context of a historical witchcraft trial. Aldous Huxley's novel *The Devils of Loudun*, John Masefield's drama *The Witch* (based on the earlier work of the Danish playwright Hans Wiers-Jenssen), and Arthur Miller's play *The Crucible* all serve as examples of this type of literary reconstruction. Many works of literature on the theme of witchcraft, both those written at the time of the witch-hunts as well as their modern counterparts, share the skepticism, if not the ambivalence, of their artistic counterparts. In this respect they perpetuate a tradition begun by classical writers, whose depictions of witches often assumed the character of satire.

Further Reading

Baldung, Hans. *Hans Baldung Grien, Prints and Drawings,* ed. James H. Marrow and Alan Shestack. New Haven, 1981.

Caro Baroja, Julio. *The World of the Witches*, trans. O. N. V. Glendinning. Chicago, 1961.

Comensoli, Viviana. "Witchcraft and Domestic Tragedy in *The Witch of Edmonton,*" in *The Politics of Gender in Early Modern Europe*, ed. J. Brink, A.P. Coudert, and M. C. Horowitz (Vol. 12 of *Sixteenth Century Essays and Studies* (1989), pp. 43–59.

Corbin, Peter and Douglas Sedge, ed., *Three Jacobean Witchcraft Plays*. Manchester, 1986.

Davidson, Jane P. *David Teniers the Younger*. Boulder, Co., 1979.

————. *The Witch in Northern European Art, 1470–1750*. Freren, 1987.

Fränger, Wilhem. *The Millenium of Hieronymous Bosch*. Chicago, 1952.

Kiesling, Nicholas. *The Incubus in English Literature: Provenance and Progeny*. Pullman, Wash., 1977.

Koch, Robert A. *Hans Baldung Grien: Eve, the Serpent and Death*. Ottawa, 1974.

Masefield, John. *The Witch*. London, 1926.

Onat, Etta Soiref, ed. *The Witch of Edmonton: A Critical Edition*. 1980.

Orians, G. Harrison. "New England Witchcraft in Fiction," *American Literature* 2 (1930–1), 54–71.

Paul, Henry N. *The Royal Play of Macbeth*. New York, 1951.

Parsons, C. O. *Witchcraft and Demonology in Scott's Fiction*. Edinburgh, 1964.

Reed, Robert R. *The Occult on the Tudor and Stuart Stage*. Boston, 1965.

Witchcraft and Demonology in Art and Literature

Art, Culture, and Mentality in Renaissance Society: The Meaning of Hans Baldung Grien's Bewitched Groom (1544)*

by DALE HOAK

For the study of early modern society, Renaissance art often provides an extraordinary means of exploring visually the values and assumptions, attitudes, and modes of perception of those who inhabited, mentally and materially, the world of traditional, preindustrial Europe. The work of Hans Baldung *dit* Grien (1484/85–1545), a Swabian painter, illustrator, and designer of stained glass,[1] illuminates one of the most familiar and yet least understood aspects of this world, the mentality of those who believed that some women were capable of influencing a man's sexual nature by means of witchcraft.

In a series of prints and drawings executed between 1510 and 1544, Baldung portrayed various aspects of the alleged activities of witches. As contributions to the iconography of witchcraft, these *Hexenbilder* were without artistic precedent. Indeed, the chiaroscuro woodcut of *Witches* (1510) about to depart for the sabbath (Fig. 1)

*A faculty research grant from the College of William and Mary supported my work on this topic in 1982. Earlier versions of the paper were presented to the Medieval History Society in the University of Cambridge, Gonville and Caius College, 3 December 1981, the Mid-Atlantic Renaissance-Reformation Seminar, Folger Shakespeare Library, Washington, D.C., 13 November 1982, and the Renaissance Society of America, Huntington Library, San Marino, California, 22 March 1984. For their encouragement, criticism or assistance at various stages I owe special thanks to Caroline Backlund, Eric Chamberlain, Miles Chappell, Miriam Chrisman, Craig Harbison, John Headley, James Marrow, Erik Midelfort, Bob Scribner, and Alan Shestack.

[1]For biographical details, cf. Carl Koch, "Hans Baldung-Grien," *Die Grossen Deutschen: Deutsche Biographie* (Berlin, 1956), I, 401–17. Thomas A. Brady, Jr. has added important new information in "The Social Place of a German Renaissance Artist: Hans Baldung Grien (1484/85–1545) at Strasbourg," *Central European History*, 8 (1975), 295–315. For a review of the earlier art historical literature, see Koch, *Die Zeichnungen Hans Baldung Grien* (Berlin, 1941), pp. 61–66. The most helpful recent assessment of Baldung's oeuvre is *Hans Baldung Grien* (Karlsruhe, 1959), a catalogue of an exhibition at the Kunsthalle Karlsruhe, to which may be added Gert von der Osten, *Hans Baldung Grien: Gemälde und Dokumente* (Berlin, 1983). In English, a brief introductory survey of Baldung's art can be found in Charles D. Cuttler, *Northern Painting from Pucelle to Bruegel* (New York, 1968), ch. 23.

1. Hans Baldung, *Witches*, chiaroscuro woodcut, 1510. Museum of Fine Arts, Boston, bequest of W. G. Russell Allen (courtesy Museum of Fine Arts, Boston)

represents the first attempt in Western high art to portray women in such a fantastic, sensational setting. The cultural myths to which the *Hexenbilder* gave visual form, however, were already well developed in fifteenth-century demonological tracts. As revealed in these tracts and in the extant records of questions put to suspects by lay and ecclesiastical interrogators in continental trials, the fantasy of the witches' sabbath combined elements of three quite distinct and very old systems of belief: the supernatural, damage-doing powers of the pre-Christian *strix*; the night-flying capabilities of certain female folk spirits; and the orgiastic, cannibalistic infanticide allegedly practiced by sects of devil-worshipping heretics.[2]

Far from merely illustrating such beliefs, Baldung's *Hexenbilder* stand as brilliantly insightful comments on the mentality of witch-hunting officialdom. Baldung's manner of portraying sorcery as a distinctly female, sexually-based phenomenon, expressively and very selectively tinged with erotically humorous, even satirical overtones, suggests that, like most intellectuals of his day, the artist refused to swallow whole the sabbath fantasy. But it would be wrong to suppose that the sexually exhibitionist, airborne nudes of the early *Hexenbilder* belied Baldung's belief in the *maleficium* of the village "sorceress": like everyone in his world, learned and unlearned alike, Baldung was probably incapable of questioning the efficacy of the system on which sorcery depended, an occult system of malevolent, supernatural powers.

Perhaps nowhere is a contemporary's acceptance of this system stated more forcefully than in the last of Baldung's *Hexenbilder*, a single-leaf woodcut known as the *Bewitched Groom*, dated 1544 (Fig. 2). In it the artist projected one of the most arresting images in all of Renaissance art. A stableman is seen lying rigidly on his back in foreshortened perspective across a pitchfork on the floor of a stable, his glassy, up-turned eyes fixed wide-open in their sockets. On the floor beside him lies a currycomb which has apparently fallen from his hand. Behind him and dominating the center of the picture is an agitated horse drawn in perspective from the rear, glowering back at the recumbent figure of the man. From a window ledge at the right a bare-breasted hag holding a flaming torch stares menacingly down at the groom.

[2]For the making of this stereotype, see Norman Cohn, *Europe's Inner Demons: An Enquiry Inspired by the Great Witch-Hunt* (New York, 1975), chs. 1–3, 8–12.

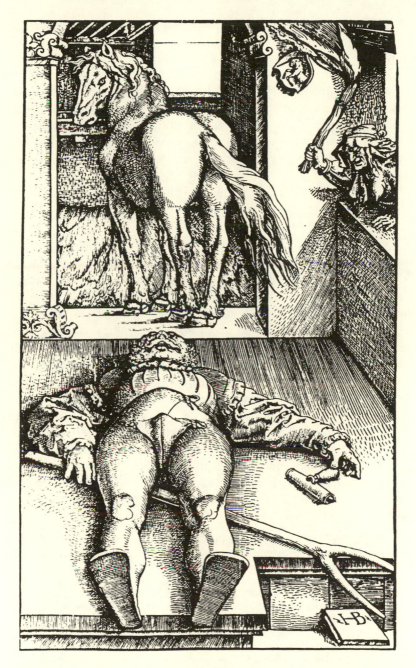

2. Hans Baldung, *Bewitched Groom*, woodcut, 1544. Cleveland Museum of Art, Mr. and Mrs. Charles G. Prasse Collection (photo: Cleveland Museum)

What is the meaning of Baldung's enigmatic portrayal of horse, witch, and groom? Has he narrated the action of some long-forgotten story, or do horse, woman, and man represent symbolic elements of an allegory or dream? The purpose of the present essay is to suggest a possible source for the image, and from it a new interpretation, one which attempts to place the *Bewitched Groom* historically in its appropriate socio-cultural context. Since this interpretation necessarily builds upon suggestions offered by other scholars, it would be well to review briefly the recent attempts to resolve Baldung's puzzle.

The groom's condition seems to hold the key to the riddle. Although Baldung gave no title to the print, the one traditionally assigned to it, *der behexte Stallknecht*—literally the *Bewitched Stable-Groom*—suggests that the woman, who is unquestionably a witch, has in some way caused the man's apparent misfortune. Has she killed him or entranced him by magical means, or by her black art caused the horse to kick him senseless? Arguments to the effect that we are looking at an allegory of death seem to be supported by what Baldung may have intended as an autobiographical allusion in the unicorn displayed on a shield on the right rear wall of the stable. Because a unicorn formed part of the municipal insignia of the town (Swäbisch Gmünd) of his birth, which coat of arms Baldung appropriated as his own, several commentators have thought the print to be a metaphorical self-portrait, the artist's nightmarish vision of his own impending death at the hands of demonic forces.[3] (Baldung died the following year, 1545.) However, in the absence of an identifiable source, this and subsequent attempts to decipher the *Bewitched Groom* necessarily have remained speculative.[4] The best guess is that the

[3]G. F. Hartlaub, "Der Todestraum des Hans Baldung Grien," *Antaios*, 2 (1960), 13–25; G. F. Hartlaub, *Hans Baldung Grien—Hexenbilder* (Stuttgart, 1961), pp. 22–24. And see James H. Marrow and Alan Shestack, eds., *Hans Baldung Grien: Prints and Drawings* (Yale University Art Gallery; University of Chicago Press, 1980), pp. 18 and 275, where variations on this theme may be found.

[4]Various allegorical interpretations have been advanced (anger, lust, sleep, artistic melancholia), but none is convincing: Gustave Radbruch, "Hans Baldungs Hexenbilder," *Elegantiae Juris Criminalis: Vierzehn Studien zur Geschichte des Strafechts*, 2nd ed. (Basel, 1950), pp. 40–41; Gert von der Osten and Horst Vey, *Painting and Sculpture in Germany and the Netherlands 1500–1600*, trans. Mary Hottinger (Baltimore, 1969), p. 222; Linda C. Hults, "Baldung's *Bewitched Groom* Revisited: Artistic Temperment, Fantasy, and the 'Dream of Reason,' " *Sixteenth Century Journal*, 15 (1984), 259–79. In his review of Marrow and Shestack (*Art Bulletin*, 64 [1982], 150–51), Craig Harbison speculated on the implications of what F. G. Pariset and J. Wirth have seen as

composition may be related to one of many contemporaneous German folk tales concerning devilry and horses.[5] If so, which one, and how?

In 1894, in his study of Baldung's preparatory drawing of the foreshortened groom (Fig. 3), Gabriel von Térey cited a folk tale about "stable-sorcery" ("Stallhexengeschichte") which he thought "somewhat similar to" the subject matter of the *Bewitched Groom*.[6] The tale was "Die Hexe als Pferd," or "The Witch in the Guise of a Horse," one of several hundred Alsatian *Sagen,* or legends, systematically collected during the early nineteenth century by August Stöber, the great student of Alsatian folk-ways. The story, as recounted by Stöber in his edition of the *Sagen des Elsasses,* first published at Strassburg in 1852, is here translated into English for the first time.[7] It runs as follows:

A man in Buchsweiler was awakened one night by a strange noise that seemed to be coming from the stable. He set out immediately [for the stable] and discovered between his own two horses a third, jet-black and with dishevelled mane, moving restlessly back and forth. He wanted to lead it out of the stable, but it bolted, and so he returned home empty-handed.

The horse was not to be seen again for several days. Some time later he heard the same noise in the stable and once again found the black horse next to his own [horses]. Noticing that it was without shoes, he roused the blacksmith who lived next to him and had the animal shod. The next morning lamentable screams in a woman's voice could be heard coming from the house next door. Rushing into the house, the man found the neighborwoman confined to her bed. She had horseshoes (*Hufeisen*) on her hands and feet.

Baldung's "Epicurean" tendencies in the 1530s: "Perhaps Baldung felt himself capable of a secularized penetration of the secrets of nature, only . . . to return to more orthodox frustration by the 1540s. The *Bewitched Groom* might thus be a kind of *Conversion of Paul* (Paul's fall brought about by the proud and angry horse) and *Lamentation over Christ* (the groom sacrificed to the howling, almost mourning witch as in Mantegna)."

[5]Marrow and Shestack, p. 275, suggested this in 1980. Charmian A. Mesenzeva, a curator at the Hermitage in Leningrad, subsequently claimed that the print was based on a late-medieval Franconian tale concerning the exploits and death of a legendary knight, William, Count Rechenberger, but the attribution is unlikely. Mesenzeva transposed elements of different versions of the fable in an attempt to make a composite version fit Baldung's image. In fact, the Rechenberger stories contain many functional details absent in the print. Most notably, however, the legends cited by Mesenzeva make no mention of a woman who is a witch; cf. Charmian A. Mesenzeva, " 'Der behexte Stallknecht' des Hans Baldung Grien," *Zeitschrift für Kunstgeschichte,* 44 (1981), 57–61. Johann Eckart von Borries summarized Mesenzeva's hypothesis in his review of Marrow and Shestack in *Kunstchronik,* 35 (1982), 58–59.

[6]Gabriel von Térey, *Die Handzeichnungen des Hans Baldung gen. Grien* (Strassburg, 1894), I, p. x.

[7]I have used the text of August Stöber, *Sagen des Elsasses* (Strassburg, 1896), II, 112.

3. Hans Baldung, *Study for the Bewitched Groom*, drawing, 1544. Kunstmuseum Basel, Kupferstichkabinett (photo: Kunstmuseum Basel)

The *Bewitched Groom* is clearly not an illustration of this tale. One doubts, in any case, that Baldung would have chosen simply to illustrate a folk narrative. Rather, I suspect that he translated in his own fashion the device on which the tale relies for its effect—the suggestive interchangeability of horse and witch. Before considering the

8

implications of this, however, one must first confront the problems posed by the use of "Die Hexe als Pferd" as a historical source. These comprehend its extant form, date, and place of origin.

Although originally generated by an illiterate peasantry, the legend has come down to us only in a written, published form. Some of the tales in the 1852 edition of *Sagen* Stöber culled from earlier printed works; others he transcribed from a variety of unnamed, local manuscript sources; still others, like "Die Hexe als Pferd," he recorded as products of "popular [i.e., oral] traditions" already more than three hundred years old in his own day. No doubt Stöber sought to preserve these legends just as he had heard them from Alsatian villagers and townspeople, but of course there is no way of knowing how stylistically intrusive was his pen at the moment of transcription. He himself represents a cultural "filter" through which all of the *Sagen* passed.

Nonetheless, it is possible that in the 1840s Stöber recorded "Die Hexe als Pferd" in substantially the form Baldung might have heard it between about 1490 and 1544. At thirty years per generation, Stöber stood ten generations removed from the artist, not a very long time historically for the transmission, in a pre-industrial setting, of orally related narratives peculiar to the type of peasant society which then characterized the villages of Lower Alsace. In the twentieth century, anthropologists and historians have verified the existence among Irish and Sicilian peasants of oral traditions dating from the later Middle Ages.[8]

Stöber traced "Die Hexe als Pferd" to Bushsweiler, presently called Bouxwiller, a town lying approximately thirty-five kilometers (or sixteen miles) northwest of Strasbourg. Baldung's known contacts with peasants in the area where Bouxwiller is located provide strong circumstantial evidence of his direct familiarity with the local witch-lore of which "Die Hexe als Pferd" is quite clearly an expression. Like many city dwellers of his class—middling *rentiers* and speculators in real estate—Baldung invested in peasant debts and bought up small parcels of property in the villages of the vineyard-covered foothills of the Vosges to the west and northwest of Strasbourg. In 1525, for example, Baldung bought property in Schiltigheim, where Baldung's father had held judicial office (1497–

---

[8] Conrad M. Arensberg, *The Irish Countryman: An Anthropological Study* (New York, 1950), ch. 6; Cohn, *Europe's Inner Demons*, p. 216.

1505), and in Balbronn the artist and his wife, Margarethe, loaned money during the 1520s and 1530s to a peasant and his son.[9]

Some of Baldung's anonymous peasant acquaintances are to be found in his art. He sketched them from life, and one, an old woman, head covered and left breast exposed, he made the sympathetically expressive subject of a black chalk drawing of c. 1535, called *The Hag* or *Witch* (Fig. 4). As Christiane Andersson has noted, this *Witch* is "generally analogous to the witch at the window in the *Bewitched Groom*."[10] In any case, the woman who sat for *The Hag* in 1535 stands as a useful reminder of a possible social source of Baldung's acquaintance with the witch-lore of the region around Strasbourg where the artist lived and worked for almost the whole of his productive life (1509–45).

Scholars have not adequately pursued von Térey's suggestion of a possible link between this Alsatian lore and Baldung's woodcut of 1544. For example, Charmian Mesenzeva nowhere mentioned von Térey's work, though she should have known about "Die Hexe als Pferd," since she cited Gustav Radbruch's essay of 1950 on the *Hexenbilder,* where there is a reference to the tale in Stöber's collection, as well as to von Térey's knowledge of it.[11] However, Radbruch, who pondered what aspect of witch-lore Baldung's woodcut might "illustrate," peremptorily dismissed the story as a possibility: "Sicher nicht die Sage 'Die Hexe als Pferd,' " he asserted.[12] More recently, Dieter Koepplin seems to have accepted an implied thematic connection between the legend and the print, though like Radbruch and von Térey, he referred to the story without discussing its contents.[13]

To my knowledge, only Maxime Préaud, Curator of Prints at the Bibliothèque Nationale in Paris, has accepted "Die Hexe als Pferd" as the source of the *Bewitched Groom* and suggested how it might be

[9]Thomas A. Brady, Jr., "The Social Place of a German Renaissance Artist," *Central European History*, 8 (1975), 300–303, and see the same author's *Ruling Class, Regime and Reformation at Strasbourg 1520–1555* (Leiden, 1978), pp. 141–143, 151, note 121. On the society and culture of Strasbourg, see two works by Miriam Usher Chrisman: *Strasbourg and the Reform: A Study in the Process of Change* (New Haven and London, 1967) and *Lay Culture, Learned Culture: Books and Social Change in Strasbourg 1480–1599* (New Haven and London, 1982).

[10]Marrow and Shestack, p. 279 and plate 89.

[11]Radbruch, "Hans Baldungs Hexenbilder," p. 39.

[12]Ibid.

[13]Dieter Koepplin, in *Hans Baldung Grien im Kunstmuseum Basel,* exh. cat. (Basel, 1978), pp. 73 and 75, n. 11.

4. Hans Baldung, *Study of an Old Woman*, drawing, c. 1535. National Gallery of Art, Rosenwald Collection (photo: National Gallery)

used to discover Baldung's meaning. Citing popular notions which held that witches could transform themselves into beasts, Préaud thought that the old woman has put the stableman to sleep in order to slip back into the shape of the horse. Alternatively, Préaud proposed that in Baldung's scene the groom finds himself at a sabbath. According to one theory of the demonologists, witches "travelled" to the sabbath in spirit only, apparently in a dream or a deep sleep. Préaud argued that the groom holds iconographic evidence for this interpretation—the pitchfork on which all of Baldung's witches make their voyages.[14]

Préaud's second suggestion may well provide a further clue to Baldung's purpose here and in some of the other *Hexenbilder*. Graphically, the groom's long-handled, double-pronged pitchfork, actually a *Heugabel* or *Mistgabel* (hay-fork or dung-fork), functions as a powerful diagonal in the composition, and Baldung has forced the viewer to concentrate on it. It cannot be accidental that this *Heugabel* is identical to the *Ofengabeln*, or oven-forks, that appear in three of the earlier *Hexenbilder*; there are five in the chiaroscuro woodcut of 1510 (Fig. 1), two in the Albertina drawing of *Witches*, dated 1514 (Fig. 5), and one (apparently) in the Louvre *Witches* of the same year (Fig. 6). Although none of Baldung's witches actually ride these forks—Préaud was wrong here—the airborne ones certainly carry them. Is the connection between the hay-fork of 1544 and the oven-forks of 1510/14 thus a matter of suggested flight? If so, flight by what means?

Fifteenth- and sixteenth-century writers knew what modern chemical analysis has revealed, that the various herbal salves concocted by the village healers of Baldung's era—historically, the very women often labelled "sorceresses"—contained ingredients with sleep-inducing, hallucinogenic properties. The sensations of flight to which some sixteenth-century peasant women voluntarily confessed after such drug-induced sleep have been corroborated by subjects in twentieth-century experiments employing unguents formulated from sixteenth-century recipes.[15]

---

[14]Maxime Préaud, *Les sorcières* (Paris, 1973), p. 2, the catalogue of an exhibition (at the Bibliothèque Nationale, Paris) of books and prints on the theme of witchcraft. Préaud paraphrased the story from Paul Desfeuilles' translation of Stöber: *Légendes et traditions orales d'Alsace* (Paris, 1920).

[15]Michael J. Harner, "The Role of Hallucinogenic Plants in European Witchcraft," in Michael J. Harner, ed. *Hallucinogens and Shamanism* (New York, 1973), pp. 125–50.

12

Pharmacology, in short, helps explain why certain miserable old women believed themselves to be capable of flight, or as Jordanes de Bergamo, a Dominican theologian, put it c. 1470–71, "the vulgar believe, and the witches confess, that on certain days or nights they anoint a staff and ride on it to the appointed place or anoint themselves under the arms and in other hairy places. . . ."[16] It has been suggested that the handles of pitchforks (among other instruments) were used to apply the atropine-containing salves to sensitive vaginal membranes.[17] The sensual nature of the application by whatever means is obvious; in his warm-toned drawing (pen on red-brown tinted paper) of *Hexen* now in Vienna (Fig. 5), Baldung concentrated on the erotic, trance-inducing power of the witches' ointment. However, this drawing of 1514 is not historical evidence of collective social practices. As the foremost historian of witch-hunting in southwestern Germany has cautioned, "pharmacology does not help prove that groups of women got together to induce by means of drugs a group experience." All of the evidence, he says, points to the use of salves by individuals. Moreover, "such evidence does not bolster the idea that [alleged] witches actually met for a sabbath." In fact, the evidence of such individual use actually explains away the notion of the sabbath.[18] Baldung's representations of witches about to depart for the sabbath thus advance an explanation of the alleged reality of such ventures, or as Jean Vincent, a learned prior of a church in the Vendée averred more precisely as early as 1475: "The Devil casts

---

The active ingredients include various plants belonging to the order *Solanaceae* (potato family), principally species of the genus *Datura*. They go by a variety of names: Jimson's weed, devil's apple, thorn apple, mad apple, devil's weed, etc. Others resembling *Datura* in their effects include mandrake, henbane, and belladonna. "Each . . . contains varying quantities of atropine and the other closely related tropane alkaloids, hyoscamine and scopolamine, all of which have hallucinogenic effects . . ."; ibid., 128. Julio Caro Baroja (*The World of the Witches*, trans. O. N. V. Glendinning [Chicago, 1965], pp. 254–55) notes that sleep could also be induced by smoking the leaves of the plants or drinking the boiled extract.

[16]From Bergamo's *Quaestio de Strigis*, an unpublished manuscript in the Bibliothèque Nationale, Paris, originally quoted in Joseph Hansen, *Quellen und Untersuchungen zur Geschichte des Hexenwahns und der Hexenverfolgungen im Mittelalter* (Bonn, 1901), pp. 195–200, and extracted in Henry Charles Lea, *Materials toward a History of Witchcraft*, ed. Arthur C. Howland (New York, 1957), I, 302.

[17]Harner, "Role," p. 131.

[18]H. C. Erik Midelfort, "Were There Really Witches?", in Robert M. Kingdon, ed. *Transition and Revolution: Problems and Issues of European Renaissance and Reformation History* (Minneapolis, 1974), p. 203; Cohn, *Europe's Inner Demons*, p. 220.

5. Hans Baldung, *Witches,* drawing. 1514. Vienna, Albertina, Fonds Albertina (photo: Lichtbildwerkstätte Alpenland)

6. Hans Baldung, *Witches*, drawing, 1514. Paris, Cabinet des Dessins, Louvre (photo: Cliché des Musées Nationaux)

people into a deep sleep, in which they dream that they have been to the Sabbath. . . . The *malefici* have philtres and unguents . . . and they also imagine themselves to be carried to the Sabbath by virtue of these."[19]

In the Albertina *Witches* of 1514 (Fig. 5) Baldung conveyed the eroticism of such "voyages" by picturing the apparently drug-induced self-gratification of some voluptuous nudes. By contrast, in the *Bewitched Groom*, the *Heugabel* transports one thematically to the fantasy of the orgiastic sabbath. In this interpretation, the groom's pitchfork signifies not merely flight, but a distinctively erotic type of demonic dream-flight. What does this suggest about the relationship of horse, witch, and groom in the woodcut? And what is the connection between this relationship and the story of "The Witch in the Guise of a Horse"?

Much depends on what one actually sees here. For example, is the groom really dead? The evidence of the print seems to deny it: for someone who has just been kicked to death by a wild stallion or (as another interpretation has it) come to grief on the end of an adversary's pitchfork,[20] he is suspiciously without marks. The mathematically cool, calculated linearity of his foreshortened figure, justly famous in studies of Renaissance perspective, does not suggest the awful tumult one must imagine, had he been felled by the horse's hoofs or impaled in the manner described. (The pitchfork is in fact his own; he has simply fallen on top of it.) Similarly, Radbruch's interpretation of the print as an allegory of ire required the discovery of a recently-kicking horse. Radbruch "found" his evidence in what he perceived to be the stallion's unnatural stance, "its right hind leg rotated outward in a peculiar manner, the hoof unnaturally transposed. With this hoof it has obviously struck the groom fatally. . . ."[21] In fact, Baldung must have carefully observed the stance of a horse at rest, for he has correctly positioned this horse's rear hoofs to take into account the partial shifting of the animal's weight to the left rear leg as it turns to the left to see what has happened to the groom (Fig. 2).

[19]Jean Vincent (Vincenti), *Liber adversus magicas artes et eos qui dicunt artibus eisdem nullam inesse efficaciam*, an unpublished manuscript in the Bibliothèque Nationale, Paris, trans. by Lea, *Materials*, I, 303, from Hansen, *Quellen*, pp. 227–31.

[20]In one version of the legend cited by Mesenzeva, " 'Der behexte Stallknecht' " 58–59, Satan's legions stormed the stable, skewering Rechenberger on the prongs of a pitchfork.

[21]Radbruch, "Hans Baldungs Hexenbilder," p. 40.

The horse's backward glance, not its right rear hoof, directs our attention to the groom's fate.

It seems to me that the witch's eyes and those of the groom tellingly reveal what has befallen him, for hers, malevolent and menacing, are directed straight at his glassy, frozen ones. Sixteenth-century viewers familiar with the alleged powers of the sorceress would have seen at once that the old woman has stunned or entranced the man by the terrible power of her glance. Baldung has pictured one of the stereotyped attributes of the witch, her diabolical ability to "fascinate" her victims, especially the male ones, by glowering at them with the proverbial "evil eye." Following the title traditionally assigned to the print, I would say that we are looking at a bewitched, or entranced, groom, not one fatally wounded by the horse.

Recognizing this, however, does not quite resolve the puzzle posed by the *Bewitched Groom,* nor does it tell us how the image may be related to "Die Hexe als Pferd." The answer, I would venture, lies in the way in which the iconography of witchcraft allows one to "read" the sexually-charged syntax of the composition. Baldung has obviously forced the viewer to comprehend the groom in a provocative way, from a particular point of view. The man's attire, as much as the angle from which he is seen, also seems to point to some sort of erotic intention: compare the fully-clad groom of the preparatory drawing (Fig. 3). Now a sixteenth-century viewer, seeing that the man was bewitched, in any case would have associated such a state with wanton sexual desire. Iconographically, the hag personifies this association. Her torch, for example, symbolizes the lust that could be induced by sorcery. As a literary device, torches, or firebrands, functioned universally as either phallic emblems or symbols of damnation,[22] and since it was commonplace to conceive of heresy in terms of sexual sin, writers of Baldung's generation, such as Sir Thomas More, used the firebrand to signify the damnable nature of a lascivious passion.[23] The torch in Baldung's woodcut looks very much like one of the common straw brooms the artist gave to some women sweeping out a church in one of his book illustrations of 1517.[24] Such broom-torches, or firebrands resembling them, consti-

---

[22] Alistair Fox, *Thomas More: History and Providence* (New Haven and London, 1983), p. 143. I thank John Headley for bringing this point to my attention.

[23] Ibid., pp. 143–44.

[24] An illustration in *Ein Kurzweilig Lesen von Dyl Ulenspiegel* (Strassburg, 1515);

tuted part of the familiar iconography of witchcraft; the nondescript witches in one of the popular woodcuts illustrating the first German-language treatise on witchcraft, Johann Geiler von Keysersberg's *Die Emeis* (Strassburg, 1517), are shown running about, holding them aloft.

Although the crone's torch could also suggest the contemporary association of witchcraft and arson[25] or even a hint of insanity—"bringing fire into a stable" was taken to be a sign of madness in one documented case of 1590[26]—her bared breast provides an unmistakeable clue to Baldung's meaning, for such was the way the artist had earlier sketched from life the old peasant woman, or *Hag* (Fig. 4), in a pose that reminds one of the figures of procuresses in German and Flemish art of the sixteenth century.[27] Procuresses and the prostitutes they employed were often among the first to be suspected of practicing witchcraft.[28] Historians of witch hunting in central Europe think that perhaps a tenth or more of all female suspects had probably committed some sort of serious sexual offense before being accused of practicing harmful magic.[29] In short, Baldung's manner of portraying the witch in this woodcut very probably constitutes a reference to the sex-linked profession or sexually suspect behavior of many of the

---

Matthias Mende, *Hans Baldung Grien: Das graphisches Werk* (Unterschneidheim, 1978), no. 235.

[25]On the suggestive connections between witchcraft and the prosecution of arson see Keith Thomas, *Religion and the Decline of Magic* (New York, 1971), pp. 533–34, 559–60; Alfred Soman, "Criminal Jurisprudence in Ancien-Régime France: the Parlement of Paris in the Sixteenth and Seventeenth Centuries," in Louis A. Knafla, ed., *Crime and Justice in Europe and Canada* (Montreal, 1980), pp. 48, 64–66.

[26]The case is that of Daniel Hoffman, 1590, from the Hospitalsarchiv Haina, "Rezeptionsreskripte von den Jahren 1500." Erik Midelfort kindly provided me with this reference. See Midelfort's discussion of this hospital, "Protestant Monastery? A Reformation Hospital in Hesse," in Peter N. Brooks, ed., *Reformation Principle and Practice: Essays in Honour of Arthur Geoffrey Dickens* (London, 1980), pp. 71–93.

[27]Christiane Andersson made this point in her discussion of Baldung's black chalk *Study of an Old Woman* of c. 1535 in Marrow and Shestack, p. 279, note 2.

[28]Gordon Andreas Singer, "La Vauderie d'Arras, 1459–1491: An Episode of Witchcraft in Later Medieval France," Ph.D. dissertation (University of Maryland, 1974), p. 95.

[29]Etienne Delcambre, "La psychologie des inculpés lorraines de sorcellerie," *Revue historique de droit français et étranger*, 32 (1954), 383–404, 505–26, as trans. and quoted by E. William Monter, ed., *European Witchcraft* (New York, 1969), p. 105; Monter, *Witchcraft in France and Switzerland: The Borderlands during the Reformation* (Ithaca, 1976), pp. 135–36.

women in his world who were thought to be capable of wielding the power of demons. The presence of an indecent, torch-bearing hag must "explain" the disturbing implications of the groom's condition: "demonic" women seduce ("bewitch") men into thinking carnally unnatural thoughts or so entrance them that they will want to perform sexually misguided acts.

Such of course was part of the stock-in-trade misogyny promoted by the early Church fathers and latterly the learned jurists, clerics, and professorial demonologists who helped elaborate the stereotype of the witch. Obviously Baldung might have said much the same thing without a horse. If I am correct, however, "Die Hexe als Pferd" allowed him to explore this assumption about women by refashioning the elements of an Alsatian tale. "Die Hexe als Pferd" narrates a variation of the familiar theme of the taming of a shrew: like a wild horse finally shod by a farrier, an ungovernable woman is at last brought to heel. Various critics have assumed that because Baldung did not "illustrate" this theme, "Die Hexe als Pferd" was irrelevant to a discussion of the meaning of the print. Surely this was to miss the point of both the legend and the image, since both rely for their effect on the mechanism of a symbol, the symbolic sexual link between wild horses and demonic women. "Die Hexe als Pferd" pithily expresses this connection in the sexual undertones of a deeply rooted popular misogyny: a heretofore unruly mare/woman is found in bed by a man; she is wearing horseshoes and so can now be "ridden." In my view, the woodcut translates this in unexpected fashion by juxtaposing the terms of the connection. We know that Baldung quite clearly associated horses with man's primitive, sexual nature: witness his engravings of *Wild Horses* of 1534 (Fig. 7). By introducing the sorceress at the window, Baldung placed the horse and groom in a satanic setting and so suggested the "source" of a bewitched man's sexual appetite—the "dream-ride" induced by the old woman's spell.

If the *Bewitched Groom* illustrates an assumption about the effects of female sorcery, it also provides an insight into sixteenth-century perceptions of the social basis of witchcraft. Attitudes about who witches were had been changing during the later Middle Ages, and the various ways in which northern artists portrayed persons suspected of witchcraft reflected those assumptions. In the mid-fifteenth century the witches imagined by artists were both male and female;

19

7. Hans Baldung, *Stallion Attempting to Mate*, one of a series of three woodcuts of wild horses, 1534. Los Angeles County Museum of Art, Museum Purchase (photo: Los Angeles County Museum)

socially, they were well-born, gentle or even noble.[30] During roughly the next hundred years—a period spanning Baldung's lifetime—accusers increasingly identified women as witches, their testimony emphasizing the allegedly demonic character of a particular type of woman, a woman of the lowest social orders. Since the appearance of lower-class women as witches in northern art dates only from about 1530 to 1540 at the earliest,[31] the *Bewitched Groom*

[30]Cf. the illustration (by an unknown artist) of heretics ("Waldensians") adoring the Devil in the form of a goat, c. 1460, MS. 11209, fo. 3ʳ, Bibliothèque Royale Albert Iᵉʳ, Brussels, reproduced in Charles D. Cuttler, "Witchcraft in a Work by Bosch," *Art Quarterly*, 20 (1957), Fig. 2, p. 133, and Cohn, *Europe's Inner Demons*, plate 1. The original MS. in Brussels is a French translation of Johannes Tinctoris, *Contra sectam Valdensium*, a tract attacking the victims of the Arras witch panic of 1459–60. A similar illustration from MS. Fr. 961 in the Bibliothèque Nationale, Paris, is reproduced in Cuttler, Fig. 3, p. 133.

[31]See the anonymous South German or Swiss pen-and-ink drawing of *Melancholics*, Cabinet Jean Masson, École des Beaux Arts, Paris, originally reproduced and discussed in R. Klibansky, E. Panofsky, and F. Saxl, *Saturn and Melancholy: Studies in the History of Natural Philosophy, Religion, and Art* (New York, 1964), pp. 393–95 and plate 139.

stands among the first Renaissance images to identify *maleficium* with a class of socially inferior women. Baldung's witch wears a floppy hat of sorts, really a cloth wrap tied loosely about her head, characteristic garb for a humble country woman or mountain dweller, precisely the sort of woman who proved to be most vulnerable to accusations of witchcraft at this time: impoverished, elderly, unmarried or widowed, a peasant or perhaps one of the displaced urban poor who lived alone. Roughly four of every five victims of the witch hunts in Germany, France, and the Lowlands proved to be women of this type, many of them the soothsayers, fortune tellers, conjurers, and isolated neighborwomen of village life to whom others resorted for "magical" charms or cures.[32] Of course in Western Europe the peak period of witch hunting lay after Baldung's death, during the socially disruptive years between c. 1550 and 1650. Historians are only just now beginning to understand why the great panics happened when and where they did.[33] As yet no one has systematically explored the impact of the graphic arts on this peculiar episode in European life.[34] Art can be an indicator, as much as a product, of social and cultural change. By allowing some to "see" witchcraft more easily, did Baldung's published *Hexenbilder* contribute to the subsequent

[32]Pierre Chaunu, "Sur la fin des sorciers au XVIIᶜ siècle," *Annales: Économies Sociétés Civilisations*, 24 (1969), 895–911; Richard Horsley, "Who Were the Witches? The Social Roles of the Accused in European Witch Trials," *Journal of Interdisciplinary History*, 9 (1979), 689–715; Robert Muchembled, "Sorcellerie, culture populaire et christianisme au XVIᶜ siècle, principalement en Flandres et en Artois," *Annales: Économies Sociétés Civilisation*, 28 (1973), 264–84; Christina Larner, *The Thinking Peasant: Popular and Educated Belief in Pre-Industrial Culture* (Glasgow, 1982), pp. 58–73. Muchembled's article has been translated by Patricia M. Ranum in *Ritual, Religion, and the Sacred*, ed. Robert Forster and Orest Ranum (Baltimore, 1982), pp. 213–36.

[33]Peter Burke, *Popular Culture in Early Modern Europe* (New York, 1978), 207–34, 241–42; Elizabeth L. Eisenstein, *The Printing Press as an Agent of Change: Communications and Cultural Transformations in Early Modern Europe*, (Cambridge, 1979), I, 433–38; Robert Mandrou, *From Humanism to Science 1480–1700* (New York, 1978), pp. 114–17; H. C. Erik Midelfort, "Heartland of the Witchcraze: Central and Northern Europe," *History Today*, 21 (Feb. 1981), 27–31; Christina Larner, *Enemies of God: The Witch-Hunt in Scotland* (Baltimore, 1981), pp. 15–28, 192–203; Larner, *The Thinking Peasant*, 21–57; Dale Hoak, "The Great European Witch Hunts: A Historical Perspective," *American Journal of Sociology*, 88 (1983), 1270–74. See also: Hartmut Lehmann, "Hexenverfolgungen und Hexenprozesse in Alten Reich Zwischen Reformation und Aufklarung," *Jahrbuch des Instituts für deutsche Geschichte*, 7 (1978), 13–70. (I am indebted to Lionel Rothkrug for this reference.)

[34]Cf. Dale Hoak, "Witchcraft and Women in the Art of the Renaissance," *History Today*, 21 (Feb. 1981), 22–26; Baroja, *The World of the Witches*, pp. 216–18.

21

"witchcraze"? Perhaps his pictures of witches helped focus the Western mind's eye in ways that he could never have foreseen. In any case, by 1544 Baldung had replaced the imaginary, high-flying voluptuaries of 1510 with the figure of a woman who might be described socially as the archetypal victim of the first great burnings in France and Germany.

The date of publication of the *Bewitched Groom* gives one pause to ponder another aspect of sixteenth-century European culture and society. Chronologically, witch hunting seems to be related (among other dynamic influences) to the history of a collective consciousness of sin in Western culture. Well before the onset of the monster trials, judges in lay and ecclesiastical courts had come to believe that since the Devil instigated sexual crime, those who confessed to such crimes (fornication, adultery, infanticide, sodomy) must already have recognized Satan as their dark lord and master. The Reformation and Counter-Reformation movements intensified an awareness of the agencies of evil and in so doing, helped shape judicial conceptions of what violated both God's law and the laws of human society.[35] As one who moved in a circle of jurists and lawyers, Baldung must have been aware after 1532 (the date of the publication of the *Carolina,* the Imperial law code of Charles V) of the reinforced association of *maleficium* and sexually suspect behavior. We know that the prosecution of sex-related crime in the sixteenth and seventeenth centuries followed the general pattern of the course and chronology of the witch hunts.[36] Although nothing can be adduced to connect this fact with the subject matter of Baldung's print, the *Bewitched Groom* nevertheless seems to be very much a picture of the historical moment: its combination of the demonic and sexually allusive is a characteristic product of Reformation mentalities.

Like the *Hexenbilder* generally, the *Bewitched Groom* confirms Baldung's obsession with the sexual manifestations of sorcery,[37] but nothing in his earlier pictures of witches quite prepares one for the

[35]E. William Monter, "La sodomie a l'époque moderne en Suisse romande," *Annales: Économies Sociétés Civilisations,* 29 (1974), 1023–33.

[36]Monter, *Witchcraft in France and Switzerland,* 197–98. See also Alfred Soman, "Les procès de sorcellerie au parlement de Paris (1565–1640)," *Annales: Économies Sociétés Civilisations,* 32 (1977), 790–814.

[37]See also Linda C. Hults, "Hans Baldung Grien's 'Weather Witches' in Frankfurt," *Pantheon,* 40 (1982), 124–30.

way he handled this theme in the woodcut of 1544. The whimsical nudity of the 1510/14 witches rendered a satanic fantasy amusing; the indecency of the 1544 witch, although dictated by artistic convention, underscores the contemporary acceptance of a certain kind of sorcery. Baldung's patrons and peers might reject the myth of Satan's orgiastic, night-flying minions—Strassburg resisted the mania that affected other parts of Alsace as well as France and Germany[38]— but like the Alsatian peasants with whom they shared elements of a common, popular culture, they thought it possible for some persons to employ occult agencies for sexually debilitating or mind-altering purposes. The *Bewitched Groom* exploits this assumption. Of course the words expressing belief in this aspect of *maleficium* have lost their originally sensational effect. Nowadays we would say that in the *Bewitched Groom* a very perceptive artist explored the sexual psychopathology of a fantasy, but to discount Baldung's acceptance of the "sympathetic" connections between sorcery and human sexual behavior would be to rob this image of a power it once had for the artist and his audience.

The iconographic device of the unicorn still leaves unresolved the question of the apparently autobiographical context of the print. If the groom is lying in Baldung's stable, is this a psychological portrait of the artist, a graphic "confession" of a sexual transgression? Or perhaps a picture of Baldung's fear of retribution for such a transgression at the hands of a known "witch"? Without additional evidence it is impossible to determine whether (or to what extent) the artist identified himself with the groom.[39]

In any case, the image does not rely for its impact on some otherwise undiscoverable aspect of the artist's private life. As art its appeal derives from what Robert Koch called its provocative, "clean-cut power."[40] Like others, Koch thought the source of the provocation enigmatic, but if "Die Hexe als Pferd" inspired Baldung, we should

---

[38]Radbruch, "Hans Baldungs Hexenbilder," p. 32 (and the note on this page for references to accounts of the Alsatian trials).

[39]Von Borries, in the review of Mesenzeva cited above, n. 5, thought that the latter's interpretation of the *Bewitched Groom* did not finally preclude the possibility that Baldung meant to portray himself in the prostrate figure of the stableman. In fact, Mesenzeva ignored the autobiographical implications of what she accepted as Baldung's coat of arms ("das Wappen des Meisters"), saying only that the unicorn was related to the Virgin Mary, a symbol of purity and salvation; Mesenzeva, 57.

[40]Robert A. Koch, *Eve, the Serpent and Death* (Ottawa, 1974), p. 22.

23

understand not only the enigma but also why the artist chose the marketable medium of the single-leaf woodcut for what proved to be his most sought-after print.[41] For Baldung's Alsatian contemporaries, learned and unlearned alike, the appeal of the *Bewitched Groom* lay not in its supposed mystery, but in its sexually suggestive play upon the familiar folkloric figure of a shape-shifting sorceress who first appeared to men in the guise of a horse.

COLLEGE OF WILLIAM AND MARY

---

[41]An impression in the Fitzwilliam Museum, Cambridge, showing the broken ridges of a well-worn and eventually reset block, suggests that copies like it were being run off well into the seventeenth century. I thank Eric Chamberlain, Keeper of Prints, the Fitzwilliam Museum, for bringing this to my attention.

THE DEVIL IN ART

THE DEVIL, perhaps even more than God, of whom he is simply a worthless imitation, is beyond our imagining. God is One: and, however incommensurable He may be, the human soul, being grounded in unity, tends towards Him, in its aspiration towards Being, as towards its First Principle. But the devil is legion: he cannot reach to such a total unity, and the essence of his condition as the Accursed One, the King of Hell, consists, of necessity, in the infinite distance that separates him from the First Principle of his being. This was the anathema that hurled his blank, disjointed soul into the abyss of Chaos, making him Lord of Hell and sovereign over discord. For this prince of all deformity and heterogeneity feeds insatiably wherever contradiction reigns.

No other sacred book has expressed this characteristic of the devil more powerfully than the *Lalitavistara* describing the assault of Mara, the devil of Tantric Buddhism, on the redeemer Bodhisattva:

"The devil Papiyan [Mara], not having done what Sârthavana had done, prepared his mighty army, four legion strong and valiant in combat, a fearful army that struck terror into the hearts of all who beheld it, an army such as had never been seen or heard of before, by men or gods. *This army had the power to take on all manner of different appearances, transforming itself endlessly in a hundred million ways.*[1] Its body and hands and feet were wrapped in the coils of a hundred thousand serpents, and in its hands were swords, bows, arrows, pikes, axes, mallets, rockets, pestles, sticks, chains, clubs, discuses, and all other instruments of war. Its body was protected by excellent breast-plates. Its heads and hands and feet turned in all directions. Its eyes and faces were flaming; its stomachs, feet and hands of all shapes. Its faces glittered in terrible splendour; its faces and teeth were of all shapes, its dog-teeth enormous, fearful to behold.

[1] Author's italics.

351

25

Its tongues were as rough as mats of hair, its eyes red and glittering, like those of the black serpent full of venom. Some were spitting the venom of serpents, and some, having taken the venom in their hands, were eating it. Some, like the *garudas*, having drawn out of the sea human flesh and blood, feet, hands, heads, livers, entrails and bones, were eating them. Some had bodies of flame, livid, black, bluish, red, yellow; some had misshapen eyes, as hollow as empty wells, inflamed, gouged or squinting; some had eyes that were contorted, glittering, out of shape; some were carrying burning mountains, approaching majestically, mounted on other burning mountains. Some, having torn up trees by their roots, were rushing towards the Bodhisattva. Some had the ears of stags, pigs, elephants—hanging ears or boars' ears. Some had no ears at all. Some, with stomachs like mountains and withered bodies made from a mass of skeleton bones, had broken noses; others had stomachs like rounded jars, feet like the feet of cranes, with skin and flesh and blood all dried up, and their ears and noses, their hands and feet, their eyes and heads all lopped off. . . .

"Some with the skin of oxen, asses, boars, ichneumons, stags, rams, beetles, cats, apes, wolves, and jackals, were spitting snake venom, and—swallowing balls of fire, breathing flame, sending down a rain of brass and molten iron, calling up black clouds, bringing black night and making a great noise—were running towards the Bodhisattva. . . ."

This lengthy extract from a text illustrated with so much colour and brilliance by the painters of Turkestan (cf. pl. 5.) is worth quoting, by way of preface, as a remarkable example of the "demonic style". This fantastic accumulation of ever-changing monstrosities never manages to be more than a sum of so many parts, a mass of fragments that can never be resolved into a unity. Ugliness, plurality, chaos—throughout civilisations most remote from each other in time and in space, these are the characteristics of diabolic art. Being himself unable to create, the lord of all impurity, who fell from grace because, for the space of a single instant, he imagined himself the equal of the demiurge, he tries to practise his delusions by turning himself into the ape of God. Artists have no difficulty in portraying this Prince of

Darkness, for he is more easily represented than God, living on what he can borrow from the faces of God's creatures, and combining, in his impotent rage, the various features in the most absurd manner. Satan creates his monsters from shattered remnants of creatures.

We must not expect to discover the most powerful manifestations of demonic art in the art of the West. In any case, if we spent much time on this branch of our subject we should probably be simply repeating what has already been so pungently stated by René Huyghe in his section of *Amour et Violence* ("Etudes Carmélitaines", 1946). In the irregular, disjointed, chaotic style which he reveals as typical of German art, we can see a clear example of the demonic, even though this is simply the reverse side of the angelic style to which this art aspired—a point which, perhaps, it would be a mistake to underestimate. This oscillation between two extremes, without ever being able to find a proper balancing-point, lies at the very heart of the German soul.

The destiny of western man has centred round the search for unity, and hence for the divine, both within man and outside him; so it is not surprising that he should have achieved so little of an outstanding nature in his representations of the devil. If we restricted ourselves to the figure of the fiend himself, we should find that only Romance art, which in any case is steeped in Orientalism, has produced pictures of any value in this respect. The meekness of the Gospel, spread abroad by St. Bernard and St. Francis, dealt Satan a mortal blow; Gothic art was too profoundly humanised to give adequate representation to him; whilst the Mystery plays helped to transform him into a comic character with childish properties borrowed from the kitchen— his fork and melting-pot, gridiron and long spoon. It is not until the Renaissance that we come across the gloomy monarch in truly demonic guise—for a man like Hieronymus Bosch (in spite of what others may have said about him) is more typical of modern times than of the Middle Ages. In a psycho-analytical study of civilisation the sudden uprush of Satanism in Bosch's paintings would be quoted as a symbol of the first onslaughts made on the faith. Catholic apologists would probably discover in it a premonition of the heresy that was to descend upon the succeeding century. For the historian of ideas, Bosch is symptomatic of the

crisis of unrealism that afflicted the fifteenth century, caught
between the faith of mediaeval times and the first beginnings of
modern rationalism. In an essay that has since become famous,
Huizinga has shown how the later Middle Ages degenerated into
a vapid unreality, how all the mediaeval ideals of courtesy and
chivalry and the divine became simply shadows of themselves.
The same thing happened to the figure who stands in everlasting
opposition to these ideals—Satan; and Bosch became the portrayer
of this dream of darkness, as Fra Angelico had been the artist
of the dream of light. In the pictures of this Dutch artist one finds
the genuinely fantastic creations of the ape of God, the forms which
the legions of the lower world assume to bring humanity to
destruction. To produce these pictures the devil, the Prince of
Anomaly, seems to have plunged both hands into the created
universe of dead and living forms, including even things created
by men, and then hurled the absurd results of his infernal industry
in all directions (cf. pl. 19). The monsters thus created,
being born of disorder, necessarily carry within themselves
malevolent powers: they are the anti-creation, with a frantic
desire to degrade the divine workmanship; but the mere name of
the one God, uttered by St. Anthony, is sufficient to bring to
nought these triumphs of the devil's wiles, these evanescent
negations of the divine creation.

The Accursed One makes a melancholy appearance in the
middle distance of an engraving by Dürer (cf. pl. 22). As is
usual in the German tradition, he is here represented in the form
of a pig. There are few pictures of the spirit of evil more striking
than this hideous snout skulking behind Death, following a man
on horseback, ready to pounce on his victim the moment he shows
the slightest sign of weakness. One wonders whether it was thus
that the Lord of Hell used to appear to haunt Luther in his night-
mares. According to the Faustian tradition, the devil has another
incarnation as a dog: in Goethe's work a sinister spaniel goes up
and down under Doctor Faust's windows, and it may be the same
creature lying at the feet of Dürer's "Melancholy". Then, as a
result of the Counter-Reformation, which restored a balance in
art, and also under the idealising influence of Raphael and his
successors, the devil disappears for several centuries. With "The
Miseries of War" he comes to life again in Goya's imagination,
and here again it is an animal that stamps the currency of man's

terror of the demonic; but this time it is a goat, the creature that figures in the "Witches' Sabbath" (cf. pl. 21). Delacroix, who was a great reader of *Faust*, also determined to try his hand at the devil, but his imagination was far too literary, and he could do no more than recreate the puppet of the Middle Ages and produce a figure to frighten the children—Mephistopheles, whom Gounod, with that ludicrous incarnation of his, finally reduced to the level of the ridiculous.

Of all the forms of art, the one most free from diabolic influence was the Greek. The Greek genius salvaged the divine element from the demonic animalism which still surrounds it in the idols of Egypt and Babylon and found the most perfect form in creation to embody it, the only form in which a spark of the divine intelligence shines—Man. Passionately devoted to the task of bringing the multiplicity of the universe, by a great effort of reason, into a unity, and thus reaching beyond the chaos of phenomena to the hidden harmony of the world, the Greek imagination, following the very principles of the structure of creation, operated in a manner that was genuinely divine. The very definition of harmony, given by Archelaus as "the unification of all that is discordant", provides a welcome antithesis to the spirit of diabolism, with its frantic desire to spread discord in the universe.

This result was not, however, achieved without patient effort. The real miracle that the Greeks accomplished lay in their triumph over the slavish state of mind that for centuries had kept man in terrified subjection to the pressure of cosmic forces. The only way man had hoped to give his life some sort of fixed basis in what was no more than a blind play of chance had been by inventing magic rites to create a system of equilibrium by which the beneficent forces in the universe could be attracted down to earth and the forces of evil repulsed, and in early Greek times the image still has its full magical significance as a prophylactic. The vase-drawings, with their black figures, have a kind of frenzied rhythm that comes from the vitality breathed into them by the devil; while on the pediments of their temples there are monsters jeering at the demons in an endeavour to drive them away. But when the luminous figure of Apollo appears on the west front of Olympia, it is a sign that the powers of darkness have been overcome; and from that time onwards the human countenance supplants the monsters and shines out, encircled with divine brightness, in its full beauty. Goya used to say that when reason sleeps the monsters are born: for thousands of years reason had been in a hypnotic trance and allowed the monsters to go on frightening mankind; but in the fifth century reason came to glorious life and put the monsters to flight. Thanks to the intellectual power of the Word, the Greeks succeeded in exorcising the devil: to chain up the bloodthirsty Erynnies, they only had to summon the benevolent Eumenides. Most important of all, they were so enamoured of beauty of form that they were able to use this as their strongest weapon to drive the devil back; for he is the antithesis of everything beautiful. The sixth century had had its satanic aspect. On the ornaments of the temples, acting as a sort of lightning-conductor to keep away the evil spirit she represented, appeared the horrible face of the Gorgon: her ugly grin leers out at you from the pediment of the temple to Artemis Gorgo, at Corfu. Often, on the sides of the black-figured vases, she can be seen in flight, like a locust out of Hades, with Perseus— a very different figure from the proud hero of the classical age—in flight before her. Perseus himself is a figure as frightening as a Tibetan devil, with his flat nose, staring eyes, wide-open mouth, boar-tusks and lolling tongue (cf. pl. 6). But with the revelation of the fifth century, the death-dealing face of the Gorgon retreats into the background, her demonic face transformed into a beautiful countenance smiling at Perseus and trying to capture him, no longer by its horror but by its charm (cf. pl. 7).

The devil's real home is the East. There, for the first time, the spirit of evil is personified as a mighty opponent of the spirit of good in the dualistic systems of Mazda and the Jews and Islam, who imagined him as a dark "double" of God, either, like Him, uncreated, or a creature who had fallen from grace. However, as these philosophic religions were opposed to the making of images, the person of the devil was given no artistic representation. It needed Christianity, with the plastic imagination it had inherited from the Greeks, before any attempt could be made to embody him out of his abstraction. But the Christian artists borrowed his features from Assyrio-Babylonian demonology. The bronze statuette of the demon Pazuzu, who appears even in the seventh century B.C. symbolised as the south-west wind bringing fever and delirium, has all the characteristics of the devil of the

Judeo-Christian tradition as he is to be seen on the wooden panels of our cathedrals and in our illuminated manuscripts (cf. pl. 2). The Mesopotamians, more haunted by the problem of evil than their neighbours the Egyptians, felt their destiny threatened by malevolent spirits which they tried to conjure away by means of magic rites. The presence of a demonic spirit can be felt deep down in the minds of the Assyrian despots who for centuries spread terror in Asia, feeding on hecatombs and tortures. For the taste for blood is one of the most undeniable signs of the

CHANG-YIN PERIOD (14th–12th cent. B.C.). Finial ornaments in the form of grotesque faces. Note the T'ao-T'ie mask.

presence of the Evil One. It is worth noticing that these old representations of the face of the devil already bear all the characteristic signs of the diabolic art whose principles we are trying to establish, for it is composed of heterogeneous elements taken from the animal kingdom, which, compared with the gods (whose faces are human), are no better than abortions.[1] The Egyptians,

[1] Dr. Contenau remarks that "on a great number of specimens there is a deep furrow running from the bridge of the nose, across the cranium, as far as the occiput. The Babylonians," he goes on, "are acquainted with the word 'dual', using it of those organs of the body which appear in pairs—the eyes, ears, etc. But they also apply it to the face, believing it to be made up of two similar halves. The way in which sculptors treated the heads of demons reflects this belief: the artist seems to have wanted to indicate the incomplete nature of the union between the two beings who

who were profoundly humanised—they seem to have been the
first civilisation to conceive of a myth of redemption—paid
practically no attention to the devil-world. Though they were
more inclined than the Chaldeans and the Assyrio-Babylonians
to see God in terms of naturalistic animal powers, they nevertheless rose far above mere bestiality by the serenity which they
engrafted upon it. In contrast with Mesopotamian art, which was
harsh and tragic, the art of Egypt, with its profound tendency
towards unity, is the first pointer towards the harmony of the
Greeks.

But it is to civilisations far beyond those which were the source
of our own, the vast countries of the extreme East, that we have
to look if we want to see man measuring himself in a titanic
struggle with the devil. In those endless stretches of country,
where the human soul seems crushed under the exuberance of
nature and the immensity of its surroundings, the concepts of
God and of the devil remained for a long time undifferentiated.
Through the mists of the ancient Chinese religion, of which we
still know practically nothing, we can glimpse a humanity bent
under the burden imposed by infernal powers. In the ritual
bronzes of the Chow period, we find a conception of the monstrous
reaching a metaphysical height such as no other civilisation has
ever known. On the sides of the *li*, the *lien*, the *touei*, the mask of
the *t'ao-t'ie* juts out, a hybrid combination of tiger, dragon, bear,
ram and owl (cf. pl. 16); "diffused in matter and only
to be perceived in flashes", the monster symbolises "the omni-
presence of a mystery always on the point of dissolving into terror".
"Two generations, convulsed by bloody tyranny (let us remember,
behind the purifying influence of Confucius, the history of the
warrior kingdoms and the opening years of Ts'in), can see nothing,
when they attempt to fathom their destiny, except the threatening
mask of *t'ao-t'ie* in the bosom of a cloud."[1] Under the hegemony
of "the wild beast of Ts'in" the history of China can be sum-
marised in a list of executions: in 331—80,000; in 318—82,000;
in 312—80,000; in 307—60,000; in 293—240,000; in 275—
40,000; in 274—150,000: finally, in 260, the record—400,000
(and yet their lives were supposed to be safe, unless they were

form the creature, the malformation of the demons, even in their physical appearance."
Cf. Dr. J. CONTENAU, *Le Magie chez les Assyriens et les Babyloniens*, p. 98.

[1] RENÉ GROUSSET, *Les Civilisations de l'Orient*, vol. iii; *Histoire de la Chine*, pp. 31 and 36.

Pl. 18.   *The Fall of the Damned*. Florentine, late 13th century. From the mosaic in the
Baptistry at Florence. (Photo. Alinari.)

Pl. 19. Hieronymus Bosch. *The Pact with the Devil*. Detail from the *Garden of Delights*. (After J. Combe, *Hieronymus Bosch*.)

enemies). In those days, "when soldiers only received their pay if they produced the heads", the leaders, to raise their prestige, "did not hesitate to throw the vanquished enemy into boiling cauldrons and then drink the dreadful mixture—or, better still, force the victims' parents to drink it".[1] Here, just as in Dürer's engraving, Death walks hand in hand with his accomplice, the devil.

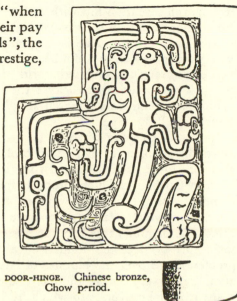

DOOR-HINGE. Chinese bronze, Chow period.

Chinese art, at the time of these sanguinary events, was animated by a rhythm genuinely diabolic. On the sides of their vases geometrical elements are juxtaposed like the fragments of a broken labyrinth or the folded coils of a truncated reptile, and yet this arabesque never creates a unity out of these scattered remnants. It is a cosmos in dissolution, even though its primordial order can be perceived behind the centripetal force that shatters its separate forms (cf. pl. 15).

To this land drenched with blood the Buddhist missionaries brought the gentleness of Kwan-yin and the smiling benevolence of the Bodhisattvas. The demonic style, and the brutal force that goes with it, passed on to another section of Asia, which had more recently emerged from the limbo of prehistory: it conquered Japan. Though at the time of Nara serenity may shine out in the countenance of the divine Maitreya, nevertheless, the "celestial emperors", whose mission is to guard the Buddhist paradise against the attacks of earth and hell, reflect the demonic cruelty of the Samurai. So strong is the diabolic tendency that this benevolent spirit has all the facial characteristics of the devil. The Shitenno of Nara (cf. pl. 9) shows a very strange

[1] RENÉ GROUSSET, *Histoire de la Chine*, p. 48.

N

iconographic relationship with a devil of Vézelay, who might be his younger brother: they have the same flaming hair, the same dilated eyes, and the same jaws open in a cry of terror. This is a very puzzling meeting to find between demonic inspiration from two extremes of the civilised world. But the terrifying power of the Japanese masterpiece leaves the little Romance puppet far behind—it could only frighten simple souls like children, on a Punch and Judy stage.

India, which gave birth to the gospel of Buddhism, investigated the problem of evil more profoundly and more intensely than any other civilisation. In the iconography of India there are very few figures which, properly speaking, can be described as demonic, even though the return to barbarism, signified by Hinduism (which was a degenerate form of Buddhism), often brings the demonic smell to our nostrils. And there is certainly some sort of demonic influence in the inorganic chaos that proliferates all over the temples of later times. For this proliferation is the very image of that endless variety of form found in the material universe, to which all beings, even the gods, are condemned, and in which the thinkers of India saw the very principle of evil. More than any other people, they emphasised the beneficent power of the one and the curse inherent in multiplicity. By what was perhaps the boldest metaphysical effort that human thought has ever made, Brahmanism tried to resolve the eternal dualism in one grandiose myth—the myth of the terrible Siva, both god and devil, mystic lover and seeker after blood, obsessed by the will to destroy and yet frantic to create: a cosmic myth, which raises evil from the level of appearance to a level of transcendental reality at which it becomes transformed into the highest good.

Though China seems originally to have been at the mercy of demonic forces, nevertheless under the influence of the later philosophers a humanism developed which had the effect of tempering these violent instincts—at least as much as was possible in a land as fierce as Asia. There was another part of the world where demonism flourished—a strange continent which followed a lonely destiny on this globe of ours, peopled by races who were brought into sudden prominence, for a moment of prehistorical time, by a brutal conquest, and then hurled back into nothingness. Here God was always portrayed in exactly the same way as the devil; and in no other country has the sign of blood, which is the sign of Satan, shone out so clearly. It is the land of America. In no other part of the world has a civilised section of mankind remained for so long cowering under the terror of superterrestrial forces; nowhere does man seem to have had a more tragic sense of the precariousness of his position in a world in which he feels an utter stranger. He is placed on earth simply to pay a toll of blood to divine powers who are athirst for it: even the sun must have a daily ration of human sacrifice if he is to consent to continue on his journey. Tlaloc, the god of rain, is no less exacting. The terrors of the year 1000 left memories which were not soon forgotten by this civilisation. Try to imagine the state of mind of a people like the Aztecs, who every fifty-two years lived in the most fearful expectation of the end of the world. Death, violent death—the death gained in battle or from the sacrificial knife—was the only means of deliverance from such a hell on earth. The ritual sacrifice of young maidens, children, and prisoners-of-war which went on in the Aztec civilisation— frequently the only reason for fighting was to replenish the altars with victims—has given it a sickening sort of notoriety. On certain feasts the priests would disguise themselves with the remains of a human victim who had previously been flayed alive, and then paint the altars and sanctuaries with fresh blood, having first been sanctified with it themselves; whilst the whole assembly would partake of a kind of communion, eating the corpses that were thrown down in hundreds from the tops of the altars. The civilisations of Peru and Bolivia, too, though more humane and less abandoned in their behaviour, performed similar ritual sacrifices. No doubt the Assyrians, the ancient Chinese and the Christian conquistadores—who were more wantonly cruel than the Indians whose customs so deeply horrified them—showed even greater contempt for human life; but no other fully-evolved civilisation has made death the first principle of a whole system of cosmology, magic and religion—as though the existence of the species could only be ensured in this terrible universe at the cost of sacrificing a large proportion of its repre- sentatives; even those who were destined to go on living being obliged to pay the same terrible toll by making blood gush from their ears or dragging a thin cord, covered with thorns, through a hole pierced in their tongue.

Peruvian works of art undoubtedly show signs of humanitarian influence. Even though the face of the lord of creation usually appears distorted and deformed on the Chimu potteries, there are some which achieve a nobility comparable to the finest portraits of the *Quattrocento*. But no breath of humanity ever reached the images of Central America. The gods portrayed by the Mayas, the Toltecs and the Aztecs are monsters, and the men are made in the image of the gods (cf. pls. 13 and 14). No other art has managed to produce such powerful symbols of the in-

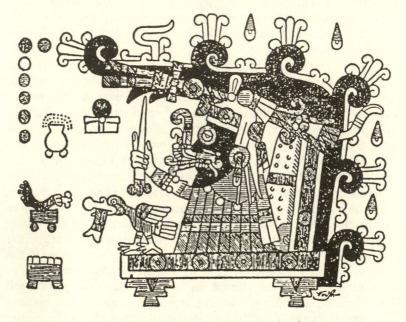

TLALOC, THE MEXICAN RAIN-GOD. (MS. drawing).

humanity of a hostile universe, or created such images of the demonic power which for primitive man is the driving-force of the world.

The strange formal structure in pre-Columbian works provides a mixed conglomeration of elements, overlapping one into another without any sort of continuity (cf. pl. 8). The key to all this is to be found in the Aztec system of hieroglyphics. Mexican writing was quite different from the Egyptian system, with its rows of picture-words and ideograms arranged in a rational sequence, for it combined all these signs together in a way that

produced veritable conundrums. This kind of writing is typical
of the "pre-logical" stage of primitive thought, when the mind,
still incapable of the deductive process which breaks things down
by analysis and then reconstructs them into a synthesis, can only
apprehend the world in a sort of global fashion as a complex of
events that are unconnected and yet simultaneous. The introduction of a principle of continuity, an order of succession, into
the chaos of phenomena, is an achievement of rational thought,
with its power of projecting intellectual lines of force into the
discordant multiplicity of the world. This intellectual gift—
which constitutes the divine element in man—is to be found in
the Egyptians and Chaldeans; it is manifested in their art quite
unconsciously—with the Greeks it became conscious—as a
realisation of certain unifying principles governing the various
structural elements that determine the composition of a work of
art and ordering them according to the laws of rhythm and
harmony and balance. In an Egyptian bas-relief all the various
poses are linked together to give them the continuity of an arabesque; even the shapes of Egyptian and Sumerian monsters are the
result of a rational choice, their arrangement being decided, in
the case of the Egyptians, in accordance with an architectural
principle of proportion and for the Mesopotamians by an internal
formal law. There is no linear continuity for the eye to follow in
an Aztec bas-relief: its unity is continually being destroyed by
sudden breaks which turn it into a chaotic medley of forms taken
from every order of nature, the only rhythm running through these
forms being like the rhythm of certain savage dances that are made
up of a series of frenzied tremblings of the body—a kind of
"seismic" rhythm, brute energy in action, ungoverned by any
intellectual principle. We know enough about Mexican cos-
mological thought to realise that for the Aztecs the universe was a
truly demonic medium of existence with no organic homogeneity.
Consequently for them evolution did not take place as the result
of any process of becoming but simply through sudden, quite
arbitrary changes. It is obvious how easily such a conception
could lead to pessimism (the oration made to celebrate the birth
of a man into the world was always a chant of woe), for optimism
develops in man when he feels it possible to order his life in a
settled environment, in which a periodic repetition of events
occurs according to fixed laws.

There is nothing analogous to this strange art of the America of pre-Columbian times except in early Chinese bronzes (cf. pls. 16 and 17). The similarity is indeed puzzling, for at times the two become absolutely identical—thus raising one of the most mysterious problems in the history of art. Some people have tried to find historical or ethnological reasons for this aesthetic parallel, but in the present embryonic state of our knowledge about the American continent—whose archaeological sites were until recently continually being ransacked by treasure-

MASK OF TLALOC THE RAIN-GOD.   Casas de las Monjas, Chichen-Itza (Yucatan).

hunters, to the great detriment of science—most scientists have wisely abandoned the attractive hypothesis of a "wrecked junk" or the idea of an Asiatic migration by way of the Behring Straits. In any case—and this fact is often forgotten—the artistic works of the two civilisations, though they manifest such strong affinities, are separated by several centuries. Possibly the simple truth is that similar conditions of life—and also, perhaps, a common remote ancestry—may have created similar effects at different points in time and space.

In our comparison of the various artistic civilisations we have seen that those of the West have been less dominated by the diabolic style than any of the others. Occasionally, however, Western artists have adopted this style by instinct, in order to represent hell as a sort of chaos. There is the unknown person, for instance, who, towards the end of the thirteenth century, created the wonderful mosaics in the Baptistry at Florence, far more important as the precursors of a new art than the work of Cimabue, which is still totally involved in Byzantine formalism (cf. pl. 18).

The fact that the West has shown so little aptitude for demonology in art makes its sudden reappearance in our own time a matter of particular concern. In the early years of 1900, in the middle of the triumphant festivities and noisy jubilations of the peoples of the West, all quite intoxicated at the thought of the coming century of Progress in which man's final happiness was to be realised, the authentic face of the Prince of Discord appears with the effect of a thunderclap. This time Satan chooses to make his appearance in negro masks, and in Picasso's "Demoiselles d'Avignon" (1907) his grin leers out in prophecy of the bestiality which was to be unleashed upon the world a few years later. But in those days nobody took any notice: the picture was looked upon simply as an artistic joke, or even as a piece of intentional mystification. Thirty years later, the same prophetic genius, inspired by the civil war that was devastating his own country, Spain, conceived, in "Guernica" (1936), the callous disintegration of the human countenance which preceded in painting the frightful outrage that man was about to perpetrate upon himself in fact. These recent pictures by Picasso, which took people by surprise and even caused a great deal of scandal, bear all the marks of the diabolic spirit, now engaged in an attack on the masterpiece of Creation itself (cf. pl. 20). Picasso takes all the separate features of the human face, which has burst into fragments as though under the effect of a high explosive, and puts them together again, but according to no principle except that of incongruity. These leering puzzles are perhaps the most typical examples that can be found of that chaotic discontinuity, that hatred of all unity, which seems to be the very essence of the demonic style. I know that if Picasso were asked about this he would maintain that he had been guided in these works by one consideration only: the search for beauty. But that is exactly the diabolic claim. "Quis ut Deus?" cried St. Michael, felling the Prince of Pride with a sudden flash of light.

Moreover, there is a whole area of modern art with its own special idiom, and this idiom is the stylised chaos that is typical of the demonic. The originators of this destructive process believed in all good faith that they were being guided by a "constructivist" instinct—but is not this very deception one of the evil Spirit's well-known ruses? As for diabolic imagery, it flourishes again in Surrealism, which, far more adeptly than Bosch, produces monsters from separate bits and pieces taken from every branch of the natural order and every element in human industry. Unnatural creation is Satan's prerogative.

After the idyllic naturalism of the nineteenth century, artists have unconsciously been driven to express the anguish of a world shaken by one of the most violent onslaughts of evil that mankind has had to endure. The red constellation which is the sign of Satan has reappeared on the horizon. The death-roll of Assyria, China and the Aztecs has been passed and now bodies are being heaped up in millions round the altars to the evil one. Modern man has outdone his predecessors in ferocity. The lampshades made from human skin that were found in Buchenwald are more devilish than the human brew on which the Ts'in generals feasted or the flayed remains with which the Aztecs disguised themselves: these had at least the excuse that they formed part of a magic ritual. Never before has Satan had such powerful means at his disposal: he now has his death-factories, laboratories of suffering in which human nature can be tortured, disfigured and degraded —that human nature which, like him, was created in the image of God, but which, unlike him, has kept the faculty to aspire towards the supreme Good, the divine Unity.

Primitive man lived in terror of cosmic forces that were always about to be unloosed upon him. Modern man, having, thanks to science, mastered nature, has freed himself from fear. But it is a brief illusion, for now we are entering upon a time comparable with the darkest periods of human history; and we tremble with anxiety under the threat of a catastrophe whose cause no longer lies in the nature of things but in ourselves. Dispossessed of nature, his former kingdom, Lucifer now seems to have installed himself at the very centre of human intelligence, which has been far too ready to put itself on a level with God, playing with the forces it has mastered without having the humility to admit that the total chain of cause and effect must always remain beyond its comprehension. Modern science is many-sided, and the knowledge it embraces far greater than any single human being could ever possibly absorb. The question is, does this prodigious sum of knowledge bring us nearer to God, or does it take us farther away from Him, and from that Unity, that state of Absolute Being, from which Satan, the Arch-Enemy, has for ever been excluded?

GERMAIN BAZIN

Great Black Goats and Evil Little Women: The Image of the Witch in Sixteenth-Century German Art

by

Jane P. Davidson
University of Nevado-Reno

Witch imagery in German Renaissance art may strike the modern observer as something incongruous in an age noted for interest in humanism, reformation, science, appreciation of beauty and the like. Nonetheless, it existed. Further, we find a number of prominent German artists who depicted witches. The operative point here is probably an interest in realism. Renaissance artists, north and south, were preoccupied with reality. To this end, their art stressed optical accuracy, factual anatomy, convincing natural details and so on.

We may not be able to accept the literary descriptions of witches from the sixteenth century as reality, but Germans did and we must also presume that the German artists did as well. In this sense witchcraft themes in art are just as much a study of everyday human activities as are any other works of genre. The German artists who depicted witches stressed the reality of witches by showing what were perceived to be accurate descriptions of the activities of witches, witches' paraphernalia, their demon associates, and witch physiognomy.

If we wish to consider the image of the witch in German sixteenth-century art, we cannot do so without placing this image in the context of contemporary literature on the subject of witchcraft. Almost every aspect of witchcraft iconography was derived from printed sources or from sermons based on such books. Only in a few cases does one see artists using their own imagination when depicting witches. A major, although not the *only* literary source, for what became a standardized popular artistic conception of the witch was the *Malleus Maleficarum* of Institoris and Sprenger.[1] The justly famous (or is it notorious) Dominican inquisitors outlined in this work of 1487 the blueprint of what witches were and how they functioned in their realms of evil. The *Malleus* was not illustrated (interestingly enough it never was even in later editions), but it contained numerous detailed descriptions of activities of witches. Institoris and Sprenger spoke graphically of night rides on pitchforks and broomsticks, of persons turning into beasts by sorcery, of sexual excesses, of *maleficia* such as bewitching cattle, causing storms, ruining grain, milking axe handles, and the like, and of the so-called witches' sabbath. In short they used all the imagery which appeared in art thereafter. Because the descriptions in the *Malleus* were so detailed, and because they were believed to be authentic and factually accurate, they were easy for artists to adapt into further "accurate" depictions of witches' activities. The imagery becomes remarkably uniform. Just as one would not add features to the face of a well-known public figure today, one would not then change around the images of what witches did. One did not tamper with facts. This uniformity is carried to the extent that one finds the exact same images being used from book to book or print to print. However difficult it may be now for a modern observer to accept, we must try to understand that these illustrations and other art works had the same effect as newspaper photographs have on us today. They represented truth. And, this "truth" most often represented the activities of women as witches. The *Malleus* did note that there were male witches. These will appear to a lesser degree in the art depicting witchcraft.

The *Malleus Maleficarum* is a notoriously misogynous piece of writing. While Institoris and Sprenger did note that men also became witches, they believed that women were far more likely to fall into the traps of Satan. This they held to be fact because women were inherently more evil, less intelligent, more talkative, more sensual, and of less value as human beings than were men.[2] To prove their point they quoted Scriptural passages and Apocrypha, such as Ecclesiasticus xxv.[3] In Part I Question 6, they state, ". . . what else is a woman but a foe to friendship, an unescapable punishment, a necessary evil, a natural temptation, a desirable calamity, a domestic danger, a delectable detriment, an evil of nature, painted with fair colors. . . ."[4]

The *Malleus* went into great detail when describing the sexual urges of women and the deleterious effect on male sexuality which a witch could cause. It went so far as to state that witchcraft stemmed from the unbridled sexual nature of women. It was no wonder then that artists immediately selected the female witch's sexual deviance and licentious behavior as a fit topic for study. This was also a part of the set of known "facts" about witches. And of course it was also a component of the Renaissance style to seek out reasons to depict the human nude. This lent itself nicely to showing examples of witches' sexual activities. So, our picture of what a witch is and what she does was well established by the beginning of printing, as the *Malleus* was both an early printed book and an early treatise on witches. The *Malleus* contributed much to this image, but did not create it entirely. Institoris and Sprenger drew upon the works of many other writers and religious theoreticians. Perhaps the very popularity of the book and its images came from the fact that it was a printed book. The *Malleus* was well-written and quite readable and this must account for part of its impact. It was reissued frequently throughout the late fifteenth and the sixteenth century and went through many subsequent editions in later centuries.

When Johannes Trithemius, the Benedictine abbot, wrote of the *Malleus* in the early sixteenth century as, "a volume against maleficent little women," he was merely echoing what had already become a prevalent idea.[5] Witches were nearly always women. Since women were the witches, one would naturally expect to see art depicting witchcraft which contained women. One might also expect to see men depicted as the *Malleus* did note that men could be witches, but the general thrust was that women were the witches. This becomes all the more interesting to consider when one notes that one of the earliest illustrated books on witchcraft contained a male witch as well as females. Ulrich Molitor's *De lamiis et pythonicus mulieribus,* in spite of its title, contained an image of a male.[6] Molitor's book was first published in Constance in 1488 in Latin. It was dedicated to Archduke Sigismund of Austria and was an immediate success. *De lamiis* was reissued in 1489, 1494, 1495, 1496, 1498 and in two editions dated about 1500. Later editions appeared in the next century as well. All fifteenth-century editions were in Latin except one German edition printed in 1493 entitled, *Von den Hexen und Unholden.*[7]

All editions of *De lamiis* contain the same illustrations. There is a series of woodcuts of male and female witches and demons repeated from book to book. These illustrations remained the same in illustrated editions until 1545. Then a new German edition was published with new prints of more elegant renaissance style. Even these new illustrations depicted the same scenes made famous in earlier editions.

The illustrator of the fifteenth-century editions of Molitor was directly guided by the descriptions of witch activities in the *Malleus.* In these illustrations one finds a witch who is shown as an ordinary peasant woman embracing her incubus who has assumed for the most part the shape of a man. His animal feet show the reader that this is the demon, for they are a visual reference to the well-known dictum of Thomas Acquinas that a demon may mimic nature, but not mimic it perfectly. Only God could create perfection. This lack of creative perfection in demons becomes a useful iconographic tool for artists.

Another Molitor illustration shows a male witch riding (probably to a sabbath) on the back of a bewitched beast. This beast could also be a demon, as demons frequently transported witches in this fashion. A third illustration depicts the flight to the witches' sabbath of three witches who have transformed themselves into beasts and who have also mounted a forked stick. The *Malleus* commented that witches flew by various means of locomotion; millstones, pitchforks, and brooms, but it was the pitchfork which these early German artists usually used when showing flying witches.

Hundreds of books dealing with witchcraft were published in Germany in the sixteenth century. However, there are only a relatively small number of these which were illustrated. The number of illustrated books increased as the end of the century approached and the witch craze expanded. But, the iconography of witchcraft remained quite uniform throughout the century.

One of the earliest sixteenth-century German treatises on witchcraft is *Die Emeis* (The Ants) written by Johannes Geiler von Kaisersberg, the cathedral preacher of Strassburg (Strasbourg). *Die Emeis* was published in Strassburg as a posthumous work in 1517. Contrary to what Rossell Hope Robbins has written concerning this book, it was not the first German treatise on witches as *Von den Hexen und Unholden* predates it by twenty-four years.[9] *Die Emeis* is a series of Geiler's Lenten sermons dealing with various topics including witchcraft and lycanthropy (people turning into werewolves). It was illustrated by several hands.

A woodcut in a rather crude style from *Die Emeis* depicts witches preparing for a sabbath. (Plate 1) This particular illustration has been frequently compared with similar prints by the contemporary Strassburg artist, Hans Baldung (Grien). This scene of a preparation for a sabbath is based on works by Baldung, but is not by his hand. We should note however that Baldung had produced illustrations for other Geiler books published before Geiler's death in 1514. As with the witch and demon scene in Molitor, these witches are not shown as anything but ordinary human women. This is all the more remarkable in an age in which persons studied physiognomy and at a time when some writers were going to great lengths to describe the peculiar physiognomy (such as ugly features) of witches as one of the "indications" (*indicia*) or guideposts to identifying a witch.[10]

The witches in this scene are preparing for flight to their sabbath. They are accompanied by a male demon who urges them on from his perch in a tree at the left. The witches have with them two pots of flying ointment — a necessary element in flight to a sabbath — a concoction of poisonous herbs, dead animal flesh or, especially prized, unbaptized baby fat, and the like. They also have wine and more palatable food as the sabbath usually consisted in part of a feast and all the food served was not necessarily fetid. One witch has a pitchfork, but another is apparently going to ride to the sabbath on her stool which she has charmed. It is literally walking into the scene. Women of several ages are shown here. This is iconographically correct as older witches were always trying to recruit younger members for the sect. This seemingly lively illustration is actually rather tame when it is compared to some of Baldung's works from which it was derived.

The *Die Emeis* illustration most closely resembles a chiaroscuro woodcut by Hans Baldung. (Plate 2) The Baldung print is inaccurately titled *Witches' Sabbath,* as it actually depicts a departure for a sabbath with witches preparing their flying ointments. The print exists in several states; a grey toned and orange toned chiaroscuro are known. It bears Baldung's monogram and the date, 1510. Witches of several ages are shown with their pots of flying ointment and foods, notably the phallic sausages draped over a witch's pitchfork and a wine vessel. Present are also two male goats and a familiar (demon) in the form of a cat. Male goats frequently symbolize Satan, but these are more likely to be lesser demons since there are more than one of them.[11]

Witches' Sabbath (Woodcut) Unknown (after Hans Baldung Grien) From J. Geiler von Kaisersberg. *Die Emeis.* 1517, Strassburg.

Witches' Sabbath (Engraving) Hans Baldung Grien, 1510.

One witch is flying on the smoke and vapor issuing from the ointment pot. This vapor itself is a fitting symbol of the magic qualities of the ointment. Another witch rides a male goat and carries with her a pot of food supported by a pitchfork. Baldung has depicted witches with their hair flying out from their heads. This iconography denotes the evil being engendered by the witches and also may depict the generally vile atmosphere of the place. In later witchcraft writings, sabbaths are often portrayed taking place in stormy weather.

Most of the Baldung witch scenes are also erotic art. A drawing from the Louvre, dated 1514, is such an example. The drawing is on green tinted paper and most likely also depicts a preparation for a sabbath. It is also traditionally titled, *Witches' Sabbath*. Witches are seen with a familiar demon, again a hellish cat, in a setting not unlike that of the previous print. They engage in sexual excesses so often the concern of contemporary writers. These witches are shown using pitchforks and sausages as phalli. An evil cupid, his foot pressing on the pitchfork, seems almost reluctant to continue his role of symbol and participant in the scene. Baldung seems to have used his depiction of witches as a vehicle for erotica and vice versa. A drawing related to the previous work is entitled, *Three Witches*. This drawing is actually a New Years design and bears the inscription, "To the clergy, a good year." Still another Baldung drawing from 1514 of a *Witches' Sabbath* also has sexual overtones. Here the imagery is more complete in the sense of showing witches cooking their feast and consorting with demonic beasts—activities part of witches' sabbaths.

Baldung's *Weather Witches* from 1523 is an elegant and erotic painting of two voluptuous nude witches and a male goat. One witch has disrobed and the other is being undraped by a cupid. She holds aloft a flask likely filled with urine. The fluid is urine-colored and not viscous. It cannot therefore be ointment, because the ointment, made of baby fat, was of necessity greasy in consistency. To influence weather, the witch usually urinated into a hole or furrow in the earth. Then, she might dip a broom into this and shake the broom at the sky as she spoke her incantations. While the *Weather Witches* is iconographically correct, it is also the artist's interpretation of the story as these witches are actually more nude studies than anything else.

A final Baldung witchcraft theme appears in the woodcut, *The Bewitched Groom* from about 1544. This is an enigmatic print. The witch is certainly depicted as a malicious being, but we do not clearly understand what Baldung is stating in this print. Perhaps the witch has caused the groom to fall into a stuporous condition, that is to say in the parlance of the day, she has "fascinated" him. Or, she may have bewitched the horse and made him kick the groom. It may also be that the groom himself is a witch and has caused himself to become unconscious by having used a drug-ladened ointment. We may be witnessing a "flight to a sabbath" induced by drugs.

Hans Baldung was not the only German Renaissance master to use the theme of witchcraft in his works. A drawing by Albrecht Altdorfer from 1506 depicts a similar scene of witches leaving for a sabbath. Again, as in the Baldung works, these are elegant and sensuous female nudes. The witches mount demonic beasts to ride to the sabbath and at least one has changed her form into that of an animal. The witch at the extreme lower right sits beside a sieve. It was frequently stated in the literature and popular lore that a witch could carry water in a sieve. Again, like Baldung, Altdorfer has been faithfully guided by literary sources.

There are two engravings by Albrecht Durer which depict witchcraft. The earliest is the *Four Witches* from 1497. A second *Witch* dates from about 1500. (Plate 3) The *Four Witches* contains iconography similar to the Baldung *Weather Witches* in that Durer was essentially studying the female nude form. The *Witch* may be identified by her flying hair and by the male goat on which she is seated. She carries a broom as well to further identify herself. She is not especially horrific, but we should note that her hair flies outward from the back of her head in contradiction to the laws of nature as the goat is flying in the same direction as her hair.

A pattern emerges in sixteenth-century German art of very exact and faithful iconographic representations of witches. The artists who worked as illustrators were extremely careful to closely follow the dictates of the printed word. Artists like Baldung and Durer may at times have felt free to use the image of the witch as a study of the nude, but even they did not invent magical paraphernalia or show deeds of witches that could not be found in the contemporary literature. This close adherence to what was known to be "true" about witchcraft is one of the best examples of how seriously most Germans took the idea that there were witches in their midst. It is interesting that the book illustrators generally depict their witches doing more awful acts like engaging in sex with demons and cooking baby corpses. One does not find such tintillating scenes in the works of the better known artists. Again, in this connection, we should note the question of the physical appearance of the witch in sixteenth-century German art. We have already mentioned that witches *generally* do not appear with extremely distorted features. The artists again seem to have adhered to the literary "reality" of the situation showing witches as real men and women, just as people believed witches to be. German Renaissance artists seem to have been very dependent on what we might characterize as the eyewitness approach to witches. This approach is clearly seen in illustrations from *Historia de gentibus septentrionalibus* written by Olaus Magnus bishop of Upsala.[12]

In this book we have detailed literary descriptions of what witches do. Following the text, the illustrators show readers male and female witches engaging with demons in a variety of acts. This book was published in Rome, written by a Swede, and dedicated to the Archbishop of Cologne. It had a great influence on German witchcraft art. The first edition of his *Historia de gentibus septentrionalibus* (1555) contained illustrations of the activities of witches and demons

The Witch (Engraving) Albrecht Dürer, about 1500.

Christlich Bedencken
vnnd erinnerung
von
Zauberey/

Woher/was/vnd wie vielfältig sie sey/ wem sie
schaden könne oder nicht/wie diesem Laster zu wehren/ vnd die
so damit behafft/ zu bekehren/ oder auch zu
straffen seyn.

Beschrieben durch
Augustin Lercheimer von
Steinfelden.
Aut assentire his, aut meliora doce.

Jetzund auffs new gemehret vnd
gebessert.

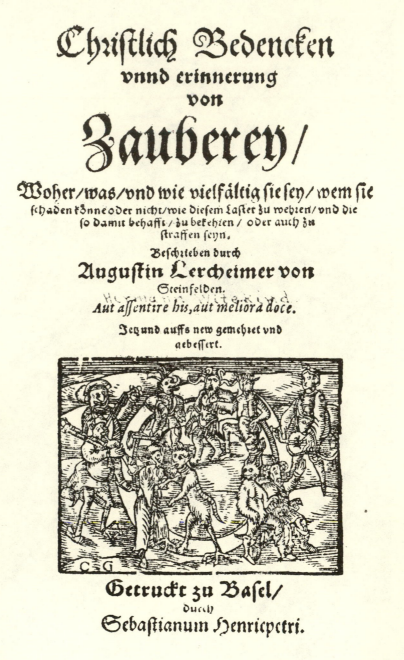

Getruckt zu Basel/
durch
Sebastianum Henricpetri.

Witches and Demons (Woodcut frontispiece) Master C.G. From Hermann
Witekind. *Christlich Bedencken unnd erinnerung von Zauberey. 1593, Basel.*

which were then copied in a second edition published in Basel in 1567. While we do not know which artists illustrated the 1555 edition, we do know the Basel illustrator only by monogram. Master C. G. based his illustrations directly on those of the earlier book. Later, he would use the Olaus Magnus illustrations in another work of an entirely different character.

The illustrations of the first and second editions of Olaus Magnus, contain matter-of-fact depictions of witchcraft. For example, one illustration shows a male witch providing favorable winds for sailors. He is shown holding a rope which is knotted in three places. This rope was an essential item for doing weather *maleficia,* such as causing storms or influencing the winds.

In another Olaus Magnus illustration a female witch has raised a dreadful tempest causing a ship to founder. She is exercising a variation of the weather making acts already described in connection with Baldung's *Weather Witches.* She has also bewitched beasts which are shown foundering in a nearby field. All the scenes in this illustration are ordinary *maleficia,* the doing of evil to one's fellow humans. Yet another illustration shows a witches' sabbath. This print, used to illustrate a chapter entitled, "De Eluarum spectorum nocturna chorea," depicts demons dancing with a male witch in a magic ring. These rather playful satyr-like demons are unusual for their neoclassical connotations and we probably should attribute them to Italianate influences in view of the fact that the book was published and illustrated in Rome. It is unusual to see a male witch dancing with male demons, although male witches were posited by Olaus Magnus and appeared in other illustrations in this book as has been noted above. This print stresses sexual imagery and the deception of demons as one holds a flower while another holds a serpent.

As noted before, these illustrations from the first edition of Olaus Magnus were copied by Master C. G. in the 1567 edition of the book published in Basel by Sebastian Henricpetri. Master C. G. also provided a frontispiece for Hermann Witekind's *Christliche Bedencken unnd erinnerung von Zauberey* (sic) (Plate 4) published again by Henricpetri in Basel in 1593. In this frontispiece master C. G. again depicted witches and demons dancing in a ring. The engraving seems obviously derived from the original in the 1555 Olaus Magnus, as it contains almost exactly the same imagery. We see the same musician demons and the same satyr-demons dancing. Some more specifically German elements are added here so that we now have a female witch included in the scene. This made it more iconographically acceptable to the German reader, as Germans would have been expecting to see female witches—more traditional depictions rather than the more neoclassical satyrs. One must wonder whether Master C .G. was acquainted with the contents of the book he illustrated for his illustration served essentially as a smokescreen for the book's central thesis. Witekind discussed witchcraft according to rather traditional sounding chapter divisions, but his point was that of criticism of the beliefs prevalent at the time. This work has been described by the historian George Lincoln Burr as "a bold and startlingly eloquent protest against the worst features of the (witch) persecution."[13] Witekind was a professor at Heidelberg and a close friend of Melanchthon. Most likely the illustration is a foil designed to molify the reader into thinking that probably after all Witekind was pretty orthodox in his views on witches. We are not saying that Witekind did not actually believe in witches, but he certainly did not succumb to all the credulity generally found in sixteenth-century German religious texts on witchcraft.

This credulity is wonderfully illustrated by the writings of the suffragan bishop of Trier, Peter Binsfeld. Binsfeld himself was responsible for the condemnation for witchcraft of probably hundreds of individuals. There has not been an exact total determined, but Binsfeld was one of the major persecutors at the height of the witch craze. In 1591 Binsfeld's *Tractat von Bekanntnis der Zauber und Hexen* was published in Munich by the well known press of Adam Berg. This was not the first edition of this book, but it was the first to be illustrated. Rossell Hope Robbins has called the *Tractat,* "a bigoted and savage work."[14] Binsfeld incorporated all the standard group of beliefs and superstitions concerning witchcraft into his book and he included a lengthy section on the justification of torture which he referred to decorously as "the painful question." The frontispiece of Binsfeld's book is by an unknown printmaker and depicts a number of different activities of female witches. (Plate 5) Once again, as we have seen in other German works, the witches are depicted for the most part as realistic-looking human beings. Here are actually well dressed witches, for it was believed that not only peasants became witches, but also members of the upper classes, the clergy, and the nobility could be followers of Satan. The illustrator depicts witches flying to a sabbath. One even issues from a chimney. A witch is shown causing a hailstorm, while another spoils wine and two witches nearby consort with demon lovers. A witch at the right of the scene is shown also with her demon familiar. Both are very elegantly dressed. At the left a witch fondles a demon dressed as a Catholic priest (Binsfeld was a Catholic). This demon may represent the Antichrist as well as a priest, as the Antichrist is often shown requiring homage from his followers in a similar fashion. Lastly, the central witch in the print is happily boiling a baby.

We see a wide range of witches' activities, the flight, *maleficia,* and the sabbath as well as sexual license. The artist of the Binsfeld *Tractat,* like German artists before him, has been absolutely faithful to the printed word in his iconography. All the scenes depicted in this frontispiece can be found described in the text. Binsfeld wrote such an intense book (a work which we feel can safely be described as bloodcurdling) that it must have been easy for the artist-illustrator to render the sort of detailed and complicated iconography which he has given us in the frontispiece.

A last example well illustrates the journalistic nature of German Renaissance witchcraft art. This is a pamphlet describing the fall into witchcraft and subsequent trial and execution of Walpurga Hausmannen in 1587.[15] (Plate 6)

Activities of Witches (Woodcut frontispiece) Unknown From Peter Binsfeld. *Tractat von Bekanntnis der Zauber und Hexen.* 1591, Munich.

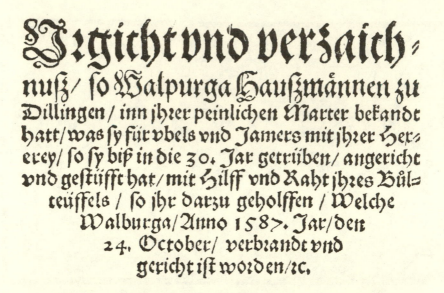

M. D. LXXXVIII.

Trial and Execution of Walpurga Hausmannen (Woodcut) Unknown, 1588, Dillingen.

This pamphlet contains an illustration of Walpurga and her demon friend has all the tabloid qualities of later broadsides such as those which were popular in England in the seventeenth century. It shows us Walpurga and the demon (whom she met at the side of the road) who convinced her to become a witch. Walpurga was primarily a practitioner of *maleficia,* but she was nonetheless tried, condemned, and burnt. Her trial comes just over one hundred years after the publication of the *Malleus Maleficarum.* Like most sixteenth-century witches, Walpurga is shown as a normal-looking woman. Illustrated trial records such as this seem to be rather rare, at least from the number of surviving representatives. However, a large number of trial accounts have been preserved and we may presume that some others were illustrated.

We began this discussion by noting that witches were real to the sixteenth-century German. We further noted that their existence was probably accepted as real by the artists who illustrated them as well. Witchcraft was a component of Renaissance Germany and witchcraft themes were a component of German Renaissance art. In another sense, these themes are also medieval. By this is meant that many ideas about witches and demons were formulated prior to this century. Even the ideas of the *Malleus Maleficarum* cannot be construed to be entirely those of the Renaissance. Institoris and Sprenger wrote out of a longstanding tradition of religious attitudes towards women and witches. It is a nice problem, this witchcraft craze in Renaissance Germany. Because the beliefs and the persecutions existed, they were a part of the period. If we have difficulty in accepting that Renaissance artists such as Durer and Altdorfer could have depicted witches and may have believed in them, it is perhaps because we are imposing on these artists our own notions about what the Renaissance was. Nothing quite so well reveals the great intellectual complexity of this period than does the presence of hundreds of German books on witchcraft and the impact that these had on art.

NOTES

1.   Editions of the *Malleus Maleficarum* consulted in this study include, the first edition (Speier, before 15 Apr., 1478), and the second edition (Speier, 1490). A workable modern translation may be obtained in M. Summers, *Malleus Maleficarum* (London, 1948).
2.   In Part I, Question 6, the *Malleus* carefully describes women as being less moral, less intellgent, and more sensual than men. Institoris and Sprenger describe in great detail the sexual dysfunction of men that witches can cause in Part I, Question 9, and to a lesser extent elsewhere in the text. They describe various witches' modes of flight such as broomsticks anointed with ointment in Part II, Question 3.
3.   The *Malleus* quotes from Ecclesiasticus xxv in Part I, Question 6, for example, "I had rather dwell with a lion and a dragon than keep house with a wicked woman. . . All wickedness is but little to the wickedness of woman. . ." Ecclesiasticus or the Book of the Wisdom of Jesus, Son of Sirach, was regarded as part of the Apocrypha by

St. Jerome, and eventually incorporated into the Vulgate. For a modern translation, see the *New Oxford Annotated Bible Revised Standard Version,* 1973. A discussion of St. Jerome's Treatment of the Ecclesiasticus can be found in Vol. I *Schaff Herzog Encyclopedia of Religious Knowledge* (New York, 1909), p. 215.

4.   *Malleus Maleficarum,* Part I, Question 6.

5.   I am indebted to Professor Noel Brann for calling this to my attention. Trithemius' comments on the *Malleus* can be found in his catalog of German luminaries, published after his death in the early sixteenth century.

6.   The British Museum owns an edition of Molitor from 1488. The earliest editions which I have been able to find in the United States are from 1489 (Constance). One is owned by the Huntington Library, another by Cornell University and a third may be found in the Library of Congress.

7.   U. Molitor, *Von den Hexen und Unholden* (Strassburg, 1493).

8.   J. Geiler von Kaisersberg, *Die Emeis* (Strassburg, 1517).

9.   R. H. Robbins, *Encyclopedia of Witchcraft and Demonology* (New York, 1959), p. 213. .

10.   Indications of witchcraft included ugly facial features, physical deformities, bad reputations, habitual cursing, and the like. They were much discussed by Roman writers on witchcraft. And they were well known and discussed by German writers as well. For example, Peter Binsfeld's *Tractatus de Confessionibus Maleficarum et Sagarum* (Trier, 1589), and editions from 1590, 1591, 1592, and 1596, describes *indicia* on pp. 232, 236, 240–43, and 248–49.

11.   The use of the male goat to symbolize the Devil may come from France. One finds, for example, trials from the early fifteenth century in which French witches confessed to having talked with or having kissed the rumps of male goats who were demons. For descriptions of such accounts see C. H. Lea, *Materials Toward a History of Witchcraft* (New York, 1957), Vol. I, pp. 231–232.

Another account is found in Robbins, *Encyclopedia,* p. 209. The poem, *Le Champion des Dames,* written by Martin le Franc about 1440, specifically mentions goats as demons in its description of a witches' sabbath. Illustrations from French fifteenth-century manuscripts concerning witches and the Waldensian heretics, such as Johannes Tinctoris' *Contra sectam Valdensium,* from about 1460 depict witches kissing a goat-demon's rump.

12.   O. Magnus, *Historia de gentibus septentrionalibus* (Rome, 1555), De Viottis.

13.   Burr made this comment in a notation on the inside cover of the original. It is also discussed in R. H. Robbins, ed., *Catalog of the Witchcraft Collection in Cornell University Library* (Millwood, N.Y.), p. liv.

14.   Robbins, *Encyclopedia,* pp. 49–50.

15.   This pamphlet was published at Dillingen (apparently Walpurga Hausmannen's home) in 1588, after her execution.

LIST OF PLATES

PLATE 1   *Witches' Sabbath* (Woodcut) Unknown (after Hans Baldung Grien) From J. Geiler von Kaisersberg. *Die Emeis.* 1517, Strassburg.

PLATE 2   *Witches' Sabbath* (Engraving) Hans Baldung Grien, 1510.

PLATE 3   *The Witch* (Engraving) Albrecht Dürer, about 1500.

PLATE 4   *Witches and Demons* (Woodcut frontispiece) Master C. G. From Hermann Witekind. *Christlich Bedencken unnd erinnerung von Zauberey. 1593, Basel.*

PLATE 5   *Activities of Witches* (Woodcut frontispiece) Unknown From Peter Binsfeld. *Tractat von Bekanntnis der Zauber und Hexen.* 1591, Munich.

PLATE 6   *Trial and Execution of Walpurga Hausmannen* (Woodcut) Unknown, 1588, Dillingen.

Photo credits
Plates 1, 4, 5, 6   Cornell University Library
Plates 2, 3   Bibliothèque Nationale, Paris

WITCH-HUNTING AND WOMEN IN THE ART OF THE RENAISSANCE

The European witchcraze was widely reflected in contemporary art. The images of women depicted as witches were varied and constitute unusual 'pieces of history' by preserving a visual record of the intellectual origins of the witchcraze

Figure 1. *Melancholy* by Lucas Cranach, 1528.

Dale Hoak

THE EUROPEAN WITCHCRAZE STANDS as a clear example of the dynamic power of a cultural myth, the myth that an earthly alliance of Satan's minions (most of them female) had conspired to destroy Christendom. The fantasy usually fed upon fear; myth became reality when the terrible, life-denying sorcery of the stereotyped witch could be made to explain unpredictable or catastrophic misfortune. For example, witchcraft might explain shipwreck, sexual impotency, or an outbreak of the plague. In each case, belief in witches assumed the efficacy of an occult system of malevolent, supernatural powers.

An important aspect of this system was the belief that the stars fatefully influenced human life and history. Medieval writers, following Arabic texts, assigned characteristic traits to certain types of people over whom the planets were said to 'preside'. The presumed influence of the planet Saturn is of special interest here, for under Saturn's sign were born those of a typically 'melancholy' visage or constitution. The crafts of the 'melancholic' included those of the conjurer and magician, and since all harmful magic belonged to Saturn, too, the black arts of witchcraft and sorcery were assigned to this planet's spell.

Northern painters such as Lucas Cranach certainly linked witchcraft, a Saturnine practice, with melancholy, the attitude or disposition of the Saturnine person. Cranach's panel of 1528 portrays

Figure 2. *Saturn and his Children* by Leroy.

Figure 3. *Witches* by Hans Baldung Grien.

Melancholy, in Renaissance fashion, as a single female figure (Fig. 1) – in this case as a contemporary German maiden whose fashionable dress and airy surroundings suggest the life of a young woman born to comfort and security. On an open terrace with her are four Italianate *putti* frolicking with a dog, their innocent play an apparently joyous distraction for the girl. But a horrible apparition overshadows this otherwise tranquil, idealised scene: out of a billowing dark cloud above rides the Prince of Darkness, sabbath-bound on a flying stallion, leading a wild charge of naked witches, almost all of them women. Equally disturbing is Melancholy's own activity. She peels a twig, the stick on which, according to one German tradition, the witch was supposed to swear allegiance to the Devil.

In Cranach's painting artistic convention and artistic imagination combine to provide a window of sorts into the men-tality of the painter's class and age. Originally court painter (after 1505) to Frederick the Wise of Saxony, Cranach became a prosperous businessman (apothecary, printer and book-seller) and member of the Wittenberg city council during the first two decades of the Lutheran Reformation. His *Melancholy* of 1528 expressed one of the cultural assumptions of the sober burgomaster's world, that the behaviour or disposition of some persons, especially some women, suggested 'melancholia' and therefore a suspicious connection with the devilish and occult. Towards the end of the sixteenth century the great French jurist, Jean Bodin, argued that, physiologically, women could not be melancholics; but on the evidence of this painting, Cranach and his contemporaries certainly believed some melancholics to be females inherently capable of practicing witchcraft and sorcery.

In the engravings of the planets which were so popular after 1550, some artists concentrated on Saturn as the patron of witches in particular. Typical of these is an engraving by Henri Leroy (Fig. 2) in which the dragons of time pull Saturn (personified as the Roman deity) in his chariot above a wild landscape dotted by people of despised or lowly occupations. Among the 'children' of Saturn are numerous witches grouped schematically according to the fantastic practices attributed to them at their sabbath: flight and orgiastic dancing here, necromancy and cannibalism there.

Such beliefs very much preoccupied Hans Baldung Grien, the illustrator of the first German-language treatise on witchcraft, *Die Emeis*, by Johann Geiler von Kaysersberg (Strassburg, 1517). Although Baldung Grien was probably the first great artist to represent an imagined sabbath, his chiaroscuro woodcut of four witches, dated 1510 (Fig. 3), essentially gave visual form to a stereotype of the witch already well developed in the questions put to suspects by lay and ecclesiastical interrogators on the Continent. In its written form, the stereotype fused elements of three quite distinct systems of belief: the supernatural, damage-doing powers of the pre-Christian *strix*; the night-flying capabilities of certain female folk spirits; and the orgiastic, cannibalistic infanticide allegedly practiced by sects of devil-worshipping heretics.

Baldung Grien's print emphasises two sensational aspects of the developed stereotype: the supposedly unrestrained sexual appetites of witches and the flight-inducing power of their magical potions. In a later version of four witches about to depart for the sabbath (1514), the artist concentrated on the erotic, trance-inducing powers of the witches' ointment. In the print of 1510, however, he intellectualised the occult source of such power: the cab-

23

balistic devices about the urn suggest his probable interest in the alchemical, astrological and numerological lore of the Renaissance magus. Much of Renaissance science was geared to explaining the unseen forces which, it was assumed, systematically connected spirit and matter, the celestial and terrestrial spheres. The Cabbala, it was believed, encoded a description of this mysterious system.

Pictorially, the streaming vapours of the witches' concoction lead the mind's eye, as it were, from the magical forces of the universe to the startling domain of

the sorceress. And what a world it is, as advertised by the wild, sexual exhibitionism of four masterless women! The fantasy of the witches' ungovernable lust finds expression too in the aerial goatdemon, sometimes pictured as the obscene object of the witches' attentions, but serving here as the bestial mount of a sabbath-bound recruit. In any case, the backward-flying, leg-kicking, erotic abandon of the airborne witch, as much as the nudity of all four, reinforces one of the stock assumptions of pre-Reformation misogynistic writers: that a woman's

sexual nature pushed her reflexively towards sin. Because she was base, inferior, of a lesser nature than the male, she was considered to be less able to resist temptation, especially the temptations of the flesh, and because her desires were thought to be insatiable, she became, in Tertullian's oft-quoted phrase, 'the Devil's gateway'. Perhaps nowhere is this view of the Christian misogynists more pointedly stated than in an anonymous woodcut of a 'Demon Lover' illustrating the text of a tract on witchcraft published at Cologne in 1489 (Fig. 4). Female sexuality is here

Figure 4.   *The Demon Lover* from Ulrich Molitor's *De Lamis et Phitonicis Mulieribus*, Cologne, 1489.

Figure 5.   *Witches transformed into Beasts* from Molitor.

Figure 6.   Detail of the Isenheim Altarpiece by Matthias Grünewald, 1515, in the Underlinden Museum, Colmar.

24

married to evil, so to speak, evil made manifest in the form of a hideously attentive gentleman-beast.

The myth of feminine evil spawned an allied assumption – that as witches, some women were able to transform themselves into beasts (Fig. 5). This was but one manifestation of the contemporary obsession with devils and demons capable of assuming animal form. The accounts of the legendary temptations of St. Anthony provide some good descriptions of such bestial demons. In the original Latin versions of the legend, a 'temptation' (from *tentatio*) could mean either something to be resisted or a physical trial or ordeal, such as an attack; and since St. Anthony himself is said to have called his temptations his 'devils' or demons, artists followed the translators of the legend by portraying the saint's suffering at the hands of 'devils which had beat him so much that he had lost his voice and hearing'. Perhaps a wing of Matthias Grünewald's 'Temptation of St. Anthony' (part of the Isenheim Altarpiece which he completed in 1515) most vividly captures the disturbingly realistic forms imagined in the texts (Fig. 6): '. . . some in likeness of bulls, and other of lions, of dragons, of wolves, of adders, of serpents and scorpions . . . and leopards, tigers and bears . . .', each of them howling, growling, hissing and wailing in a fearsome manner.

Grünewald's devils purposefully threaten a religious vision of life. Evil moves and breathes, his art declares, and like St. Anthony, one must wilfully combat evil's dangerous life-forms.

Sometimes St. Anthony's demons put him to a different test: sometimes he encountered devils in the form of seductive

(Above) Figure 7. 'The Temptation of St. Anthony': triptych by Hieronymus Bosch, c. 1500–05: detail from the central panel – The Devil Queen.

(Left) Figure 8. Detail from the left-hand panel of 'The Temptation of St. Anthony' showing the saint being carried by demons.

25

women inciting him to surrender to the sinful temptations of the flesh. In a fantastic version of 'The Temptation of St. Anthony', a detail of the central panel of the triptych he executed about 1500–05, Hieronymous Bosch specifically emphasised the demonic quality of the woman who tempts men so: she is demonic because she is a beast (Fig. 7). Bosch unmistakably fixes her demonic nature by giving her a reptilian tail, though her kneeling pose and monastic attire suggest a woman of very different qualities.

In fact, Bosch's lizard-tailed lady is supposed to be the legendary Devil Queen, St. Anthony's chief female protagonist in a group of stories added to the *corpus* of the legends in 1342. In the most popular of these stories, the Devil Queen plays the part of the archetypal temptress, on one occasion inviting the saint to bathe with her and her nude attendants. When he overcomes the temptation, she dresses and attempts to persuade him of her miraculous powers, especially her extraordinary ability to heal the sick. The first illustrated manuscript version of this story, dated 1420, was produced specifically for the Hospital Order of St. Anthony. To the hospitals of St. Anthony came those who were suffering the torments of St. Anthony's Fire (probably ergotism, a widespread ailment in Bosch's day). The hospitallers gave such patients the famous *saint vinage* – wine which, because it had been poured over the saint's relics, was believed to be a medicine of miraculous curative power. In Bosch's painting, the Devil Queen appears to mock this aspect of the Order's good works by offering her own shallow cup of wine to the seated figure on the right. Moreover, she kneels before an altar, so Bosch seems to be saying her sorcery denies Christ's sacrifice, her demonic magic confounds the faithful.

The art historian Charles Cuttler has established a clear connection between Bosch's Devil Queen and the witchcraft

allegedly practiced in the Netherlands during the late fifteenth century. The artist himself stated this connection in various motifs appearing on the interior wings of the same triptych. In the upper portion of the interior left wing, Bosch painted a fantastic group of aerial demons, one bearing a praying St. Anthony, the other carrying a ship whose curious complement includes an oversized, naked passenger peering between his legs at St. Anthony (Fig. 8). Professor Cuttler discovered that in the image of the ship borne aloft by a beast, Bosch combined two familiar artistic and literary motifs of western European popular and learned culture. In medieval bestiaries, errant sailors sometimes beached their vessel on a half-submerged whale, mistaking its sand-covered back for an island. Of course the 'island' came to life with disastrous results for both ship and crew. Bosch replaced the whale, which did not fly, with a sawfish, which readers of the bestiaries believed to be capable of flight. Now the bestiaries identified the flying sawfish with the Devil, likening the destructive power of such a monster to the more deceptive but equally destructive power of both Devil and heretic, who, 'through their pleasant speaking and the seduction of their savor, tempt the simple and those who are wanting in judgement'.

Bosch's sawfish thus introduces us to the world of pre-Reformation heresy, the alleged heresy of the witches burned after the 'vauderie' of 1459 at Arras, near Bosch's homeland. The connection between Bosch's *Temptation of St. Anthony Triptych* and the witch-hunts at Arras is fixed by an illustration – the only illustration – accompanying the text of a contemporary tract (dated about 1460) attacking the victims of the Arras panic (Fig. 9). This miniature shows what the authorities imagined a witches' sabbath to be like – an assembly where the initiates worshipped the Devil in the form of a

goat. Bosch carried over part of this illustration (the part showing witches riding aerial demons to the sabbath) to the interior right wing of his triptych, a panel linked thematically to the heretical crew of the ship carried off course by the sawfish-Devil.

In such pictures we are of course still inhabiting a world of stereotypes. An anonymous south German or Swiss pen-and-ink drawing of two 'melancholics', dated about 1530–40 (Fig. 10), brings us closer to the realities of sixteenth-century life. A ragged and barefoot old man sits on a barrel on the right; his dishevelled, tattered female companion stands on the left. The influence of Albrecht Dürer is clearly at work in the figure of the man who holds his head in sad reflection, surrounded by symbols identifying him as a melancholic of the contemplative type. In the case of the old woman, however, our artist, unlike Dürer and Cranach, abandoned the form of Melancholy as an idealised female. Rather, he followed the illustrators of late-medieval almanacs who portrayed the melancholy 'children of Saturn' as very realistic social types – peasants, woodsmen, vagabonds, beggars, thieves, cripples, criminals and such like. But unlike the late-medieval illustrators, he invested his melancholics, especially the female one, with new meaning. The old woman warms herself with a brazier, an instrument traditionally carrying occult, magical associations. The suspicion that she practices magic, and demonic magic at that, is confirmed by the parchment, or fragment of paper, at her feet. On it one can see a six-sided star and other devices of the conjurer. The message is clear: like Cranach's melancholic maid, she is a witch.

Of course, like the figure in Cranach's painting, she is also the product of an artistic tradition. But such traditions in art do not exist independent of society. Art is both a product and an indicator of social and cultural change. Unlike the stereotyped witches of imagined sabbaths, this woman could actually represent many of the impoverished women who were accused of witchcraft in early modern Europe. In this sense, the image of her allows us to look at both a mentality and a society, the mentality of those who discovered witches among women of a particular social class. Such images therefore constitute unusual 'pieces of history': they preserve a visual record of the social and intellectual origins of the great European witch-hunts.

NOTES ON FURTHER READING

Charles D. Cuttler, *Northern painting from Pucelle to Bruegel* (New York, 1973), chapters on Bosch, Grünewald and Cranach; R. Klibansky, E. Panofsky and F. Saxl, *Saturn and Melancholy: Studies in the History of Natural Philosophy, Religion and Art* (New York, 1964).

26

THE LUCIFER MOTIF IN THE GERMAN DRAMA OF THE SIXTEENTH CENTURY

Hugo Bekker
University of Oregon

There are few literary figures whose prestige has been as prolonged and as imposing as that of the Prince of Darkness.[1] It is the very slowness of his descent that makes Lucifer interesting. At least in drama, his portrayal presents better than almost any other the gradual secularization of a motif that originally was strictly confined to the realm of religion. In the twenty-odd centuries of his recorded existence as a being that figures importantly in Hebraic and Christian thought, he soon emerges as the abhorred and dreaded propagator of evil. And he ends by receiving complete rehabilitation, or by becoming — through the poet's sympathy — a sufferer whose first enemy, God, must now be negatively depicted. The portrayal of Lucifer follows a line of development that accurately mirrors the history of Western thought and civilization.

Before entering dramatic literature, Lucifer had already traversed centuries during which he changed considerably. In his beginnings, that is, in the pre-Messianic era, man's conception of him betrayed the influences of Persian-dualistic and cabalistic views. This dualism made him a demon and at the same time a spiritual principle. But this view of Lucifer could not be accepted by Christianity, for he now became the adversary, not only of the Father, but also of the Son. Not only Justice, but also Love was now his opponent. This confrontation could not fail to contribute to Lucifer the principle of Hatred, thus making him a figure that became increasingly negative and lacking in majesty.

In the early period of Christianity, however, such philosophers as Origen[2] and Gregory of Nyssa[3] still thought of Lucifer appreciatively and found room in their systems for his ultimate redemption. But the views of these philosophers did not prevail. When Manichaeism ended with the stigma of the Church's disapproval on it, the representation of Lucifer changed of necessity.

But although the conception of Lucifer became thus more narrowly confined by the dogma and religious feelings of the Church, the rebel who once had been the highest and foremost of God's creatures continued to move men because of his somber lot, and to confront the thinkers with the problem of his nature. The theological view that evil had originated in this creature and thus had entered the world did not

---

[1] The material presented in the following pages is based on the study of some twenty dramas, selected as being representative and pertinent to the subject.

[2] Origen, *First Principles*, tr. G. W. Butterworth (London: Society for Promoting Christian Knowledge, 1936), Book I, chap. vi, par. 3, p. 55; Book III, chap. vi, par. 5, p. 250.

[3] Gregory of Nyssa, *Catechetical Oration*, tr. J. W. Srawley (London: Society for Promoting Christian Knowledge, 1917), chap. vi, pp. 5, 9.

stop the search for the how and why, for the meaning and portent of that event. On the contrary, from Tertullian (c. 155-230) onward, there is an uninterrupted line of Church fathers who occupied themselves with the riddle of Lucifer.

When Lucifer entered the drama, he began by playing a silent and symbolical role. However, in this new realm he had to take on at least some measure of concreteness and individualization. Another factor that was influential in Lucifer's emergence as a character in drama was the increasing tendency of the authors to take liberties with the Bible texts. This freedom became increasingly effective in the fourteenth century when the drama had completely separated from the Church and the laity had taken possession of it. In this century the hell scenes begin to occupy an increasingly important place in the drama. They introduce Lucifer in his intimate surroundings, and — familiarity breeding contempt — the Devil thereby begins to lose his ability to inspire horror and terror. However, the customary review of sinners in these scenes remains a potent reminder that the Fiend keeps the condemned in his clutches.

Despite Lucifer's animosity to Christ and man, and despite his becoming the object of ridicule, a dark tone of regret in the lamentations of the ruined archangel often betrays the poet's sensitivity regarding his lot. This sympathy was greater in the measure that the authors were poets rather than teachers. The fall of the angel who had been created good and glorious could not fail to evoke a deeply human echo; for it was with him, and not with Adam, that the original unity of the world first was marred. The rift in God's perfect world (the fall of the rebellious angels) is usually a prerequisite to the creation of man, a creature whose body imposes restrictions upon his soul. Lucifer's beginnings, by way of contrast, show him as a pure spirit. And they are accompanied by the first songs of glorification, sung to the Creator of a universe without blemish. In such portrayals the first Seraph is a being of a magnitude that is the expression of divinity — albeit self-assumed. The reasons for his claims to equality with the Deity suggest again and again that it is the very loftiness of his state that makes him think that his aspiring to divinity is a very natural matter.

In the Corpus Christi plays, and also in the works of the *Meistersinger*, this idea continues to live on, misunderstood maybe and unappreciated, but nevertheless strangely effective in its dogmatic environment. The Eger Corpus Christi play [4] finds a picturesque expression for this trait by having Lucifer identify himself with the sun (vv. 93 ff.). The incomprehensible change of the angel into the Devil is presented with the same simple impressiveness. Only the exhortations of his lieutenant Satan are able to call Lucifer out of his maddening sorrow, and to make him adopt a more sober state of mind. This unfathomable remorse of the Prince of Hell which makes him in many plays a quite passive figure

[4] *Egerer Fronleichnamsspiel* (Ms. of 1480), ed. G. Milchsack (BLSV, no. 156; Tübingen, 1881).

is used in the late Middle Ages as the last sign of his heavenly origin. In a single instance — in the Eger Corpus Christi play — he even pleads for mercy and forgiveness (vv. 141 ff.).

There are long choruses of lamentation in which Lucifer's voice is raised among those of his companions as in alternate chant. It is again the Eger Corpus Christi play in which such a lament receives the most meaningful wording. Thinking of his former glory and bewailing his pride, Lucifer calls upon God, Heaven, the sun, moon, and stars, as well as on the grass and the flowers, to witness his sorrow (vv. 181 ff.). The lament ends with the popular motif of the tree studded with knives and reaching from Hell into Heaven, along which Lucifer would gladly climb if it would effect his reinstatement as an archangel.

However, the moment Lucifer assumes the traits of the Evil one, the attitude of man as represented by the author changes into mere defense. The late Middle Ages have no psychological interest whatsoever in the Devil who thirsts for revenge. In God and Christ it celebrates the victory over the powerless enemy whose punishment is justified by undoubted, divine justice, while dramatic justification follows through the pathos of the struggle between good and evil. This explains the pitiless attitude of many of the poets, as reflected in the triumphant inflexibility of the good angels when the rebel is punished.

Even in Immessen's *Sündenfall*,[5] a drama in which an attempt is made to motivate psychologically the actions of the characters, Lucifer serves, for instance, as the tempter of Cain, who is thus persuaded to kill his brother. However, no attempt is made to motivate the actions of the Prince of Hell himself.

The last result of divine superiority in the late-medieval drama is the ludicrous change of Lucifer into a morose and peevish, mentally somewhat limited, ruler of Hell, who relies heavily on his minister Satan, a devil who never despairs and always "knows" a way out of difficulties. With a liberating laugh man elevates himself above a power the threat of which is already taken away by the divine promise of redemption.

In such situations, Lucifer becomes the clown of the spectators, and even of the lesser devils, who on occasion castigate their master, since he is such a nuisance and kill-joy.[6] Ridicule and scorn become Lucifer's part; at most there is then in his situation something of the pathetic, never of the tragic or imposing. His main purpose is no longer to inspire fear — although he continues to do so — but to amuse an audience which is no longer preoccupied with him as the being whose act of rebellion threw the world out of joint.

[5] Arnold Immessen, *Der Sündenfall* (c. 1480), ed. O. Schönemann (Hannover, 1855), pp. 1 ff.

[6] Cf., for instance, vv. 169-174 of *Alsfelder Passionsspiel* (1501), ed. R. Froning (Deutsche Nationalliteratur, XIV; Stuttgart, 1891), 562 ff.

The Humanists were not preoccupied with the Lucifer motif. The very fact that it was traditional and deeply entrenched in the religious drama of the era that had drawn to a close made it less "interesting" than the new possibilities that were found in the riches of ancient Rome and Greece. This indifference to the Lucifer motif is marked by the fact that, with the exception of a host of traditional and popularized Passion plays stemming from late medieval versions, the Lucifer was not treated between 1480 and 1538. After this year those poets with humanistic training who elaborate the motif do so as Lutherans rather than as Humanists.

In this group the schoolmaster Hieronymus Ziegler is the only Catholic. His *Protoplastus* [7] reads like a historical drama, not written for ulterior purposes. And Ziegler is the first poet — and remains practically the only one in the sixteenth century — who seems to ask himself how it is possible that the angel Lucifer came to choose evil, what was in his mind when he made his decision. This is the first sign, ever so intriguing (albeit weak and here only touched peripherally), that in course of time Lucifer's "Seelentragödie" may come into its own, and that the inner action may some day loom larger than the outer one.

This combination of Catholicism and Humanism involved some seemingly paradoxical aspects, since the place of the individual in the one differed from that in the other — or, at least, was of a different orientation. However, that dualism was more a matter of theory than of practice. For Catholicism and Humanism could be said to be of a classical mold. Both adhered to the essential unity of the world, albeit for different reasons and on different levels. And because also the Church of Rome was prepared to take that unity for granted, it, like Humanism, could afford to turn its attention to the individual in that unity on the level of life on earth. Catholicism could therefore peacefully dwell with Humanism without painful changes in the practical implications of its dogma.

Catholicism in the first part of the sixteenth century was as yet unconcerned by the fact that the spirit which made Humanism flourish was the same that would soon fan the opposition against the medieval tradition of ecclesiastical unity. It is interesting to note that the Church of Rome, which on the surface seemed the diametrical opposite of the spirit of Humanism, could so readily amalgamate it, while early Protestantism, which at first glance seemed to stem from the same individualistic orientation as Humanism, was actually irreconcilable with the new view of life.

If we may judge by the one Catholic dramatic product treating the Lucifer motif after the outbreak of the Reformation, it appears, then, that Humanism would provide a more natural development from the medieval

[7] Hieronymus Ziegler, *Protoplastus* (1545). In *Dramata Sacra* (Basilae, 1547). Copy in Herzog August Bibliothek, Wolfenbüttel.

approach to the modern than could be expected at first sight. The reason lies at the core of this particular motif. It is intrinsically connected with the basic tenets of Christian dogma and as such is a guarantee that the Humanists who used it for literary purposes and who still were so aware of the transcendental world would only gradually begin to change the emphasis and manner of interpretation of the figure of the Fiend. [8]

The dichotomy in the combination of Lutheranism and Humanism, on the other hand, resulted in the supremacy of faith over intellectual training. In so far as the Humanism of the Protestants became effective at all, it was put to the service of religion. It was inevitable that this supremacy of faith became a factor detrimental to the development of the Lucifer portrayal.

The figure of Lucifer decreases in stature whenever faith in the essential unity of the world holds sway, and he generally makes his appearance in an epoch of upheaval when an old world crumbles and a new one is in the throes of birth.

Such a period was the Reformation; in it, the great religious, spiritual, social, and political frictions which absorbed all energies in Germany, absorbed those of the dramatists as well. It is significant that in the wake of Luther's teachings a flood of literature on the Devil appeared, and that the German dramatists who used the Lucifer motif in the period of the Reformation belonged with the one single exception of Ziegler to the Protestant camp. This suggests that Protestantism tended to be more concerned with the problem of evil as personalized in the Devil than Catholicism, and that the contrast between Heaven and Hell was more marked in Wittenberg than in Rome. One reason for this may have been that Catholicism could afford to be lenient and indulgent to the follies of man since it had Purgatory as a means to blunt Lucifer's final effectiveness. The Protestant, on the other hand, had to meet his Maker for the immediate and final decision.

The (contingent) individualism resulting from the personal nature of this confrontation may not have been consciously intended, for the Reformation decreased the importance of the subjective element which played a role in the Catholic doctrine of justification; instead, the Reformation placed man's destiny in the hand of the Most High.

But the man of the Reformation, whose salvation was to a degree none of his own business, could not help being very much aware of the forces that battled for his soul. Man of the Reformation *knew* that "at the other side of the Cross stands the Devil," and that the dwelling place of the Divinity, man's heart, becomes the target of the Evil one, and that all are called to the Kingdom of Heaven, but not all are chosen.

[8] For the small but very important role which Humanism played as a link between medieval and seventeenth-century Lucifer portrayals, cf. pp. 205 ff. of my unpublished dissertation, "The Lucifer motif in the German and Dutch drama of the sixteenth and seventeenth centuries" (Ann Arbor, 1958).

This "accidentally" evolving individualism was perhaps fed by the humanistic view of life, of which the individualistic element was directed toward the present.

However it be, the Reformation did not continue to decrease the influence of Lucifer on man as the (Catholic) Humanists did. If we judge by Ziegler's *Protoplastus*, the Catholics were not so much concerned with Lucifer's relation to man, and could therefore be the first to turn their attention elsewhere, or to begin groping for a psychological understanding of the Devil. The Reformation, on the other hand, lent the fallen archangel greater power than was attributed to him in the previous century. He looms formidable in the life of the individual.

And yet, in the sixteenth century, Lucifer is no longer the same awesome being of the early Middle Ages, when he was tinged with a stark somberness and melancholy majesty. In the era of early Christianity he had come close to being identified with the Greek Pluto of the underworld (a god in his own right, delivering battle against his brother-god Zeus), and thus he acquired magnitude. Now, in the Reformation, the figure of the archangel whose fall represents the causal event of the history of salvation, retreats in favor of a satanic power that is to be understood from the point of view of man's wrestling for faith; the celestial rebel has become man's adversary to a degree which the writers of the medieval drama could not have conceived. With them, Lucifer had first and foremost been the opponent of Christ rather than of the individual who found shelter in the protection of His Church.

In addition, Luther warned against the dangers involved in presenting Christ's passion in drama.[9] His followers no longer confronted Lucifer so much with the God-man as his opponent, but with *man*. The change is of consequence. Whereas Lucifer in his dealings with man formerly attacked him in order to attack God, it now happens that he takes it upon himself to be the prosecuting attorney, demanding justice and requesting that man be punished for his trespasses against a divinely decreed code of conduct. He thus pretends to represent the law, and he appears before the judgment seat with the register of sins.

Such trial scenes are very popular in the Reformation. They were also in the Middle Ages. However, formerly it was Lucifer who sat in judgment and pronounced sentence. Such scenes did not only convey a warning to the audience but soon began to serve comical purposes. Now, in the sixteenth century, it is the Deity who sits in judgment, while Lucifer must be content with the souls allotted to him.[10]

[9] Cf. J. E. Gillet, "The German Dramatist of the Sixteenth Century and his Bible," PMLA, XXXIV (1919), 471.

[10] The trial scene is employed by the following sixteenth-century dramatists: Hans Sachs (1558); Sebastian Wild (1561); Lucas Mai (1562); Georg Schmid (1565); Petrus Meckel (1571); Philip Agricola (1573); Vitus Garleb (1577); Bartholomeus Krüger (1580); Joachim Arentsehe (1587); Georg Pontanus (1589). However, Lucifer does not occur in all of these dramas. In some he is represented by the allegorizations of justice or law.

The fact that Lucifer uses the register of sins and the law of justice as his aids does not mean that the Reformation acknowledges readily the old Christian view according to which evil is the necessary counterpart to the good, made to contribute to the fulfillment of the divine command in spite of its factual opposition. However, the fact that Lucifer now confronts man as an enemy *per se* accounts for the change in the Devil's stature. He begins to acquire some of the characteristics that will later go into the make-up of the eighteenth century sophisticate, Goethe's Mephisto. His gestures become ampler, and he swaggers a bit. There is a leer in his knowing eyes; the skin of his ageless face has not *quite* begun to fade. He seems to portray in his endeavors the effects of some thousands of years spent in a new walk since he decided to be the Devil. He is smaller and meaner, but also shrewder and cleverer than he was at the outset of his career. In short, he is no longer the tremendous being of the medieval presentations when he was still capable of dealing in noble thoughts and high arguments, and at least betrayed his stature in his lamentations.

Man of the Reformation is inclined to imagine all evil powers in demonic forms, and the Prince of Darkness is for him the sum total of all forces hostile to his beliefs. Lucifer is so much seen as the Enemy and as Evil *per se* that he is no longer framed in human dimensions. His greatness disappears because he has no vastness of motives imputed to him. However, the potential threat of his power remains, and he fills man of the Reformation with dread.

There is a new meanness about this lawless lawkeeper who wants to tie God down to His own laws and ordinances. His noblest feeling is disappointment; he is volatile; it is rather that he enjoys an occupation than that he conducts an enterprise brimming with masterful resolve. Also, the sixteenth century accepts Lucifer's reality too unconditionally to have room for feelings of empathy with the Devil's fate. That is why the psychological interest in Lucifer is very slight in this period; his fall is mentioned or portrayed only in short scenes in a few dramas. [11]

As in the Middle Ages, then, the portrayal of Lucifer fuses with the spiritual currents of the day. It is again the religious point of view that determines his character. This is inevitable for an age in which the drama stands by and large in the sign of The Book. However, the concern of the Reformation is not to impregnate man's mind with undoubted religious tenets and traditional beliefs which once have the individual security, but rather, it is the struggle of a new religion to replace those tenets and beliefs with its own, as it is for Humanism a struggle for new insights.

[11] This is the case in the following works: Hieronymus Ziegler, op. cit.; Valten Voith, *Ein schön lieblich Spiel von dem herrlichen Ursprung* (Magdeburg, 1538), ed. H. von Holstein (BLSV, no. 170; Tübingen, 1870); Jakob Ruf, *Adam und Heva* (Zürich, 1550), ed. M. Kottinger (Deutsche Nationalliteratur, XXVI; Quedlinburg, 1848); Bartholomeus Krüger, *Eine Schöne und lustige newe Action von dem Anfang und Ende der Welt* (1580), ed. J. Tittmann, *Schauspiele des sechzehnten Jahrhunderts*, II (Leipzig, 1858), 11-120.

Even the ethical-pedagogical endeavors of the Reformation (that happen to coincide with the educational principles of the Humanists) are religiously motivated, and they can therefore be included in the effective range of the religious orientation.

It is this religious orientation that causes many authors to elaborate the predominance of divine grace over fulfillment of the law. With such a writer as Valten Voith, who turns the stage into a pulpit from which he woos the man in the street, this results in his placing the allegorized figure of the law (Gesetz) in the camp of Lucifer. While the latter leans heavily on advice given to him, not having a mobile mind of his own, *Gesetz* appears as the most important antagonist. He goes so far as to counsel Lucifer regarding the possibilities of luring mankind (Cayn) into breaking the law so that Hell may increase the number of its denizens. A lawlessly acting *Gesetz* becomes thus the awkward result of Voith's Lutheran enthusiasm.

Also the drama of Jakob Ruf becomes a powerful reminder that man must struggle to keep on the difficult path leading to the gate of Heaven. When also those who do strive are conquered by evil, they serve as an indication that even the purest individual needs divine grace.

Even the Bohemian Stephani, [12] who makes a conscious attempt to blend the two fundamentally alien strains of Humanism and Lutheranism, argues the importance of grace over law or justice. However, he does not elaborate his commitment, and his aim is not polemical. Stephani seems to be mainly concerned that his fellow men be aware of the folly of sinful behavior, which can result only in disaster and therefore must be avoided as a very poor investment for eternity.

That same religious orientation makes of Lucifer a tool with which to engage in polemics. It is in the drama of Naogeorgus [13] that the polemically employed Devil sets the tone for the Lucifer portrayals in the Reformation. In *Pammachus*, Hell and Rome are working together to subjugate the world. The Holy See is regarded as the seat of the anti-Christ. Toward the end of the fourth act Christ calls on Luther to do battle against the powers of Hell. There is no fifth act. Instead, the audience is told that the struggle is still going on and that the outcome will not be known until the world is about to end. Thus, Naogeorgus places at the end of his drama a question mark, a more powerful didactic device than any other he could have employed.

And so, in the Reformation drama, the spoken word is full of the passion of religious strife. But the characters, Lucifer included, do not participate in it. They merely speak the words but lack life. Elaboration

[12] Clemens Stephani, *Geistliche Action, wie man des Teufels Listen und Einge —
ben furnemlich in Sterbens-Stund und Zeiten entfliehen soll* (Nürnberg, 1568). Copy in University Library, Göttingen.

[13] Thomas Naogeorgus, *Pammachus* (1538), ed. J. Bolte-E. Schmid, in *Lateinische Literaturdenkmäler des sechzehnten und siebzehnten Jahrhunderts*, III (Berlin, 1891).

without imagination does not lead anywhere. The aim is, so to speak, to gather the partisans, who are to be edified.

This lack of dramatic characterization is very pronounced with Voith. In the monologue that introduces his play, Lucifer dwells on his celestial origin and his pride which aroused him to aspire after divinity for himself. It is a strange speech for one who presumably has just risen from his fall out of Heaven. There is no indication of remorse in his words, and no evidence that he is aware of the tremendous impact of the event in which he was the protagonist. He simply relates now in an aloof fashion what happened. The only purpose of the detachedly spoken report is to get the action started and to tell the audience how he is going to work against Heaven.

Here, at the outset, Lucifer is already the Devil pure and simple, deciding on his future role without hesitation. His change from fallen angel into the Prince of Darkness has no problematical aspects. Almost at once, Voith's Lucifer turns himself, so to speak, into a devil with an old face. He is the Fiend as he will become typical of the sixteenth century. But in this monologue he is placed at the beginning of man's history, and as such he becomes an anachronism.

Even with Naogeorgus, one of the more gifted of the Lutheran dramatists, the Prince of Hell remains unreal. What differentiates this Devil from his medieval brothers is a lack of realization of his *raison d'être*. He does not for a moment think of the glory that was his in the long ago when he was still one of the peers of the Kingdom. There is nothing left, not even a dim echo, of his past, or a hint of an awareness that he has much to remember. As we have seen (*cf. supra*), in the late-medieval drama the Devil often did bewail his fate in a few traditionalized lines in which he revealed that he was indeed memory-possessed. But then, Naogeorgus' Fiend is a highly successful devil. He gains one victory after another, and his abode is a merry place in which he feels perfectly comfortable. And to be sure, the dynamic drive of Naogeorgus' Devil pushes the development of the action so that it appears that he is quite alive and knows what he wants. But he himself remains static, and although he has more spirit than Voith's Lucifer, there is nothing tragic or even problematical about him.

In the characteristic Protestant drama the struggle is of course fought in the wake of Luther's doctrine. A Pauline reference which the Reformer liked to quote (Ephesians vi. 10-11) was influential in making popular the presentation of the Christian Knight,[14] who does not become a shining example until the Reformation period, although the theme of the Knight was already known in the Middle Ages.

In a manly attitude, the Knight withstands all the attacks of the evil enemy and carries the victory. Thus man rather than Lucifer stands in

[14] Some poets who treated the Christian Knight theme in drama: Caspar Huberinus (1545); Alexius Bresniver (1553); Friedrich Dedekind (1553); Clemens Stephani (1568); Bartholomeus Krüger (1580).

the center of the dramatist's attention. And it is not God or the Christ who deals the final blow to the Devil, but man himself. To be sure, it is all a portrayal of the power of faith in God, whose protecting arm holds up the battling warrior. And the intention of the authors is thoroughly Lutheran. Nevertheless, it is revealing that after the treatment of the trial scene has had its heyday, the theme of the Christian Knight continues to receive successful treatment. It is more man-centered and more of an expression of man's self-awareness and self-reliance than had been possible or deemed advisable heretofore.

Since the era no longer thinks of Lucifer as of the stuff that makes for dramatic grandeur, it is very natural that it see the rise of a profuse devil literature in which Lucifer himself is often not even mentioned, but is represented by Satan or by one or more of his minions.

Because Lucifer is usually unsuccessful in his endeavor to lure man away from his faith and his trust in God, so that perseverence in what is a good cause from the Devil's point of view turns out to be but stubbornness in a bad one, he becomes the foolish devil, held up to ridicule and contempt. He acquires the characteristics of the fool, clowning on the stage, hilarious and often vulgar, linking scenes that otherwise would have no connection.

That means that Lucifer during the Reformation goes through the same stages which he traversed in the Middle Ages. And to be sure, this development is natural enough. It is even inevitable for it is based on a contradiction that lies at the core of the being of Lucifer as he appears in the drama of the sixteenth century. Because he occurs as negation pure and simple, and because, albeit often not until belatedly, his scheme falls through, he must of necessity perish as the result of the complete negativism with which the dramatist endows him. Such utter negativism, says the Philosopher, [15] is but the complete absence of the good, and therefore cannot stand by itself. This decay of Lucifer, then, is the result of the view of a time that conceived of Lucifer as pure evil. And so, the Devil of the sixteenth century succumbed as a dramatic character before Lutheran theology could modify his status and reappoint him his place in Reformed thought.

Also, in spite of all fear of Lucifer and his band, there persisted in the Reformation a glimmer of the awareness that man is superior after all to the physical and spiritual forces of evil. Man's innate knowledge was that he stood above them — not that he was inclined to seek that superiority within himself, as emanating from him. The times were as yet too God-centered for that. But man's feelings and reasonings led him back unerringly to God's grace, and it was this very orientation toward the eternal that nourished his self-awareness. Luther himself had provided the

[15] Thomas Aquinas, *Summa Theologica*, ed. A. C. Pegis (New York, 1945), chap. iii, qu. 49, art. 3, p. 478.

possibility for that feeling of ultimate superiority by teaching that the best weapon against the Devil was to despise and deride him. [16]

Thus, as in the late-medieval period — albeit for different reasons — Lucifer receives toward the end of the sixteenth century the treatment he cannot abide at all: he is being laughed at. The Devil thus gains in scenic importance, but he loses his aesthetic significance.

To be sure, the casting of Lucifer in the role of the laugh-provoking Devil had been going on without much interruption in the Shrovetide plays, and it was not merely due to a specific development of the Lucifer portrayal toward the end of the Reformation period. But the thought occurs that, when the era draws to a close, Lucifer deteriorates. When the first religious fervor of the Reformation has abated and the new religion begins to take stock of its assets, or simply begins to take its position for granted, Lucifer finds himself in the backwash of religious enthusiasm, bleaker and robbed of much, if not all, of his erstwhile grandeur.

It is only with the one dramatist with truly poetic feeling that this superiority on the part of man leads to the expression of empathy and understanding with the Prince of Hell. In the last scene of Krüger's monumental *Action vom Anfang und Ende der Welt* Lucifer is desperate when Christ on the judgment day rejects all those who have forsaken him, or only have paid lip-service for purpose of personal gain. The Devil does not delight in the large number of those who are sent to their perdition. Instead, he bewails the fact that Hell did not have a Redeemer. How gladly would he and his underlings have used the opportunity to obtain forgiveness! There is no tone of bitterness in Lucifer's words or any indication that he feels unjustly treated. In fact, it is Lucifer himself, and not the man-judging Christ, who speaks his doom. The dark tone of regret that Krüger imputes to Lucifer was never before heard in the Reformation. This poet is the first Lutheran to find room for sorrow about Lucifer's lot. With him, the Devil becomes a lonely sufferer who acquires the reflectiveness that becomes part of his elaborate make-up in the seventeenth century.

And so, the Reformation, while still dealing with the Prince of Darkness in religious contexts, begins to show the first, faint, glimmerings of a personalized approach, whereby Lucifer's portrayal is about to be increasingly determined by the disposition of his respective creators. By this time he stands at the portal of a new and modified orientation in German literature — the Baroque.

[16] Cf. M. Osborn, *Die Teufelliteratur des sechzehnten Jahrhunderts* (Berlin, 1893), p. 45.

THE DEVIL AND HELL
IN MEDIEVAL FRENCH DRAMA :
PROLEGOMENA

The modern interest in demonology is explainable in various ways, even justifiable from some points of view. If it is taken seriously, however, it should be investigated in terms of its sources. Then, perhaps, it might be possible to throw some light on the most important causes for this phenomenon of our time.

Supernatural forces have occupied man's imagination since the dawn of mankind ; our modern ideas of the devil and hell have been shaped essentially, however, by thought, art, and literature of the Middle Ages. During the period of Christianization, certain pagan deities such as Sylvanus, Diana, and Saturnus (to name but the most influential) had been assimilated to Christian thought, and, as a result, demons became part of medieval man's ontological universe. The Bible and the Saints legends supported popular imagination and furnished the devil and various demons, which often seem to act by divine command.

Thus, until the age of heresy, demons (good and evil) co-existed with the more saintly deities, and if it had not been for the development of a systematic reinterpretation by the scholastics, itself only the result of reinforcing tendencies in the church, our modern views of the devil, witchcraft and hell might have been quite different from what they actually are [1]. In the absence of early

---

1. On witchcraft in the Middle Ages, and on the role of the scholastics in the development of demonology, see Charles E. Hopkin, *The Share of Thomas Aquinas in the Growth of the Witchcraft Delusion*, Philadelphia, 1940 ; H. R. Trevor-Roper, *The European Witch-Craze of the Sixteenth and Seventeenth Centuries*, New York, 1969 ; J. B. Russell, *Witchcraft in the Middle Ages*, Ithaca, 1972 ; A. C. Kors and E. Peters, *Documentary History of Witchcraft in Europe, 1100-1700*, Philadelphia, 1972.

demonographic sources, the historians describing thirteenth century demonology rely on popular as well as theological writings, and they have done remarkably well. However, these sources may be insufficient when it comes to reconstructing what medieval man really felt and believed about the devil and hell, and what the essential role of these concepts might have been in his life. Medieval art yields further clues, as far as it is available ; on the other hand, perhaps because of the impact of the inquisition, it must be realized that the iconography proper of demonology and witchcraft is fairly recent.

Medieval drama presents to us both devil and hell ; in fact, according to M. Rudwin, « Diabolus was undoubtedly the most popular actor in the mystery plays, calling forth half-terrified interest and half-enthusiastic respect » [1]. Closely connected to the liturgical texts in its origins, as well as to Saints legends, the medieval religious theatre can be investigated in perfect isolation, i. e., relatively uncontaminated by either popular or theoretical sources. The influence of medieval art on drama is, of course, recognizable especially in the topography of hell, and undoubtedly there has even taken place a reciprocal impact, in that certain dramatic representations have in turn influenced medieval paintings [2].

While this study is limited to French medieval theatre, which could have been most immediately affected by scholastic teaching, it might be worthwhile to investigate, on another occasion, whether other European dramatic literatures of the time would yield similar results.

The scene of the devil's temptation in le *Jeu d'Adam* (end of twelfth century) has been given a masterly treatment by E. Auerbach [3]. A minor shift of emphasis only is needed to analyze the figure of Diabolus, in order to highlight this first literary specimen of medieval French demonology.

---

1. *The Devil in Legend and Literature*, 1931 ; rpt. New York, 1970, p. 274.

2. Cf. G. Cohen, *Histoire de la mise en scène dans le théâtre religieux français du moyen âge*, Paris, 1926, p. 104 ff. ; L. Dubech, *Histoire générale illustrée du théâtre*, Paris, 1931, II, 9-105.

3. *Mimesis*, Bern, 1946, p. 141-168.

The role of Satan in this scene is limited to that of a tempter :
to induce man to eat of the apple of knowledge and be like God.
He tempts first Adam, then Eve, each by a method well calculated to impress, and, of course, he succeeds. Arousing Adam's
curiosity as to how his lot might be improved (« Poet estre
mielz » [1]), Satan early tests the lord-servant relationship between
his victim and God (« Criens le tu tant ? » [l. 135]). Skillfully he
extracts from Adam information on what he (Satan) might call
the only weak point in Paradise : the forbidden fruit. Quickly this
apple is then associated with superhuman wisdom, to make it
desirable : « Ço est le fruit de sapience, / De tut saveir done science »
(l. 157-158) ; and science leads to power and godlikeness (« Tu
regneras en majesté, / Od Deu poes partir pöësté » [l. 193-194]).

The method reserved for Eve is one of subtle flattery. Diabolus
appeals to her intelligence (« Tu as esté en bone escole » [l. 220])
and calls Adam a fool because of his inflexibility. She concedes :
« Un poi est durs » (l. 222), and Satan, to prepare his victim for
his final assault, details his promise of power over all the universe (« Del soverain et del parfont » [l. 256]), in other words, even
over the realm of demons. When Eve tries to persuade herself
(« Ja me fait bien sol le veoir » [l. 260]), Satan's battle is practically won. Later, at an opportune moment, he reappears as a
serpent, precipitating Eve's decision to present the apple to her
husband. They eat — and experience a state of lucidity and heightened awareness. Ever since this moment in the history of civilization, critics of knowledge and progress have used the moral
argument in order to buttress their opinion.

Growing from the Biblical tradition, le *Jeu d'Adam* does show
a considerable amount of *inventio* : the conscious attempt of its
unknown author to present the Biblical story to a medieval
audience in a framework well adapted to the playgoers' needs.
As for the figure of Satan, it is obvious that he has become the
speaker of the group of demons which, according to the scenic
remarks, « courent en tous sens à travers la place, faisant les gestes
qui conviennent » (p. 35). In the course of the play, he is polarized with God, although he never claims to be a sort of anti-God.

---

1. This passage (l. 115) and the following quotations ware taken
from P. Aebischer, ed., *Le Mystère d'Adam*, Genève, 1963.

That Satan acts even with divine permission is very clear from the scenic instructions at the end of the play : the procession of prophets indicates that the Fall was a necessary link in the chain of events, and that there can be no Redemption without original sin. Satan, then, is at most a kind of Lucifer, a fallen angel, in the *Jeu d'Adam*.

He does not characterize himself in any way. His words seem more like afterthoughts, reactions, as it were, of Adam and Eve, as they ponder the mysterious command of the Lord, not to eat of this fruit. The figure of Satan in this piece, who has indeed amplified the role played by the serpent in Genesis, is therefore a dramatic incarnation of what could have been the first couple's own thoughts, one part of their complex personalities. Hence, from the linguistic point of view, we would hardly expect a semantic field of diabolical terminology in this early play ; and, indeed, there is none.

Almost one century later, the devil in medieval French drama has taken on much more distinct features. Rutebeuf's *Miracle de Théophile* introduces a devil who has been conjured up by a magician and « infidel » with the Arabic name Salatins. Polarization with God is very obvious : the devil has become a feudal over-lord whose contractual agreements are comprehensible and respectable to medieval man, even though they are not acceptable from the religious point of view. Thus, logically, a miracle has to happen, in order to absolve Théophile from the bondage contracted at an earlier time.

The well-known Faustian pact between frustrated Théophile and the feudalized devil was explicit and somewhat resembled a commercial transaction, with the man's soul as a pawn. Demonographers of the time, among them Thomas Aquinas, distinguished between implicit and explicit pact [1]. Aquinas verified only cases of implicit pact (concluded according to hearsay) and doubted records of explicit bondage. Naturally, from the Christian point of view, no pacts with demons should be solicited at all [2] ; but what is interesting is that there was never any doubt in

---

1. Cf. Thomas Aquinas, *Opera omnia*, Parma, 1854, VIII, 391 ; I, qu. 110, art. 4 ; II, 2, qu. 92-96.

2. Cf. Deuteron. 18 ; St. Paul, I Cor. 10 ; St. Augustine, *De Doctrina christiana*, 2.

the minds of most scholastics that demons and devils existed in reality.

As can be expected, the specific form of bondage in our text is entirely within the feudal frame of reference : « Or joing / Tes mains, et si devien mes hon ; / Je t'aiderai outre reson » [1]. In this « classic » form it seems eons removed from the more perverse types of devil worship which were practiced by certain heretic groups long before the first official mention of a witches' sabbath (Toulouse, 1330), complete with infamous kiss, orgies, and promiscuity [2]. Once feudalized, the devil has indeed become an Anti-God, and this dualism is very obvious in the linguistic structure of Rutebeuf's text. The devil's conditions for service, we find, are not only receipt of Théophile's soul after death, but rather, as in true (Germanic) vassalage, an entire change of life, outlook, orientation. The use of the future tense in « Je te dirai que tu feras. / Ja mes povre homme n'ameras » (l. 258-259) is intentionally vague in meaning. There is a sense of obligation (« You do as I tell you ! »), but also the implication of a self-imposed future attitude, as well as even the possibility of action necessitated by the circumstances (« You will necessarily never love the poor any more »). This triple ambiguity only enhances the stature of a devil who is truly Godlike in his own (anthropomorphic) way and therefore all the more dangerous.

After this careful testing of his victim's psychological readiness, the commandments of the devil are unequivocal (imperative, familiar), linked to three specific situations :

> (1)   Se povres hom sorpris te proie,
>   Torne l'oreille, va ta voie.
> (2)   S'aucuns envers toi s'umelie,
>   Respon orgueil et felonie.
> (3)   Se povres demande a ta porte,
>   Si garde qu'aumosne n'en porte.
>
> (l. 260-265)

Then, without further ado, the devil states his negative attitude towards the Christian virtues :

---

1. G. Frank, ed., *Rutebeuf, Le Miracle de Théophile*, Paris, 1925, l. 239-241.

2. Cf. Préaud, *Les Sorcières*, Paris, 1973, p. 52-53.

Douçor, humilitez, pitiez,
Et charitez et amitiez,
Jeüne fere, penitance,
Me metent grant duel en la pance,

(l. 266-269)

followed by a paraphrase of the above, and summed up by the
statement : « Cil qui fet bien si me tormente » (l. 279). The devilish life amounts thus to a complete reversal of values : « Lai les
biens et si fai les maus » (l. 281). From now on, the devil continues,
good judment would not only be folly in itself, but would also be
directed against him (the devil) — yet another type of folly. In
the last two lines of his long admonition, the devil uses the condi-
tional tense, in order to indicate the possibility of something that
had better not happen, again working on the psychological sensitivity of his victim.

There is no doubt that Rutebeuf's devil is every bit as clever
as the tempter of the *Jeu d'Adam* ; but as a dramatic figure he is
a being « of flesh and bone », in comparison to the « afterthought
personified » in the earlier play. He is at least man's equal and no
longer a fallen angel. In addition, he is a true feudal lord, and
the reorientation which he requires is in the realm of moral values
— though diametrically opposed to the Christian way of life.

Rutebeuf's hell is barely sketched, and not for its own sake
but in order to project the horrible fate of Théophile's soul :

Ele sera arse en la flame
        d'enfer le noir.
La la covendra remanoir.
Ci avra trop hideus manoir,
        Ce n'est pas fable.
En cele flambe pardurable
N'i a nule gent amiable ;
Ainçois sont mal, qu'il sont deable :
        C'est lor nature ;
Et lor mesons rest si obscure
C'on n'i verra ja soleil luire ;
Ainz est uns puis toz plains d'ordure.

(l. 109-120)

Hell is thus a place characterized by fire and darkness ; it is
hideous, inaccessible to the sun, a well of filth.

The process of inversion, begun in Rutebeuf's work, is continued and detailed, as it were, in the *Passion du Palatinus* (beginning of the fifteenth century). Its Sathanas characterizes himself
as a manipulator of cardinal sins personified :

> Je qui le feu d'enfer atise
> De luxure et de couvoitise,
> Je sai de traïtour la guise [1].

Using the words of Pilate, Sathanas embroiders upon the « traï-
tour de Galilee ; / Qui se faisoit apeler Crist » (l. 1238-1239). He
describes the passion story from the devil's point of view : « Veëz
le mort a grant viltance / Entre deus larrons crucefiez » (l. 1244-
1245). By the same inversion of values, Judas becomes « nostre
ami », whose transaction for thirty pieces of silver is to be admi-
red : « Onques si bele lecherie / Ne fit deable ne maufé » (l. 1258-
1259). Jesus is defined as « fel truant », « lozengier », and « lerres »,
who has been killed in an especially bloody manner (insisting
repetition) :

> Li ai fet sanc issir a tas.
> L'ai fet sallir et par destraice
> Le sanc.
>
> (l. 1263-1265)

While the world is mourning and even nature is in cosmic disorder
(according to the gospel),

> Or n'i a que du faire feste,
> Joie, soulas et rigolage
> De bon cuer et de bon courage
> D'enfer toute la compaignie.
>
> (l. 1267-1272)

However, Satan's joy is short-lived. Already, Enfers (personified) sees the Redeemer approaching hell and realizes, step
by step, that Satan's work has not only been useless, but has
been turned into a necessary link in the chain of events. In
vain, Enfers tries to rally the « inmates » of hell behind him in

---

1. G. Frank, ed., *La Passion du Palatinus*, Paris, 1922, l. 1285-
1287.

defense, enumerating them according to their former offices and
thus creating the kind of canon already familiar to us from the
Dances of Death, late-medieval elegiac and didactic poetry :

> Li roy, li conte et li princier,
> Li apostoile et li legat,
> Li cardinal et li prelat,
> Li moine noir, li jacobin,
> Li cordelier, li faus devin,
> Li avocat, li amparlier,
> Li robeür, li usurier,
> Clers et lais de par tout le mont
> Qui dedens le feu d'enfer sont
> Soient a mon commandement !
>
> (l. 1314-1323) [1]

Enfers finally resigns himself with : « Je m'en vois, ne m'en doy
retraire. / Si entrera li roys de gloire » (l. 1394-1395).

The Satan of this passion play is shown in his natural habitat,
in hell. He reinterprets the figures of Jesus and Judas, thereby
continuing the tradition of contrast and inversion which had
begun in the thirteenth century. Gone, however, is the feudal
relationship between devil and man ; rather, we have here a confrontation of two different groups, « nostre gent » and « cil... qui
le tenoient a seigneur ». Satan does not strike us as particularly
clever ; on the contrary, his vocabulary is rather naïve, almost
vulgar :

> Je ferai a Jhesucrist la moe,
> Se je ceans venir le voy.
> Tant li jeterai fiens et boue
> Que je le ferai tenir quoy,
> Certainement ne par ma foy,
> S'il est si hardiz qu'il i viegne !
>
> (l. 1350-1355)

He speaks with the certainty of having ample personnel who
can back him up — by words, and, if necessary, by deeds. This

---

1. In later mystery plays, these imprisoned souls are blended
with the cardinal sins personified ; in South Germany, the genre
develops into didactic diabolical literature which, similar to the fools'
allegories, is used in satiric intention (sixteenth century).

Satán is not dangerous ; the character is drawn by the author in the firm knowledge that Redemption is « just seconds away », and, of course, the medieval playgoer, who knew the outcome of the story beforehand, enjoyed seeing a devil depicted as clumsy foolish, and slightly scatological — in short, as a comic figure.

In the final confrontation with « li esperiz Jesu », Sathanas loses his power once and for all : the « sires des infernaus » finds that in this critical moment, his « companie » has vanished (a parallelism to the episode at the Mount of Olives ?), and he decides to go to the only place where evil can be done without interference :

> Or m'en irai en Lumbardie
> A touz jours mais user ma vie,
> En despit du roy Jhesucrist.

> (l. 1418-1420)

Thus, the devil has characterized himself as an Anti-Christ, king (in exile) of hell. As yet, however, we hear very little about the actual topography of hell. As outlined by Grace Frank, the *infernus* often occupied a separate structure among the scenic props of passion plays, and was located at the right of the spectators with its gates visible to the audience : « Smoke arises from the structure, and the rubrics provide that the demons, clamorously rejoicing within and beating on kettles and cauldrons, should do so loudly enough to be heard outside » [1].

In Gréban's *Mystère de la Passion* (1450), hell is fully « furnished » linguistically, and detailed descriptions of it as well as of the devils leave little doubt as to the Dantean inhospitableness of the place. Furthermore, the comic and the musical possibilities of a scene in hell have been fully written out. Lucifer uses vocabulary rich in grotesque exaggeration and distortion to describe hell and his fellow devils as essentially ugly (in aesthetic terms), as opposed to paradise and its inhabitants. Dark colors prevail (noirs, obscurs), and the two *epitheta ornantia* « horribles » and « hideux » characterize the infernal scene. The sense of smell, is involved (« feu », « souffre »), and the enumeration of the devils' accessories, « tools of their trade » to inflict pain, includes sharp

---

1. G. Frank, *The Medieval French Drama*, Oxford, 1954, p. 83.

objects, animals, and even the elements : « chaisnes », « crochés », « gibés », furnaces, serpents, dragons, molten metal. Here Gréban's octosyllabic verse accumulates descriptive terms without attention to meter or rhythm : it is intentionally rough, uneven, in order to project the entire unwholesome image of hell. We are reminded of a mountainous landscape with deep grottos and cliffs, indeed an inhospitable place for fifteenth-century city dwellers who are beginning to experience some of the luxuries that can be traded in for money. Here is the passage in question :

Lucifer

Saultez hors des abismes noirs,
des obscurs infernaulx manoirs,
tous puans de feu et de souffre,
deables, sailliez de vostre gouffre
et des horribles regions :
par milliers et par legions
venez entendre mon procés.
Laissiez les chaisnes et crochés,
gibés et larronceaux pendans,
fourneaux fournis, serpens mordans,
dragons plus ardans que tempeste ;
ne vous bruslez plus groing ne teste
a faire ces metaulx couller :
faictes moy bondir et crouller
tout le hideux infernal porce,
de haste de venir a force
oÿr ma proposicion [1]

Lucifer himself howls like a famished wolf, according to his servant, Sathan. He characterizes himself by inversion :

Quand est de mes ris et mes chans,
Ilz sont malheureux et meschans,
Ma noblesse et ma grant beaulté
Est tournee en difformité,
Mon chant en lamentacion,
Mon ris en desolacion,

---

1. G. Paris and G. Raynaud, eds., *Le Mystère de la Passion d'Arnould Gréban*, Paris, 1878, p. 47, l. 3705-3721.

> Ma lumiere en tenebre umbrage,
> Ma gloire en douloureuse rage,
> Ma joye en incurable dueil.
>
> (l. 3727-3735)

The musical interlude that follows uses inverted vocabulary to describe the ugliness of the demons' song, which comes closer to the croaking of old birds than to the human voice :

> Gringotez et croquez vos notes
> Et barbetez comme marmotes
> Ou vielz corbeaux tous affamés.
>
> (l. 3845-3847)

The actual « motet d'onneur », a rondel, sings eternal death for the damned souls. A comic touch : Lucifer stops the singing, since the disharmony is worse than even he can stand.

As in the *Passion du Palatinus*, Judas becomes the devil's servant (tierce journee), who calls on Despair personified, another inhabitant of hell. She suggests suicide by hanging, and Judas, continuing inversion, renders his spirit to the devils : « ... en l'eternelle flamme / vous habandonne corps et ame / sans jamés espoir d'eschapper » (l. 21975-21977). Then, in a lament of almost classic style, he describes the geography of hell in two complex images. One pictures hell as an abode of Despair, a bastion on a steep cliff, to which he addresses his words :

> haulte tour de desesperance
> bastillee de cris piteux,
> couverte de pleurs despiteux,
> enclose de mur pardurable
> forgé et fait de main de deable,
> fossoyee de puis parfons,
> d'abismes sans rive ne fons,
> dont les salles pour tout soulas
> sont paintes tout de las, helas,
> attens moy, terrible manoir ;
> par dedens toy m'en vois manoir ;

Then he turns to an abysmal cleavage in the earth :

> attens moy, tres horrible gouffre,
> car sans fin en l'eternal souffre
> vois mourir de mort douloureuse ;
> attens moy, chartre rigoureuse,

> fourneau rouge de feu ardant,
> fosse de serpens habondant,
> riviere de puant bourbier :
> a mon grief dueil et destourbier
> par dedans toy plonger m'en vois ;
> mes au partir a haulte voix,
> deables, dont j'ay fait les commandz,
> et corps et ame vous commandz.
>   Icy se pend Judas.
>
> (l. 21986-22008)

From the structural point of view, the action of the devils in this fifteenth century passion play forms a logical counterpoint to the Biblical story, by inversion in its purest form. Not only that : the counterpoint reinterprets the events of the « main » action in its own (diabolical) sense and philosophy. Each of the two actions has its own level, its own logic, its own protagonists ; but the villains in the Gospel story (Judas, Pilate, the Jews) are the heroes of the devils' clan, while Christ is, of course, their villain and much feared adversary.

Gréban, as the reader soon notices, ran into two problems ; one was linguistic, the other more attached to logical reinterpretation of content. Necessarily, since the language of the devils is inverted and negative, a blessing given by Lucifer to a departing devil is expressed as : « Or va, que le deable te maine / a peine et terrible misere ! » (l. 10719-10720). How, then, does Lucifer sound when he is really angry ? An example : Sathan exclaims to another devil, who seems to admire Jesus, when He is fasting in the desert, « Tes toy, tu me fais enrager / quand tu m'en parles grain ne goute » (l. 10461-10462). There is no distinction, no emotive nuancing possible in the inverted language of Gréban's devils.

Second, Lucifer, who is afraid of Jesus' redemption of sinners in hell, sends Sathan to Pilate's wife, in order to have him appear to her in a dream and cause her to stop Jesus' execution. Sathan thus becomes God's instrument at the same time — which is plausible from the Gospel point of view, but which destroys the structural logic of diabolical action :

> A la femme Pilate iras,
> qui encore en son lit sommeille,

et luy monstre par grant merveille
que tous ceulx qui entenderont
et couppables se renderont
de la mort Jhesus le prescheur
seront condampnés.

(l. 23398-23405)

These few remarks may suffixe to sketch Gréban's treatment of devil and hell in his monumental work.

The « fall of the devil» has now been traced through four medieval French plays. Starting as a fallen angel and tempter, the devil does not take on a quasi-human shape until the four-teenth century, when acting like a human being in a feudal context. At first following divine command, the devil gradually becomes an Anti-Lord (Anti-Christ) and is placed in hell. The more he is polarized with God, the more he develops into a comic figure, or, in Rudwin's words, « he was at once the great fallen archangel of heaven and the painted clown of the country-fair » [1].

The dramatic incarnation of the devil remains linked with then Bible stories and Saints legends through the entire period : there has been virtually no contamination from popular demonology with its beliefs in incubi, succubi, night flight of demons and witches. An exception is the scene of the fairies' visit in the *Jeu de la feuillee*, which could be interpreted, however, as parody.

The literary techniques used in the treatment of the devil and hell can be summarized as follows. From the very beginning, in the *Jeu d'Adam*, the devil opposes his opinion to that of God : he claims the forbidden fruit is *good*. Contrasting and (moral) inversions are continued in the *Miracle de Théophile*, to outline moral conduct following the devil's set of values. In the *Passion du Palatinus*, then, the devil reinterprets the Gospel events again by inversion, while Gréban's masterwork opposes an entire inverted action to that of the Biblical stories, which interacts, as it were, in those parts requiring diabolical influence. No new vocabulary is needed to express the devils' thoughts, as the exis-ting words are merely placed in opposite context. It can there-fore be said that the technique of inversion alone is the most

---

1. *Op. cit. supra*, n. 2, p. 275.
Romania, 100.   12

important linguistic means used by all four authors in order to characterize the devil.

Hell, on the other hand, is merely sketched in Rutebeuf's play and is not really treated until the *Passion du Palatinus*. Its inmates of hell, however, are familiar figures from the Dances of Death and other « serial » works of the Middle Ages. A detailed topography of hell appears finally in Gréban's play, which uses a multitude of descriptive terms all in the realm of the grotesque and the aesthetically repulsive, including instruments of torture, underground animals, and uncouth elements. An almost pre-baroque, pre-romantic insistence upon frightening detail is calculated to remind every Christian of what is waiting for him at the end of a sinful life. At the same time, the elements of imaginary horror accumulated in this many-faceted account of hell present an early reward, as it were, for the good man who anticipates what will be spared to him. As a by-product, Gréban gives us a description of (savage) nature in his geography of hell; perhaps one of the first treatments of nature in French literature, not counting certain passages in the *romans courtois*.

In the broadest sense of interpretation, then, the devil in medieval drama had at first a role within a context of psychomachia, while he was used later on to maintain a dualistic universe, or — at least in Thomistic thinking — to demonstrate the defeat of such a universe by the power of God, his adversary. To characterize the devil and hell, elements of the grotesque and the fantastic were used which were henceforth connected with the entire sphere of the demonic. These elements retained therefore a negative connotation, which was reinforced by classicism and not abandoned till the nineteenth century. It is clear that our modern fascination with the demonic is still linked to both of these functions, or basic human needs : 1) to probe the evil for either its intrinsic or its temporary (episodic) value ; 2) to explore the realm of fantasy in yet another reaction to an overemphasis on rational approaches to life and its problems.

If literary evidence can indeed be used to complete our knowledge and understanding of medieval civilization, medieval French drama tells ut that the devil was thought about in somewhat anthropomorphic terms ; that the language of the devil was negative in contents, contrasting positive values, particularly

Christian values ; and that, finally, devil and hell were placed into a fantastic frame of reference, a setting even more inhospitable and horrifying than early Biblical allusions had indicated. In tracing the two concepts through medieval drama it becomes evident not only to what extent it had emancipated itself from the theological tradition, but also, on the other hand, that it always remained faithful to its liturgical origins.

Edelgard DuBruck.

WITCHCRAFT IN THE NOVELS OF
SIR WALTER SCOTT

By Mody C. Boatright

Though Scott did not compose his *Letters on Demonology and Witchcraft* until he had worked out the more profitable veins of his ore, they concern a subject which had fascinated him from his youth. He had spent years in gathering and mastering what Lockhart speaks of as "perhaps the most curious library of *diablerie* that man ever collected."[1] Scott's mastery of this library bore its richest fruit, not in the *Letters*,[1a] which came in 1830, after Scott's physical and mental decline, but in the novels, where Scott, living in the nineteenth century, found not only means of picturing vividly the beliefs of the past, but also, as Professor Hugh Walker has observed, "a sort of gateway for the awful and supernatural, which can no longer be introduced by the older device of witchcraft."[2] This paper is a study of how Scott employed the lore of witchcraft in his double capacity of artist and student of *Culturgeschichte*.

Scott in 1827 made the following entry in his journal:

July 22—Rose a little later than usual and wrote a letter to Mrs. Joanna Baillie. She is writing a tragedy on witchcraft. I shall be curious to see it. Will it be real witchcraft—the *ipsissimus diabolus*—or an imposter, or the half-crazed being who believes herself an ally

---

[1] John Gibson Lockhart, *Memoirs of the Life of Sir Walter Scott,* Boston, 1901, IV, 118.

[1a] That is, from a literary point of view. Mr. Lewis Spence, the only anthropologist of note whose judgment on the *Letters* I have found recorded, has high praise for the work. He writes ("Sir Walter Scott as a Student of Tradition," in *Sir Walter Scott To-day*, edited by H. J. C. Grierson, London, 1933, p. 123) : *"The Letters on Demonology and Witchcraft* are so many doors opening on the treasure-house of a life-time's gleaning, and, Lockhart's criticism notwithstanding, nothing they contain in the richness of their hoard is more astonishing than the superior insight distinguishing the accompanying comment."

[2] Hugh Walker, *Three Centuries of Scottish Literature*, Glasgow, 1893, II, 230.

of condemned spirits and desires to be so? That last is a sublime subject (II, 10).

Scott himself created witches of the second and third types mentioned, and drew characters the reality of whose witchcraft he left in poetic uncertainty; but he also drew on his knowledge of witchcraft in other ways.

Often he makes effective use of withered hags who are not even charged with witchcraft, but in whose lineaments the feature of the traditional witch are clearly discernible. They may be active agents in the plot, or they may serve chiefly as stage property. This is true, for example, of the three old women who in the opening scene of *The Surgeon's Daughter* "might be observed plying their aged limbs through the single street of the village of Middlemas towards the honoured door, which, fenced off from the vulgar causeway, was defended by broken palings, inclosing two slips of ground, half arable, half overrun with an abortive attempt at shrubbery" (p. 30).[3] The old women are not witches, and they are merely rushing to secure employment as nurses, but they recall a famous meeting on the blasted heath near Forres. More definitely witch-like is Elspeth in *The Antiquary*, whose function in the plot is to clear up certain secrets concerning the chief personages. Oldbuck and Hector find her "sitting 'ghastly on the hearth, . . . wrinkled, tattered, vile, dim-eyed, discolored, torpid' " (p. 405). She dies without religious hope, in her delirium answering the call of her deceased, wicked mistress, with whom she has been associated in crime. Of the same type are Hannah Irwin and the old woman with whom she lodged in *St. Ronan's Well.* The latter especially exhibits the misanthropy usually associated with witches, by her refusal to admit Clara to her hut. She was one whose heart "adversity had turned to stone," and who was "impelled by a

---

[3]References to the *Waverley Novels* are to the edition of P. F. Collier and Sons, New York, n. d. The text of the Collier edition is that of the *Dryburgh Edition*, A. and C. Black, London, 1892. *The Surgeon's Daughter* was printed first in the volume entitled *Castle Dangerous.*

general hatred of the race" (p. 462). The most vivid character of this type, however, is Ulrica in *Ivanhoe*. She is a witch in everything but the compact with Satan and the consequent supernatural power. Prematurely old and ugly, and inured to crime herself, she hated Rebecca for being young and beautiful. Her chief comfort is that in dying "we leave behind us on earth those who shall be as wretched as ourselves" (p. 259). She is so repulsive that Cedric orders her out of his presence, using the witch formula: "I bid thee avaunt!" (p. 290). Although she says nothing of a compact, she sees no hope for herself in Christian redemption, and dies chanting a pagan rhyme. As she appears on the turret of the burning castle, her long, dishevelled grey hair flying back from her uncovered head, the inebriating delight of vengeance contending in her eyes with the fire of insanity (p. 354), she suggests an evil spirit, with witch-like exterior, hovering over hell.

Another class of characters involving witchcraft are those who are suspected of sorcery or formally charged with it, but who themselves make no pretense to supernatural powers. A situation growing out of a charge of this sort may be treated either comically or pathetically. The former treatment is exemplified in *Waverley*, where old Janet Gellatley is suspected on "the infallible grounds that she was very old, very ugly, very poor, and had two sons, one of whom was a poet and the other a fool" (p. 120). She is imprisoned for a week, tortured into a confession, and is being tried by a synod of Presbyterian divines. By exclaiming that the Evil One is in the midst of the assembly, she breaks up the trial.

The pathetic case of Rebecca is too well known to require review here. Less spectacular, because related with more restraint, but more penetrating, is the suffering of Madge Wildfire at the hands of a mob in *The Heart of Midlothian*. The infuriated villagers, after Meg Murdockson has been executed and is beyond the reach of their resentment, turn on her crazed daughter, and "swim" her in the Eden to determine whether she is a witch. Madge dies as a result of the exposure and ill-treatment.

More often the persons who make no claims to witch-craft are not brought to an accounting. When Elshie in *The Black Dwarf* builds his house on ill-famed Mucklestane Moor, he is immediately associated with sorcery, and he himself encourages the popular conception of his character. He tells fortunes and gives advice on diseases of men and cattle and on the affairs of the heart. Hobbie Elliott goes to this "warlock" to secure aid in recovering his stolen property and his abducted *fiancée*. Elshie causes Hobbie's property to be restored and his sweetheart to be rescued, but his means, it is always clear, are natural. He affects witchcraft because he delights in gloating over the super-stitious fears of his countrymen.

Suggestions of a different aspect of witchcraft are fre-quent in the treatment of Meg Murdockson in *The Heart of Midlothian*. This woman commands no supernatural powers, and stands rather for those malicious hags who, Scott thought, were the witches of sacred history.[1] Some of these suggestions come through the insane prattle of Madge:

> "Hear till her," said Madge. "But I'll wun out a gliff the night for a' that, to dance in the moonlight, when her and the gudeman will be whirrying through the blue lift on a broomshank, to see Jean Jap, that they hae putten intill the Kirkcaldy tolbooth; ay, they will hae a merry sail ower Inchkeath, and ower a' the bits o' bonny waves that are poppling and plashing against the rocks in the gowden glimmer o' the moon, ye ken" (p. 224).

On one occasion she thus addresses the horse upon which she and her mother are riding: "Come naggie, trot awa', man, an as thou wert a broomstick, for a witch rides thee" (p. 337). Again, in camp Meg is described "seated by the charcoal fire with the reflection of the red light on her withered and distorted features, marked by every evil pas-sion," as the "very picture of Hecate at her infernal rites" (p. 342). It was Meg's destiny to die on the scaffold, not for sorcery, but for having taken "an active part" in an "atrocious robbery and murder" (p. 555). The mob, how-ever, which glories in her death rejoices not because a

---

[1]*Letters on Demonology and Witchcraft*, pp. 53 ff.

murderess has been extinguished, but because another witch has gone to her master.

Scott here introduces a communal chorus, which was one of his most effective devices in dealing with the supernatural:

> "She has gone to ho master, with ho's name in her mouth," said another. "Shame the country should be harried wi' Scotch witches and Scotch bitches this gate; but I say hang and drown."
> "Ay, ay Gaffer Tramp, take awa yealdon, take awa low; hang the witch, and there will be less scathe amang us; mine owsen hae been reckan this towmont."
> "Silence wi' your fule tongues, ye churls," said an old woman who hobbled past them as they stood talking near the carriage; "this was nae witch, but a bluidy-fingered thief and murderess."
> . . . .
> "Ay, ay, neighbour," said Gaffer Tramp, "seest thou how one witch will speak for t'other—Scots or English, the same to them."
> His companion shook his head and replied . . . , "Ay, ay, when a Sark-foot wife gets on her broom-stick, the dames of Allonby are ready to mount, just as sure as the bye-word gangs o' the hills" (pp. 465, 466).

In Meg Murdockson Scott presents the criminal as witch. In Magdalen Graeme, in *The Abbot*, he presents the religious fanatic as witch. Magdalen's abstracted demeanor and mystic language were enough to fix upon her the suspicion of the vulgar, a suspicion which she was willing to encourage if she might thereby further the cause nearest her heart, that of a Catholic restoration in Scotland. She prescribed remedies, was reputed to be a prophetess, and at one time was in danger of being tried for sorcery. Her willingness to be suspected grew out of the conditions of the time, which made it safer for her to be thought a witch than to be thought what she was, a plotter for the Catholic cause.

Some of the suspected persons in Scott's novels turn their evil reputations to gain. The cleverest of these imposters is Wayland Smith in *Kenilworth*, a character based on the old legend of Wayland the Invisible Horse-shoer. Smith had been a disciple of the charlatan Alasco. Having detected the frauds of his master, he abandoned alchemy and set up as a farrier; but because of this former connection with Alasco, he had difficulty in securing customers. He met the situation by playing upon the credulity of the peasantry. He took into partnership an urchin of the village, whom he called "Flibbertigibbet." This lad would guide the customer to the vale where Smith's forge was concealed in a cave. He would then direct the customer to tie his horse at a certain spot and place his fee on a certain stone. The boy would then signal, and he and the customer would withdraw, to return later and find the horse shod and the money gone.

More impressive than Smith, who is a comic character, is Elspat MacTavish in *The Highland Widow*. Whatever comes to this woman as a result of her supposed witchcraft comes through the fear of her curse, and not from any service rendered. After she had been the cause of the death of her son, she withdrew to her mean hut near a large tree and became known as the Woman of the Tree. Ill luck was supposed to attend those who approached too near the tree, even long after she was dead. We are told that:

> If . . . Elspat was repelled when she demanded anything necessary for her wants, or the accommodation of her little flock, by the churlish farmer, her threats of vengeance, obscurely expressed, yet terrible in their tenor, used frequently to extort, through fear of her malediction, the relief which was denied her necessities; and the trembling goodwife who gave meal or money to the widow of MacTavish Mhor wished in her heart that the stern old carline had been burnt on the day her husband had his due (pp. 472, 473).[5]

If, however, Elspat had the power to bring harm by malediction, there is no recorded instance of her using it except against her own son. She had wanted him to follow the profession of his father, that of cateran, and when he went away to enlist in the army of the Hanoverian king, she addressed him in the following language:

> "Stay, I command you . . . , stay or may the gun you carry be the means of your ruin—may the road you are going be the track of your funeral" (p. 476).

---

[5]In the volume entitled *The Betrothed*.

It was the gun that he carried which he afterwards used to slay his comrade, and it was the road that he was traveling that led to the scene of his execution. Scott leaves the supernaturalism of the curse and its fulfillment without comment. There is no evidence that Elspat, or any of the other characters so far considered, believed herself endowed with supernatural power.

This is not true of another group of women whom Scott introduced into the *Waverley Novels*. It will be recalled that, in the journal entry quoted at the beginning of this discussion Scott wrote of "the half-crazed being who believes herself an ally of condemned spirits and desires to be so" as a "sublime subject." In the *Waverley Novels* he has introduced two such beings, to whose characterization he devoted considerable care.

The more famous of these is Meg Merrilies, an important force in the action of *Guy Mannering*. Essentially she is a protector of the hero. A gipsy spae-wife, she had at his birth tried his fortune, predicting the outlines of his life as they are revealed in the subsequent action. But despite her love for the hero, she came to regard herself as the cause of his misfortunes. For political reasons the Laird expelled the gipsies from his estate. In her indignation Meg cried out:

> "Ye have riven the thack off seven cottar houses; look if you ain roof-tree stand the faster. . . .
> "Ride your ways, Ellangowan. Our bairns are hinging at our weary backs; look that your braw cradle at hame be the fairer spread up; not that I am wishing ill to little Harry, or to the babe that's yet to be born—God forbid—and make them kind to the poor, and better folk than their father!" (p. 79).

When Harry is kidnapped, Meg superstitiously connects this event and other misfortunes of the house with her anathema, and she dedicates the remainder of her life to the restoration of the heir.

She is able to restore Harry's inheritance primarily because she is in possession of the secret of his kidnapping and has the means of identifying him; and, though her reputation for witchcraft stands her in good stead, her means of extricating the hero are purely natural, and Scott does not, even for purposes of suspense, suggest that they are not. Being under sentence of banishment, she must of necessity move in secret, but her movements are accounted for. Before she returns to the Ellangowan estate, she expresses her determination to serve the hero, and the reader is not surprised to find her there. She makes a prophecy, and it is fulfilled; she curses a house, and it falls. She herself regards her curse as supernatural. Upon her return, she says:

"Here I stood on this very spot . . . ; here I stood when I tauld the last Laird of Ellangowan what was to come on his house; and did that fa' to the ground?   Na, it hit even ower sair!" (pp. 376, 377).

And upon her death-bed she confesses:

"I am a sinfu' woman; but if my curse brought it down, my blessing has taen it off!" (p. 454).

Meg Merrilies is a demented gipsy woman who comes to think of herself, first as one having the power to curse, and then as an instrument of fate. She may be the instrument which she conceives herself to be, for she was privy to the destiny of the house and of the hero; but if so, the fate whose tool she is employs only natural means.

A rôle somewhat similar to that of Meg Merrilies is that played in *The Pirate* by Norna of Fitful Head, "the most fearful woman in all the isles." Her function in the plot is not to restore a house which she has cursed; it is to mitigate the severity of the fate which Mourdant Merton brings upon himself by saving a drowning man. She claims supernatural powers, performing her "part with such undoubting confidence . . . that it would have been difficult for the greatest sceptic to have doubted the reality of her enthusiasm, though he might smile at the pretensions to which it gave rise" (p. 72). This "enthusiasm" had been of long duration. By disobeying her father she had unwittingly caused his death. She had erected her offense into a crime of the first magnitude, even imagining that she had trafficked with spirits, — not Satan, indeed, but with the "drows," fairy-like creatures of the North, and with the old deities of Norse mythology.

Norna's claims are extensive. Her ability to influence weather is several times alluded to, and the reader is allowed one demonstration. She watches a storm for several minutes, then begins an incantation, which gradually becomes more subdued in its cadence, the storm abating as the song subsides. She professes to command the local genii with which, according to Zetland superstition, the islands were haunted. It was said of her that "she kens a'thing that happens in these islands . . . muckle sooner than other folk, and that is Heaven's truth" (p. 305). Her movements are a mystery to the uneducated. "Wha kens how she travels?" asks Swertha, the serving woman.

Norma is not, however, a supernatural character. I agree with Scott (introduction to the 1831 edition) that anyone who will "take the trouble of reading *The Pirate* with some attention" will see in her "the victim of remorse and insanity, and the dupe of her own imposture, her mind, too, flooded with all the weird literature and extravagant superstition of the north." Scott, indeed, leaves some of her exploits unexplained, but he accounts for a sufficient number of them to reveal her technique. "I heard you sing . . . and I saw the tempest abate," said Mourdant. But Norna examined the cloud carefully before she began her incantation, and "it was not improbable that the issue had been for some time foreseen by the pythoness" (p. 78). She "made herself familiarly and practically acquainted with all the secret passages and recesses, whether natural or artificial, which she could hear of . . . , and was, by such knowledge, often enabled to perform feats which were otherwise unaccountable" (p. 454).

Scott admitted that there was "great improbability" in "the statement of Norna's possessing power and opportunity to impress on others that belief in her supernatural gifts which distracted her own mind. Yet," he continues in the 1831 introduction, "amid a very credulous and ignorant population, it is astonishing what success may be attained by an imposter who is, at the same time, an enthusiast."

The improbability to which Scott refers exists only for readers devoid of historic imagination. The general atmosphere which Scott pictures as surrounding an isolated agricultural and fishing people untouched by the rising science of the seventeenth century is ample explanation of Tronda's advising her master to "say an *oraamus* to St. Ronald and fling a saxpence ower [his] shoulter" (p. 82) after Norna has been in the house; of the pedlar's reluctance to pronounce her name (p. 216); of old men's asking that their sons be remembered at sea (p. 455);[6] and of old women's blessing themselves as she passes (p. 456).

In the introduction to the 1831 edition of *The Pirate* Scott protested that those critics who saw in Norna a mere copy of Meg Merrilies had not read attentively; and he had some grounds for the protest. Each is a demented creature sincerely claiming supernatural powers. Each displays her gifts of prophecy, and each has a prophecy fulfilled. Each is friendly to the hero, and mitigates the severity of an announced fate. But there are also differences. Meg is an ignorant gipsy whose claims extend no further than fortune-telling and the command of a few charms. After her curse has apparently brought ruin upon the Bertram family, she thinks of herself as an instrument of destiny, and thinking herself such an instrument, she becomes one. Norna, on the other hand, is a woman of birth and education. Meg's delusion proceeds from a simple-minded acceptance of the traditions of her tribe. She executes her plans by good fortune and native shrewdness. Norna's dementia grows out of a parental disobedience which a tendency toward monomania has magnified into a heinous crime. The superstitions of her country and the books she has read give form and content to her mental disorder. Her plans are executed with studied thoroughness, and her claims are far more pretentious: she even threatens her gods with compulsion. Norna is the more ambitious and lofty conception,

---

[6]According to Sir James George Frazer (*The Golden Bough*, one-volume edition, New York, 1922, p. 81), "Shetland seamen still buy winds in the shape of knotted handkerchiefs or threads from old women who claim to rule the storms."

but Meg, being more human and less threatrical, will probably remain the favorite among readers of Scott.

Scott's use of "real" witchcraft (but perhaps it is only apparent witchcraft) is confined to *The Bride of Lammermoor,* in which witches, next to old prophecy, constitute the most important agency through which the fates of the characters are announced.

Blind Alice is approaching the close of a long life on the Ravenswood estate, now under a new lord. She is the "best authority" on the traditions of the old Ravenswood family (p. 58). Lucy Ashton observes that, although Alice is blind, "she has some way of looking into your very heart" (p. 58). She warns Ashton that Edgar Ravenswood is not a man to be persecuted. "My lord," she says, "take care what you do; you are on the brink of a precipice" (p. 59). Knowing the enmity between the Ravenswood and the Ashton families, she is profoundly astonished to find Edgar and Lucy together:

"Young man, he who aims at revenge by dishonorable means—"

"Be silent, woman!" said Ravenswood, sternly; "is it the devil that prompts your voice? Know that this young lady has not on earth a friend who would venture farther to save her from injury or from insult."

"And is it even so?" said the old woman in an altered but melancholy tone, "then God help you both!" (p. 207).

And she goes on to speak of "either . . . fatal revenge or . . . still more fatal love" (p. 209). Edgar offers her gold to appease her wrath. "In the slight struggle attending his wish to force it upon her, it dropped to the earth":

"Let it remain an instant on the ground," said Alice, as the master stooped to raise it; "and believe me, that piece of gold is an emblem of her whom you love; she is as precious, I grant, but you must stoop even to abasement before you can win her. For me, I have as little to do with gold as with earthly passions; and the best news that the world has in store for me is, that Edgar Ravenswood is an hundred miles distant from the seat of his ancestors, with the determination never again to behold it" (p. 210).

It is this very coin which Edgar and Lucy afterwards break as a symbol of their fatal troth (p. 217).

It is clear that Alice is aware of the fate which hangs over Ravenswood and Lucy. The source of her information is treated with poetic indefiniteness. Her acquaintance with three generations of Ravenswoods gives her a thorough knowledge of the family temper. She is quick to apprehend Lucy's love for Edgar. "A thousand circumstances have proved it to me," she says (p. 211). The uneducated think her a witch, a charge which she neither affirms nor denies. When she hears Henry Ashton say that she should have been burned at Haddington, her reply is, "If the usurer, and the oppressor, and the grinder of the poor man's face, and the remover of ancient landmarks, and the subverter of ancient houses, were at the same stake with me, I could say, 'light the fire in God's name' " (p. 208). She does claim extraordinary, though not necessarily supernatural power of looking into the future, for she tells Edgar, "If my mortal sight is closed to objects present with me, it may be that I can look with more steadiness into future events" (p. 209). She makes no use of images, mirrors, crystals, or other devices of soothsaying. Whatever her powers, whatever the sources of her information, she is clearly the mouthpiece of fate.

Three other old women, unlike Alice in that they are wholly repulsive, function in the story as a witch chorus. As Professor Wilmon Brewer observes,[7] these old hags appear after the climax and deliver only fate's minor decrees." But they heighten tremendously the tragic effect.

The first appearance of the chorus of witches was upon the death of Alice. Ravenswood had found her dead and was watching by the corpse until help should come from the village. The three hags reached Alice's hut "sooner than he could reasonably have expected, considering the distance betwixt the hut . . . and the village, and the age and infirmities of the three old women" (p. 258). They saluted Ravenswood with a "ghastly smile, which reminded him of the meeting between Macbeth and the witches on the

---

[7]Wilmon Brewer, *Shakespeare's Influence on Sir Walter Scott*, Boston, 1925, p. 283.

blasted heath near Forres" (pp. 258, 259). He was glad to quit a "company so evil-omened and so odious" (p. 259), but he could not help overhearing the following "croaking" dialogue concerning his own fate:

"That's a fresh and full-grown hemlock, Annie Winnie; mony a cummer lang syne wad hae sought nae better horse to flee over hill and how, through mist and moonlight, and light down in the King of France's cellar."

"Ay cummer!" but the very deil had turned as hard hearted now as the Lord Keeper and the grit folk, that hae breasts like whinstanes. They prick us and pine us, and they pit us on pinnywinkles for witches; and, if I say my prayers backwards ten times ower, Satan will never gie me amends o' them."

"Did ye ever see the foul thief?" asked her neighbour.

"Na!" replied the other spokeswoman: "but I trow I hae dreamed of him mony a time, and I think the day will come they will burn me for't." . . .

"He's a frank man, and a free-handed man, the Master," said Annie Winnie, "and a comely personage—broad in the shoulters, and narrow around the lunyies. He wad mak a bonny corpse; I wad like to hae the streiking and winding o' him."

"It is written on his brow, Annie Winnie," replied the octogenarian, her companion, "that the hand of woman, or of man either, will never straught him; dead-deal will never be laid on his back, make your market of that, for I hae it from a sure hand."

"Will it be his lot to die on the battle-grounnd, then, Ailsie Gourlay? Will he die by the sword or by the ball, as his forbears hae dune before him, many ane o' them?"

"Ask nae mair questions about it—he'll no be graced sae far," replied the sage.

"I ken ye are wiser than ither folk, Ailsie Gourlay. But wha tell'd ye this?"

"Flashna your thumb about that, Annie Winnie," answered the sibyl. "I hae it from a hand sure eneugh."

"But ye said ye never saw the foul thief," reiterated her inquisitive companion.

"I hae it frae as sure a hand," said Ailsie, "and frae them that spaed his fortune before the sark gaed ower his head."

"Hark! I hear his horse's feet riding aff," said the other; "they dinna sound as if good luck was wi' them."

"Mak haste, sirs," cried the paralytic hag from the cottage, "and let us do what is needfu' and say what is fitting; for if the dead corpse binna straughted, it will girn and thraw, and that will fear the best o' us" (pp. 260–261).

The three come on the stage again at the marriage of Lucy and Bucklaw, and take their place among the poor who have assembled in the churchyard to receive the wedding dole. After the hags have complained about the inferiority of their portions, they reveal, in a dialogue similar to the one above, the fate of the bride. Four days later they gather at Lucy's funeral, and there engage in their "wonted unhallowed conference," the third one, the burden of which is their pleasure in the death of Lucy, and in the fact that "ane of the company," Ravenswood, will "no be lang for this world." Thus from their introduction to the catastrophe, these three hags are ever hovering in the background of the action, and give to *The Bride of Lammermoor* an atmosphere of supernatural tragedy that would be lacking without them.

Moreover, the chief of these hags, Ailsie Gourlay, had been instrumental in bringing about Lucy's insanity, and perhaps had natural grounds for predicting the early death of the bride. Dame Gourlay was sometimes called the "Wise Woman of Boden" (p. 319). She had a considerable reputation for skill in healing, in which art she employed herbs selected in planetary hours. In private she traded more deeply in the occult sciences. She "spaed fortunes, read dreams, composed philtres, discovered stolen goods, and made and dissolved matches as successfully as if, according to the belief of the whole neighbourhood, she had been aided by Beelzebub himself" (p. 320). She claimed her power, however, not from that prince, but from a "harmless fairy" (pp. 319, 320). This old woman, repulsive in appearance, vindictive in disposition, and obscene in mind, preyed upon Lucy's worries and fears and gradually deprived her of her reason. She convinced Lucy that there was a fate on her attachment to Ravenswood. She expounded her dreams, and professed to show by a mirror that Edgar had bestowed his affections elsewhere.

In treating Ailsie Gourlay and her companions, Scott exemplifies the same indefiniteness we have seen in his treatment of Alice. He neither affirms nor denies their supposed supernatural powers, and Ailsie is the only one who lays claim to them. Her control of Lucy, Scott explains, is to be accounted for by rational psychology. But, wherever the hags go, they pollute the atmosphere and cause a general shuddering. Whether or not they are witches conscious of supernatural powers, they are the agents of fate, whose decrees they announce.[8]

Let us now look at our subject as a whole.

One of the most obvious generalizations we can make is that in his prose fiction Scott put the traditions of witchcraft to a variety of uses. They were traditions which the author of the *Waverley Novels* in his capacity as historical novelist could not ignore, and on numerous occasions witchcraft is alluded to apparently for no other reason than to make more nearly complete the picture of the past. As artist, however, Scott knew how to turn the materials of the witchcraft tradition to the uses of comedy, of pathos, and of tragedy. The former is of least importance. Humor occurs in numerous passing references to the belief in witchcraft, in the scene in *Guy Mannering* where Sampson comes upon Meg cooking a pot of stew which he imagines must be hell-broth, and in the report of a witch trial in *Waverley*. More generally, however, witchcraft is a source of pathos or of tragedy, as in *The Heart of Midlothian, The Bride of Lammermoor*, and *The Highland Widow*.

Scott introduces various types of witch-like characters. An impressive group of such characters is that of the withered and malicious hags, who, though not accused of witchcraft, seem to exude evil. Famous among the examples is Ulrica in *Ivanhoe*, whose affinity with the devil is symbolized by her death-scene, where she is shown hovering

---

[*]Professor Brewer (*op. cit.*, p. 283) says: "Moreover, unless when Ailsie Gourlay announces repeatedly in regard to her messages, 'I have it from a sure hand,' we are to suppose that she means the Devil they work without supernatural power." There seem to me to be two other possibilities. She may refer to the fairy, not mentioned until chapter XXXI. But since she uses this phrase only in relation to her prophecies concerning Ravenswood, she may refer to Thomas the Rhymer, whose doleful lines about the last Laird of Ravenswood both she and Caleb know.

over a burning castle like a fiend over hell. Many characters obviously innocent are suspected of witchcraft. The types so suspected are numerous, but most of them are unusual in some way: they are religious fanatics, glee-maidens, criminals, dwarfs, and the like. There are several imposters who do not believe themselves endowed with supernatural powers. Only one of these characters, Wayland Smith in *Kenilworth,* can we admire for his cleverness. Two of Scott's witches, Meg Merrilies in *Guy Mannering* and Norna in *The Pirate,* are demented creatures who sincerely believe themselves possessed of the powers they claim. Old women in one work, *The Bride of Lammermoor,* seem to be real witches, but their treatment is such as to make a categorical statement impossible. The only witch the reality of whose witchcraft is asserted is one occurring in an old legend embodied in *The Black Dwarf.* Scott often allows supernaturalism in old legends told as such which he would not allow in the plot proper.

Other specific devices than the old legend used in Scott's presentation of witchcraft are what I shall call the communal chorus and the witch chorus. The former is exemplified in *The Heart of Midlothian,* where a group of villagers comment on the hanging of Meg Murdockson, and in several other novels. The latter is brought to a high state of artistic development in *The Bride of Lammermoor,* where three withered hags gather on three different occasions to comment on the action and to announce the approaching doom of the chief personages in the story.

Besides acting as a chorus, the witch-like characters may perform various functions in the plot. In *The Surgeon's Daughter* they serve merely as stage scenery. Meg and Norna are indispensable agents in the plots, and the former thinks herself, and may be considered, a chosen instrument of destiny. It is Alice's function in *The Bride of Lammermoor* to announce the fate of the chief characters. After the warning is disregarded, she drops out of the action. Ailsie Gourlay has a part in the bringing on of Lucy's insanity. But in every case where a witch-like character influences the action, she does so by natural means. Scott is careful to show how Elshie recovers Hobbie's property and to explain that Lucy's insanity is not due to bewitchment.

In his treatment of witchcraft, Scott is usually careful to build up an appropriate atmosphere. He reminds us that Butler lived in an age when laws against witchcraft were in force and had recently been acted upon. In *The Pirate* he brings in numerous minor superstitions to show that to the inhabitants of Zetland the external world was an unfriendly, mysterious, and capricious place. *The Bride of Lammermoor* opens with a funeral. Omens are mentioned, and fate is talked about. Unfortunately, however, Scott, at one point in the story, allows the foolery of Caleb, which he had introduced for relief, to continue too long. But, in general, witchcraft in Scott is accompanied by an appropriate atmosphere.

I have noted that witch-like characters work by natural means. Usually it is clear to the reader at the time that the means are natural. But when witch-like characters deliver prophecy, the information seems to come from a supernatural source. Meg foretold the fall of the Ellangowans and the troubles of the hero. Alice knew that the love of Edgar and Lucy would be fatal. Ailsie knew that no woman or man would have the winding of Ravenswood's body. There is no explanation of how they came by the information.

Witch-like characters, especially Meg and Norna, who have important parts in the action, may be kept a great deal before the reader, but not in their supernatural capacities. When Alice's message has been emphatically delivered, she dies, her ghost lingering a moment for a final warning. The witch chorus is limited to three appearances.

Witch-like characters may be definitely described as to personal appearance, or only generally characterized. An epithet like "leathern chops" may suffice. But there is about the character an element of mystery, indicated by the attitude of other characters toward her. Even Guy Mannering thinks Meg a remarkable woman. But chiefly Scott attains the indefiniteness which he thought essential to the artistic use of the supernatural by so treating the characters that it is impossible to say categorically whether they are witches or not. This is not true, of course, of the persons clearly pictured as innocently accused and of imposters.

In his treatment of witchcraft Scott adhered to the traditions of his country. He followed the popular tradition more closely than the theological one. His witches are not all evil. Meg and Norna in the working out of the plots align themselves on the side of moral order. Alice attempts to show others how evil may be averted. Some of the witches in Scott's novels, then, are "white witches." Again Scott followed the popular tradition by allowing two of his witches to claim power from fairies, or other spirits than evil ones.

I do not know of any body of fiction which deals more satisfactorily with the sociological aspects of witchcraft than the *Waverley Novels*. The treatment, however, is incomplete in that it contains no instance of unjust legal condemnation. It is true that Madge Wildfire dies at the hands of a mob, but innocent people legally accused escape punishment. In his studies of the deluded witch Scott was successful in the relatively simple Meg Merrilies, but when he essayed the more complex psychology of Norna, he attempted what was not his forte. Scott is at his best when dealing with relatively simple characters like Jeanie and Davie Deans, Balfour of Burley, or Mucklebaket. In using witchcraft as an adjunct to tragedy Scott attained a high degree of success. To find an English tragedy of the supernatural more impressive than *The Bride of Lammermoor*, one has to go to Shakespeare; and the superiority of *Macbeth* to *The Bride of Lammermoor* lies not in its treatment of witchcraft, but in its more profound characterization.

Archaeological
Institute
of America

THE SERPENT WITH A HUMAN HEAD IN ART AND IN MYSTERY PLAY

ONE of the most noteworthy examples of the close relationship between religious drama and Christian art is to be found in the correspondence between pictured and dramatic representations of the serpent in the Garden of Eden. I call it noteworthy because in the field of art we shall find ourselves ultimately concerned with some of the great masters of the renaissance, and especially with one of the greatest works of one of the greatest masters—The Ceiling of the Sistine Chapel by Michelangelo.

Who has not noted with curiosity, in the picture of the temptation on that ceiling, the strange serpent almost wholly woman? Was this the result of some queer freak of misogyny on the part of the terrible Florentine? Or was there some old legend, now lost sight of, that might account for such a monster? Certain lines of Keats and Rossetti, perhaps, floated vaguely in the mind, and one dismissed the matter as probably having something to do with Lilith and Lamia.

It is my purpose, however, to show:—that the representation of the serpent in Eden as having a human head was common to drama and iconography; that it is first noticeable in the thirteenth, or the early part of the fourteenth century, being then a startling innovation in art; and that in all probability it was the mystery play which, to facilitate the dialogue between Eve and the serpent, first adopted it, from a literary source.

Let me first state in simple terms the problem a consideration of which has brought me to this point of view. The human-headed serpent, it would seem, must derive in one or other of the following ways:

A. The literary source gives rise *independently* to the dramatic and iconographic representation;

B. The literary source gives rise *first to the art form*, and that in turn brings about the dramatic;

C. The literary source gives rise *first to the dramatic*, and that

American Journal of Archaeology, Second Series. Journal of the Archaeological Institute of America, Vol. XXI (1917) No. 3.

255

113

in turn brings about the art form; or, as would seem only remotely
probable,

D. The *dramatic form preceded* all, occasioning first the literary and then the art form.

That the art form might have preceded the other forms is a
possibility that I have deemed hardly worthy of enumerating in
this series of hypotheses. The artists before the thirteenth century so seldom originated anything, so persistently followed
tradition or the direction of more learned men, that in the
absence of any evidence that the serpent was represented with a
human head before the thirteenth century, I am satisfied that
we have in this case no original art source.

My first hypothesis, that the literary source might have given
rise independently to the dramatic and art forms, is also proposed
rather for the sake of completeness than with any serious expectation of its proving fruitful.

In the absence of immediately convincing evidence on this
point, we must reason from probabilities. It does not seem likely
that the thirteenth century artists,—who, as was observed of
their predecessors, followed an ancient and fairly rigid tradition,
—should in the case of the temptation and fall of man suddenly
have been influenced to change their mode of representation
purely by a literary source. There does not appear to be any
sufficient reason for their doing so. In the efflorescence of art
in the thirteenth century, which sought,—as Didron pointed out
and Émile Mâle has further explained,—to give a complete
mirror of human and divine affairs, it is true that many new
iconographs appeared. But new and old were intended to teach
doctrines, or to fix in the mind principles of knowledge and
belief. Thus we have new episodes of the Bible story together
with the ancient symbols, we have the Platonic as well as the
Christian virtues, and personifications of all branches of knowledge. But the only explanation we have for the human head on
the tempter is that this head, this woman's face, was assumed
the better to ensnare Eve, since *similia similibus applaudunt*.[1]
Neither this nor any other of the literary sources seems to have
in it a germ of doctrine or belief such as to have caused one di-
recting the work of artists to make them break their ancient
tradition.

[1] Petrus Comestor, *Historia Libri Genesis*, in Migne, *Patrol. Lat.* CXCVIII,
1072.

What appeals to the artist far more powerfully than learned commentary, however, is the direct impression received by his sensitive and observant eye. If then he should see the serpent represented in a mystery play, he would be stimulated to represent it in his next picture to some extent as he saw it, especially if the play seemed to have the Church's approval.

The second hypothesis,—that the literary source gives rise first to the art, and that in turn brings about the dramatic form— is answered by the argument against the first.

These somewhat weak negative arguments lead naturally to the favorable consideration of the third hypothesis,—that the literary source gives rise first to the dramatic, and that in turn brings about the art form. But to establish this as the true line of derivation it will be necessary to present methodically the whole body of the evidence. The documents and iconographs, because it is impossible to assemble them into a complete and continuous chronological record, present many difficulties. Gaps of time and place, the possibility of lost plays and demolished pictures, must be allowed for.[1]

I

The Literary Sources

Taking up the evidence as nearly as possible chronologically, I must begin with the literary sources.

Petrus Comestor in his comment on Genesis[2] (*Historia Libri Genesis*) says of the serpent in the garden of Eden, *tunc serpens erectus est ut homo,* and goes on to tell how Satan (*Lucifer*, he says), *Elegit etiam quoddam genus serpentis, ut ait Beda, virgineum vultum habens, quia similia similibus applaudunt.*[3]

[1] If at any time new evidence should come to light supporting the hypothesis that the art form was earlier than the dramatic, nothing would give me more pleasure. For such a relationship, inasmuch as it is far more unusual, is by so much the more interesting.

I treated the most striking example of the indebtedness of the mystery play to art, in my article on the Hegge play of the *Radix Jesse*, the Tree of Jesse, *Pub. of Mod. Lang. Assoc. of Amer.*, XXIX, 1914, pp. 327 ff.

[2] Migne *Patrol. Lat.* CXCVIII, 1072.

[3] I have not been able to find in Beda anything remotely suggesting the phrase which follows Comestor's *ut ait Beda.* Is it possible that the *ut ait Beda* refers solely to the clause *elegit quoddam genus serpentis*, which is entirely in agreement with Beda's explanation that the serpent was merely the instrument of Satan, not wise in itself?

I cannot refrain from attacking the text of Comestor, though it may appear

As Comestor died about 1173 A.D., his commentary may be regarded as nearly contemporaneous with the Anglo-Norman play of *Adam*. Inasmuch, therefore, as the play of *Adam*, which is the oldest extant vernacular French mystery play, does not present the serpent with a human head, and as there is no other Adam play in any language which does so present it in the twelfth century, we are obliged to regard Comestor as par excellence the literary source.[1]

After Peter Comestor, Vincent de Beauvais (*ca.* 1190—*ca.* 1264 A.D.) is the next source. In the *Speculum Naturale*, Lib. XX, Cap. XXXIII (Vol. I, Col. 1478 in the Douai edition of 1624), we read: *Draconcopedes serpentes magni sunt, et potentes, facies virgineas habentes humanis similes, in draconum corpus desinentes. Credibile est huius generis illum fuisse, per quem diabolus Euam decepit, quia (sicut dicit Beda) virgineum vultum habuit. Huic etiam diabolus se coniungens vel applicans ut consimili forma mulierem alliceret, faciem ei tantum ostendit, et reliquam partem corporis arborum frondibus occultavit.*

In the *Historia Destructionis Trojae* of Guido delle Colonne[2] (1287), Beda is (as in Comestor and Vincent) cited as authority for the human headed form of the tempter. In summarizing Guido's narrative, after speaking of the fall of the rebel angels, Gorra writes: "Questo diavolo fu Satana, o quel Leviatham, che primo cadde dal cielo e che gli Ebrei chiamano Beenoch, vale a

---

that my suggestion is a wild one. But as so far I have not been able to find the reference in Beda, I will venture the following hazardous guess. In one passage of the apocryphal Beda, the text reads: "*Serpens per se loqui non poterat . . . nisi nimirum illum diabolus utens, et velut organum per quod articulatum sonum emitteret*"—etc. (Migne, *Patrol. Lat.*, XCIII, 276).

Is it possible that Comestor having before him the above passage in an ancient and somewhat difficult manuscript partly obliterated by age, made the revolutionary blunder of reading the two words "*velut organum*" as "*vultum virgineum*"? In twelfth century writing similarity in the appearance of these two phrases is a possibility.

C. Hippeau in a note in his edition of *Le Bestiare d'Amour*, p. 148, asks— "Bède le Vénérable ne dit-il pas que le serpent, pour parler à Ève, avait pris le visage d'une jeune fille?" His source, however, may be Comestor, or Vincent of Beauvais, rather than Beda himself.

[1] As to the supposed tradition linking Hebrew *Lillin* and classical *Lamiae* with a monster half woman and half serpent, see page 290, note 2.

[2] E. Gorra, *Testi Inediti di Storia Troiana;* Introduzione,—Sulla Leggenda Troiana in Italia. Cap. II,—Guido delle Colonne, p. 135. The complete Latin text of Guido has not been accessible.

dire animo bruto, cioè serpente tortuoso, o anche drago (Isidore, *Orig.* VIII, ch. 11) del quale parle anche Davide. Di questo serpente che tentò sotto forma d'uomo i nostri primi padri, parla il Genesi 'secundum Mosaycam traditionem,' ma 'secundum traditionem sacrarum scripturarum catholice universalis ecclesie ratum est, ut scripsit Beda, quod diabolus elegit tunc quendam serpentem de quodam genere serpentum, virgineum habens vultum,' e questo noi dobbiamo credere aver tentato il primo uomo."

Next comes the anonymous and exceedingly popular *Speculum Humanae Salvationis*,[1] the date of which Paul Poppe fixes as about 1324.[2] This work has sometimes been erroneously attributed, in addition to his already enormous bulk of volumes, to Vincent de Beauvais. In the first chapter the author, after briefly mentioning the fall of Lucifer and the rebel angels from heaven, continues as follows:

11 *Quapropter diabolus, homini invidens, sibi insidiatur*
Et ad praecepti transgressionem ipsum inducere nitebatur:
Quoddam ergo genus serpentis sibi diabolus eligebat.
Qui tunc erectus gradiebatur et caput virgineum habebat:
15 *In hunc fraudulosus deceptor mille artifex intrabat,*
Et per os eius loquens, verba deceptoria mulieri enarrabat.
Tentavit autem mulierem tanquam minus providam,
Reputans prudentem et cautum esse virum Adam.
Accessit autem ad mulierem solam, sine viro· exsistentem,
20 *Quia solum facilius decepit diabolus, quam socios habentem.*

The same idea naturally appears in the fifteenth century translations of the *Speculum* into French, English and German.

---

[1] J. Lutz et P. Perdrizet, *Speculum humanae salvationis. Texte critique: Traduction inédite de Jean Miélot* (1448), etc. Mulhouse 1907. 2 vols.

The Latin text is from a Munich MS. (Clm. 146) of the middle of the fourteenth century. This is one of the oldest MSS. of the Speculum, and contains 192 pen drawings, which are published, along with a number of other illustrations of the Speculum in volume II. See below, p. 267.

[2] "Wahrscheinlich um das Jahr 1324 von einem trotz aller Forschungen bis Heute unbekannt gebliebenen Verfasser in lateinischer Sprache verfasst, erlangte es schnell eine ungeheure Verbreitung." Paul Poppe, *Über das Speculum Humanae Salvationis*, Berlin, 1887.

Lutz and Perdrizet, *op. cit.* I, p. 249, argue at some length that the *Speculum* was composed early in the fourteenth century at a Dominican convent in Strasburg by a Dominican of Saxon origin, whom they tentatively identify with a certain Ludolph of Saxony, a Dominican, who later became a Carthusian.

Piers the Plowman is the next source after the *Speculum Humanae Salvationis,*—of course antedating the fifteenth century translations. In *Piers the Plowman* the serpent which tempted Eve is described as

y-lik a lusard, with a lady visage[1]

Having considered the foregoing literary sources for the origin of the human-headed serpent,—the earliest scarcely earlier than the first play of Adam and Eve, and the latest possibly a generation later than the first Adam play in which the serpent is given a human head,[2] I wish now to cite some of the important works

---

[1] *Cf.* W. W. Skeat, *Notes* on *Piers the Plowman*, Oxford, 1886, note on Bxviii. 355.

Is Chaucer, in the *Man of Lawes Tale*, possibly thinking of the same thing when he apostrophizes the wicked sultaness?

O sowdanesse, rote of iniquitee,
Virago, thou Semyram the secounde,
O serpent under femininitee,
Lyk to the serpent depe in helle y-bounde,
O feyned womman, al that may confounde
Vertu and innocence, thrugh thy malyce,
Is bred in thee, as nest of every vyce!
—(*Man of Lawes Tale*, B. 360 ff.)

There is nothing more than a figure of speech in this comparison of the wicked woman with the serpent tempter; there is no direct suggestion that the serpent took the face of a woman in order to trick Eve. Yet Skeat does so interpret this passage, and thinks the line,

Thyn instrument so, weylawey the whyle!

in the following stanza has special significance:

O Satan envious sin thilke day
That thou were chased from our heritage
Wel knowestow to wommen the olde way!
Thou madest Eva bringe us in servage.
Thou wolt fordoon this cristen mariage.
Thyn instrument so, weylawey the whyle!
Makestow of wommen whan thou wolt begyle.

It seems to me that though possibly there may be an allusion here to the human-headed serpent of art, it is at best a rather shadowy one. Surely it is a common enough comment upon the story of the fall of man, and one characteristic of the middle ages, that Satan tempted Eve first because she was weaker than Adam, and that since Adam's fall was due to Eve, all men should beware of the falsely alluring beauty of women? The stanza just quoted I believe implies no more than this.

In the *Persones Tale* Chaucer tells the story of man's fall without even the vaguest allusion to anything like a human-headed serpent.

[2] That is, the Chester play, probably by Ranulf Higden, *ca.* 1328.

in which the temptation of man is recounted or alluded to without any hint that the serpent had a human head. This will serve to show how little probable it is that the artists were directly indebted to any literary source.

Seventh to Eighth Century.—From the apocryphal Beda,—since Beda is given as an authority for the human-headed tempter,—I quote a relevant passage:[1] *Serpens per se loqui non poterat, nec quia hoc a Creatore acceperat assumpsit, nisi nimirum illum diabolus utens, et velut organum per quod articulatum sonum emitteret: per illum nempe verba faciebat, et tamen hoc etiam ille nesciebat.*

In the several discussions attributed to Beda, both those classified by Migne as *dubia et spuria* and also the *exegetica genuina*, the same idea concerning the serpent is conveyed: that the devil used the serpent as his instrument or organ of utterance (*Patrol. Lat.* XCIII, 229 and XCI, 211). As I have already said, I find nothing in Beda to bear out Comestor's reference to the *virgineum vultum.*

Eighth to Ninth Century (?)—In Genesis B, the Anglo-Saxon poem formerly attributed to Caedmon (edited by Klaeber, Heidelberg, 1913), the tempter assumes the form of a serpent.

Eleventh or Twelfth Century.—Onulphus, *Poema Biblicum.*[2] The dialogue between Eve and the serpent is given without any description of the serpent's appearance.

Twelfth Century, ca. 1100.—Rupertus Abbas Tuitiensis (Migne, *Patrol. Lat.* CLXVII, 290) speaks of "*Sathanas, ipse draco magnus et serpens antiquus est.*"

Thirteenth Century.—St. Martinus Legionensis (Migne, *Patrol. Lat.* CCVIII) quotes St. Augustine, and it will be observed says just about the same thing that the venerable Beda said. This, then, seems to be the ancient and firmly established exegesis.

The author of the *Ancren Riwle* (Camden Society, London, 1853) in speaking of the temptation of Eve, gives no description of the serpent.

In another passage he describes the scorpion in the manner of the *Bestiary:*

Þe scorpiun is ones cunnes wurm Þet haueð neb, ase me seið, sumdel iliche ase wummon 7 is neddre bihinden, makeð feir

[1] Beda Venerabilis, *Dubia et spuria* in Migne, *Patrol. Lat.* XCIII, 276.

[2] Karl Young, 'The Poema Biblicum of Onulphus,' *Publications of the Modern Language Association.* Vol. XXX, 1915, pp. 1 ff.

semblaunt, 7 fikeᵹ mid te heaued, 7 stingeᵹ mid te teile. Þet is lecherie: Þet is Þes deofles best, Þet he let to chepinge 7 to euerich gaderinge, 7 cheapeᵹ hit forto sullen, 7 beswikeᵹ monie Þuruh Þet heo ne biholdeᵹ nout bute Þet feire heaued.

This passage may have some bearing, as Skeat suggests, upon the human-headed serpent, but the author of *Ancren Riwle* does not make any connection between the scorpion and the tempter of Eve.[1]

Fourteenth Century.—Dante, *Purgatorio* VIII, 97 ff., significantly describes the serpent, which he sees in the Valley of the Princes, as a real zoölogical serpent, yet says it was perhaps such a one that gave Eve the bitter food. Sordello in pointing it out, moreover, calls it the adversary:

"Vedi là il nostro avversaro."

In all the account of the earthly paradise which fills the concluding cantos of the *Purgatorio* there is no allusion to a human-headed serpent.

Speculum Gy de Warewyke, circa 1310, tells nothing of the form of the serpent in the passage about the fall of man.

Clannesse, circa 1370 (in *Early English Alliterative Poems*, London 1869), contains nothing about the form of the serpent. Nor is there anything in the following: Þe *lyff of Adam and Eve*, (*circa* 1375) (C. Horstmann, *Sammlung altenglischer Legenden*, Heilbronn, 1878–81); and *Canticum de Creatione*, (*circa* 1375) (Horstmann, *Sammlung*, etc.).

Chaucer, as I have already observed, expounds the story of the temptation and fall of man without the least hint of anything like a human-headed serpent.

Summing up, we find that the only literary sources for the tradition prior to its appearance in the mystery plays are: Peter Comestor, Vincent de Beauvais, Guido delle Colonne, and,—if it is really earlier than the Chester play,—the *Speculum Humanae Salvationis.*

Though these are very important works, and works no doubt consulted by the writers of plays,—especially Comestor and the

---

[1] Note also that Chaucer, in *The Marchantes Tale* (E 2057–60), employs the figure of the scorpion in his apostrophe to 'sudden hap' or fortune:

O sodeyn hap, O thou fortune instable,
Lyk to the scorpioun so deceivable,
That flatterest with thyn heed when thou wolt stinge;
Thy tayl is deeth, thrugh thyn enveniminge!

Speculum,—it is doubtful, in view of the evidence before us, whether their popularity was sufficient to affect the traditions of artists. If such learned men as Dante, Chaucer, and the author of *Ancren Riwle,* ignore the picturesque and startling notion of Comestor, I cannot regard it as probable that artists, a century or more after Comestor's death should suddenly decide on his account to break their own tradition of more than a thousand years.

II

THE ART FORM

That the artists' tradition was simple and unbroken for more than a thousand years, is readily seen if one takes up the representations in art of the serpent tempter, from the earliest down to Michaelangelo's and Raphael's frescoes, and the painting of Titian. Art in the first centuries of the Christian era, it will be remembered, was almost entirely symbolic. I have found no example of a narrative treatment of the story of the temptation earlier than the ninth or tenth century.

Adam and Eve with the tree of knowledge and the serpent, were represented in art from the early centuries of Christianity as the symbol of original sin. That is to say, the iconograph turned the mind of the devout believer to the thoughts of his inherited wickedness, the curse of labor, the coming of death, and the need of a redeemer.

Thus on the famous sarcophagus of Junius Bassus, now in the crypt of St. Peter's, Adam stands on one side of the tree holding a sheaf of wheat; Eve on the other holding a sheep; each holds a fig-leaf as being conscious of shame; the serpent twined about the tree trunk is a simple zoölogical serpent. The design is purely symbolic, the sheaf and sheep indicating, with an appropriate division of labor, labor's primal curse; the tree and serpent, the first cause of man's mortality. It is not a representation of the tempting and fall of man within the Garden of Eden, nor of his toil without the gates, but a symbol of both. Thus it is suitable on the sarcophagus of a Christian, in a series that is dominated triumphantly by symbols of the redemption and resurrection.

From the second century to the eighth century, inclusive, whether in gold-glass decoration, medal, plate, sarcophagus, or fresco, the design is symbolic and the serpent is purely zoölogical. With the beginning of the ninth century there is a suggestion of a representative or narrative treatment in the picturing of the

serpent as apart from the tree, erect on the tip of his tail. Thereafter the artists take slightly more liberty with the subject, but
it is not until the thirteenth or the beginning of the fourteenth
century that we find the tempter represented with a human head.
Even after the introduction of the human head, however, the
temptation is very commonly shown with a simple zoölogical
serpent, the same artist sometimes—Lukas Cranach for instance
—impartially giving, in separate pictures, both types.[1]

The human-headed serpent in art flourishes in the fourteenth,
fifteenth, and sixteenth centuries—that is, at the same time as
the mystery plays.

Though I have relegated to a footnote (p. 290) the discussion
of possible influences of classical and oriental mythology upon
the formation of the monstrous woman-headed serpent in Christian art, yet because of their striking similarity to much later
forms I shall begin my list of the human-headed serpent in art
with two or three examples that I believe have nothing to do
with that tradition of the fourteenth, fifteenth, and sixteenth
centuries which gave the serpent in Eden a human head.

Bronze Statuary.—Egypt. Ancient bronze figures of Isis and
Serapis[2] in the form of cobras with human heads. Isis wears a
royal headdress, has the hair and face and also the *mammae* of a
woman, the latter being on the anterior or ventral surface of the
cobra's distended "hood," or neck.

Gem.—Rome (?) in the earliest epoch of Christian art. A
Christian,—or Christ (?)—with a monogram cross bends as
though exorcising a serpent-like monster on which he stands.
The monster has the head and arms of a human being, but ter-
minates in a barbed tail. The ventral surface is covered with

---

[1] The following works give much information, accompanied by a wealth of
cuts, illustrative of the old traditional representation of Adam and Eve and
the Serpent: O. M. Dalton, *Byzantine Art and Archaeology*, Oxford, 1911;
Jean Ebersolt, 'Sculptures Chrétiennes Inédites du Musée de Constantinople,'
R. Arch. Vol. XXI; R. Garucci, *Storia dell' Arte Cristiana*, Prato, 1879; Carl
Maria Kaufmann, *Handbuch der christlichen Archäologie*, Paderborn, 1913;
Kaufmann, Mogk, Hirt, etc., *Kulturgeschichte des Mittelalters*, Leipzig, 1897;
H. Leclercq, *Manuel d'Archéologie Chrétienne*, Paris, 1907; Walter Lowrie,
Monuments of the Early Church, New York, 1901; Orazio Marucchi, *Guida
del Museo Cristiano Lateranense*, Rome, 1898; J. O. Westwood, *Palaeographia
Sacra Pictoria*, London [1843–45].

[2] Roscher, *Lexikon der griech. und röm. Mythologie*, II, p. 538, *s.v.* Isis.
Roscher speaks of similar treatment on silver armlets from Naucratis, and
refers to the *Third Memoir of Egyptian Exploration Fund*, London, 1888.

numerous *mammae*. (Didron, *Christian Iconography*, English translation II, p. 201, Fig. 226.)

Coin of Valentinian III, Roman Empire, fifth century. A figure holding in the left hand a globe surmounted by a small Victory, and in the right a long staff tipped with a Greek cross, stands with the right foot upon the human head of a serpent. The human-headed serpent may represent the barbarians or other enemies of the Empire. (Cohen and Feuardent, *Descr. historique des Monnaies frappées sous l'Empire Romain*, VIII, p. 212, No. 19.)

The above designs have obviously nothing to do with Adam and Eve, and could only by a very remote possibility have had any influence upon the artists of the fourteenth century.

THIRTEENTH CENTURY

1. *Sculpture.*—Amiens, Notre-Dame. A dragon-like monster with claws and a female head is represented beneath the feet of the Virgin. This is probably in illustration of the fulfillment of the prophecy of Genesis III, 15: "And I will put enmity between thee and the woman, and between thy seed and her seed; it shall bruise thy head, and thou shalt bruise his heel." If so, this is the serpent of the temptation, and perhaps the earliest case in which it is represented with a human head. (Viollet-le-Duc, *Dictionnaire Raisonné de l'Architecture*, IX, p. 369.)

THIRTEENTH OR FOURTEENTH CENTURY

2. *Illumination* (Fig. 1).—*Biblia cum Figuris*, Paris, Bibl. Nat., MSS. Fr. No. 9561, fol. 8a.[1] Adam and Eve are on opposite sides of the tree,—Eve at the left and Adam at the right, and each is tasting an apple. The serpent, whose enormous folds seem thicker than the trunk of the tree he entwines, bifurcates near the anterior extremity and bears two human heads!

This unique[2] representation causes the good Didron to remark:

[1] Omont, *Cat. Général des Manuscrits Français*, No. 9561. "Partie d'une "Bible historiée toute figurée." Miniatures italiennes à chaque page. XIV• siècle. Parchemin. cf. *Hist. litt. de la France*, XXXI, pp. 246–251." This manuscript is assigned to the year 1340 in the list of illustrations in the English translation of Didron, *Christian Iconography*, II, p. 437. This list of illustrations seems to be a compilation of the translator (cf. II, p. 84). It may be added that the portion of the translation relating to these representations of the Fall (pp. 139–140) is somewhat abridged from *Annales Archéologiques*, I, pp. 131–132, where the number of the manuscript is not given.

[2] Didron cites no other example, and I know of none.

"The serpent has occasionally two heads, one female with which to address the man, the other male with which to address the

FIGURE 1.—FROM MS. IN PARIS
(After Didron)

woman." Peter Comestor's dictum, "*similia similibus applaudunt*" is thus reversed. But unless the original be very different from the cut Didron gives, it would seem hopeless to attempt to distinguish male from female in these little faces.

A much simpler explanation of the duplication of the human head on this serpent would be that the artist wished to suggest motion, the serpent watching both Adam and Eve after the temptation. Progressive action suggested by repeating a figure in the same composition is, of course, familiar in mediaeval art: there is an example of it in the next picture I shall discuss. The difficulty lies in the fact that only the head and neck are duplicated, not the whole serpent. This is strange, indeed, and I believe unique. But as the most ancient tradition held the serpent twined about the tree, the artist could not very well repeat the whole serpent's body. If this explanation seem strained, I can only add that to me it is not half so bizarre as the idea that the miniaturist intended to represent the tempter as having two human heads. To have given him even one human head was surely a sufficient innovation. (Didron, *op. cit.* II, p. 139; *Annales Archéologiques*, I, p. 132, fig. 5, where, however, the design is reversed.)

3. *Illumination.*—France.   Paris, Bibl. Nat., MSS. Fr. No. 9561, fol. 8.   The serpent in this design has head and arms that are human, the head being with its calm features and long hair almost the exact counterpart of Eve's.

Eve is shown first in the conventional position at the right of the tree, receiving an apple from the serpent; and again at the left of the tree tempting Adam, who kneels on one knee with his back to the tree and serpent, and looks over his shoulder at Eve. In this part both Adam and Eve have apples in both hands. Here the repetition of the figure of Eve within the frame and composition of one little miniature is, clearly enough, an indication of action. It would not occur to anyone to say that the artist had represented two Eves! (Didron, Vol. II, p. 140; *Annales Archéologiques*, I, p. 132, fig. 6.)

4. *Illumination.*—England, British Museum MS. Reg. 2Bvii, Queen Mary's Psalter. Adam is at the left of the tree; Eve at the right reaches up to seize an apple.

The serpent has the "head of a beautiful woman and the body of a dragon," says Wright. The serpent tail is entwined about the trunk of the tree; the "body" is small and seems to be furnished with only one pair of limbs,—hind legs of the mammal quadruped type. It is interesting to compare this with the type shown in the French MS. cited by Didron, which gives the tempter only one pair of limbs—the arms of a woman; and also with that picture of van der Goes which gives four limbs to the human-headed monster, all four being reptilian. Three demons are represented in this illumination besides the serpent tempter. (Wright, *History of Caricature*, p. 73; Warner, *Queen Mary's Psalter*, pl. 5.)

5. *Illumination* (Fig. 2).—Munich, MS., Clm 146. The oldest manuscript of the *Speculum humanae salvationis*. Here, as in the many other illustrated manuscripts of this work,[1] the artists naturally followed the text in representing the tempter with a woman's head. (Lutz and Perdrizet, *Speculum humanae salvationis*, II, pl. 2.)

6. *Painting* (Fig. 3).—Hamburg. The Grabower altar from St. Peter's, by Master Bertram, 1379; now in the Hamburg Museum.

Two of a series or cycle of little paintings on the so-called *Grabower altar* show the serpent tempter with a human head. The cycle as a whole (as I shall endeavor to show in another article) has a most important bearing upon the mystery plays. (A. Lichtwark, *Meister Bertram*, Hamburg 1905.)

7. *Painting* (Fig. 4).—Italy, by an unknown artist. The main

---

[1] Lutz and Perdrizet, *op. cit.* I, pp. ix–xvii record 205 Latin manuscripts, over 60 of which contain miniatures. The general type of the miniatures of the Temptation is described (I, p. 184) as follows: "Le 'Serpent' est représenté par les miniaturistes du *Speculum* comme une bête monstrueuse, à corps de dragon ailé, à long col, et à tête de jeune fille. Dans la miniature de A, ses ailes sont entrouvertes, et de sa bouche sort un dard bifide, indiqué par un léger trait de minium. Même serpent dans C que dans A, sauf qu'il lui manque le dard." A and C are closely related fourteenth century manuscripts in Paris (Bibl. Nat., MSS. Lat. 9584; Arsenal, MSS. Lat. 593), written in an Italian hand, and with miniatures showing Giottesque influence.

FIGURE 2.—FROM SPECULUM HUMANAE SALVATIONIS: MUNICH.

FIGURE 3.—GRABOWER ALTAR: MASTER BERTRAM.

FIGURE 4.—FROM AN ITALIAN PAINTING: CLEVELAND.

subject is a Madonna suckling the infant. Below, in a horizontal panel, Eve is shown reclining, and near her the serpent with a female head. (Lent to the Cleveland Museum by Mrs. L. E. Holden.)

8. *Stained Glass.*—Mulhouse. The choice of scenes seems influenced by the *Speculum humanae salvationis,* and naturally the serpent has a human head. (Lutz and Perdrizet, *op. cit.* II, pl. 101.)

FOURTEENTH OR FIFTEENTH CENTURY

9. *Illumination.*—Germany or Austria. Vienna Hofbibliothek, MS. No. 2980 (Ambras 259) *Lutwins Adam und Eva.*[1] The picture, of which no reproduction is given, is thus described by the editors of the manuscript: "Bild: In der Mitte ein Baum mit Blättern und Früchten (Äpfeln?); darum·die Schlange mit menschlichem Antlitz und Krone gewunden; Eva hat bereits eine Frucht in der Hand."

FIFTEENTH CENTURY

10. *Painting.*—Florence, Brancaccio Chapel in the Church of the Carmine, by Masolino, *ca.* 1425. The tempter is a serpent with a rather small human[2] head. (Woltmann and Woermann, II, p. 277; Venturi, *Storia dell' Arte Italiana,* VII, Part I, p. 103.)

11. *Relief.*—Bologna, San Petronio, by Jacopo della Quercia, *ca.* 1426–1438. The temptation scene is one of a series giving the whole story of Adam and Eve. The serpent has a human head. It is interesting to note that to della Quercia even the great Michelangelo is said to have been indebted. (Venturi, *op. cit.* VI, pp. 87 ff.)

12. *Relief.*—Florence, Baptistery, the famous bronze doors by Lorenzo Ghiberti; 1424–1447 (second door). On the second door, Ghiberti's masterpiece, are depicted in one composition the creation of Adam and of Eve and the story of the temptation. The serpent in the temptation scene has a human head. (*Iconographic Encyclopedia,* Philadelphia, 1887, Vol. III, pl. 23, Fig. 4.)

13. *Illumination.*—Paris, Bibl. Nat., MSS. Fr., 6275. Miélot's

---

[1] Konrad Hofmann und Wilhelm Meyer aus Speyer, *Lutwins Adam und Eva,* Tübingen, 1881.

[2] In this case as in a good many others, the head, though it might be called a woman's because of its mild expression and its locks, is not necessarily feminine.

French translation (1448) of the *Speculum humanae salvationis.* (Lutz and Perdrizet, *op. cit.* II, pl. 129.)

14. *Woodcut.*—Germany, xylographic copy, of the *Biblia Pauperum, ca.* 1440–1450,[1] in the Heidelberg University library. The serpent with human head appears twice in this book: (1) Plate I,—The Annunciation, which is accompanied by the explanation that it was foretold in God's words to the serpent, has as a "type" beside it a picture of God cursing the serpent. (2) Plate X,—The Temptation of Christ has as a "type" the temptation of Adam and Eve. In this the serpent is crowned. (*Biblia Pauperum* [facsimile], Graphische Gesellschaft, Berlin, 1906.)

15. *Illumination.* Venice, Breviary Grimani, Bibl. Marc. The Fall: The devil is human, but for his claw feet and long tail. He stands on the ground, hiding behind the tree. (Facsimile edited by Zanotto, pl. 45.)

16. *Illumination.*—Savoy, the *Très riches Heures* of the Duke de Berry illuminated by Jean Colombe, illuminator of the ducal court of Charles I of Savoy; now in the Musée Condé, Chantilly. A decorative structure resembling a monstrance occupies the centre of the design; possibly representing the *tree of life*(?). At the left is the tree of the knowledge of good and evil, with the serpent. The serpent has the head, arms, and bust of a woman. (Durrien, *Les très riches heures de Jean de France, Duc de Berry,* pl. XVIII; Venturi, *op. cit.* VII, Part I, p. 133.)

17. *Painting* (Fig. 5).—Ghent, by Hugo van der Goes, now in the imperial gallery at Vienna. Adam and Eve stand at the left of the tree and the tempter at the right. The "serpent" is here a lizard with a child's head, standing upon its hind legs, supporting itself by holding the tree trunk with its forelegs, and gazing almost wistfully up at Eve, who, quite ignoring it, reaches calmly with her left hand for an apple. The child-faced tempter is furnished with two little pigtails which stick up absurdly over the temples—and what hard heart will not receive it for a horned demon? I shall have more to say of this remarkable picture. (J. Destrée, *Hugo van der Goes,* pp. 32 (pl.), 38–40; E. Heidrich, *Alt-Niederländische Malerei,* Jena, 1910, pl. 72.)

---

[1] The date of the first *Biblia Pauperum* was perhaps as early as the twelfth century. I shall discuss this elsewhere, in considering the significance of the work in its relation to other cyclic treatments of Bible story.

This Heidelberg *Biblia Pauperum* is, according to Paul Kristeller, the oldest xylographic copy. The pictures are made on movable wood-blocks so that groups of woodcuts may be variously assembled and printed together. The text, however, is filled in by hand.

2

18. *Painting.*—In the library of Schloss Frens. It is the work of a painter of the Netherlands living at the end of the fifteenth

FIGURE 5.—THE TEMPTATION, HUGO VAN DER GOES: VIENNA.

century, and closely related to Hugo van der Goes. It is very like the Vienna painting, but represents Adam and Eve in Paradise, while the devil, who is almost the same as van der Goes', is hiding behind a tree in the background, apparently planning the temptation. (P. Clemen, *Die Kunstdenkmäler der Rheinprovinz,* IV, 3, p. 70, pl. VII.)

19. *Painting.*—Florence, decorative detail in the Annunciation by Lorenzo di Credi, in the Uffizi, *ca.* 1480. The influence of the *Biblia Pauperum* is seen in this association of the Old Testament type with the New Testament story,[1] indicating that the prophecy made in the Garden of Eden is about to be fulfilled in the incarnation of Christ. The three panels under di Credi's Annunciation show (1) the creation of Eve, (2) the temptation, and (3) the expulsion from Eden. The serpent tempter has a human head. (Venturi, *op. cit.* VII, Part II, p. 798.)

20. *Woodcut.*—Venice, in the *Supplementum Chronicarum* of Jacobus Philippus, 1486–1491. The serpent has a human head. (Jacques Rosenthal, *Incunabula Typographica,* p. 71.)

21. *Painting* (Fig. 6).—Padua, The Madonna of Victory by Andrea Mantegna, 1496; now in the Louvre. Adam and Eve are represented in a relief upon the magnificent throne on which the Madonna is seated. The composition is according to the most approved tradition—Adam standing at the left, Eve at the right, the serpent twined about the tree in the middle—save that the serpent has a human head. (*Masters in Art,* VI, Part 64.)

Figure 6.—Mantegna.

22. *Woodcuts* (Fig. 7).—These woodcuts were printed in an edition of the *Speculum humanae salvationis* by Peter Drach of Speier in 1479. Pl. 4 shows Eve and the serpent, who has female head and breasts; Pl. 5 shows Eve giving Adam the apple, while the serpent is coiled on the tree; it has a female head. The illuminator of the Munich manuscript (No. 5) has omitted the

---

[1] "And the Lord God said unto the serpent, Because thou hast done this, thou art cursed above all cattle, and above every beast of the field: upon thy belly shalt thou go, and dust shalt thou eat all the days of thy life: And I will put enmity between thee and the woman, and between thy seed and her seed; it shall bruise thy head, and thou shalt bruise his heel." *Genesis,* III, 14, 15.

serpent in this scene. (H. Naumann, *Die Holzschnitte des Meisters von Amsterdamer Kabinett zum Spiegel menschlichen*

FIGURE 7.—FROM SPECULUM HUMANAE SALVATIONIS, 1479.

Behaltnis. Strassburg, 1910. *Studien zur Deutschen Kunstge-schichte*, Heft 126.)

23. *Woodcut*.—Geneva, initial letter 'M' on title page of the Missal of Bellot. Adam is at the left and Eve at the right of the tree. The serpent, wound about the trunk and looking out from a fork in the branches, offers the apple to Eve. It has human head and arms. (O. Jennings, *Early Woodcut Initials*, London, 1908, p. 164.)

SIXTEENTH CENTURY

24. *Tapestry*.—Brussels, by an artist or artists of distinction not certainly identified, *ca.* 1500; now in the possession of Baron de Zuylen de Nyevelt de Haar, Château de Haar, Belgium. This is one of a famous group of tapestries, unfortunately now widely separated, which clearly reflect the influence of religious drama.[1]

The serpent in the temptation has four limbs, the hind legs, on which it stands, apparently more like those of a dog than of a

[1] D. T. B. Wood, 'Tapestries of the Seven Deadly Sins' *Burl. Mag.* XX, p. 210, says: "Through all of them run two leading motives: the religious history of the Redemption as it appears in various cycles of Miracle Plays, and the moral allegory of the conflict of Virtues and Vices."

reptile—but I cannot be sure of this. It has a woman's head with long flowing hair, and human arms. Wood comments on the kindly expression of its face. (*Burl. Mag.* XX, p. 215.)

25. *Illumination.*—Munich, Bavarian National Museum, No. 861. A prayer book of the end of the fifteenth or beginning of the sixteenth century. The serpent has a woman's head and arms; the upper part of the body is hidden behind the tree, around which the serpent is coiled. (L. von Kobell, *Kunstvolle Miniaturen und Initialen aus Handschriften von IV–XVI Jahrh.*, p. 92.)

26. *Painting.*—Rome, Sistine Chapel, ceiling by Michelangelo, 1508–1512. To describe Michelangelo's design of the temptation would, I suppose, be a work of supererogation. It is to be noted, however, that the tempter is a woman to the hips, and that the voluminous folds of the serpent portion encircling the tree strongly suggest a duplicate tail. If the serpent portion is really intended to be double, then Michelangelo is creating a new type,—possibly being influenced by the bifurcated mermaidens of classical art, or the Scylla[1] of Virgil:

[1] Whoever has studied Virgil in Greenough and Kittredge's edition will remember the cut illustrating the description of the monster Scylla. See p. 290, note 2, in which I discuss Lilith, Lamia, etc.

Milton speaks of the serpent in the temptation as "Mere serpent in appearance," and describes it with some particularity, thus:

> "So spake the Enemy of Mankind, enclosed
> In serpent, inmate bad, and toward Eve
> Addressed his way—not with indented wave,
> Prone on the ground, as since, but on his rear
> Circular base of rising folds, that towered
> Fold above fold, a surging maze; his head
> Crested aloft, and carbuncle his eyes;
> With burnished neck of verdant gold, erect
> Amidst his circling spires, that on the grass
> Floated redundant."
>
> *Paradise Lost*, Book IX, ll. 494–503.

But in the second book, when describing the monster at the gate of Hell personifying Sin, though avowedly borrowing from Virgil's description of Scylla, Milton may have had a shadowy recollection of some of the numerous examples of Christian art in which the serpent tempter is given a form half woman and half serpent:

> "The one seemed woman to the waist, and fair,
> But ended foul in many a scaly fold,
> Voluminous and vast—a serpent armed
> With mortal sting. About her middle round
> A cry of Hell-hounds never-ceasing barked—"
>
> *Paradise Lost*, Book II, ll. 650–654.

At least Milton makes this spawn of Satan end in serpent, not in dolphin tails.

Prima hominis facies et pulchro pectore virgo
pube tenus, postrema immani corpore pristis, [i.e. pistrix]
delphinum caudas utero commissa luporum.

Æneid, III. 426–428.

I think it will be clear to the reader now that Michelangelo was following a tradition in making the serpent half woman, a tradition by this time about two hundred years old. (*Masters in Art*, II, part 17.)

27. *Painting* (Fig. 8).—Rome, fresco in the Camera della Segnatura of the Vatican, by Raphael, 1511. Adam is seated at the left of the tree, and Eve stands at the right holding a branch with her left hand as with her right she proffers the apple to Adam. The serpent is simply a serpent as far as it appears below the fork of the tree, but above the fork it assumes the face and shoulders of a woman, bending an expectant glance toward Adam. (Champlin and Perkins, *Cyclopedia of Painters*, 1892; E. Müntz, *Raphael*, English transl., London 1888, p. 276.)

FIGURE 8.—RAPHAEL.

28. *Terra-cotta relief* (Fig. 9).—Florence, from the workshop of the Della Robbias, *ca.* 1515; now in the collection of Mr. Henry Walters, Baltimore. Adam and Eve are conventionally arranged on either side of the tree; the serpent has a human head. (*Burl. Mag.* XX, p. 36.)

29. *Painting* (Fig. 10).—Rome, fresco by pupils after Raphael's designs, in the loggie of the Vatican, 1516–1518. This design resembles the Adam and Eve by Raphael in the Camera della Segnatura in its general composition, save that the figures are reversed: Eve is at the left, and Adam seated at the right. The serpent (unlike the serpent of the Camera) has no shoulders, —only the head, which is charmingly feminine, being human.

30. *Painting.*—Saxony. A large composition giving the whole story of Adam and Eve, by Lukas Cranach, 1530; now in Vienna.

This composition is remarkable because Cranach has several times painted Adam and Eve without any human-headed serpent— *e.g.* his Adam and Eve in the Dresden gallery. The whole story

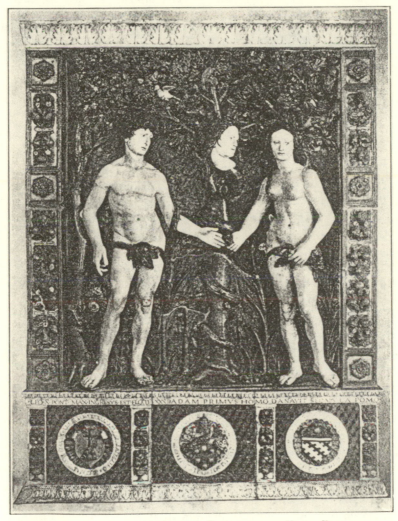

FIGURE 9.—TERRACOTTA RELIEF: SCHOOL OF THE DELLA ROBBIA.

being given in one composition, it is perhaps the more natural to suppose that this painting might have come under the influence of the plays. The serpent has the head, bust, and arms of a woman. (Ed. Heyck, *Lukas Cranach, Künstler-Monographien,* Leipzig, 1908.)

31. *Woodcut.*—Bavaria, "Dance of Death" designed by Hans Holbein the Younger, *ca.* 1538.

FIGURE 10.—SCHOOL OF RAPHAEL

In the Adam and Eve design the serpent, which is coiled above with head down, has a woman's head. (G. Hirth, *Kulturgeschichtliches Bilderbuch,* Munich, 1883, II, p. 651.)

32. *Stained Glass.*—Rouen, Saint-Vincent's church *ca.* 1550; subject, the *Triumph of Sin.* On the triumphal car the serpent, with the head and bust of a woman, is entwined about the trunk of the tree, and has floating above it a banner decorated with the image of Death. (E. Mâle, *L'Art Religieux de la Fin du Moyen Age,* p. 309.)

33. *Woodcut.*—Antwerp, by an artist employed by Plantin, 1569. The serpent has a human head. ('A Booke of Christian Prayers,' in *Fine Art Quarterly Rev.,* 1867, p. 157.)

34. *Painting.*—Venice, by Titian, 1570; now in the Prado, Madrid. The serpent has a child's head and arms, and duplicate tail. (A. Weese, *Der Schöne Mensch,* II, pl. 39 A.)

35. *Painting.*—Holland, by Cornelisz van Haarlem, 1592; now in the Rijks Museum, Amsterdam. The serpent with human head and arms leans down to offer Eve the apple. (R. Muther, *Geschichte der Malerei,* Leipzig, 1909, p. 65.)

III

THE PLAYS

Though the artists before the fourteenth or fifteenth century could not be assumed to be sufficiently learned or independent to search out old commentators and from their texts derive new forms and modes of pictorial representation,[1]—for with all their

[1] G. Cohen, *Histoire de La Mise en Scène dans le Théatre Religieux Français du Moyen Age,* pp. 129–131;   E. Mâle, 'Le renouvellement de l'art par les Mystères,' *Gaz. B-A.* XXXI, 1904, four articles.

talents 'these fine folk knew no Latin,' and followed only what was before their eyes or was dictated by more learned men,— on the other hand the authors of the plays were necessarily learned. To quote M. Cohen, "the clerks, chaplains, bishops or doctors who dictated what was needful to the artisans were also those who made, organized, and put on (*montaient*) the mystery plays, whether in the choir, in the nave, or in public places. Their material was drawn either directly from the Bible, or more often from Scholastic Histories, Bestiaries, Lectionaries, the Compendia (*les Sommes*) of every sort; they searched in the apocryphal works of Bede and St. Augustine, in Isidore of Seville, Peter Comestor, Honoré d'Autun, Vincent de Beauvais, or in the *Meditations* of St. Bonaventure."

Just one point of difficulty remains to be cleared up. If the artists were not responsible for the sudden introduction of the human-headed serpent into Eden because they were too unlettered, it may seem strange that the "producers" of the mystery plays, who were undoubtedly learned, and generally pious in their intentions, should have sanctioned such an unprecedented and undoctrinal monster.

"Satan chose," says Peter Comestor, "a certain kind of serpent, as Beda, says, having a virginal face, because like things applaud like." Here is a comment of no doctrinal value, a sort of thing ignored by even such learned poets as Dante and Chaucer. Had it any practical value for the stage managers of the primitive drama? That is logically the next question.

To answer this question let us consider the presentation of the Anglo-Norman *Jeu d'Adam*, which is generally conceded to belong to the mid-twelfth century, just Comestor's time.[1] It is at all events the oldest vernacular Adam play, and, indeed, semi-liturgic in character.

In this charming little play, Satan first comes on the stage *in propria persona* in order to converse with Eve, and only after this attempt has failed does the serpent play its part. At first the dialogue takes great freedom with Scripture, the seductive Satan flattering Eve with many pretty words, calling her a frail and tender thing, more fresh than a rose and more fair than crys-

---

[1] The dissenting opinion of Paul Meyer is cited by Cohen (*op. cit.*, p. 51): "Je ne vois pas, écrit le savant romaniste, de raison positive pour attribuer à l'Angleterre ce petit mystère qui ne paraît pas antérieur à la première moitié du XIIIe Siècle. (*Romania*, 1903, p. 637.)"

tal; but when the time comes for the fatal dialogue of Genesis, the play is obliged to omit it because the serpent is mechanical and cannot speak. Eve bends to listen, but no words are audible:

"Tunc serpens artificiose compositus ascendit juxta stipitem arboris vetite. Cui Eva propius adhibebit aurem, quasi ipsius ascultans consilium; dehinc accipiet Eva pomum porriget Ade. Ipse vero nondum eum accipiet, et Eva dicet"—etc.

A charming tableau truly, but not a complete success, is achieved.[1] It must have been a disappointment to the pious author not to be able to include in the climax the very scripture of the temptation scene.

It is easy to imagine that this same disappointment stimulated some later author to seize upon Peter Comestor's text with its apparently ancient and venerable sanction in Beda. Thereafter and particularly in such plays as included the story of the fall of the angels, it would be but natural to have the youth who played the rebellious Lucifer[2] put on the "sort of serpent" skin or costume, while adapting himself to the rôle of tempter in Eden. A fair-faced lad with flowing hair would equally well present the glorious angel before his fall, and the "sort of serpent with a virginal face" approved by Comestor. Other advantages besides the facilitation of the dialogue are apparent. The serpent would be able to walk and stand before the curse compelled him to crawl upon his belly—that is, in those cases in which he took the form of a lizard; and he would be instantly recognized by the audience as identical with Lucifer, both by his face and voice. and sometimes by his crown.

If the pictures we have considered actually reflect the influence of the plays, it would seem that there were two distinct types of presentation of the serpent:

(1) That in which it is simply a serpent below, with no hind legs; and human above, sometimes the head alone, and sometimes with arms and more or less of the trunk;

(2) That in which it has the body, or at least the hindquarters

---

[1] Cohen, *op. cit.*, p. 60, commenting on the fineness of suggestion in the directions, says there are other gestures so exquisite that one might believe they were indicated by a painter. Adam receiving the apple that Eve proffers reminds him of the famous panels of Van Eyck. Does he momentarily forget that the actors are gowned and standing behind curtains which screen them to the shoulders?

[2] Or one like him, if the *Temptation* were given by a different guild.

and tail of a dragon or lizard; and the head, or head and trunk, human.

In the case of (1) there could be no walking about on the stage, but the player would be obliged to lie concealed at the foot of the tree until his cue came to crawl up the trunk. This is precisely the stage direction of a Lucerne play of 1583 in the case of a human-headed, four-limbed serpent. After the curse, however, he is directed to crawl on all fours away to Hell (vff allen Vieren wider durch die Hell hinweg), *i.e.*, out through Hell-mouth.

In the case of (2) I think that, except in some continental stationary performances, the player generally walked on his "hind legs." In the Gréban Passion play—Eden scene,[1]—and in plays expounded by Klimke and by Brandstetter it is expressly stated that this is not to be done; but in the English Chester play the fallen angel puts on his serpent disguise and enters Eden while or just after speaking a soliloquy; in the York play the *directions* imply walking; in the Hegge play it seems necessary; the serpent's costume in the Norwich play seems to be adapted thereto; a sixteenth century Breton play which indicates that the serpent had feet and hands before the curse,—though after it he has to be carried out by fellow demons,—seems to imply that at first he walked; the Low-German play by Arnold Immessen says that Lucifer enters paradise and climbs the tree as a serpent *in specie virginis*.

It is to be noted that in both pictures and plays the serpent is sometimes crowned. This is the case in the temptation scene in the *Biblia Pauperum*. But let the plays themselves now give their testimony.

It is possible that the play described by the Regensburg Annals as including the creation of the angels, the fall of Lucifer, the creation and fall of man, and the prophets, anticipated the method of presenting the serpent which we find in the English Chester play more than a century later, but I am unable to say that it is probable. The notice in the annals gives the date of this play as February 7, 1194; according to Carl Klimke this is the earliest mention of a Paradise play in Germany.[2]

In the thirteenth or fourteenth century, a Viennese Passion-play describes the tempter in the Garden of Eden thus: "*Adam*

---

[1] "*Icy s'en va Sathan a quatre piez comme un serpent entortiller autour de l'arbre.*" Edition of Gaston Paris.

[2] Carl Klimke, *Das Volkstümliche Paradiesspiel*, Breslau, 1902.

et Eva sint in paradyso, et serpens dyabolus clam veniens ad Evam et introspiciat sicut dicens—" [1] but gives no further description. Perhaps we may infer from the *clam veniens* and the *dicens* that this moving and speaking serpent is furnished with a human head. The manuscript, according to Froning, though in a hand of about 1320–1330, is doubtless a copy of a thirteenth century play.

This brings us to the probable time of the composition of the Chester plays, the oldest of the English cycles.[2]

In the following tabulation of evidence from plays, I cannot defend as logical my method of classifying by centuries. For the most part I classify plays according to the date of the earliest manuscript. In the case of the Chester plays I take the liberty of attributing the origin to the fourteenth century, to which very likely other of these plays also belong.

FOURTEENTH CENTURY

1. Chester, probably composed 1328, by Ranulf Higden. Earliest MS., 1591.

The second Chester play (it follows the play of the *Fall of Lucifer*) includes the creation of the world, divided according to the six days; the creation of Adam and Eve; the temptation and fall; the expulsion from Eden; the story of Cain and Abel.

The Demon tempter,—evidently Lucifer, for he says he was formerly the brightest angel,—approaches Eden soliloquizing.[3] He says he must disguise himself:

> A manner of an Adder is in this place,
> that wynges like a byrd she hase,
> feete as an Adder, a maydens face;
> her kinde I will take.
>
> .   .   .   .   .
>
> Therefore, as brocke I my pane,
> my adders coate I will put on,
> and into paradice will I gone,
> as fast as ever I may.

---

[1] R. Froning, *Das Drama des Mittelalters*, Stuttgart, 1891.

[2] E. K. Chambers, *The Mediaeval Stage*, Oxford, 1903, Vol. II, pp. 145, and 348–352: discussion of date and evidence for authorship.

[3] The *direction* in one MS. is, *"et veniet serpens ad paradisum positum in specie Demonis et ambulando dicat"*; and in the three other MSS., *"the serpente shall Come up ovt of a hole and the deuille walkinge shal saye."* See H. Deimling, *The Chester Plays*, London, 1892.

(*Versus: Spinx Volucris penna, serpens pede, fronte puella.*) [1]
After the fall, questioned by God, Eve says,

    This adder, lorde, shee was my foe
    and sothelie deceaved me thoe,
    and made me to eate that meate.

Then God pronounces the curse and the prophecy, and the serpent goes out hissing,[2]—*Tunc recedet serpens, vocem serpentinam faciens.* Unquestionably, fulfilling the curse, the serpent glided out upon his belly.

2. Cornwall, play of fourteenth century.[3]

The play opens with the creation, but lacks the fall of Lucifer. A Latin note (at the end of the fifth day of creation), however, indicates that this was probably played from another manuscript: *hic ludit Lucifer de celo.* Norris interprets this as meaning merely that Lucifer appears at this point!

In the temptation scene the *direction* for the serpent reads: *diabolus tanquam serpens loquitur ad euam in arbore scientie et dicit male ad euam.* The *direction* for Eve reads: *Tunc accipiet pomum et deferet ad adam et dicit Eva.*

In speaking to Adam of the tempter, Eve calls him the 'angel' (*el*); in speaking to God, she calls him the 'serpent' (*sarf*). God, in cursing him, says he shall be cursed above all beasts:—*a gertho war an nor reis*, which Norris translates *which go on the face of the earth*.

In this play, then, we have the tempter described as a *devil like a serpent*, as an *angel*, and as a *serpent*. He speaks, and gives the apple to Eve,—which she *receives*.

FIFTEENTH CENTURY

3. Einbeck, Prussia, MS. of the first half of the century; by Arnoldus Immessen.[4]

In this play the scene of the temptation follows a rather splendid play, or opera, of the revolt and fall of Lucifer, the creation of man, and conspiracy in Hell, wherein Lucifer announces his intention of going to Eden.

---

[1] Thus Deimling; Wright, following other MSS., gives it: *superius volucris penna, serpens pede, forma puella.* What Deimling reads "Spinx" may also be intended for *superius: superius* is the reading in all other MSS.

[2] Or, possibly, merely making a cry in a "small voice": cf. the Norwich serpent.

[3] Edwin Norris, *Ancient Cornish Drama*, Oxford, 1859.

[4] O. Schönemann, *Der Sündenfall und Marienklage*, Hanover, 1855.

The *direction* which shows the entrance of the serpent gives him specifically the name *Lucifer*, though indicating that the part may be taken by another actor: *lucifer intrat paradifum et afcendit arborem vel aliud nomine ipfius et dicit ferpens in fpecie virginis.*

The audience then is expected to recognize in this walking (?) serpent, Lucifer himself—not merely one of his minions, but the glorious archangel, son of the morning,[1] fallen from Heaven down to that bad eminence, the lordship of Hell. Though a serpent, he wears his serpent guise with a difference,—*in specie virginis.*

Note that he *enters* Paradise and *gets up into* the tree. At the conclusion of his speech of temptation he *gives* the apple to Eve; he has forelimbs then, either reptilian or human:

> Num, wíf, den appel unde love minem done.

Et dat fibi pomum

4. Paris, *Misière du Viel Testament,*[2] ca. 1450.

In this monumental work the tempter in Eden is thus described:

Icy doit estre Sathan vestu d'un habit en manière de serpent et le visage de pucelle.

5. Paris, play of ca. 1452, by Arnoul Gréban.[3]

In this play, in the temptation scene, Satan says:

> D'aller en ce point,
> on verroit trop tost ma falace;
> je prendrai virginalle face
> les piez et le corps serpentin.

The *directions* explain the manner of his entrance: *Icy s'en va Sathan a quatre piez comme un serpent entortiller autour de l'arbre.*

6. Lincoln (?)[4]. Ms. of 1468, known as the *Hegge* Mysteries.[5]

The play of the temptation and fall of man is the second of the *Hegge* plays: it is preceded by a play of the days of creation and the fall of Lucifer.

---

[1] "How art thou fallen from Heaven, O Lucifer, son of the morning!" *Isaiah*, XIV, 12. This and the following verses constitute the basis for the plays of the revolt of Lucifer.

[2] Edition of J. de Rothschild and E. Picot, in publications of *Société des anciens textes français*, Paris, 1878–1885.

[3] *La Nativité, la Passion, la Resurrection de N.-S. J.-C. par Arnoul Gréban*, edition of Gaston Paris and G. Raynaud, Paris, 1878.

[4] Cf. Hardin Craig, 'The Coventry Cycle of Plays,' *Athenaeum*, August 16, 1913.

[5] J. O. Halliwell, *Ludus Coventriae*, London, 1841.

No stage directions indicate the entrance of the serpent, but the speeches suggest that he accosts Eve with an apple held out toward her:

> *Serpens.* Heyl ffayr wyff and comely dame!
> This ffrute to ete I the cownselle,
> Take this appyl and ete this ssame
>
> .   .   .   .   .
>
> Take this appyl in thin hond,
> And to byte therof thou ffond,
> Take another to thin husbond.

Eve describes the serpent to Adam as a "ffayr aungelle"; and to God as a "werm with an aungelys face," adding "I suppose it was Sathanas."

God in cursing the serpent, and the serpent in replying, intimate that before the curse this serpent walked upright:

> *Deus.* Thou wyckyd worm fful of pryde,
> ffowle envye syt be thi syde,
> Upon thi gutt thou xalt glyde
>   As werm wyckyd in kende.
>
> .   .   .   .   .
>
> *Diabolus.* At thi byddyng ffowle I falle,
> I krepe hem to my stynkyng stalle,
>
> .   .   .   .   .
>
> ffor this ffalle I gynne to qweke,
> With a ——— my breche I breke
> My sorwe comyth ful sone.

Evidently he falls on his belly and glides out.

7. Eger, play of *ca.* 1480.[1]

After the fall of Lucifer, and the creation, Lucifer and his comrades confer. Then Satan, who is here a different person from Lucifer, goes to tempt Eve: *transit ad paradisum dicens Evam.* . . . After his speech, the *direction* calls him a serpent: *Eva respondit serpenti.*

He has hands, for he plucks the apple giving it to Eve: *Et tunc Sathanas frangit pomum dans Eve.* But Eve in speaking of him to Adam calls him "die Schlang"; and speaking to God, "die beese Schlang."

God in cursing him also calls him so: *dicit ad serpentem*

---

[1] G. Milchsack, *Egerer Fronleichnams-spiel*, Tübingen, 1881.

O Schlang, du solt verflucht sein:
Das weiplich pildt das schwechet dich,
Dein gang sei nimer aüffrichtigklich,
Also der weiplich nam dich krenckt;
Hinfuer kreüch auff dem paüch gesenckt.

SIXTEENTH CENTURY

8. Lucerne, play of 1545 discussed by Renward Brandstetter.[1]
In this play the serpent tempter is described as,—*Mit eym wybischen Angesicht, bekrönnt, sonst alls ein gifftiger Wurm.*

9. Brittany, play of *ca.* 1550, discussed by l'Abbé Bernard.[2]
In this Celtic play the tempter appears in three different forms: first, as a leopard, second, as an old man; and third, as a serpent. From his position in the tree he addresses Eve, telling her that he is an angel of Heaven. Doubtless the face which appeared from the tree was such as to bear out this assertion. Apparently this serpent had four limbs,—the upper probably human, for God in cursing it says explicitly not only that it shall go on its belly, but that it shall go *without feet or hands* (*Hac nep na dorn na troat*). Then the serpent in the tree cries out, and his fellow demons come to rescue him and carry him away, *because he can no longer walk* (*pa na hell quet querset*).

10. Norwich, MS. of 1565.[3]
The Norwich play of the Temptation and the Expelling of Adam and Eve out of Paradise is supplied with two prologues,— one to be used in case no other play preceded it in performance; the other, in case the play of the creation of Eve (or some other play of the fall of the angels and creation?) were given first. It was performed by the Grocers.

The serpent is not described in the *directions* of the play, but we learn from the Grocers' accounts that he wore a wig, a crown, and "a cote with hosen & tayle steyned." We learn, moreover, that the player who for the sum of 4d. played the serpent in this play in 1534 was named Edmund Thurston.[4]

In the speech of the serpent, before the temptation, and in his

---

[1] R. Brandstetter, 'Die Luzerner Bühnen-Rodel,' *Germania*, XXX, pp. 205 ff.

[2] l'Abbé Bernard, 'La Création du Mond,' *Revue Celtique*, IX, X, and XI.

[3] O. Waterhouse, *The Non-Cycle Mystery Plays*, London (Early English Text Soc.), 1909.

[4] Waterhouse, *op. cit.* p. xxxiii.

mode of addressing Eve, we get some hints of his characterization: he says that to catch the man and woman he will use subtlety and appear as an angel of light; and he cries to Eve, "Oh lady of felicite, beholde my voyce so small!" When Eve is questioned by God she says, "The Serpente diseayvyd me with that his fayer face."

11. York, MS. of 1583.[1] Plays were given at York as early as 1378.

The fifth York play gives the story of the temptation. It follows plays of the creation, the fall of Lucifer, creation of man, and the introduction of Adam and Eve into Eden.

Satan begins by expressing his envy of Adam and his determination to betray him. Then he says,

> In a worme likness wille y wende,
> And founde to feyne a lowde lesynge.
> Eue, Eue!

To which Eve replies, "Wha es þare?"

> *Satanas:*　"I, a frende.
> And for thy gude es þe comynge,
> I hydir sought."

When Eve asks who he is that counsels her to eat of the forbidden tree, he replies, "A worme þat wotith wele how þat yhe may wirshipped be."

When Eve is at last convinced, the *direction* reads, *Et tunc debet accipere pomum.* Satan bids her bite on boldly, and goes out: *Tunc Satanas recedet.* Eve describes him both to Adam and to God, as "a worme." God in cursing him says,—

> "A! wikkid worme, woo worthe þe ay
>
> .　　.　　.　　.　　.
>
> And on thy wombe þan shall þou glyde."

But apparently the York serpent was not proficient in gliding off on his belly, and, having already receded, does not illustrate the biblical curse.

It is to be noted that Satan first says he *will go* in a *worm's likeness* to betray man, and forthwith begins to call "Eve! Eve!" He apparently comes forward to meet her when she asks "Who is there?" and proffers the apple, for the *direction* says she *receives*[2] it. When she has done so, and he sees she is

---

[1] Lucy Toulmin Smith, *York Mystery Plays,* Oxford, 1885.
[2] *accipere,* not *capere.*

3

beginning to eat, he goes out. This is evidently a walking and speaking serpent after the manner of the Chester play. I am satisfied, in the light of the *directions* of the other plays, that this serpent is of the lizard-with-a-lady's-face type.

12. Lucerne, play of 1583.[1]

In this play the serpent tempter appears, *Alls ein vierfüssiger gifftiger Wurm angethan vnd gerüst, mit wybischem Angsicht vnd Stimm, ein Huben vnd Cron vff dem Houpt.*

This is the serpent, of which I have already spoken, that lies concealed until its cue comes to appear, but nevertheless crawls off to Hell after it is cursed; it is significant that it lies concealed in the Mount of Olives,[2] where Christ suffered agony and bloody sweat: *Sy zücht nit yn vff den Platz, sonder verbirgt sich frü jn den Oelberg bis es an sy kompt zereden vnd so sy den Fluch emphangen, krücht sy vff allen Vieren wider durch die Hell hinweg.*

13. Lucerne, play of 1597.[3]

In this play, as in the Lucerne play of 1583, the serpent lies concealed until his cue to appear: *Zücht ouch nit vff sonder verbirgt sich morgens frü jn Oelberg bis es Zyt jst, macht sy sich vff den Boum.*

Seventeenth Century

14. Cornwall,[4] play of 1611, by William Jordan of Wendron.

In this play of the Creation of the world, which probably preserves an old tradition, Lucifer is transformed into,—*A fyne serpent made wth a virgyn face & yolowe heare upon her head.*[5]

IV

How Far the Artists Were Influenced by the Plays

It would be a mistake to suppose that the artists who represented the serpent with a human head were slavishly imitating the figure as presented in the plays, or that one could take any of the pictures and say of it that it showed exactly how the play

---

[1] R. Brandstetter, *op. cit.*, p. 325.

[2] Adam in this same play lies concealed until his creation in the same spot which is later to be the sepulchre of Christ. This served not only convenience but symbolism.

[3] Brandstetter, *op. cit.*, p. 342.

[4] Edited by Davies Gilbert, with Keigwyn's translation.

[5] O. Waterhouse, *op. cit.*, p. xxxiii; E. K. Chambers, *op. cit.* II, p. 142.

was given. Even those pictures which come nearest to doing so are also somewhat controlled by the older tradition of the artists. The nude figures of Adam and Eve are more lifelike than the leather suits or fleshings worn by the actors could have appeared; the fatal tree, the landscape, often with wild animals, are of a size and elaboration in detail quite beyond the reach of the stage; and the serpent, human head and all, often too diminutive possibly to represent an actor. We shall have to be content to say that the artist in depicting the old familiar scene had altered it solely with regard to what he doubtless considered a matter of fact. He was not trying to show how the plays were given, but to make a devotional picture, and merely relied a little too much on the authority of the writers of the plays.

The temptation scene from the Grabower altar of *Master Bertram* (Fig. 3) is an excellent example of the extent and nature of the play's influence upon the artist. I am convinced that in this case the influence is immediate, because a good many points of contact between plays and art are observable in the cycle of paintings on the Grabower altar. In the temptation scene the serpent is twined about the tree in the middle of the composition, Adam standing on the left reaching for an apple, Eve on the right' eating an apple and pointing toward the tree. Except for the human head on the serpent, the whole is almost exactly the arrangement of the ancient tradition in art. The serpent and the human head are obviously too small to represent an actor. The artist has taken the supposed fact of the human head, but has reduced the scale to something like the true dimensions of a serpent. Some secondary influences of the play are perhaps to be found in the stiff trees, the conventional star-sown sky of the background, the bit of architectural detail in the lower right-hand corner (which we know from other pictures in this cycle represents the wall of the Garden of Eden), and the unlifelike-ness of the nude figures. Of the last point too much should not be made, for the church until a much later date did not countenance the picturing of complete nakedness.

The serpent in *Hugo van der Goes'* painting (Fig. 5) seems to have been painted from a model posed in the very costume of the play—as a four-footed poisonous serpent with a virgin's face. It is a child, most likely a boy, who essays the rôle. Choir-boys from time immemorial had sung the *Gloria in excelsis*, and since the first brief plays of the Nativity, had represented the angelic choir, singing from the rood-loft or some other elevated place. Now the serpent, being Lucifer himself or one of the defecting angels, comes to tempt Eve with his fair face and small persuasive voice. His adder's coat (with hosen and tail stained, *i.e.* painted) gives him the general appearance of a lizard. His demonic nature is further attested by his little horn-like pigtails. Certainly no artist is under the necessity of suggesting horns in this manner.[1] Goat's horns, characteristic of devils and satyrs, could just as easily have been painted; any sort of small corneous processes peeping through the golden locks would be more suggestive. But anyone who has had the mortifying experience of dropping half a moustache in a theatrical performance will realize the great superiority of horns such as this little devil wears, over any artificial goat's horn attached with fish glue. The pigtail horns are for me the strongest assurances that this serpent is painted directly from an actual performer in a mystery play of Adam. Adam and Eve in the same picture are, on the other hand, evidently painted from nude models and not from performers as they appeared in the play.

I am convinced that the human-headed serpent of Christian art was derived, not from myth or tradition,[2] but from a conven-

---

[1] The woodcuts of the *Nuremberg Chronicle* show Moses with horns that are apparently locks of hair, but not braided. This, in 1493, about the same time as van der Goes' painting, seems to me to point to a probable influence of a Moses play. The fifteenth century *Biblia Pauperum* shows Moses (Transfiguration scene) in the same manner.

[2] As to Lilith, Lamia, and other female monsters, I have not been able to find any evidence that they were thought of, or represented, in the middle ages, as being half serpent and half woman. Rossetti emphasizes the baneful nature of Lilith, the demon wife of Adam, by making her a partner with the serpent in seeking the Fall of Adam. But Lilith is not, either in Rossetti or in the Hebrew tradition so far as I am able to ascertain a serpent woman. She is a female spirit of the night, sometimes taking the form of a cat, and sometimes that of an owl. The passage in Isaiah (xxiv, 14) which in the King James version reads, "the screech owl also shall rest there, and find for herself a place of rest" has this comment on *screech owl,*—"or, *night monster.*" In the Hebrew, the word is *Lilith;* in the Vulgate, it is *Lamia.* Wyclif follows the Vulgate, and the marginal comment in the Wyclif Bible is, "lyk a womman above, and hath horse feet bynethe and sleeth hir owne whelpis."

J. Lempriere, in the article *Lamiae* in his *Bibliotheca Classica* (New York, 1833) describes the creatures thus: "Certain monsters of Africa, who had the face and breast of a woman, and the rest of the body like that of a serpent. They allured strangers to come to them; and though they were not endowed with the faculty of speech, yet their hissings were pleasing and agreeable."

tion of the mystery play stage, a convention much more common and widespread than has heretofore been recognised: indeed, it seems to me, with the exception of the Anglo-Norman *Adam* play, almost universal.

JOHN K. BONNELL.

UNITED STATES NAVAL ACADEMY,
  ANNAPOLIS, MD.

And he gives the following citations: *"Philostr. in Ap.—Horat. Art. Poet.* v. 340—*Plut. de Curios.—Dion."*

But in all these references the only thing suggesting the serpent is Apollonius' warning to Menippus: "σὺ μέντοι" εἶπεν "ὁ καλός τε καὶ ὑπὸ τῶν καλῶν γυναικῶν θηρευόμενος ὄφιν θάλπεις καὶ σὲ ὄφις." (IV, 25).

But to say, "You cherish a serpent and a serpent cherishes you," is not by any means to imply that the physical form of the beautiful witch Lamia is half serpent. Her loveliness, on the contrary, is implied throughout the story. See also *Diodorus Siculus,* Lib. xx: and Blaydes' note on Aristophanes' *Frogs,* v. 293. Compare also Roscher, *Lexikon der griech. u. röm. Mythologie,* s. v. Lamia, Vol. II, cols. 1819 ff.

The classical Siren may have had some influence on our human headed monster—the wings, the virginial face, the persuasive voice, are certainly closely parallel.

Witchcraft and Domestic Tragedy in
The Witch of Edmonton

Viviana Comensoli

THE *WITCH OF EDMONTON* (1621) DRAMATIZES the historical execution of Elizabeth Sawyer for witchcraft on April 19, 1621. The play's immediate source is *The Wonderfull Discouerie of Elizabeth Savvyer a witch,* a pamphlet written by Henry Goodcole, chaplain of Newgate prison, and entered in the Stationers' Register on April 27 of the same year. The pamphlet records Goodcole's "interviews" with Elizabeth Sawyer shortly before her execution. Goodcole's question-and-answer scheme is essentially a tract against the dangers traditionally associated with witchcraft. Elizabeth's answers form a conventional catalogue of descriptions about the causes and effects of demonology, revealing little about the personality of the woman or the social roots of witchcraft. In the account of Elizabeth's covenant with the Devil, for example, Elizabeth's replies, like Goodcole's questions, are mechanical and predictable, their sole function being to underscore her guilt:

> *Question.* What sayd you to the Diuell, when hee came vnto you and spake vnto you, were you not afraide of him? if you did feare him, what sayd the Diuell then vnto you? *Answere.* I was in a very greate feare, when I saw the Diuell, but hee did bid me not to feare him at all, for hee would do me no hurt at all, but would do for mee whatsoeuer I should require of him . . . .[1]

Dekker, Ford, and Rowley, on the other hand, initially portray Mother Sawyer as knowing nothing about witchcraft. Unlike Goodcole's compliant prisoner, she forcefully insists on her innocence. In addition, she is endowed with a powerful eloquence that deflects the accusations of her enemies. During her first appearance on stage, Mother Sawyer's soliloquy reveals a bold and agile mind:

> And why on me? why should the envious world
> Throw all their scandalous malice upon me?
> 'Cause I am poor, deform'd and ignorant,
> And like a Bow buckl'd and bent together,
> By some more strong in mischiefs then my self?
> Must I for that be made a common sink,

---

[1]*The Wonderful Discouerie of Elizabeth Savvyer a witch,* C1v-C2; quoted in Cyrus Hoy, *Introductions, Notes, and Commentaries to Texts in "The Dramatic Works of Thomas Dekker"* Edited by Fredson Bowers, 4 vols. (Cambridge: Cambridge University Press, 1980), 3: 248-49.

151

For all the filth and rubbish of Men's tongues
To fall and run into?

(II.i.1-8)[2]

In breaking with theatrical decorum by having a poor, uneducated female describe with considerable rhetorical acumen her status as a social outcast, the dramatists elevate and dignify the character, enhancing the audience's sympathy for her.

Unlike the other domestic "witch plays" of the period,[3] namely the anonymous *Merry Devil of Edmonton* (c. 1599-1604), *The Wise Woman of Hogsdon* (c. 1604), and Heywood and Brome's *The Late Lancashire Witches* (c. 1612-1634), in which the magical roots of witchcraft are treated as unproblematic, *The Witch of Edmonton*, with its undertone of pain and bewilderment, makes a bold statement about demonology: Mother Sawyer is not an agent of supernatural powers but a victim of an entrenched social code that relegates old and poverty-ridden spinsters to the Devil's company. A handful of commentators have noted the non-magical treatment of witchcraft in the play,[4] although its scrutiny of the social dynamics of the witch phenomenon has been more fully appreciated by those who have

[2]*The Witch of Edmonton*, in *The Dramatic Works of Thomas Dekker*, ed. Fredson Bowers, 4 vols. (Cambridge: Cambridge University Press, 1953-1961): 3. Subsequent references to the play will be to this edition.

[3]The play has been classified as a domestic or homiletic drama because it includes four major components of the genre: it treats a topical event; it concerns the tragedy of common people; like many domestic plays, it deals with the subject of witchcraft, combining popular beliefs in sorcery and its influence on family affairs; and it incorporates (at least ostensibly) what Henry Adams, *English Domestic or, Homiletic Tragedy 1575-1642* (New York: Columbia University Press, 1943), 141, has defined as the genre's major scheme, that is, a pattern of "sin, discovery, repentance, punishment." For Adams "the most noteworthy characteristic of *The Witch of Edmonton* is its careful adherence to the customary practices of homiletic drama." A qualified view is offered by Andrew Clark, in *Domestic Drama: A Survey of the Origins, Antecedents and Nature of the Domestic Play in England, 1500-1640*, 2 vols. (Salzburg: Universität Salzburg, 1975), 1: 209, 210, who also notes the play's homiletic structures but claims that "it would be inaccurate to suggest that [it] is a dramatized homily," in that it "achieves tragic power in its sympathetic insight into human weaknesses and the sufferings of the characters, its sense of irony and the moving pathos of the later scenes."

[4]Katherine M. Briggs, *Pale Hecate's Team: An Examination of the Beliefs on Witchcraft and Magic among Shakespeare's Contemporaries and his Immediate Successors* (London: Routledge & Kegan Paul, 1962), 99, although claiming that "there is little doubt that the witchcraft of which . . . [the play] treats was believed by its authors," proposes that Elizabeth's "complaints are too well imagined to have been written without some sympathy." Etta Soiref Onat, "Introduction," *The Witch of Edmonton: A Critical Edition* (New York and London: Garland, 1980), 72, 73, for whom Mother Sawyer's "pact and the *maleficia* which confirm it" imply that she "is responsible to Heaven," notes that from the outset of the play until Mother Sawyer "goes to the scaffold, surrounded by her malicious and credulous neighbors," the dramatists intend "to place on cruelty and superstition the chief guilt in the process of witch-making." Larry Champion, *Thomas Dekker and the Traditions of English Drama* (New York: Peter Lang, 1985), 119, suggests that Mother Sawyer "exercises free will in choosing evil," but that she is "victimized by external pressures that render her ability to withstand temptation all the more difficult." Similarly, Michael Hattaway, "Women and Witchcraft:

staged the play. "It is Dekker's eternal credit," wrote Edward Sackville-West of the Old Vic Theatre's 1936 production, "that he should have realized . . . the underlying [social] causes of witchdom."[5] More recently, the Royal Shakespeare Company performed the play as "subversively . . . show[ing] [Mother Sawyer] as a wretched old woman shunned by the community who force the role of witch on her before she has done anything more than steal firewood."[6] Mother Sawyer's personal tragedy arises from an inextricable link between her persecution and her internalization of the community's brutality: "Some call me Witch," she declares, "And being ignorant of my self, they go / About to teach me how to be one" (II.i.8-10). Feeling "shunn'd / And hated like a sickness: made a scorn / To all degrees and sexes" (II.i.96-97), she resolves to take revenge against an abusive world since "'Tis all one, / To be a Witch, as to be counted one" (lines 113-14). When Mother Sawyer finally summons the "Familiar" or "devil" her desire for revenge is a coherent response to the violence she can no longer endure.

The subversive structures of the Mother Sawyer plot locate the roots of witchcraft in the external conditions of class, misogyny, and poverty.[7] These structures, moreover, inform the ways in which the play as a whole

---

The Case of *The Witch of Edmonton*," *Trivium* 20 (May, 1985): 55, argues that unlike *The Masque of Queens*, in which Jonson "accepts the nature of witches as given" (51), *The Witch of Edmonton* makes the devil "responsible for the acts of will that lead to sin, for turning intent into effect," thereby "arous[ing] compassion for his victims." Jonathan Dollimore, *Radical Tragedy: Religion, Ideology and Power in the Drama of Shakespeare and his Contemporaries* (Chicago: University of Chicago Press, 1984), 176, commenting on Mother Sawyer's madness, writes that the play is "remarkable for the way it depicts how habit, socially coerced, becomes another – or rather 'anti' – nature."

[5]Edward Sackville-West, "The Significance of *The Witch of Edmonton*," *The Criterion* 17 (1937): 24.

[6]Irving Wardle, "*The Witch of Edmonton*: Other Place," *The Times*, 17 September 1981, 9.

[7]In this context, *The Witch of Edmonton* corroborates recent historical and sociological accounts of the witch phenomenon of the sixteenth and seventeenth centuries. Keith Thomas, for one, in *Religion and the Decline of Magic* (New York: Scribner's, 1971), 520, writes that "the judicial records reveal two essential facts about accused witches: they were poor, and they were usually women." In her analysis of the witch craze in Scotland, Christina Larner, *Enemies of God: The Witch-hunt in Scotland* (Baltimore: The Johns Hopkins University, 1981), 91, notes that "Suspects were . . . from the settled rather than the vagabond or outcast poor," and, as in the rest of Europe, "they were predominantly women." Yet the "stereotype" of the woman as witch, notes Larner, was prevalent "long before there was a witch-hunt. The stereotype rests on the twin pillars of the Aristotelian view of women as imperfectly human . . . and the Judaeo-Christian view of women as the source of sin and the Fall of Man" (92). For further discussions of the link between witchcraft and misogyny see Joseph Klaits, *Servants of Satan: The Age of the Witch Hunts* (Bloomington: Indiana University Press, 1985), ch. 3; Ben Barker-Benfield, "Anne Hutchinson and the Puritan Attitude Toward Women," *Feminist Studies* 1 (1972): 65-96; and E. William Monter, "The Pedestal and the Stake: Courtly Love and Witchcraft," in *Becoming Visible: Women in European History*, ed. Renate Bridenthal and Claudia Koonz (Boston: Houghton Mifflin, 1977), 119-36.

displaces conventional schemes of domestic or homiletic tragedy. While the Mother Sawyer plot debunks popular notions of witchcraft, the marriage plot involving Frank Thorney and his wife, Susan, identifies the witch phenomenon as part of the broader cultural need to punish those who transgress social boundaries. The two plots are loosely integrated by the influence of the supernatural on the protagonists. The marriage plot combines domestic tragedy with the supposed effects of black magic. Although already secretly married, Frank Thorney yields to familial and social demands and marries Susan, the daughter of a rich yeoman. Frank consoles himself with the thought that a wise woman, "Known and approv'd in Palmestry," (II.ii.116) has foretold he would have two wives. But as the result of a sudden demonic impulse, attributed by society to the evil influences of the "Witch" Sawyer (V.iii.21-27), Frank ruthlessly kills Susan. The link between the two plots through Mother Sawyer and her supposed witchcraft has been consistently viewed as a melodramatic device which undermines the tragic potential of the events dramatized. George Rao, for one, writes that "the popular belief in witchcraft is made one of the chief reasons for the domestic crime," Mother Sawyer being "the source of mischief."[8] A close analysis of the action, however, reveals considerable complexity in the portrayal of the connection between witchcraft and domestic crime. The popular explanation for Susan's demise, namely Frank's bewitchment, is undermined by a number of complications, foremost of which is Frank's admission that he is defeated primarily from within. Moreover, we shall see that Susan, the paragon of wifely patience and humility, dies, like Mother Sawyer, at the moment when she is most assertive. The link between witchcraft and assertive women was frequently drawn by Protestant commentators. As Allison Coudert observes, witches were frequently "women who rebelled," and in Puritan circles in particular "rebellion was routinely equated with witchcraft and rebellious wives with witches."[9] That Mother Sawyer and Susan meet similar ends underscores the general fear of female behavior that threatened patriarchal authority.

In locating the witch craze within this larger framework, the play's treatment of witchcraft claims a unique position in English Renaissance drama. In addition, the dramatists go well beyond not only the play's analogues but also the pious indictments of both continental and English skeptics. The play's rational perspective had been current in a number of

---

[8]George Rao, *The Domestic Drama* (Tirupati: Sri Venkateswara University Press, 1978), 187. George Herndl, *The High Design: English Renaissance Tragedy and the Natural Law* (Lexington: University Press of Kentucky, 1970), 272, complains that in the Frank Thorney plot "the action is so presented that the motive of the 'sin' is hardly felt to lie within the will of the sinner, which is paralyzed by the power of evil," while in the Mother Sawyer plot "tragic emotions dwindle into sentimentality."

[9]Allison Coudert, "The Myth of the Improved Status of Protestant Women: The Case of the Witchcraze," in this volume.

discourses on demonology since the latter half of the sixteenth century. This perspective was most forcefully articulated by the physician Johann Wier, whose *De praestigiis daemonum* (1563) was published at the time when witch prosecutions in Germany were entering their most intense phase. While not rejecting the reality of witchcraft, Wier claimed that the confessions for which women were being executed were illusions incited either by devils or by melancholia. Wier's misogynist bias, however, is evident in his proposal that women are easier prey than men to the sleights of demons because women are inherently prone to delusion.[10] Since the Middle Ages, the notion of women's credulity had been current in European writings about women as the "weaker" sex. In witchcraft treatises it appears as early as the *Malleus Maleficarum* (1487), the first printed encyclopedia of demonology, whose authors Heinrich Kramer and Jacob Sprenger described women as "more credulous" than men, "naturally more impressionable, and more ready to receive the influence of a disembodied spirit."[11] Critiques similar to Wier's were later put forth by Neoplatonists, Hermeticists, Paracelsians, and even a few Aristotelian commentators, all of whom claimed that sorcery was founded upon illusion and was therefore harmless.[12] In England, Wier's arguments were refined in 1584 by Reginald Scot, who cast doubt on the prevalent belief in *maleficium* by offering non-magical theories of its causes. Dekker, Ford, and Rowley's sympathetic portrayal of Mother Sawyer suggests their possible debt to Scot's *The Discovery of Witchcraft*, an influential treatise which provoked James I in 1597 to write his *Daemonologie*, a tract against witchcraft, denouncing as well those who professed a disbelief in witches.[13] Scot claimed that witchcraft was essentially a myth created

---

[10]*De praestigiis daemonum*, in *Histoires Disputes et Discours des Illusions et Impostures des Diables*, ed. J. Bourneville (Paris, 1885), 1: 300. The debate on demonology is well documented in D.P. Walker, *Spiritual and Demonic Magic from Ficino to Campanella* (London, 1958); H.R. Trevor-Roper, *The European Witch-Craze of the Sixteenth and Seventeenth Centuries* (New York and Evanston: Harper, 1967); and Sydney Anglo, "Melancholia and Witchcraft: The Debate Between Wier, Bodin, and Scot," in *Folie et déraison à la Renaissance* (Brussels: University of Brussels, 1976), 209-28. A useful survey of the play's intellectual background is found in Etta Soiref Onat, "Introduction," *The Witch of Edmonton*, 1-23.

[11]Henricus Kramer and Jacobus Sprenger, *Malleus Maleficarum*, trans. Montague Summers (London: Pushkin Press, 1928), 43-44.

[12]Trevor-Roper, *The European Witch-Craze*, 132-34. Thomas, in *Religion and the Decline of Magic*, 579, claims that it was easier for Neoplatonists "to advance a 'natural' explanation for the witches' *maleficium* than it was for those who had been educated in the tradition of scholastic Aristotelianism" which frequently supported diabolical explanations.

[13]Stuart Clark, "King James's *Daemonologie*: Witchcraft and Kingship," in *The Damned Art: Essays in the Literature of Witchcraft*, ed. Sydney Anglo (London, Henley, and Boston: Routledge & Kegan Paul, 1977), 164-65, notes that before coming to England, James I dealt cautiously and even skeptically with accusations of witchcraft; however, he later "became a witch-hunter and demonologist" apparently "to satisfy political and religious pretensions at a time when they could be expressed in few other ways." He "found in the theory and practice of witch persecution a perfect vehicle for his nascent ideals of kingship," among which was the duty of the king to be "the people's teacher and patriarch." Elsewhere, "Inversion, Misrule

by the faithless: "The fables of Witchcraft have taken so . . . deepe root in the heart of man, that fewe or none can (nowadaies) with patience indure the hand and correction of God. For if any adversitie, greefe, sicknesse, loss of children, corne, cattell, or libertie happen unto them . . . they exclaime uppon witches."[14] For Scot, the persecutions of those believed to be witches conflicted with the Protestant idea of Providence whereby neither good nor evil could occur without God's will: "certeine old women heere on earth, called witches, must needs be the contrivers of all mens calamities, and as though they themselves were innocents, and had deserved no such punishments."[15] Scot considered Wier's assertion that melancholia induced women to confess to impossible acts as only one naturalistic cause among others. Many aged women, he pointed out, were physically ill and in urgent need of medical and financial assistance, their vulnerability making them easy targets. *The Witch of Edmonton* echoes Scot's critique of witch persecutions as a denial of divine providence. The play also upholds the skepticism of George Gifford, who in 1593 wrote that legal convictions were founded on doubtful evidence and conjecture, and that the more gruesome the punishments the more people were wont "to thirst even in rage after innocent blood."[16]

By 1621 skepticism had gained widespread acceptance, as is evident from the growing number of accusations both of imposture on the part of those claiming demonic possession and of judicial fraud.[17] However, the link which Dekker, Ford, and Rowley draw between witchcraft, domestic crime and the threat to the established order represents a radical point of departure from the skeptical tradition. Whereas Reginald Scot had dismissed witchcraft primarily on theological grounds, *The Witch of Edmonton* forces the audience to confront the destructive effects of marginality and patriarchal claims on the individual.

---

and the Meaning of Witchcraft," *Past and Present* 87 (May, 1980): 117, Clark suggests that James's "attempt in 1590-91 to write into the confessions of the North Berwick witches a special antipathy between demonic magic and godly magistry had been a way of authenticating his own, as yet rather tentative initiatives as ruler of Scotland."

[14]Reginald Scot, "The Fables of Witchcraft," in *The Witchcraft Papers: Contemporary Records of the Witchcraft Hysteria in Essex 1560-1700*, ed. Peter Haining (Secaucus, N.J.: University Books, 1974), 67. Four years prior to the publication of Scot's treatise, Bishop Thomas Cooper, *Certaine Sermons* (1580), 176, had warned that "Whensoever misery or a plague happeneth to a man, it cometh not by chance or fortune, or by a course of nature, as vain worldly men imagine, but by the assured providence of God."

[15]Scot, "Fables of Witchcraft," 67.

[16]*A Dialogue concerning Witches and Witchcraft* (1593); quoted in Katherine M. Briggs, *Pale Hecate's Team*, 34.

[17]Wallace Notestein, *A History of Witchcraft in England from 1558 to 1718* (1909; rpt. New York: Crowell, 1968), 143.

A number of modern historians have pointed out that the witch beliefs of early modern Europe were generated not by aged women practicing sorcery in different villages (they had more or less always been tolerated) but by inassimilable women – old or diseased spinsters, widows, prostitutes, obstreperous wives, healers, and midwives.[18] As *The Witch of Edmonton* makes clear, the marginality and rebelliousness of such women posed a problem for those intent on preserving the patriarchal structure of the family and society. In addition, because these women were essentially powerless they easily became scapegoats. From the outset the play discredits supernatural causation. Long before Mother Sawyer's pact with the "Familiar" or "devil," she is accused of "Forespeak[ing]" her community's cattle and of "bewitch[ing] their Corn" and "their Babes at nurse" (II.i.12-13). Demonology is thus used to explain away both the community's economic hardship and behavior which poses a disturbing challenge to moral and cultural codes. It is essentially through desperation that Mother Sawyer conforms to society's expectations to the point where she becomes consumed by "madness" (IV.i.152). Her madness attests to what E. William Monter claims witchcraft itself had become, that is, "a *magical* form of violent revenge, practiced by exactly those persons who could not employ physical violence."[19] Marginalized women suited this description especially well: "They had many grievances; they wanted revenge; yet recourse to the law often was beyond their economic power, and successful physical violence was beyond their physical power."[20] They gained revenge by arousing their accusers' fear of magic.

Just as medieval and Renaissance demonologists depicted witches "as usually poor, old, solitary, and female,"[21] the social stigma which branded Mother Sawyer as an outcast are her age, her gender, her physical deformity, and her poverty. Mother Sawyer's demise epitomizes what awaits those in her world who "feel / The misery and beggary of want; / Two Devils that are occasions to enforce / a shameful end" (I.i.17-20). Her strategy of survival shares with certain revenge plays of the sixteenth and seventeenth

[18]Midwives, notes Mary Nelson, "Why Witches Were Women," *Women: A Feminist Perspective*, ed. Jo Freeman (Palo Alto, California: Mayfield, 1975), 346, 347, were "expert in methods of birth control, and most likely cooperated in abortions and infanticides" with families who were either too poor to sustain many children, or who "did not wish to jeopardize their new prosperity." Allison Coudert, "Witchcraft Studies to Date," unpublished MS, 21, suggests that the "early association of the term *maleficium* with abortofacients and sterilizing potions, together with the almost universal assumption that the users of such potions would be women, helped to feminize the crime of witchcraft and to associate it with the women healers and midwives."

[19]Monter, "Pedestal and Stake," 134.

[20]Ibid. Cf. Thomas, *Religion and Decline of Magic*, 522, "Although the witch might expect to gain some material benefits from her diabolical compact, these were subordinate to her main desire, to avenge herself upon her neighbors. Such a desire was to be found at all levels in society, but it was usually only the poor and helpless who hoped to attain it by witchcraft, because for them the normal channels of legal action or physical force were not available."

[21]Ibid., 21.

centuries a definition of revenge as a response to social dislocation. In his study of the radical Elizabethan and Jacobean revenge play, Jonathan Dollimore notes that the protagonists, once alienated from society, become "bereaved, dispossessed, and in peril of their lives, . . . suffer[ing] extreme disorientation" as they "are pushed to the very edge of mental collapse."[22] The dark side of seventeenth-century England is represented by the villagers of Edmonton, including prominent citizens, all of whom exploit Mother Sawyer's deprivation. The dramatists' portrayal of the overlap between the upper and lower classes' attitude toward witchcraft foregrounds the historical paradox that "in the witch trials, members of the elites and ordinary folk found a common cause."[23]

The accusations against Mother Sawyer are initiated by her landlord, Old Banks, who calls her "Witch" (II.i.17) and "Hag" (line 17) and beats her when she refuses to return the "few rotten sticks" (line 21) she has gathered from his property. (The incident is not recorded in Goodcole.) It is significant that the spectator first sees Mother Sawyer collecting bits of firewood from her landlord's property. In England, witchcraft trials coincided with the enclosure laws, which "broke up many of the old co-operative village communities,"[24] increasing the numbers of poor people, many of them widowed and elderly, and depriving them of any means of subsistence. The enclosure movement further coincided with "the bureaucratization of poor relief under the Elizabethan Poor Laws" which "divested the individual of responsibility for charity."[25] Although the clergy insisted on the ethical imperative of Christian charity, many townships now strictly prohibited alms-giving.[26] The poor and elderly women indicted for witchcraft were usually those whose names were listed as having been dependent upon the old custom of parochial charity.[27]

The play stresses the absence of neighborly support. Mother Sawyer is repeatedly rebuked as a burden to Edmonton and a threat to the community's well-being. That she first invokes the Familiar during the beating by her landlord – "What spells, what charms, or invocations, / May the thing call'd Familiar be purchased?" (II.i.35-36) – challenges the conventional notion requiring the witch's private pact with the devil to stem from arcane practices. Instead the pact is rooted, as it was for many of those accused

[22]Dollimore, *Radical Tragedy*, 40.

[23]Klaits, *Servants of Satan*, 51.

[24]Thomas, *Religion and Decline of Magic*, 552.

[25]Larner, *Enemies of God*, 61.

[26]Thomas, *Religion and Decline of Magic*, 563.

[27]J.F. Pound, "An Elizabethan Census of the Poor," *University of Birmingham Historical Journal* VIII (1961-62): 138, 141.

of witchcraft, in the need for security and self-esteem.[28] The Familiar's shape immediately underscores the play's concern with madness as a response to dispossession. Once Mother Sawyer resolves to "Abjure all goodness" (II.i.107) the Familiar manifests itself as a black dog, directly corresponding to her mental image of Banks as a "black Cur" (line 111). The Familiar promises to take "just revenge" against Mother Sawyer's enemies (line 124). He also does to her precisely what she has accused Banks of doing, that is, "suck" her "very blood" (line 112) but with a startling result: the Familiar's drawing of her blood is a gratifying experience. The creature's appearance in the likeness of Mother Sawyer's image of Banks demystifies the supernatural, maintaining the spectator's interest in Mother Sawyer as an isolated human being desiring her community's approval. As a mental image of Banks, the Familiar is clearly a wish-fulfillment of material comfort and social status. The dog is also a projection of a profound desire for one who loves her and who soothes her suffering and anger:

> *Sawy.* My dear *Tom*-boy welcome.
> I am torn in pieces by a pack of Curs
> Clap'd all upon me, and for want of thee:
> Comfort me: thou shalt have the Teat anon.
>   (IV.i.148-51)

The emotive component of Mother Sawyer's relationship with the Familiar substantiates the role of the dog as a demon lover emphasized in the 1962 production of the play (by the Mermaid Theatre in London), in which Mother Sawyer was depicted as "a pitiable old woman who turns to the Devil because no one else will have her, and whose contract is undisguisedly a love relationship."[29] The pathos surrounding the fantasy, however, challenges the myth of the sexually potent and threatening witch figure encountered in Renaissance treatises on witchcraft. Since the Middle Ages, women had been considered naturally disposed toward lust, which made them easy prey for the devil. In the *Malleus Maleficarum* we read, "All witchcraft comes from carnal lust, which is in women insatiable . . . Wherefore for the sake of fulfilling their lusts they consort even with devils."[30] While in medieval demonology lust was only one among many causes leading women to worship demons, in the sixteenth and

---

[28]"Seventeenth-century English women at the margins of society," writes Larner, *Enemies of God*, 95, "did not expect that their soul would qualify them for silk and riches. Instead they said that the Devil promised them mere freedom from the extremes of poverty and starvation." Thomas, *Religion and Decline of Magic*, 520, writes: "The Devil promised that they should never want; he offered meat, clothes and money, and was ready to pay their debts."

[29]"Fascinating Rag-Bag of Dramatic Idioms," *The Times*, Thursday 22 November 1962, 15.

[30]Summers, ed., *Malleus Maleficarum*, 47.

seventeenth centuries "sexual overtones became the leading theme of demonological imagery," as witch hunters emphasized the sabbat as the expression
of perverse sexual practices.[31] However, the witches' sabbat, wherein the
devils' worshippers "blasphem[ed] against God, copulat[ed] with their master,
and indulg[ed] in orgies of sexual promiscuity,"[32] is never mentioned in
the play. Rather than exploit a popular motif for its sensational appeal, the
playwrights depict the relationship between Mother Sawyer and the Familiar
in terms of its psychological interest: in reality Mother Sawyer's physical
needs are thwarted by her age, deformity, and poverty; in the sexual fantasy,
however, she exerts a form of power over the source of her degradation.
The fantasy, moreover, corroborates historical evidence indicating in both
Scotland and England that "the fear of witchcraft bestowed power on the
powerless,"[33] relieving their feelings of "impotence and desperation."[34]

The scenes which follow stress Mother Sawyer's persecution rather
than her sorcery. After summoning the dog, she orders him to carry out
a series of vengeful tricks which provoke the villagers to burn her thatch,
a common ritual designed to prove witchcraft. According to Goodcole, the
thatch "being so burned, the author of . . . mischiefe should presently
then come."[35] Even Goodcole recognizes that the custom is irrational,
although he does not go as far as to disparage it. On the one hand, he
describes it as "old" and "ridiculous," and the community's suspicions as
"great presumptions"; on the other hand, he writes that the court learned
the custom worked because Elizabeth came "without any sending for." In
the pamphlet the thatch is burned after the sudden death of infants and
cattle. In the play Mother Sawyer's power to influence nature and human
behavior is portrayed in such a way as to undermine conventional ideas
about witchcraft through parody and farce. The first set of reasons given
for the thatch-burning climaxes in a theatrical *reductio ad absurdum*: 1) a
villager has caught his wife and a servant with stolen corn, a theft readily
attributed by the wife to her bewitchment by Mother Sawyer (IV.i.5-9);
2) Old Banks' horse has contracted a fatal disease, which Banks blames on
"this Jadish Witch, Mother *Sawyer*" (line 4); 3) Banks has been plagued
by an uncontrollable urge to raise his cow's tail and kiss its behind, a habit
which has made the community of Edmonton "ready to be-piss themselves
with laughirg" him "to scorn" (lines 57-58). The broad comedy elicited
by the ric' .andowner's predicament exposes not only the folly of the
villag   lictiveness against Mother Sawyer, but also the social tensions
at the heart of the community between elite and popular culture. At the

[31]Klaits, *Servants of Satan*, 53.

[32]Ibid., 2.

[33]Larner, *Enemies of God*, 95.

[34]Thomas, *Religion and Decline of Magic*, 520.

[35]Goodcole, A4-A4v; quoted in Hoy, *Introduction, Notes, and Commentaries*, 3: 258.

same time, the epithets hurled at Mother Sawyer, in particular "Hag" (II.i.27) and "hot Whore" (IV.i.24), together with the villagers' frenzied ritual in carrying out the thatch-burning amid the chant "Burn the Witch, the Witch, the Witch, the Witch" (IV.i.15) and the chilling refrain "Hang her, beat her, kill her" (line 29), sustain the focus on the social causes of her dislocation.

A more serious charge concerns Mother Sawyer's apparent hand in the madness and death of Old Ratcliff's wife, Anne. The Anne Ratcliff episode takes place moments after the villagers have burned Mother Sawyer's thatch. Exasperated and "dri'd up / With cursing and with madness" (IV.i.152-53), Mother Sawyer reminds the Familiar about Anne Ratcliff, "Who for a little soap lick'd by . . . [Mother Sawyer's] Sow, / Struck, and almost had lam'd it" (lines 169-70). This incident further explores a classic precondition of sixteenth- and seventeenth-century witch trials, namely village quarrels, usually involving household disputes, which would give rise to accusations of witchcraft. In England the targets of these accusations were frequently elderly women who sought charity.[36] Having been refused charity by Anne Ratcliff, Mother Sawyer wonders whether the Familiar has "pinch[ed] that Quean to th' heart" (line 171). Her comment is followed by the stage direction, *Enter Anne Ratcliff mad.* A number of critics have commented on the ambiguity surrounding Anne's madness, although the episode has not been explored in detail. David Atkinson observes that "the play does not make it entirely clear whether or not the witch really is responsible for the death of Anne Ratcliff," and suggests that "the episode was probably imperfectly assimilated from the source."[37] Etta Soiref Onat, on the other hand, points out that Mother Sawyer's Familiar rubs Anne Ratcliff after she has gone mad, and proposes that "her suicide might very well have been caused by nothing more than a coincidental madness, not the result of demonic possession at all."[38] Michael Hattaway also offers an insightful, although cursory, reading: "the text makes it legitimate to conjecture that [Anne's] madness arose independently of the devil's action," the "motives for action aris[ing] out of social transactions" while the "chains of causation are left incomplete."[39] The structural indeterminacy, I believe, crystallizes the interplay between the social and psychological construction of both Mother Sawyer's and Anne Ratcliff's madness. Beneath the surface conflict, the dramatists create a number of structural links between the two characters. To begin with, economic destitution is a source of mental anguish for both women. Just as Mother Sawyer's indigence is

---

[36]Klaits, *Servants of Satan*, 86-88.

[37]David Atkinson, "Moral Knowledge and the Double Action in *The Witch of Edmonton*," *Studies in English Literature* 25, no. 8 (Spring, 1985): 431.

[38]Onat, "Introduction," *The Witch of Edmonton*, 94.

[39]Hattaway, "Women and Witchcraft," 53.

of mental anguish for both women. Just as Mother Sawyer's indigence is responsible for the trespass of her sow, poverty has led Anne to injure the animal. Although the two women are enemies,[40] Anne's jabber about privation echoes the cynical perspective which Mother Sawyer has maintained, namely that there is no justice for the dispossessed:

> *Ratc.* Hoyda! a-pox of the Devil's false Hopper!
> all the golden Meal runs into the rich Knaves
> purses, and the poor have nothing but Bran. Hey
> derry down! Are not you Mother *Sawyer?*
> *Sawy.* No, I am a Lawyer.
> *Ratc.* Art thou? I prithee let me scratch thy Face;
> for thy Pen has flea'd off a great many mens skins.
> . . . I'll sue Mother *Sawyer,* and her own Sow
> shall give in evidence against her.
> *Sawy.* Touch her.   [Dog *rubs her.*]
>
> (IV.i.176-82)

Significantly, the Familiar "rubs" Anne when, like Mother Sawyer, she is emotionally vulnerable and railing against the disparity between the rich and the poor. The verbal exchange between the two women highlights their mutual estrangement. Although the dog touches Anne during her delirium, Mother Sawyer believes she has induced Anne's madness. The old woman delights in inverting the power structure of her world by fancifully assuming the role of "Lawyer." As she rails at Anne for being uncharitable – "That Jade, that foul-tongu'd whore, *Nan Ratcliff*" (IV.i.168) – Mother Sawyer ironically denounces her enemy with epithets identical to those which the community had formerly levelled at her, namely "Jadish" and "whore" (IV.i.4; 24). Eager to take credit for Anne's social and mental disorientation, Mother Sawyer strips the married woman of her socially sanctioned identity, taking revenge upon the community that has been responsible for her own suffering. However, that Anne's derangement has also stemmed from social coercion is suggested by the sudden and unsettling interpolation of society's need to link women and madness:

> *O. Bank.* Catch her [Anne] fast, and have her into
> some close Chamber: do, for she's as many Wives are,
> stark mad.
>
> (IV.i.193-94)

[40]Thomas, *Religion and Decline of Magic,* 561, observes the striking irony that "Essentially the witch and her victim were two persons who ought to have been friendly towards each other, but were not. They existed in a state of concealed hostility for which society provided no legitimate outlet. They could not take each other to law; neither could they have recourse to open violence."

[*Countryman*] 2.   Rid the Town of her, else all
   our Wives will do nothing else but dance about . . .
   Country May-poles.
[*Countryman*] 3.   Our Cattel fall, our Wives fall,
   our Daughters fall, and Maid-servants fall . . . .
                              (IV.i.10-14)

Anne's nameless anxiety, which she and the community can attribute only to supernatural causes, is thus fundamentally related to a type of "madness" experienced not only by Mother Sawyer but also by many women in Edmonton.

Following Anne Ratcliff's suicide Old Banks spearheads the move "to burn . . . [Mother Sawyer] for a Witch" (IV.i.215). During the arraignment scene, Mother Sawyer is momentarily spared by the intervention of a Justice and Sir Arthur Clarington. In a significant addition to Goodcole's description of this event, the episode initially stresses the Justice's wisdom and compassion in reprehending the villagers for their violent actions, which he labels "ridiculous" (IV.i.40) and "against Law" (line 51). "Instead of turning [Mother Sawyer] into a Witch," he warns, "you'll prove your selves starke Fools" (line 42). The villagers' fury subsides when the Justice insists on treating the old woman with mildness. Mother Sawyer, however, continues to vilify her detractors. When Sir Arthur, a libertine and a schemer, joins the interrogation, she exposes his false rectitude and denounces a concept of honor based on class and privilege: "Men in gay clothes, whose Backs are laden with Titles and Honors, are within far more crooked than I am; and if I be a Witch, more Witch-like" (IV.i.86-88). Her boldest denunciation is reserved for the court where, she claims, are found "painted things . . . / Upon whose Eye-lids Lust sits blowing fires / Upon whose naked Paps, a Leachers thought / Acts Sin in fouler shapes than can be wrought" (lines 103-107). Henceforth, the accusations against Mother Sawyer abruptly shift from conspiracy with the devil to insubordination. Ironically, her spirited and vituperative self-defense, which the Justice calls her "sawcie[ness]" and "bitter[ness]," (IV.i.81) rather than her alleged crimes, secures her imprisonment.

Although virtually the entire community shares in the responsibility for Mother Sawyer's death, and although most of the prominent citizens are themselves guilty of moral backsliding, none of the villagers is punished through any real or symbolic intervention of Divine Providence, as would be expected in homiletic tragedy. And while in the denouement Mother Sawyer utters the conventional public-repentance speech of the genre (V.iii.50-51), the implication is that in the world of the play she has been condemned irrevocably. Henry Adams writes that the Mother Sawyer plot "is unusual" in its treatment of the redemption scene, and that Mother Sawyer's "well-chosen words against the court anticipate a development many generations in the future."[41] David Atkinson, on the other hand, while noting "some doubt as to Mother Sawyer's ultimate fate," nonetheless argues for homiletic closure: "As she goes to her execution" no one "expresses the conviction that she will achieve salvation. But the onlookers are deeply prejudiced against her . . . ," so that "it is perhaps just to believe that she can still benefit from the mercy of God."[42] From the outset, however, the Mother Sawyer plot has been moving toward an indeterminate ending. Mother Sawyer's fate cannot be accommodated to the typical conclusion of homiletic tragedy because only Mother Sawyer is tried and executed for her transgressions, suggesting the universe has become indifferent to human action. The complication forestalls the melodramatic effect of Mother Sawyer's pitiable death, attesting to authorial doubt about the genre's ability to provide solutions for human conflict.

*   *   *

The dramatists' uneasiness with homiletic schemes connects the Mother Sawyer action and the marriage plot, where the relationship between power and gender, as it bears upon the witch phenomenon and on domestic conduct in general, is further explored. Under profound emotional strain, Frank Thorney commits bigamy rather than defy his father's and the community's wishes that he marry Susan, whose wealthy family makes her a respectable catch. Rather than confess his clandestine marriage with another woman, Frank submits to a series of inescapable compromises, indulging in a painful web of lies in order to retain his father's and the world's approval until, in a sudden demonic rage, he kills Susan. Frank's inability to reconcile personal and social claims underlies Susan's murder, which thematically unifies the two plots. The cruelty to which Susan is subjected directly parallels that experienced by Mother Sawyer and, by implication, Anne Ratcliff. Like the conventional patient wife, Susan enters marriage believing that a wife's duty is to be passive and solicitous, and above all to yield to her husband's will (II.ii.79-88). Susan's notions of wifely perfection lead her to blame herself for Frank's discontent, a reaction based on a set of conventional moral prescriptions governing conjugal behavior.[43] When Susan finally thwarts convention by passionately asserting

[41]Adams, *English Domestic*, 141.

[42]Atkinson, "Moral Knowledge," 432-33.

[43]Contemporary literature providing instruction on marital relations was extensive. While the general consensus was that harmony should serve as the natural solution for all marital disputes, wives were admonished to practice absolute patience and self-abnegation, and husbands to exert their authority courageously but firmly. See Ian Maclean, *The Renaissance Notion of Woman: A Study in the Fortunes of Scholasticism and Medical Science in European Intellectual Life* (Cambridge: Cambridge University Press, 1980), 55ff. For an overview of how Elizabethan and Jacobean domestic drama absorbed these prescriptions, see Andrew Clark, *Domestic Drama*, 1: 27-99; and George Rao, *The Domestic Drama*, passim.

her sexual desire, Frank reproaches her for undermining her role as a "perfect Embleme of . . . modesty" (II.ii.104). Her ardent speech on Frank's "power / To make me passionate as an *April-day*" (II.ii.89) elicits a startling reply:

> *Frank.*   Change thy conceit, I prithee:
> Thou art all perfection: *Diana* her self
> Swells in thy thoughts, and moderates thy beauty.
>
> . . . .
>
> . . . still as wanton *Cupid* blows Love-fires,
> *Adonis* quenches out unchaste desires.
> (II.ii.94-106)

Susan's passion shocks and confuses Frank, whose response embodies two cardinal contemporary notions of ideal male and female behavior: he denies Susan's sexuality by viewing her as an emblem of chastity, and he upholds the husband's duty to command by instructing his wife on how to be decorous. Before Susan reveals her passion, Frank cannot even contemplate her death:

> . . . thou art so rare a goodness,
> As Death would rather put it self to death,
> Then murther thee. But we, as all things else,
> Are mutable and changing.
> (II.ii.138-41)

As a paragon of modesty, Susan is exempt from mutability; as a flesh-and-blood woman, Susan, like Mother Sawyer and Anne Ratcliff, pays dearly for her humanity.

Ignoring her husband's command to be silent, Susan persists in her importunities (lines 107-110), her romantic notions making her an easy victim: "till this minute," Frank charges, "You might have safe returned; now you cannot: / You have dogg'd your own death" (III.iii.37-39). In Frank's claim that Susan has "dogg'd" her own death, there is an inescapable association between Susan and carnality as represented by the dog who courts Mother Sawyer and who independently paws Frank prior to Susan's murder (III.iii.15). In making the association, Frank instinctively articulates the widespread suspicion about female sexuality challenged in the Mother Sawyer plot, namely that women are inherently disposed toward lust. Woman "is more carnal than a man," write the authors of the *Malleus Maleficarum*, "as is clear from many carnal abominations" for which "there are more women than men found infected with the heresy of witchcraft."[44]

---

[44]Summers, ed., *Malleus Maleficarum*, 44-47.

Susan dies because she fails to fulfill Frank's expectation that chastity is an essential aspect of female virtue, as defined by contemporary culture.

The conclusion of the marriage plot is notable for its resistance to homiletic closure. Lying seriously ill as a result of a self-inflected wound designed to make others believe he was attacked by Susan's murderers, Frank is overcome with remorse and guilt. He sleeps badly, eats little, and hallucinates about death, for which he longs. Unable to envision a better life, he muses on the possibility of suicide (IV.ii.20-27). In prison, he is forced to realize that he cannot escape divine justice, and his repentance speech (lines 134-42), which brings about society's forgiveness, conforms with the stock scaffold speeches of domestic tragedy, sharing with them the recognition of "the justice of earthly punishment."[45] Frank's speech also includes the conventional didactic address to the audience, but his advice to the world to marry for love and not for material gain (V.iii.107-10) has a hollow ring when juxtaposed with Susan's murder. Frank's repentance is further qualified by his spiritual malaise, for only the certainty of death gives him the inner strength to face his punishment.[46]

The final scenes, moreover, do not end in praise of the mysterious workings of Providence as do typical domestic tragedies. Instead, the play foregrounds society's role in the tragic events we have been witnessing. On his way to Frank's hanging, Susan's grief-stricken father meets Mother Sawyer, who is being executed simultaneously for witchcraft. Without cause, Old Carter blindly accuses her of having been the "instrument" (V.iii.21) of Frank's murder of Susan. A few moments later, however, when face to face with Frank, Old Carter acknowledges that social claims are the root cause of his daughter's demise: "if thou had'st not had ill counsel, thou would'st not have done as thou didst" (lines 116-18). Ironically, the "ill counsel" to which Old Carter refers is neither palmistry nor witchcraft but his and Old Thorney's enforcement of Frank's marriage to Susan.

In different but related ways, then, the deaths of Frank, Susan, Anne Ratcliff, and Mother Sawyer are brought about by the characters' psychological fragmentation, which is portrayed as a direct response to social barriers created by class, poverty and misogyny. By locating the witch phenomenon

---

[45]Adams, *English Domestic,* 136.

[46]Leonora Leet Brodwin, "The Domestic Tragedy of Frank Thorney in *The Witch of Edmonton," Studies in English Literature* 7 (1967): 322. Elsewhere Brodwin, *Elizabethan Love Tragedy 1587-1625* (New York and London: the University Presses, 1971), 174, contends that Frank's "final desire is that death may extinguish the despair which [his] ultimate self-recognition has brought." Etta S. Onat, "Introduction," *The Witch of Edmonton,* 86, while conceding that Frank's repentance is "not the mere stock convention of homiletic drama," claims that it is "dramatically credible" because "Frank has been characterized as a man of some conscience and feeling."

in the complex dynamics of social and domestic life, the two plots of *The Witch of Edmonton* inscribe a subversive discourse about witchcraft which exposes the limits of tidy homiletic conclusions in mitigating tragic events.

LEGENDS OF LUCIFER IN EARLY ENGLISH AND IN MILTON.

The richness and variety of the Lucifer legends preserved in Early English writings — especially those of the Middle English period — cannot fail to strike the student of the literature of the England of Cædmon and Laȝamon and Chaucer and Lydgate. In the course of an examination of the medieval Mystery Plays, I encountered the many and varied legends of the Fall of Lucifer and the Angels that find expression in the several English and Continental Mysteries, and I was moved to inquire a little more closely into the adoption of these legends in the narrative and, generally, non-dramatic literature of Old and Middle English. And it was but natural to be constantly reminded in the course of such an investigation of how particular legends had found or not found acceptance in that later monument of learning and genius, *Paradise Lost.* From the comparisons being at first instituted haphazardly and as memory prompted, they gradually usurped a larger and larger share of my attention, and this paper is the result, — partly an exposition of the multifarious legends of Lucifer prevalent in Early English and, partly, a comparative study of the Early English versions of the angelic revolt on the one hand and Milton's version of it in *Paradise Lost* on the other.

Having said so much about how this paper originated and what it is, I may as well, to leave no room for misunderstanding, make it clear what it is not. It is not an attempt to catalogue or consider comprehensively all Old and Middle English references to the Fall of the Angels. I could not have done this even if I had wanted: facilities for research in Early English literature are very limited in India. How-

ever, I trust that the references I have been unable, or have
failed, to take account of are but minor and incidental ones.
Again, this paper is not an attempt to discover or discuss
Milton's medieval sources. In fact, it is not concerned with
sources as such at all. I have, indeed, when I have been able,
suggested an early authority for an occasional belief held
whether by Milton or by his medieval predecessors, but I have
been chary of glorifying such authorities into immediate sources
of the particular form of the legend in question.

I. The Creation of the Angels.

Milton's views on the question of the creation of the
Angels are clearly put forward in a long passage in his posthumous *Christian Doctrine.* He writes:

> "It is generally supposed that the angels were created at the same
> time with the visible universe, and that they are considered as com-
> prehended under the general name of *heavens.* That the angels
> were created at some particular period, we have the testimony of
> Numb. xvi. 22. and xxvii. 16. 'God of the spirits,' Heb. i. 7. Col. i. 16.
> 'by him were all things created ... visible and invisible, whether
> they be thrones,' &c. But that they were created on the first, or
> on any one of the six days, seems to be asserted (like most received
> opinions) with more confidence than reason, chiefly on the authority
> of repetition in Gen. i. 1. 'thus the heavens and the earth were
> finished, and all the host of them,' — unless we are to suppose that
> more was meant to be implied in the concluding summary than in
> the previous narration itself, and that the angels are to be considered
> as the host who inhabit the visible heavens. For when it is said
> Job xxxviii. 7. that they shouted for joy before God at the creation,
> it proves rather that they were then already in existence, than that
> they were then first created. Many at least of the Greek, and some
> of the Latin Fathers, are of opinion that angels, as being spirits,
> must have existed long before the material world; and it seems even
> probable, that the apostasy which caused the expulsion of so many
> thousands from heaven, took place before the foundations of this
> world were laid." (Chap. VII. — *P. W.* IV, pp. 184, 185).

In *Par. Lost,* accordingly, the Angels are represented as
created long before the World and Man. But there is more
to it than this. No doubt Abdiel is right in reminding the
blasphemous Lucifer, as does St. Paul the Colossians (*Coloss.*
I, 16, 17), that it was through "the begotten Son" that all
the Angels were made —

> "by whom
>
> As by his Word, the mighty Father made
> All things, even thee, and all the Spirits of Heaven."[1])
>
> (V. 835—837).

Nevertheless it is clearly indicated in Book V that the Angels existed long before even the Son of God, as Son, was begotten, the interval between their creation and the day on which the Almighty announces:

> "This day I have begot whom I declare
> My only Son",   (V. 603, 604).

being apparently nothing less than "Heaven's great year", — in other words, Plato's *Annus Magnus*, learnedly computed as being a period of thirty-six thousand years. For, that the Angels were created at the beginning of a previous such natural cycle is to be gathered from the words of Raphael in V, 577—605 and Lucifer's boast:

> "We know no time when we were not as now;
> Know none before us, self-begot, self-raised
> By our quickening power, when fatal course
> Had circled his full orb, the birth mature
> Of this our native Heaven, Ethereal Sons." (V. 859—863).

I may parenthetically remark that though Lucifer here, talking for victory, anticipates Manichaeism and claims to be self-begot and, similarly, later in a mood of "bursting passion" doubts if the Angels are really created by God (IX, 145—147), yet in the quietness of thought even he cannot disguise from himself the fact that God is his Creator (IV, 42, 43).

Now, Milton's Arianism, coupled with his desire to make the action of *Paradise Lost*, no less than that of *Paradise Regained*, centre round the person of Christ[2]), seems to have been responsible for this view of the creation of the Angels. The view is not shared by the majority of medieval writers on the subject, or even by the poet's beloved "original", Spenser.[3]) It is true that the Greek Fathers, as a rule, and the Latin ones, sometimes, held that the making of the Angels preceded at least that of the rest of the World, so that they were used, as Plato declared of his daemons, and as Milton suggests

---

[1]) Cf. *P. L.* III, 383—391 and *Christ. Doctr.* V (*P. W.* IV, pp. 80, 81).
[2]) See also *P. L.* III, 412—415.
[3]) See his *Hymne of Heavenly Love*, 22 ff.

the faithful angels were used (VIII, 228 ff.), at the creation
of the World.[1]) And we find the so-called Caedmonian *Genesis*
(ll. 112 ff.) maintaining that the Angels were created and fell
as well, just as in *P. L.*, before the World was even contemplated. And much the same view finds expression in the
M. E. *Deuelis Perlament*, when Christ is made to say:

> "I seie þee, lucifer, y schal þee telle,
> Or euere ony þing was wrought —
> Heuene or erþe, eir or helle, —
> Forsoþe þoo y made þee of nought". (329—332).

However, it is not this, but rather the other belief, rejected
by Milton in the above-cited *Christ. Doctr.* passage but held by
Augustine and medieval theologians like Hugo St. Victor,
Aquinas, Bonaventura and Alexander Hales[2]), the belief that
the Angels were created along with the rest of creation, that
is most commonly adopted in medieval literature. Even so the
question remains: On what day of Creation were the Angels
made? Most widely accepted was the doctrine that they were
created on the first day of the creation of the World. This
belief, dating at least as far back as the *Book of Jubilees*, II 2,
and held emphatically by teachers like Augustine (*De Civ.
Dei*, XI c. 9), is the one that is almost always adopted in
Middle English literature. Nevertheless, those medieval writings
that accept this in the main differ among themselves in their
details, for the simple reason that their authorities, the theological doctors, were themselves not always agreed. Thus, in
the opening play of the cycle known as *Ludus Coventriae*,
the work of Creation begins with the making of Heaven and
the Angels (ll. 30—39), but there is no mention of the fashioning
of Earth or the fiat regarding Light; so that the second
pageant opens:

> "Now hevyn is made ffor Aungell sake
> Þe fyrst day and þe fyrst nyth,
> The secunde day watyr I make,
> The walkyn also full fayr and bryth."

---

[1]) See, e. g., Gregory Nazianzen, *Oratio* XXXVIII, 9.

[2]) Hagenbach, *Compendium of the History of Doctrines*, Vol. I, p. 493.
Nothwithstanding Saurat (*Milton, Man and Thinker*, pp. 273 f.), Milton does
not adopt Augustine's view; rather, as we have seen, he vigorously combats
it. Indeed, Saurat is inclined to make too much of Milton's indebtedness
to Augustine. (See also Hanford, *A Milton Handbook*, p. 193, fn. 30.)

On the other hand, in the York and Chester Lucifer plays, though the Angels are created on the first day as soon as Heaven is made, their creation is followed immediately by that of the World and Hell (*York* I, 25—27; *Chester* I, 51, 52). As far as the creation of the World at this stage is concerned, *Cursor Mundi* rightly cites Augustine as the authority for this belief:

> "Als austin sais, þe hali man,
> Als we in his bok writen find:
> First þan wroght he angel kind,
> Þe werld and time, þir things thre
> Byfor al oþer thyng wroght he." (360—364).[1]

For, Augustine, commenting in his *De Civ. Dei*, XI c. 33, and *Gen. ad Litt.* I, 1, 3, on the opening words of *Genesis*, emphasizes the simultaneous creation of the Angels and the Earth.

But a slightly different tradition, which too has, more or less, the authority of Augustine himself, is followed elsewhere. In the thirteenth century *Story of Genesis & Exodus* and in the fourteenth century prose *Lyff of Adam and Eue* not only is Earth no less than Heaven made before the Angels, — and this seems to be implied also in the later Cornish play of *Creation* by William Jordan[2]) — but also the making of Light precedes that of the Angels. The account in *Genesis & Exodus* runs:

> "In firme bigini[n]g, of nogt
> Was heuene and erðe samen wrogt;
> Do bad god wurðen stund and stede,
> Ðis middes werld ðor-inne he dede,
> Al was ðat firme ðrosing in nigt,
> Til he wit hise word made ligt;
> Of hise word, ðu wislike mune,
> Hise word, ðat is, hise wise sune,
> Ðe was of him fer ear bi-foren
> Or oni werldes time boren;
> — — — — — — — — —
> Do so wurð ligt so god it bad,

---

[1]) See Augustine, *De Civ. Dei* XI c. 6. Cf. Sir Thomas Browne: "Time we may comprehend; 'tis but five days elder than our selves, and hath the same Horoscope with the World" (*Religio Medici* I, sect. 11.); and Plato's *Timæus*. But Milton believed that Time existed before our World was made. See *P. L.* V, 579—582 and *Christ. Doctr.* VII (*P. W.* IV, p. 185).

[2]) See Gilbert's Edition (1827) pp. 3, 7. Curiously enough, in this play Light is regarded as made on the second day.

> Fro ðisternesse o sunde[r] sad;
> Dat was ðe firme morgen tid,
> Dat euere sprong in werld wid.
> Wið ðat light worn angles wrogt,
> And in-to newe heuene brogt,
> Dat is ouer dis walkenes turn,
> God hem quuad ðor seli suriurn." (39 - 48; 57—64).

Similarly the *Lyff of Adam and Eue* opens:

> "Alle þat bileeuen on Jhesu Crist, lusteneþ and ȝe mowen heere
> how muche is þe miht of vre heuene kyng! Furst he schop heuene,
> & siþen þe eorþe, to beren treo and gras. Þe eorþe was druyȝe
> & wiþouten moisture; þer nas no þing þat was quik, neiþer more
> ne lasse. Þe holigost was euere wiþouten biginning, & schal be
> wiþouten endyng. God as his wille was, behihte to make liht. And
> þo he made angelus, of a swiþe fair bleo. Sachel was þe furste
> angel þat Crist made, and siþen he hihte Lucifer, þat þorw pruide
> was forloren." [1] (Horstmann, *Sammlung Alteng. Leg.* p. 220).

Does not Augustine in *De Civ. Dei* repeatedly suggest that
the light that was made on the first day of creation is
identical with the Angels, even though he also inclines to
the belief that the one day of light includes all the six days
of creation? [2]

But at least one Middle English author placed the creation
of the Angels later than the first day, — indeed, placed it,
if I read him aright, as late as the fifth, notwithstanding
Job, XXXVIII 7 (*Sept.*), which had appeared conclusive to
Augustine as proof that they were created at least before
the fourth day when the stars were made. [3] In the Slavonic
Secrets of Enoch (Chap. XXIX) and other Jewish writings —
e. g. *Bereshith Rabba* — the Angels are represented as created
on the second day; but the author of the Creation play of
the so-called Towneley cycle — who is the author I am
referring to — seems to adhere rather to that other Hebrew
tradition that the Angels being winged creatures were made
on the fifth day when all winged creatures were made. [4]

---

[1] It will be noticed that in both the passages quoted above Christ
is distinctly mentioned as the Creator of the Angels. Cf. also *Piers
Plowman*, B I 105; *Deuelis Perlament*, 329 ff; *Colossians*, I, 16.

[2] *De Civ. Dei* XI c. 9 etc. Cf. also Chrysostum, *Homil. in Genesis*;
Bede, *In Pent. Comm.* — *Genesis*; and see *Religio Medici* I, sect. 33.

[3] *De Civ. Dei* XI c. 9.

[4] See Wace's Edition of *Apocrypha*, Vol. 1, p. 175. But perhaps
we have in the Towneley play no more than want of proper chronological

I may conclude this section with remarking that if we are to take the Elizabethan author of *The Times' Whistle* literally, we must understand that the Angels were created at least not earlier than the third day. For he writes:

"After the fabricke of heaven, earthe & seas
Were gloriously composde, it then did plesse
High Ioue (e're he began man's operation)
To give vnto the Angels their creation." (877—880).

II. The Angelic Orders.

Without going into a detailed history of the traditions regarding the number of the angelic orders, we may content ourselves with recalling how belief in the existence of several distinct orders, taking its rise possibly in the two pseud-epigraphic Books of Enoch known as the Ethiopic and the Slavonic, and finding expression in canonical writings like St. John's *Revelation* and the epistles of Saints Paul and Peter[1]), filtered into early patristic literature. Augustine, indeed, in the latter half of the fourth century disclaims all knowledge of the supernatural and most beatific society of angels[2]), but his contemporary, Gregory Nazianzen[3]), boldly enumerates nine orders: — Angels, Archangels, Thrones, Dominions, Principalities, Powers, Brightnesses, Ascensions and Incorporeal Mightinesses or Virtues. And about a hundred years later, Pseudo-Dionysius[4]) is even able to subdivide the nine orders into three hierarchies of three orders each, — Seraphim, Cherubim and Thrones making the first hierarchy, Dominions, Virtues and Powers the second, and Principalities, Archangels and Angels the third. This enumeration Dante, in his *Paradiso*, XXVIII, 92 ff., not only adopts, but con-

arrangement, as often in narrative accounts of the Fall of the Angels. The Angels may thus only seem to be created on the fifth day, because their fall is handled at this stage. See Lyle, *The Original Identity of the York and Towneley Cycles*, p. 71. No M. E. author that I know of has gone the length of Philo in postponing the creation of the Angels to the seventh day.

[1]) See *Revelation*, IV; *Colossians* I, 16; *Ephesians* I, 21; *Romans* VIII, 38; *I Peter* III, 22.

[2]) *Enchiridion*, 58.

[3]) *Orat.* XXXVIII, 31.

[4]) *De Coelesti Hierarchia*, VI, VII.

siders the only true one; and hence he is severe upon Gregory the Great for venturing to set up a rival to it. For one thing, Gregory, "dissentient", does not distinguish the orders into three hierarchies; for another thing, in his thirty-fourth Homily, starting from the order of Angels, he counts backwards up to Seraphim and, even so, makes the Virtues and Principalities of Pseudo-Dionysius change places with one another. And lastly, — and this is most significant of all — in his *Moralia*, XXXII, Gregory suggests that there was also a tenth order, the one that fell. In thus speaking of ten orders, however, Gregory had the support of the Slavonic *Secrets of Enoch*, XX, 3:

> "And all the heavenly troops would come and stand on the ten steps according to their rank and would bow down to the Lord."

Now let us see how far the teachings of the Fathers with regard to nine orders or ten, on the one hand, and the hierarchic division, on the other, influenced medieval literature and Milton.

In medieval references to the story of Lucifer the number of the angelic orders, or, for that matter, the very existence of such orders, is often (it need hardly be said) overlooked. Thus, the O. E. *Genesis*, the M. E. *Genesis & Exodus*, the Vernon MS *Lyff of Adam and Eue*, the *Ludus Coventriae 'Lucifer'* and the account of the angelic rebellion in *The Destruction of Troy* (4395 ff.) pass silently over the question of the angelic orders. But elsewhere there are references to them, sometimes to Pseudo-Dionysius' and Gregory Nazianzen's nine orders, at other times to Gregory the Great's ten. In the Medieval Drama mention of nine orders of angels was, it would appear, commoner than that of ten. Like the French Mysteries of the *Viel Testament* (44 ff.) and the *Passion* of Arnoul Ereban, and the Cornish *Creation* of Jordan (pp. 5, 19), the *York* cycle and the *Chester* one (at least according to the MSS representing the younger redaction) speak consistently of but nine orders. On the other hand, the more primitive version of the *Chester 'Lucifer'*, the one preserved in the best, if the latest, MS, persists in holding to the ten-orders tradition, and in this it is followed by the *Towneley 'Creation'* and the morality *The Castell of Perseverance* (3497 f.) in the field of Drama, and outside that it is supported by the author of the

Later Genesis (246—8), by Aelfric (*De Initio Creature*) and by Langland (*Piers Plow.*, B. I, 105 f.; C. II, 105 f.). The author of *Cursor Mundi* appears at first sight to have been unable to decide between the rival traditions; for, in one place he says that God would be served by orders "thrice three", and yet later declares that Man was made to take the place of the tenth order that fell. But a closer examination of the passages in question — ll. 411—432 and 511—516 — reveals that what the author evidently means is that God in His foreknowledge knew that He would ultimately be served by (only) nine orders of Angels supplemented by an order of Men, which order would be created in place of the tenth angelic order that was destined to fall. Similarly, in *Adrian and Epotys*, after the nine existing orders are enumerated we are informed that

> "The x ordyr schall mankynd ben,
> That xall fulfyll the place ageyn,
> In heuyn be that ylke syde,
> That Lussyfer fell owte for hys pryde." (103—6).

In fact, we are not to conclude rashly that all references to, or enumerations of, the nine orders are necessarily in the line of the Pseudo-Dionysian tradition. Mention of no more than nine orders occurs, for instance, in *Ormulum*, 1050 f; *Ancren Rewle*, p. 30; Myrc's *Instructions for Parish Priests*, 766; Lyndesay's *Dreme*, 524; and possibly in many other places; but it will be discovered that the majority of such references are concerned, not with the number of orders originally created, but with the number in existence, and therefore offer no evidence for determining their adherence to either of the rival doctrines.[1])

We have seen how not all medieval authors were prepared to commit themselves to either of the rival views regarding the angelic orders. Not all, again, of those who sided definitely with one or other of these traditions deemed it necessary to name the several orders. The *Later Genesis* and *Cursor Mundi*, for example, are satisfied with merely stating the number of

---

[1]) Thus, the *Boke of St. Albans* (*Lib. Armorum*) talks repeatedly of nine orders, but it is always understood that reference is to the nine existing orders; for we are distinctly told at the very outset that originally there were ten.

orders; the *Towneley* playwright mentions only Cherubim, the *York* one no more than Cherubim and Seraphim, and Langland's ten orders are vaguely:

"Cherubyn and seraphin suche seuene and an-othre".[1]) (B I, 106).

The reason why Cherubim and Seraphim are so often specifically mentioned when the other orders are not is evident from the following lines, Pseudo-Dionysian in ultimate inspiration, of *Ormulum*:

"All ennglepeod to-dæledd iss
    o niʒhenn kinne þeode;
& Cherubyn & Seraphyn
    sinndenn þa tweʒʒen þeode
þatt sinndenn Drihhtin allre nest
    & hehʒhesst upp inn heoffne." (1050—55).

But in such widely different writings as the *Homilies of Aelfric, Adrian and Epotys,* the *Chester 'Lucifer', The Myroure of Oure Ladye* and Lyndesay's *Dreme,* not to mention others, the nine orders of Pseudo-Dionysius and Gregory are distinctly specified though not always in a strictly Dionysian or Gregorian manner. Aelfric, in his homily, *Dominica IIII post Pentecostam,* the author of the *Myroure* and Lyndesay, indeed, adhere rigidly to Gregory's version in his thirty-fourth homily. In his homily, *De Initio Creature,* however, Aelfric deviates slightly from the account in Gregory's *Moralia,* XXXII,[2]) while the *Chester* and *Adrian and Epotys* versions, which agree among themselves, would have been identical with the latter one of Aelfric's if their Cherubim and Seraphim had not taken the place of the Angels and Archangels in Aelfric's scheme and so come first instead of last.

---

[1]) Curiously enough the corresponding line in one of the MSS of the A type runs:

"Cherubin and Seraphin an al þe foure ordres".

[2]) Caxton's *Golden Legend* also follows this arrangement except that it omits the Virtues and so mentions only eight orders. Spenser too, in his *Hymne of Heavenly Beavtie,* 85—89, enumerates only eight orders, omitting the Virtues. Sometimes the order of Principalities is also omitted, leaving seven orders. (See Peacock's note to *Myrc's Instructions for Parish Priests,* 766.) Burton speaks of some writers dividing aetherial spirits or angels into only seven orders corresponding to the seven planets (*Anatomy of Melancholy,* I, 2, i, 2.).

However, neither Aelfric, nor the author of *Adrian and Epotys*, nor the *Chester* dramatist has troubled to arrange his orders in hierarchies of threes. As far as the last-named is concerned, this is particularly remarkable, for a hierarchic enumeration is present in the French *Viel Testament*, which has often been regarded as the original of the Chester cycle of plays. But, for his part, Lyndesay makes it clear, in his *Dreme*, that

"Thir ordouris nyne thay ar full plesandlye
Deuydit in to Ierarchies three." (524, 525).

And among prose writers we may mention Wycliff (*Sel. Works*, II, p. 338), Trevisa (*Bartholomeus*, '*De Proprietatibus Rerum*') and the author of the *Myroure* as acceptors of the tradition of the three hierarchies. The Cornish *Creation*, too, makes a hierarchic division of the heavenly host, but it is strikingly original and far from Pseudo-Dionysian. Cherubin, Seraphin and Lucifer are said to form the "first degree", Principality, Power and Domination the second, and Lordship, Virtue and Angels the third. But still more curious is the division of the existing angels into just two classes (the first inferior, the second superior) in the *Book of St. Albans* (*Cote Armour*, a iv), where it is stated:

"Ther be ix orderis of angelis, v Ierarchie & iiii Tronly. The v Ierarchye be theys: Angelis, Archangelis, Virtutes, Potestates & Dominacones. The iiii Tronly be theys: Principates, Trony, Cherubin, and Seraphyn."

Turning to Milton, we observe that while in Early English writings specific mention of nine orders or ten is frequently made, nowhere in *Paradise Lost* are we directly told the number of the angelic orders. Nowhere, in fact, in the entire course of the epic are more than five of the orders mentioned together by name, not even in passages like the following where, if anywhere, we should expect a full-dress enumeration. The Almighty, announcing the begetting of His Son, begins:

"Hear, all ye Angels, Progeny of Light,
Thrones, Dominations, Princedoms, Virtues, Powers,
Hear my decree, which unrevoked shall stand." (V. 600—2).

Similarly, Abdiel, contending with the Faithless, affirms:

"the mighty Father made
All things, even thee, and all the Spirits of Heaven
By him created in their bright degrees,

> Crowned them with glory, and to their glory named
> Thrones, Dominations, Princedoms, Virtues, Powers."
>   (V. 836—40).

In two other passages — V, 772, and X, 460 — Satan addresses his followers in the same manner: "Thrones, Dominations, Princedoms, Virtues Powers". In the only other place where as many as five orders are specified the list is differently given:

> "Cherub and Seraph, Potentates and Thrones,
> And Virtues, winged Spirits". (VII, 198, 199).

However, evidence furnished by the mention in all of no more than the usual nine names of the orders, and the references to the mixed character of the portion of the angelic host that fell with Lucifer — of which more later — make it certain that in Milton's conception there always were but nine angelic ranks and that those that fell never constituted a separate tenth order by themselves.[1]

And then there is that division into hierarchies, which, somehow, does not seem to have been very frequently made in medieval references to angelology. The two fullest references in *Paradise Lost* to the hierarchic organization are in I, 734—37 and in V, 586—91. In the first of these the poet declares that in Heaven

> "Sceptred Angels held their residence,
> And sat as Princes, whom the supreme King
> Exalted to such power, and gave to rule,
> Each in his hierarchy, the Orders bright."

The second passage recounts the assembling of the empyreal host at a Divine summons:

> "Forthwith from all the ends of Heaven appeared
> Under their hierarchs in orders bright,
> Ten thousand thousand ensigns high advanced,
> Standards and gonfalons, 'twixt van and rear
> Stream in the air, and for distinction serve
> Of hierarchies, of orders, and degrees."

Now, neither in a reference to the angelic organization in his *Reason for Church Government*[2]), nor anywhere in the

---

[1]) Ll. 131, 132 of the *Nativity Ode* may be cited as further evidence of this:
> "And with your nine-fold harmony
> Make up full consort to the angelic symphony."

[2]) "Yea, the angels themselves . . . are distinguished and quaternioned into their celestial princedoms and satrapies according as God himself has

posthumous *Christian Doctrine* [1]) does Milton definitely assert
that the angels were arranged in ternaries or, what Spenser
calls, "trinall triplicities". [2]) He, however, comes very near
making such an assertion, if, indeed, he does not actually
make it, in the following three lines of *Par. Lost*, describing
the flight towards the limits of the North of Satan and his
aspiring band of followers:

> "Regions they passed, the mighty regencies
> Of Seraphim and Potentates and Thrones
> In their triple degrees". [3]) (V, 748—50.)

It may incidentally be pointed out that the mention precisely
of Seraphim, Potentates and Thrones is perhaps not accidental;
for, in one of Gregory the Great's two enumerations — the
one in his *Moralia* — these three are the ninth, sixth and
third orders respectively. Moreover, from other occasional
indications the discerning reader of *Par. Lost* can safely come
to the conclusion that, in Milton's angelology, not only were
there three, and only three, hierarchies, but also Michael,
Lucifer and Raphael were the leaders and princes of them.
For, only to these three does the poet allow the proud title
"hierarch": Michael is the "princely hierarch" (XI, 220) and
Raphael the "winged hierarch" (V, 468), and, as for Lucifer,
is not his standard of revolt "the great hierarchal standard"
(V, 701)? It is worth while pausing to note here that Milton
has dethroned Uriel from his traditional place as one of the
hierarchs and exalted Raphael to that lofty position. I suspect
that this displacing of Uriel by Raphael is deliberate. Deliberate
or not, it certainly serves to raise the dignity of Unfallen
Man and gives the story of the loss of Paradise an additional
importance; for, as the epic goes, Man is warned by Raphael,
is tempted and deceived by Lucifer, is finally expelled by
Michael; and these are no inferior spirits but are hierarchs all.

---

writ his imperial decrees through the great provinces of heaven." (*Prose Works*, II, p. 442.)

[1]) In *Christ. Doctr.* VII, he contents himself with saying: "They are distinguished one from another by offices and degrees" (*P. W.* IV, p. 186).

[2]) *Faerie Queene*, I, xii, st. 39; *Hymne of Heavenly Love*, 64.

[3]) Cf. Tasso, *Gier. Lib.* XVIII, 96:
> "Tre folte squadre, et ogni squadra instrutta
> In tre ordini gira."

So much having been said about the marshalling of the heavenly hosts in *Par. Lost*, it must be added that Milton makes no attempt to distinguish the various angelic orders very clearly, but often employs their names indiscriminately as so many grand, mouth-filling variants for the generic terms "angels", "spirits". Occasionally, moreover, titles like Virtues, Dominations, Thrones and Powers are treated as mere personifications of goodness and majesty. Thus, the captains and leaders of the Fallen Angels are called

"godlike Shapes and Forms
Excelling human; princely Dignities;
And Powers that erst in Heaven sat on thrones." (I, 358—60).

Satan calls his followers variously, "Celestial Virtues" (II, 15) and "Empyreal Thrones" (II, 430); and after the grand council in Pandemonium is over, it is "the ranged Powers" that are said to disband (II, 522). Elsewhere, these same misguided spirits are referred to as "the rebel Thrones" (VI, 199), and "the aspiring Dominations" (III, 392), and "Seraphim" (I, 129, II, 750), and "Cherubim" (I, 665). And, likewise, Raphael, "the affable Archangel" (VII, 41), is not only a "Seraph winged" (V, 277); he is also "the angelic Virtue" (V, 371) and the "godlike Power" (VIII, 249).

If Milton uses any title sparingly it is the title "Archangel". Only Lucifer (I, 243, etc.), Michael (VI, 203, 257, etc.), Uriel (III, 648) and Raphael (VII, 41) are expressly called Archangels, and for each of them our poet has the authority of a long-standing tradition behind him.[1]) And when the Archangel Uriel is said to be

"one of the seven
Who in God's presence, nearest to his throne,
Stand ready at command, and are his eyes
That run through all the Heavens, or down to Earth
Bear his swift errands over moist and dry,
O'er sea and land" — (III, 648—53),

Milton is adhering strictly to the doctrine of the number and functions of the supreme Archangels established in the Ethiopic *Book of Enoch* XX; in *Revelation* I, 4, V, 6, VIII, 2, etc.; in

---

[1]) For Michael, biblical authority: *Jude*, 9; for the others, various apocrypha: for Lucifer, the Slavonic *Secrets of Enoch*, XXIX, 4; for Raphael, the Ethiopic *Enoch*, X, 4, and *Tobit*, XII, 15; for Uriel, the Ethiopic *Enoch*, XXI, and *2 Esdras*, IV, 36.

Tobit XII, 15, and followed in more recent writings like Spenser's *Hymne of Heavenly Beavtie*, 97, 98, Reginald Scot's *Discourse of Divels*, X, and Heywood's *Hierarchie of the Blessed Angels*, p. 194.[1])

It is therefore all the more remarkable that Gabriel should, neither in *Par. Lost* nor in Heywood's *Hierarchie*, be given equal rank with Michael, Uriel and Raphael as he is in long-established tradition; see, e. g., Ethiopic *Enoch* IX, XX, XL; *Hali Meidenhad*, p. 45; *Ormulum*, 13 512; *Gesta Romanorum* I, xliii, 143. For, notwithstanding the Almighty's words:

> "Go, Michael, of celestial armies prince,
> And thou, in military prowess next,
> Gabriel,"[2]) (VI, 44—46)

it will hardly do to day that Milton means that we should reckon Gabriel among the Archangels, even though he does not happen expressly to call him one. It is surely not an accident that Gabriel is variously introduced as no more than "the winged warrior" (IV, 576) or "the warlike Angel" (IV, 902) or "the warrior Angel" (IV, 946).[3]) And at best he is regarded as a Cherub (IV, 971) taking his orders from Uriel (IV, 574, 589), who, like Raphael (V, 277) and Lucifer (I, 539)[4]) and doubtless Michael too, is a Seraph (III, 667).

What exactly is implied by this last distinction? It must first be observed that in Milton's usage the terms "Seraph", "Seraphic", "Cherub", "Cherubic" are a grand, if general, mark of distinction and are applied to spirits above the average, regardless of the precise orders to which they may, strictly considered, belong. Thus, in the very first Book a distinction is made between "the great Seraphic Lords and Cherubim", who, in their own dimensions, sit godlike within in secret conclave, and the undistinguished crowd of Fallen Spirits, who are constrained to reduce themselves to smaller forms before they throng the outer hall of Pandemonium (I, 777 ff.). Thus, again, as pointed out already, Uriel, Raphael

---

[1]) Cf. *Christ. Doctr.* IX (*P. W.* IV, pp. 215, 216).

[2]) Cf. Ethiopic *Enoch* X, 9, 10; XL, 9, and the Cornish *Creation*, p. 25.

[3]) Likewise, Origen considers Gabriel the angel of war. See E. de Pressensé, *The Early Years of Christianity*, Vol. II.

[4]) For Lucifer as a Seraph, cf. the quotation from the *Faust Book* on p. 228.

15*

and Lucifer, who are Archangels, are also Seraphim, and, likewise, every one of the lesser spirits deemed worthy to be mentioned by name is definitely either a Seraph or a Cherub; Abdiel is a Seraph (V, 804 f., 875), and Gabriel, Uzziel, Ithuriel, Zephon (IV, 778, 844, 971) and Zophiel (VI, 535) are all Cherubim.

Evidently, then, Milton ranked the Cherubim and Seraphim very high in the celestial hierarchy as did Spenser in his *Heavenly Beavtie* (92—98), if indeed he did not, as did Pseudo-Dionysius, give them absolute pride of place. Evidently, also, of these two orders Milton ranked the Seraphim above the Cherubim. Perhaps the phrase "the great Seraphic Lords and Cherubim", suggests this, and so too, surely, does the fact that the Archangels are Seraphim but their lieutenants are Cherubim, — that, for instance, Lucifer is a Seraph, but Beelzebub and Azazel are Cherubim (I, 157, 534). And we have seen already how the "mighty regencies" that the Rebel Angels passed in their northward flight were those of "*Seraphim* and Potentates and Thrones" (V, 749). Further, is it not significant that Milton's Uriel is a Seraph when the Uriel of popular medieval tradition is a "St. Cherubin"?[1] The point need not, however, be laboured, for the superiority of the Seraphim was traditional ever since Pseudo-Dionysius formulated his hierarchies[2] and is no peculiarly Miltonic invention. Dante (*Paradiso* XXVIII) and Lyndesa yamong earlier writers recognized it, and, among the Elizabethans, Spenser (*Heavenly Beavtie*, 92—5) and Bacon (*Advancement of Learning*, Bk. 1) and the writer of the popular English *Faust Book*, with which Milton was very probably familiar.[3] The relevant passage in this last is worth quoting, as having perhaps suggested to Milton the Seraphic nature of Lucifer:

"But how came lord and master Lucifer to have so great a fall from Heaven? Mephistophiles answered, My lord Lucifer was a fair

---

[1] See *Dict. of Christ. Doct.* I, 89/2 and *N. E. D.* s. v. *Cherub*. Note also how Satan, disguised as a "stripling Cherub", bows low to the Seraph Uriel, "As to superior spirits is wont in Heaven" (III, 737 f.), though here the stripling may be regarded as bowing to the Archangel.

[2] It may indeed be traced further back than Pseudo-Dionysius, through Gregory Nazianzen to the Slavonic *Secrets of Enoch*, XIX, XX.

[3] On the other hand, in Jordan's *Creation*, p. 5, the Seraphim come below the Cherubim, who are the highest in rank.

angel, created, of God as immortal, and being placed in the Seraphims, which are above the Cherubims, he would have presumed upon the Throne of God."[1])

To return, then, to the Cherub Gabriel, all the evidence points unmistakably to the conclusion that, at least in *Par. Lost*, Gabriel is not an Archangel but a spirit inferior.[2])

III. Angeli Boni et Mali.

First the Arch-Adversary. From very early times the reference in *Isaiah*, XIV, to the fall of Lucifer, the morning-star, was interpreted by the Fathers as a veiled allusion to the Fall of the Rebellious Angel from Heaven.[3]) And yet, till we come to the eleventh century it is rare to find the Devil identified by name with Lucifer. Eusebius, indeed, in the fourth century, expressly called him Lucifer, and so also did Jerome, but never their contemporary Augustine. And even Avitus, whose share in the development of the legend has perhaps been exaggerated, does not call the Adversary Lucifer, though the features of his rebellion, as narrated in *De Originali Peccato*, are distinctly Isaiahian. We are not surprised, therefore, when the name Lucifer is not given to the Rebel Leader of the O. E. *Genesis* (*A* and *B*) or, for that matter, of the much later M. E. alliterative poem, *Cleanness*.

But by the time of Anselm and Peter Comestor the name *Lucifer* had come to be almost synonymous with *Satan*, with commonly just this distinction that *Lucifer* was rather the glorious Angel's name and *Satan* the fallen Devil's. It is true that often in the religious drama — as, e. g., in the *York, Towneley, Ludus Coventriae* and *Viel Testament* Lucifer scenes, and in the Cornish *Creation* and *Origo Mundi*, — the Adversary is Lucifer both before and after his fall. But nevertheless the

---

[1]) Thoms, *Eng. Prose Romances*, III p. 184.

[2]) Since the zealous and faithful Abdiel is a Seraph, it would seem that Gabriel is inferior even to him.

[3]) See Tertullian, *Contra Marrionem*, V, 11, 17; Origen, *In Ep. ad Rom.*, Lib. V; Jerome, *Adv. Jovin.*, Lib. II, c. 3; Augustine, *De Civ. Dei*, XI, c. 15, *De Gen. ad Litt.*, XI, c. 24; etc. See also *Jewish* and *Catholic Encyclopedias*, s. v. Lucifer; Hagenbach, *Hist. of Doctrines*, I, p. 495; *Notes & Queries*, 3rd Ser. XII, pp. 110 f.

distinction is frequently made. Thus, O. E. *Genesis*, 343—5, says that God named the fallen leader Satan. That the change was from an earlier name, Lucifer, is elsewhere distinctly stated. For instance, we read in *Cursor Mundi*:

> "Þis was þe fend that formest felle
> For his pride from heuen to helle,
> For þenne his name chaunged was
> Fro lucifer to Sathanas."　　　(Trinity MS, 477—80.)

and in Chaucer's *Monkes Tale*:

> "O Lucifer, bryhtest of angels alle,
> Now artow Sathanas, that maist not twinne
> Out of miserie in which that thou art falle"
> 　　　　　　　　　　(*Cant. Tales*, B. 3194—6.)

Similarly in the *Canticum de Creatione* (Auchl. MS, 38) "Satanas is now his name", it is said, of the hell-sunken Liȝtbern; and in the York cycle, it is Lucifer who falls in the first pageant, but Satanas who takes the stage again as "Diabolus" in the fifth.[1])

Milton, consequently, is in the best medieval tradition when he indicates the Apostate Angel by the name Lucifer (VII, 130; X, 425) but also makes it clear that he is now to be called Satan:

> "Satan — so call him now; his former name
> Is heard no more in Heaven".　　　(V, 658—9.)

It must be observed, however, that in early references to the story of the Prime Devil, neither are Lucifer (or its medieval englishing, Lightber or Lightbern[2])) and Satan (or Satanas) the only names, even if we exclude appellations like Demon, Serpent, Dragon and the like, by which he is known, nor is Satan always the same fallen spirit as Lucifer. Thus in the prose *Lyff of Adam and Eue* the original name of Lucifer is said to have been Sachel:

> "Sachel was þe furste angel þat Crist made, and siþen he hihte
> Lucifer, þat þorw pruide was forloren."　　(*S. A. L.*, p. 220.)

---

[1]) In the Chester cycle, Lucifer, once fallen, is known as Demon. See I, 209; II, 161.

[2]) See *Poems of Wm. of Shoreham*, VII, 385; *Cant. de Creat.* (Auchl. MS), 8, 21; *Ayenbite of Inwit*, p. 16; *Gen. & Exod.*, 271; and Cushman, *The Devil and the Vice in the Eng. Dramatic Lit. before Shakespeare*, p. 18. Note, however, that in the *Chester 'Lucifer'*, Lightborne is not Lucifer, but a *Secundus Malus Angelus*.

This name for the proud Archangel, which does not, as far as I know, occur elsewhere in Early English literature, may be a corruption of *Zaqiel*, the name given in early Jewish angelology to one of the leaders of the Fallen Angels, or even of *Saraqael*, the name of one of the seven Archangels.[1]) But, then, neither of these names seems to have been employed in such writings for the Adversary, who is, at one time, Semjaza, at another Azazel, at a third Sammael.[2])

If the author of the *Lyff of Adam and Eue*, or his authority, drew upon rabbinical material for a new name for Lucifer, the author of the *Destruction of Troy*, Osbern Bokenam and Lydgate went no further than the Bible for other names not often expressly given to him. In the *Destr. of Troy* and in Bokenam's *Lives of Saints*, along with the common ones, Satan and Dragon, two less known "post-exilic" names are applied to Lucifer. On the strength, obviously of *Isaiah*, XXVII, 1, and *Job*, XL, XLI, and, in the Troy poem, avowedly of Isidore, the ruined Archangel is dubbed Leviathan and Behemoth. The passage in the *Destr. of Troy* runs:

> "Tis fende was the first þat felle for his pride,
> And lost has his lykyng, þat lyuyation is cald.
> And for the case is vnknowen be course to þe lewd,
> Here sumwhat I say, er I sew ferre.
> And ysidre in ethemoleger openly tellis, —
> þat bemoth in Ebrew ys opunly to say, —
> 'A Roid beste vnreasonable, þat no Rule holdes.'" (4422—28.)

And in Bokenam's *Lives* we read:

> "By the envye deceyvd of hys enmy,
> Clepyd serpent, behemoth or levyathan." (150—1).

The identification of the Prime Demon with Behemoth occurs also in at least one French medieval play — *Le Chevalier qui donna sa femme au Diable* —, but elsewhere Behemoth and Leviathan are regarded as two of the lieutenants of the Devil.[3])

---

[1]) See, e. g., Ethiopic *Enoch*, VI, 7; XX, 6.

[2]) See Ethiopic *Enoch*, VI, 1; LXIX, 2; X, 4—8; XIII, 1; LIV, 5; LV, 4; *3 Baruch*, IV, 8; *Martyrdom of Isaiah*, I, 8. In *Par. Lost*, I, 534, Azazel appears, but as the standard-bearer of Satan. Saurat (*Milton*, pp. 255 f.) rightly traces this back to the Ethiopic *Enoch*, VI—XI.

[3]) See Wieck, *Die Teufel auf der mittelalterlichen Mysterienbühne Frankreichs* (Leipzig, 1887), pp. 8, 11. In *Par. Lost*, I, 200 ff., the fallen Archangel, "prone on the flood", is compared to:

For his part, Lydgate, in *The Pilgrimage of the Life of Man*, renders *Revelation*, VIII, 10, 11, and declares that the "star" that fell was "Absinth":

> "And Abisinthium men hym calle,
> Be cause he doth sygnefye,
> Thorgh hys pryde and ffals envye,
> The bryhte aungel that ffel so ffer, —
> I mene the Aungel Lucyffer —
> ffro the heuene into dyrknesse;
> And he hath ek mor bytternesse
> Than any woormood growyng here." (12574—81).

But that Lucifer should have several names in medieval times[1]) is not as remarkable as that he should be differentiated from Satan as a leader from his lieutenant. We find this done sometimes in the French Mysteries — witness *Viel Testament*, 444, Ereban's *Passion*, 648 ff. — and in medieval Cornish drama — witness *Origo Mundi*, 541; *Passion*, 3037; *Resurrection*, 2307. But, because of the distinction made in the *Gospel of Nicodemus*, XV ff., between Satan, the prince of death, and *Inferus*, the prince of hell[2]), it is observable also in the Harrowing of Hell scenes in the *York* and *Towneley* cycles and, outside the drama, in *Cursor Mundi*, *Piers Plowman* and *The Deuelis Perlament*.[3])

But to return to the name Lucifer, it was agreed by all that Lucifer was so called because of his extreme beauty. "Dictus est autem Lucifer", says Bonaventura (*Compend.* II, 28), "quia prae ceteris luxit." Lines 441, 442 of *Cursor Mundi*, read almost like a translation of this, and (to pick only one out of a multitude of possible passages) the Cherubim in the *Towneley 'Creation'* exclaim:

> "that sea-beast
> Leviathan, which God of all his works
> Created hugest that swim the ocean-stream."

---

[1]) Belzebub is a name for Satan in some of the French Mysteries; see Wieck, *op. cit.*, pp. 11, 12; cf. *Matthew*, XII, 24 ff.; *Gospel of Nicodemus*, XVIII, 14; *O. E. Homilies*, I, p. 55. Zabulon in *Lud. Cov. 'Radix Jesse'*, 6, is the "devyll of helle" and so this is perhaps another nonce name for the demonised Archangel. This name, applied to a devil, occurs also in the French *Passion* of Jean Michel.

[2]) Cf. *Gospel of Bartholomew* (James), p. 168.

[3]) If ll. 245 ff. of *The Deuelis Perlament* suggest that Lucifer is not Satan, ll. 393 ff. suggest that he is.

> "We loue the, lord, bright ar we,
> bot none of vs so bright as he;
> He may well hight lucifere,
> ffor lufly light that he doth bere." (ll. 69—72).

In like manner, Raphael, in *Par. Lost*, calls the fallen Rebel Lucifer, because he was

> "brighter once admist the host
> Of Angels than that star tha stars among."[1]) (VII, 131—2.)

It was agreed too in a general way by Milton and his medieval predecessors that Lucifer's shining beauty was damaged by his fall. But there is nevertheless a difference to be noted between the frank acceptance of this view by the medieval mind and the artistic use made of it by Milton. In the medieval handling of the legend Lucifer's beauty is always regarded as totally and immediately destroyed at his expulsion from Heaven, so that the most lustrous of the heavenly ones, equally with his followers, is suddenly translated into a fiend fearful and black; see, e. g., *O. E. Genesis*, 68 ff., 304 ff.; *O. E. Homilies*, I, p. 219; *Christ and Satan*, 68 ff.; *York 'Lucifer'*, 99—101; *Towneley 'Creation'*, 136 ff.; *Chester 'Lucifer'*, 229 ff.; *Lud. Cov. 'Lucifer'*, 77 f.; *Genesis & Exodus*, 283 ff.; *Piers Plowman*, B I, 113 ff.; *Adrian and Epotys*, 388. In *Par. Lost*, on the other hand, Satan's beauty, and his powers generally, suffer but gradual diminution. Immediately after the Fall he is darkened, but is none the less Archangelic:

> "His form had yet not lost
> All her original brightness" (I, 591, 592).

It is not till after he has wrought the fall of man that he is metamorphosed into

> "A monstrous serpent on his belly prone" —

the Dragon of the Apocalypse and the horrid Demon of popular imagination.

The Light-bearer's slow declension from archangelic splendour was artistically inevitable in Milton's epic scheme. The protagonist of *Par. Lost* could not have been successfully introduced into the poem as a fiend already in the lowest depths of degradation. But there was nothing in epic tradition

---

[1]) Cf. *Macbeth*, IV, iii, 22: "Angels are bright still, though the brightest fell."

to prevent the poet from following the current conception of Lucifer's pristine power and definitely regarding him as having fallen, not merely from his high — indeed very high — archangelic estate, but from the absolutely highest. And yet Milton somehow hesitates to so regard him. He is apparently uncertain whether he should give Lucifer clear pre-eminence in heavenly place and power, no less than in beauty. The most that may be said is that he is inclined to do so. Satan's scornful retort to the questioning guards may mean very much:

> "Know ye not me? Ye knew me once no mate
> For you, there sitting where ye durst not soar!
> Not to know me argues yourself unknown,
> The lowest of your throng." (IV, 828—31).

So also may Raphael's testimony to his influence and power:

> "Great indeed
> His name, and high was his degree in heaven."
>
> (V, 706, 707).

But when we look for anything more definite, all we discover is that Lucifer was not inferior in Heaven to Michael and Uriel and Raphael:

> "He of the first,
> If not the first Archangel, great in power,
> In favour and preeminence." (V, 659—61).

But neither the Renascence nor the medieval writers on the subject seem to have had any doubts about Lucifer's absolute pre-eminence among all created beings. Doubtless there are references to Lucifer in which the exact determination of his place in the angelic army is ignored, but whenever the question has been considered the verdict has been given loud and bold: Lucifer is then clearly the first-created or the first-placed in honour and glory, or both. Heywood, in his *Hierarchie*, emphasizes Lucifer's priority in birth and "super-eminence" and unequivocally asserts that though Michael and Gabriel and Raphael are great,

> "Yet aboue these was Lucifer instated,
> Honour'd, exalted, and much celebrated." (p. 337.)

The *Faust Book*, too, has it that Lucifer

> "was so of God ordained for shape, pomp glory, authority, worthiness and dwelling, that he far exceeded all the other creatures of God."
>
> (Thoms, *English Prose Romances*, III, p. 187).

Of similarly emphatic medieval statements of Lucifer's supremacy among the angelic hosts we may content ourselves with recalling some seven — O. E. *Genesis*, 252 ff.; *York 'Lucifer'*, 33 ff.; *Towneley 'Creation'*, 139 ff.; Jordan's *Creation*, p. 5; *Viel Test.*, 65 ff.; *Lyff of Adam and Eue*, p. 220; and *Destruction of Troy*, 4401 ff.[1] — and quoting one:

> "Bot þe angel he wroght formast
> Of all he gaf an pouste mast;
> For þof þai all war fair and wis,
> And sum of less and sum mare pris,
> He gaf an mast of all sele
> If he cuth hafe born it wele,
> And sette him heist in his hall,
> Als prince and sire ouer oþer all;
> And for þat he was fair and bright
> Lucifer to nam he hight."

(Cursor Mundi, 433—442.)

Had not Gregory the Great in his *Moralia*, XXXII, c. 23, observed, "Prima et nobilior creatura fuit angelus qui cecidit."?[2]

Of the names and identities of the other Angels, good or bad, there is next to no mention in Early English accounts of the angelic revolt. In only one of the four extant Lucifer scenes in the English Mystery Cycles is even a single one of them sought to be identified. This is in the *Chester 'Lucifer'*, where a mistakenly-conceived Lightborne is indicated as siding actively with the Arch Rebel. Apart from this solitary attempt at particularization, it is just Angelus Malus or Angelus Bonus or Secundus Angelus Deficiens, or the like. In fact, in medieval versions, dramatic or non-dramatic, of the legend, Lucifer bestrides the world of Angels so like a Colossus that he monopolizes the author's attention. To my knowledge the only other celestial spirit who figures individualized in M. E. accounts of the Fall is Michael, and he too, in spite of *Revelation*, XII, 7, is a rare occurrence. The only medieval

---

[1] In the E. E. T. S. Edition of the *Destr. of Troy*, ll. 4401, 4402:
> "But on the oddist of other ordant our lord,
> Brightest of bemes in blisse for to dwelle" —

are marginally explained as referring to Christ. But the subsequent reference to *Isaiah*, XIV, 13 and *Ezekiel*, XXXI, 8, 9, shows that *lord* is the subject (not the object) of *ordant* and that *Brightest of bemes* is in apposition to *on* (and not to *lord*) and refers to Lucifer.

[2] See James, *The Apocryphal New Testament*, pp. 119, 175, 178.

English versions of the Fall I have so far found him in are
Cursor Mundi, 469 ff., and, in the role of persuader rather
than of pursuer, in the prose *Lyff of Adam and Eue*, p. 221.

To find mention of other angelic personalities we must
either wander outside Old and Middle English references to
the Fall or turn to accounts of it in other languages. Thus,
in the Lucifer episode in the Cornish *Creation* of Jordan,
Michael and Gabriel are particularized, while in corresponding
scenes elsewhere — as for example in the French *Viel Testament*
and the German Creation play performed at Freiberg in the
fifteenth century[1]) — a third angel, Raphael, also appears.
But in Early English literature we must look for the emergence
of Gabriel and Raphael, not in stories of the angelic revolt,
but in other connections, as in the *Lyff of Adam and Eue*
version of the creation of Man, where Michael, Gabriel, Raphael
and Uriel are commissioned to find a name for man. (*S. A. L.*
p. 221.)

I have so far, it will be noticed, said nothing of the
names that were given to the wicked Angels after they had
fallen and were metamorphosed into Demons. Here, again, of
Old and Middle English versions of the legend the *Chester
'Lucifer'* is the only one known to me which specifies even
a single subordinate demon, and then he is naively enough
called merely Ruffian (l. 239). For denominated demons too
we must either move outside Early accounts of the legend in
English or go to those in other literatures. The French *Viel
Testament* alone, in its dramatization of the legend, specifies
seven of the Arch Demon's followers, — *Sathan, Astoreth,
Cerberus, Mammon, Asmodeus, Leviatan*, and *Aggrapart*. We
do find a good many named demons in M. E. writings, but
they figure in other contexts. Thus Beelzebub and Belial appear
in the *Ludus Coventriae 'Temptation of Christ'*; Tutivillus plays
a considerable part in the *Towneley 'Judgment'*; Belial, Astrot
Anaball, Bell, Berith[2]), and the more homely Ragamuffin,
Coltyng, Goblin, and Ribald[3]) occur in the Harrowing of Hell

---

[1]) See Rothschild's *Viel Testament*, Vol. I, pp. xlvii f.

[2]) Perhaps we should read *Bellberith* (Towneley) or *Beleberit* (York)
as sometimes in the French Mysteries. See Wieck, *Die Teufel*, p. 8. For
Berith, however, see James, *Apocryphal N. T.*, p. 468.

[3]) Cf. Belcher in Marlowe's *Dr. Faustus*, sc. iv.

episode in *Piers Plowman* and in the *York* and *Towneley* cycles. And if we look beyond both the legend and Early English we discover that the number of identified Devils in French medieval drama alone is legion. For, the Bible, the Apocrypha, Greek and Roman mythology, history, personal fancy, all furnish the French playwrights with their Devils.[1]

Milton too uses Biblical, Apocryphal, mythological and fanciful names for his Demons, and, what is more, he draws upon fancy as well as upon sacred writings for his Angels too. Consequently, his parade of Angels and Demons, in *Par. Lost*, exceeds by far that of any medieval English or French work. Specific mention is made in Milton's epic of no fewer than nine Angels, — Michael, Gabriel, Raphael, Uriel, Uzziel, Ithuriel, Zephon, Abdiel and Zophiel. When I speak here of nine Angels, it will be seen that I refer to the faithful ones only. For, of the names of the others, says Milton,

"in Heavenly records
Be no memorial, blotted out and rased
By their rebellion from the Books of Life." (I, 361—3).

However, later as Demons these fallen spirits got new names on earth, when they misled men into adoring them for deities and, generally inveigled them into idolatory:

"Then were they known to men by various names,
And various idols through the heathen world." (I, 374 f.)

In thus identifying the deities of heathendom with the degraded Angels, Milton was only adopting a very common theological notion. We may compare *Deuteronomy*, XXXII, 17; *Psalm* CV, 37; *Baruch*, IV, 7; Ethiopic *Enoch*, XIX, 1, XCIX, 7; Jerome, *Contra Vigilantium*, X; and Tertullian, *De Idol.*, IV.[2]) Of medieval expressions of the belief I may draw attention to the long passage in the *Destr. of Troy* (4280—4394), which,

---

[1]) See Wieck, *Die Teufel*, pp. 7—11.

[2]) See also Hooker's *Ecclesiastical Polity*, Bk. I, c. iv, 3:
"These wicked spirits [i. e. the Fallen Angels] the heathens honoured instead of gods, both generally under the name of *dii inferi*, 'gods infernal'; and particularly, some in oracles, some in idols, some as household gods, some as nymphs: in a word, no foul and wicked spirit, which was not one way or other honoured of men as God, till such time as light appeared in the world and dissolved the works of the Devil."

by reference to the worship among heathens of Baal and the gods of the Greek Pantheon, illustrates how

> "ffor lacke of beleue þai light into errour,
> And fellen vnto fals goddes, & faithly honourt
> With worship on all wise as weghis vppon lyue;
> Þat no pouer hade plainly but of pale fyndes
> Þat entrid into ymagis euer for dissayet,
> Spekand to specyals, þat spede for to aske,
> Thurgh falshede of fyndes þe folke to dissayue,
> And to ert hom in errour euermore to lenge."[1] (4287—94)

Of the names so acquired by the Demons Milton cites many in *Par. Lost*.[2]) Several of them can be paralleled in medieval, particularly French, literature: Beelzebub (I, 79 — M. E. *passim*), Moloch (I, 392 — *La Passion par Jean Michel*), Baalim (I, 422 — *La Passion par Arnoul Greban*), Astoreth (I, 438 — *Piers Plow., Viel Test.*), Isis, Jove (I, 478, 514 — *Destr. of Troy* [?ysum, Jubiter]), Belial (I, 490 — M. E. *passim*), Mammon, Asmodeus (I, 678, VI, 365 — *Viel Test.*).

The rest, — Chemos (I, 406), Thamuz (I, 446), Dagon[3]) (I, 462), Rimmon (I, 467), Osiris, Orus (I, 478), Titan (I, 510), Saturn (I, 512), Azazel (I, 534), Andramelech (VI, 365), Ariel (VI, 371), Arioch, Ramiel (VI, 372), and Nisroch (VI, 447) — I have yet to find in medieval writings.[4])

IV. The Rebellion.

We may at the very outset put aside that view of the Fall of the Angels which maintained that their apostasy consisted in leaving their high heavenly estate to mate with the daughters of men. This view was based on the interpretation of *"filii Dei"* in *Genesis*, VI, 2 as the Angels of God, an inter-

---

[1]) According to Burton's *Anatomy of Melancholy*, I, 2, i, 2, the false gods of the Gentiles constitute only the first of the nine orders into which, in Pseudo-Dionysian style, the bad spirits are divided by Schoolmen and Divines. Cf. also Heywood, *Hierarchie* p. 436.

[2]) Cf. also the *Nativity Ode*, 173—228.

[3]) Dagon, Bel, Astertes, Baal, Isis, Osiris, are mentioned in Burton's *Anatomy*, I, 2, i 2, as "terrestrial devils", while Arioch occurs in Nash's *Pierce Penilesse* as the spirit of revenge.

[4]) Although I include Azazel and Ramiel among the Demon-names, they should perhaps be regarded as true Angel-names; at least, they occur as such in the Ethiopic *Enoch*, VI, 7, among the names of the angels who fell.

pretation suggested by the Septuagint reading ἄγγελοι τοῦ Θεοῦ, accepted unquestioningly in Hebrew apocrypha and pseudepigrapha, and adhered to, among the Fathers, by Philo, Clement of Alexandria, Tertullian, Eusebius, Ambrose and others. That the interpretation was, however, a proper one Chrysostum, Cyril of Alexandria and Augustine denied, and Philostrius even went so far as to number it among the heresies.[1]

Not lasciviousness and intemperance, but pride — less commonly pride coupled with envy — was in the popular medieval conception the cause of the Fall of Lucifer. Pride is indicated as the cause in *Isaiah*, XIV, 12—14 and *Ezekiel*, XXVIII, 7[2]), and emphasized by the Fathers. „Inflatio, superbia, arrogantia,“ says Origen (*Homil. in Ezek.*, IX, 2), „peccatum diaboli est, et ob haec delicta ad terras migravit de coelo.“ Augustine (*De Civ. Dei*, XII, c. 6) and Eusebius (*Demonstr. Evang.*, IV, 9), too, attribute the apostasy to pride, while others, like Gregory Nazianzen (*Orat.*, XXXVI, 5) and Cassian (*Collat.*, VIII, 6), add envy as a further cause.

About Lucifer's pride at least the medieval handlers of the legend had no doubt. Almost every Old and Middle English reference to his downfall expressly states that it was brought about by his pride.[3]) Indeed, in the Lambeth MS *Mirror of the Periods of Man's Life*, Pride is identified with Lucifer:

> "'Bi waar', quod Meekenes, 'how pride doop wys';
> He ȝeueþ but woo & wyssche to wage;
> Of aungelis bewte þe prijs was his,
> In heuene on þe hiȝest stage;
> He wolde haue peerid with god of blis
> Now is he in helle moost loopeli page." (137—142)

---

[1]) See Hagenbach, *Hist. of Doctrines*, I, p. 348. Milton rejects the old interpretation in *Par. Lost*, XI, 620 ff., but avails himself of it in *Par. Lost*, V, 446—8, and *Par. Regained*, II, 178—181.

[2]) Cf. also *1. Timothy*, III, 6.

[3]) See, e. g., O. E. *Genesis*, 22 ff., 261 ff.; *Christ and Satan*, 50 ff.; *Salomon and Saturn*, 450; *O. E. Homilies*, I, p. 219; *Gen. & Exod.*, 65 ff.; *Lyff of Ad. & Eue*, pp. 220 f.; *Cant. de Creat.*, 14; *Adrian & Epotys* 383 ff.; *Fall and Passion*, 17; *Piers Plow.*, B I, 125; *Destr. of Troy*, 4409; *Curs. Mundi*, 448, 465, 478; *Pricke of Consc.*, 378; *Conf. Amantis*, I, 3297 ff.; VIII, 22 f.; *York*, I, 49 ff.; II, 5; *Towneley*, I, 152; *Lud. Cov.*, I, 66; *Chester*, I, 113, 145 ff.; *Castell of Persev.*, 2096 f.; *Pilgrimage of Man*, 12576 ff.

Moreover, it is frequently declared that it was the consciousness of his surpassing beauty which inflated him with pride. Thus, it is said of the Rebel Angel of the *Later Genesis* that he

> "cwæð, þæt his lic wære leoht and scene,
> hwit and hiowbeorht. Ne meahte he æt his hige findan,
> þæt he Gode wolde geongerdome
> þeodne þeowian." (265—268.)

And similarly the Lucifers of the medieval Mysteries cannot away with their beauty (see *York*, I, 49 ff.; *Towneley*, I, 77 ff.; *Chester*, I, 105 ff.), nor, indeed, can their counterparts in such diverse pieces as the O. E. *Christ and Satan* (58 ff.), the didactic *Cleanness* (209 f.), and the romantic *Destr. of Troy* (4409). Does not Bonaventura, in a passage already partly quoted, say: "Dictus est autem Lucifer, quia prae ceteris luxit, suaeque pulchritudinis consideratio eum excaecavit"? Indeed, did not the lamentation on the fallen King of Tyre contain the verse, "Et elevatum est cor tuum in decore tuo; perdidisti sapientiam tuam in decore tuo" (*Ezekiel*, XXVIII, 17)?

But, as I have hinted already, the Adversary of God was according to some, impelled by envy as well as by pride. In the curious opening lines of the fifth *York* play, he is represented as unable to endure the thought of Man's being made in the image of God. For, though it is as a fallen Satanas that the speaker is introduced, he is, it appears, referring to a time before his fall and to Man as yet only contemplated, not made.

> "For woo my witte es in a were,
> That moffes me mykill in my mynde,
> The godhede þat I sawe so cleere,
>   And parsayued þat he shuld take kynde,
>   of a degree
> That he had wrought, and I denyed þat aungell kynde
>   shuld it noȝt be;[1])
> And we were faire and bright,
>   þerfore me thoght þat he

---

[1]) So Miss Toulmin Smith in her Edition of the Cycle, but perhaps these lines should be read thus:

> "That he had wrought, and I dedyned
>   þat aungell kynde shuld it noȝt be."

See my note on these lines in *Mod. Lang. Review*, XXI, p. 427.

> The kynde of vs tane myght,
> And þer-at dedeyned me.

> The kynde of man he thoght to take,
> And theratt hadde I grete envye,
> But he has made to hym a make,
> And harde to her I wol me hye."[1]) (1—15.)

These lines — if indeed I interpret them aright — would seem, when taken along with the version of the angelic rebellion in Play I, to make both pride and envy the cause of the rebellion. But a less doubtful instance of the combination is furnished by the Lucifer scene in the Cornish *Creation* of Jordan. Here Lucifer at first rebels out of sheer presumption but adds to it the sin of envy when God threatens to hurl him out of Heaven and fill his room with Man. He exclaims:

> „Wouldst thou that the Son of man,
> When he is made of filthy slime,
> Should possess for a stayne
> My room, that can find no peer
> > Here in heaven?

> This would be a vile thing;
> A man, which thou wilt make of clay,
> To come here into my place,
> Who am full of glory;
> > For this worthy not is he." (p. 21.)

In both these dramatic pieces it is of man unmade that Lucifer, as yet unfallen, is represented as becoming jealous, but it is of man already made that he is shown as being envious and so losing his heavenly abode, in the *Canticum de Creatione* and the parallel prose *Lyff of Adam and Eue*.

> "And þo Liʒtbern hade seyd so,
> Mani þousend angels and mo
> Sayd: þai nold in no manere
> Anour Adam no Eue, his fere.
> Þus in heuen pride bigan
> While god in erþe made man."
> > (*Cant. de Creat.*, Auchinl. MS., 21—26).

---

[1]) Were it not for the last two lines, we should be certain that Satan is referring to the envy of the Angels at a revelation of the Incarnation. (See *Catholic Encyclopedia* under 'Devil'.) As it is, however, there seems to be an identification of Adam with the Son of God, as in certain Jewish writings. (See Bousset, *Die Religion des Judentums im neutestamentlichen Zeitalter*, p. 558.)

Such accounts of the Fall of the Angels may be traced at least as far back as the apocryphal Latin *Vita Adae et Evae*, in which in Chapters XII—XVI the Devil relates to Adam the story of how, when Adam was made, he, conscious of his angelic nature, refused to worship one so inferior to himself, though urged by Michael and commanded by God, and how consequently he and his followers were expelled from Heaven.

It was evidently with such a version of the angelic revolt in view that Cyprian, in his *De Dono Patient.*, declared:

"Diabolus hominem ad imaginem Dei factum impatientur tulit; inde et periit primus et perdidit."[1])

Augustine, however, challenges such a doctrine.

"Nonnulli enim dicunt" (he writes in *De Gen. ad Litt.*, XI, c. 14) ipsum ei fuisse casum a supernis sedibus, quod inviderit homini facto ad imaginem Dei. Porro autem invidia sequitur superbiam, non præcedit; non enim causa superbiendi est invidia sed causa invidendi superbia."

And he concludes that Satan's pride caused his fall and thereafter he envied Man. Accordingly, in most M. E. references to Satan's envy of Man, that envy is regarded, not as the cause of his fall, but rather as the sequel to it. As Lydgate Milton-wise allegorizes it in his *Pilgrimage of Man*, Pride, the daughter of Lucifer, brought about his fall, and Envy was born later of the incestuous relation between Pride and her parent (14029 ff.; 14826 ff.).[2]) Of course, most commonly this envy is begotten in Satan at the Creation of Man — see, e. g., O. E. *Genesis*, 364 ff. and *Towneley 'Creation'*, 260 ff., the first two references that come to mind — but a curious instance, in which the Fallen Archangel envies the yet unmade race of Man, deserves separate mention. This occurs in the *Chester 'Lucifer'*, where Primus Demon is made to vow:

"And therefore I shall for his sake
showe mankind great Envie;

---

[1]) Cf. also *Gospel of Bartholomew*, IV, 52 ff., and *The Koran*, VII, 10 ff. XX, 115.

[2]) It is obvious from this that there is no need to go to the *Zohar* as Saurat does (*Milton*, pp. 284, 285), to explain "the repulsive idea of incest" in Milton's allegory of Sin and Death. If Lydgate can fable thus, surely a Milton, especially when he has *James* I, 15 before him, may be relied upon to do at least as much.

> as sone as ever he can him make,
> I shall send him for to destroye." (233—236.)

So much about pride, coupled occasionally with envy of Man, as the cause in medieval legends of Lucifer's revolt. Let us now consider the form which, in those legends, that revolt takes.

The general nature of the revolt had been determined once for all by *Isai.*, XIV, 13, 14:

> "In coelum conscendam, super astra Dei exaltabo solium meum: sedebo in monte Testamenti in lateribus Aquilonis; (14) Ascendam super altitudinem nubium, similis ero Altissimo."

These words were the starting-point of the tradition that the Apostate Angel left his place and coveted God's throne. The Slavonic *Secrets*, XXIX, 4, took it up, and *Jude* 6, and Avitus (*De Orig. Peccato*) and Bede (*Hexameron*, Lib. I), and all the rest of them. And references to it in Early English literature abound; see, e. g., *Chr. and Saturn*, 187 f.; *Sal. and Sat.*, 452 f.; *Cleanness*, 211 ff.; *York*, I, 87 ff.; *Towneley*, I, 99 ff.; *Chester*, I, 109 ff.; *Lud. Cov.*, I, 56 ff. In the three last-named pieces it will be further observed that Lucifer does more than aspire to God's throne; he, dramatically enough, occupies it during the absence of his Master. But in the *Deuelis Perlament*, most curiously of all, the divine seat is given for a while by the Almighty Himself to Lucifer, whose sin consisted in thenceforth deeming himself as worthy of it as the Ruler of Heaven:

> "I took þe my seete ful stille,
> It to ȝeme þou were ful prest;
> And while y wente where me list,
> And come aȝen a-noon in hiȝe,
> Þou seidist þat þou were worþiest,
> And to sitte þere as weel as y." (339—344.)

Isaiah's specific mention of the North as the region in which Lucifer desired to establish his kingdom is often passed over unnoticed; thus, none of the medieval Mysteries just mentioned takes cognizance of it. Nevertheless there are medieval writings, both dramatic and non-dramatic, which reproduce this particular of the Isaiahian lament. Of such are O. E. *Genesis*, 32 ff., 275 ff.; *Gen. & Exod.*, 277 ff.; *Poems of Wm. of Shoreham*, VII, 385; *Curs. Mundi*, 457 ff.; *Piers Plow.*, B I, 117 f., C II, 112 ff.; *Destr. of Troy* 4410 ff.; and the French Mysteries of the Passion and the Nativity.

16*

If we now cross over to Milton we shall notice that while he too draws upon the popular Isaiahian version of the nature of Lucifer's rebellion, he blends with it the version of *Apoc.*, XII, 7 ("Et factum est proelium magnum in coelo") and, moreover, adds many subtle touches of his own for the sake of greater realism and effect. Thus, Lucifer's purpose is

> "With all his legions to dislodge and leave
> Unworshipped, unobeyed, the throne supreme,
> Contemptuous." (V, 669—671.)

And to that end he marches northwards with all his host. But observe that in *Par. Lost* the North is regarded as the home and peculiar region of Lucifer. Accordingly, he sends word to his followers to haste

> "Homeward with flying march, where we possess
> The quarters of the North;" (V, 688, 689.)

and thus they all come to the limits of the North,

> "and Satan to his royal seat
> High on a hill, far-blazing, as a mount
> Raised on a mount." (V, 756—758.)

It is sometimes said that Milton, in placing Satan's domicile in the North, is shrewdly girding at his pet aversion, at Presbyterianism, which had its headquarters in Scotland. But though, as Langland says in *Piers Plow.*, C II, 112 ff., northmen may feel offended, the fact is that the North has, from ancient times, been associated in Oriental and in Teutonic folk-lore with physical and moral darkness. In Norse mythology Niflheimr, the dreary abode of Hela, is a cold misty region beyond the northern ocean[1]), and ancient Talmudic tradition held that the North was the region of the demons, just as the East was God's, the South the Angels', and the West Man's. Consequently Beelzebub, in the *Faust Book*, and Asmenoth, in Greene's *Friar Bacon*, xi, 109, are rulers of the North, while the fiend in Chaucer's *Freres Tale*, 115, declares that his home is "fer in the north contree", and Shakespeare speaks of evil spirits as being "under the lordly monarch of the North" (*1. Hen VI*, V, iii, 6). Likewise the author of *Oure Ladyes Myroure* in his exposition of the Latin hymn, *Celestis erat Curia*, writes:

---

[1]) Cf. "niðr ok norðr liggr Helveger" in the Icelandic *Gylfaginning* (cited by Skeat in the Clarendon Press *Piers Plow.*, Vol. II, p. 26).

"Fyrste ye shall understande that the northe wynde ys colde and bytyng, and maketh fayre flowres som tyme to fade. And therfore by the northe ys understoded the fende lucyfer, that by coldenesse of hys malyse caused other anngels that are lykened to fayre flowres to falle from blysse."[1] (p. 189.)

But not content with holding the North, Milton's Prime Rebel further contemplates open war with the Lord of Heaven. A foe is rising, the Almighty warns His Son,

> "who intends to erect his throne
> Equal to ours, throughout the spacious North,
> Nor so content, hath in his thought to try
> In battle what our power is, or our right." (V, 725—728.)

The Battle of the Angels that ensued occupies Raphael's attention throughout Book VI. I must hasten to add that a "proelium magnum" is not always absent in earlier writings. In both the texts, A and B, of the O. E. *Genesis*, the revolt is conceived as taking the form of an armed mutiny. It is obvious, however, that the inspiration for this came, not from *Revelation*, but from the conditions of contemporary life, which necessarily imposed an atmosphere of Teutonic feudalism upon these poems. Accordingly, in them, God is the Overlord and dispenser of treasure, the Angels are his thanes, and some of these stout-hearted heroes break allegiance and thirst for battle. But the same cannot be said about the mutiny in the Cornish *Creation*. The author of this play has undoubtedly the Apocalypse in mind when he makes Lucifer offer battle against the powers of God. "I and my company", declares the Rebel,

> "By the sword will dispute it,
> That I am more worthy." (p. 25.)

It is when we come to examine Milton's reasons for the mutiny in Heaven that we discover that he has elected to stray wide from the most commonly accepted medieval notions on the point. It is true Milton's Lucifer, no less than the one of popular tradition, is filled full with overweening pride and ambition:

> "Lifted up so high,
> Disdained subjection, and thought one step higher
> Would set me highest." (IV, 49—51.)

---

[1] Cf. also *Jeremiah*, I, 14, and see Verity's note to *P. L.*, V, 688, 689.

We read in Book I, as clearly as anywhere else, that

> "his pride
> Had cast him out from Heaven, with all his host
> Of rebel Angels, by whose aid, aspiring
> To set himself in glory above his peers,
> He trusted to have equalled the Most High,
> If he opposed and, with ambitious aim,
> Against the throne and monarchy of God
> Raised impious war in Heaven and battle proud
> With vain attempt." (I, 36—44.)

It is true also that the Rebel's pride stirs up envy in his heart. But it is not envy of Man, made or to be made, that he nurses in his angelic bosom; such envy is aroused in him only after his fall: see, e. g., I, 650 ff.; II, 345 ff. His envy, while he is still unfallen, is directed against the Son of God, and here it is that Milton parts company with the majority of his medieval forerunners in the handling of the legend. In the medieval writings, that we have so far considered, either it is the making of Man that acts as the spur to Satan's self-esteem and rouses envy within him or, more commonly, it is just a vain consciousness of his unparalleled power and beauty that urges him to proud revolt. But in *Par. Lost* the outburst of pride and envy in him is occasioned by the creation of a Divine Vicegerent superior to himself. Lucifer cannot brook the thought of the Son of God being placed above the angelic host and, hence, he seeks redress in mutiny:

> "He of the first,
> If not the first Archangel, great in power,
> In favour and pre-eminence, yet fraught
> With envy against the Son of God, that day
> Honoured by his great Father, and proclaimed
> Messiah, King Annointed, could not bear,
> Through pride that sight, and thought himself impaired."
> (V, 659—665.)

I have said already that Milton's Arianism, coupled with a desire to make the action of *Par. Lost* no less than that of *Par. Regained* centre round the person of Christ, may have been responsible for his view of the creation of the Angels. It may be responsible also for his choosing to adopt this particular view of their revolt. However, that Milton, as I say, merely adopted one of several views on the question is evident from a passage in Reginald Scot's *Discourse of*

Divels, where, after pointing out how the Schoolmen "differ much in the cause of Lucifer's fall", the author mentions, as one of the beliefs, that Lucifer's "condemnation grew here-upon, for that he challenged the place of the Messias."[1]) If Milton, then, did not create the legend, neither, it seems, was he the first English writer to employ it. He had been anti-cipated long ago by the poet of the Junian MS *Christ and Satan*, a poem with which was possibly familiar. In this poem, if nowhere else in Early English versions of the angelic revolt, does the revolt appear to have been inspired by envy of the Messiah. For, though here (as in so many other Early English texts) the Father and the Son, the Shaper of the World and the Saviour of it, are not always kept distinct, yet we have reason to believe that when the Rebel Angel is said to have challenged "wuldres leoman, bearn helendes" (ll. 85, 86), or "sunu meotodes" (l. 173), the poet has said exactly what he meant. For, when the fallen angels complain:

> "Seʒdest us to soðe þæt ðin sunu wære
> meotod moncynnes,"[2])   (63, 64)

it is obvious that this son of Lucifer was run by him as a rival, not to God Himself, but to the Son of God.

V. The Expulsion.

Under this head we shall consider (a) The Manner of Expulsion, (b) The Number of the Fallen, (c) The Date of the Fall, (d) The Duration of the Fall, and (e) The New Abode.

(a) *The Manner of the Expulsion.* — Few medieval accounts regard the war-version of *Revelation*, XII, 7 ff., in which Michael and his Angels are presented as battling with, and ultimately overthrowing, the Dragon and his host.[3]) Milton makes use of it, but puts an unusual and unorthodox interpretation on it. In *Par. Lost*, Michael, indeed, assisted by all his Angels including Gabriel, fights with the Rebel Army, but he is

---

[1]) Nicholson's *Edition*, p. 423. See also *Catholic Encycl.*, s. v. *Devil* and Saurat, *Milton*, p. 262. This view is apparently based on *Heb.* I, 6.

[2]) A reference to Lucifer's "ofspringe" occurs also in the *Chester* 'Lucifer', 129—32.

[3]) Michael's being entrusted with the task of punishing the leader of the apostates can be traced back to earlier apocryphal tradition; see, e. g. the Ethiopic *Enoch*, X, 11—16.

unable to vanquish it. That is reserved for Christ to do. The
battle of the Angels rages for two days and is still undecided
when on the third day Christ, single-handed, overawes the Sons
of Darkness and roots them out of Heaven. A suggestion for
this glorification of Christ may have been got from *Revel.* XII, 11;
in any case that it is Milton's private conviction, and not
merely a matter of epic expediency, is obvious from the following passage in the ninth chapter of his *Christian Doctrine*:

> "It is generally thought that Michael is Christ. But Christ vanquished
> the devil, and trampled him under foot singly; Michael, the leader
> of the angels is introduced in the capacity of a hostile commander
> waging war with the prince of the devils, the armies on both sides
> being drawn out in battle array, and separating after a doubtful
> conflict." (*P. W.*, IV, p. 216, 217).

As for the Miltonic conception of the war in Heaven lasting
for three days, it may be compared with the opinion of those
medieval Schoolmen who held, as Scot expresses it in his *Discourse*, that

> "it stood with God's justice to give them three warnings; so as at
> the third warning Lucifer fell down like led to the bottom of hell."
> (p. 423.)

In none of the versions of the legend in M. E. literature,
so far as my knowledge of it goes, is there any indication of
either the three warnings, or a three days' fight, or the
Messiah's intervention in the conflict. In such an elaborate
narrative account as the one in *Curs. Mundi* we find at most
a plain straight-forward rendering of *Revel.*, XII, 7, 8:

> "Sent micheal, for þare aller right,
> Rais a-gain him for to fight,
> Again him gaf a batell grim,
> Out of þat hei curt kest him;
> Lucifer first dune he broght,
> And sithen þat till him helded oght,
> And schurd þat curt o þam sa clene,
> Þat sithen þar sted was neuer sene." (p. 469—476.)

So likewise in the French *Viel Test.*, 416 ff., Michael is commissioned by the Almighty to eject the rebels, which he does
without much ado. An amplification of these versions occurs
however in the Cornish *Creation*, where Gabriel too is definitely
represented as playing a leading part in the enemy's over-
throw. He is made to rally the powers of Goodness; thus:

> "Let us work, all that are in Heaven,
> Let us go chase him away
>   To Hell, to darkness;
> And you and all his company,
> Come you along also with him;
>   Beat him with your swords."
>   (p. 25.)

In the O. E. *Genesis* (*A* and *B*), too, the expulsion of the rebels takes the form of a battle, but, as has been said already, the picture presented is purely Teutonic and, consequently, no Michael from the apocalypse figures in the struggle. At the same time it is remarkable that at least in *Genesis B*, though we are prepared for a great battle by the words of Satan:

> "Bigstandað me strange geneatas; þa ne willað me æt þam striðe geswican
> hæleþas heardmöde; hīe habbað mē tō hearran gecorene,
> rofe rincas;"   (284—286.)

yet that there was actual fighting is revealed only parenthetically and retrospectively by the words:

> "Lāgon þā ōðre fȳnd on þām fȳre, þe āer swā feala hæfdon
> gewinnes wið heora Waldend."   (322, 323.)

In some twenty forceful lines — ll. 47—77 — of *Genesis A*, however, the clash is vividly depicted.

But few Middle English writings pay any heed to the apocryphal vision of War in Heaven[1]), and none at all (with the exception of the *Boke of St. Albans*[2])) presents the expulsion as a Teutonic overlord's subjugation of mutinous thanes. The author of the late sixteenth century *Times' Whistle* speaks of "Jove" striking the wicked angels with lightning down to Acheron, just as Milton speaks of Christ rooting them out with "ten thousand thunders" (VI, 834 ff.); but Spenser is

---

[1]) We speak cenfidently of a war in Heaven, but Scot in his *Discourse* says:

"Now where this battell was fought ... there is great contention. The *Thomists* say ... in the empyrean heaven where the abode is of blessed spirits ... *Augustine* and manie others saie ... in the highest region of aier; others saie, in the firmament; others in paradise." (Cited from Verity's *P. L.*, II, p. 510.)

[2]) See *Lib. Armorum*, A ii b etc., where each of the faithful angels is said to have served "in his kynges batayll of heuen whan they faught with Lucifer."

nearer the common medieval view of the expulsion when, in
his *Heavenly Love*, 87, he declares of the refractory angels that
God "with his onely breath them blew away". Thus, in the
Lucifer scenes of the *Chester* and *Lud. Cov.* cycles and the
French Passion play of Arnoul Greban, the Divine Fiat is
the only evicting force. Indeed, even this is not always deemed
necessary. If the *Deus* of these plays has to exclaim:

> "Thu lucyfere ffor þi mekyl pryde
> I bydde þe ffalle from hefne to helle,
> And all þo þat holdyn on þi syde,
> in my blysse nevyr more to dwelle,"
>
> (*Lud. Cov.*, I, 66—69.)

his counterpart in the *York* and *Towneley* cycles has not to
utter even a word; the wicked ones just fall. At one moment
it is

> "Owe! what! I am derworth and defte"

with Lucifer; at the very next it is:

> "Owe, dewes! all goes downe!
> My myghte and my mayne es all marrande,
> Helpe, felawes! in faythe I am fallande!"
>
> (*York*, I, 91—93.)

(b) *The Number of the Fallen*. — What proportion or
number of the celestial spirits fell with Lucifer? According
to the Apocalypse, the Great Dragon drew after him "the
third part of the stars of heaven" (XII, 4). Once more Milton
adheres to the biblical version of the matter. We are, in
reading *Par. Lost*, to discount Satan's exaggerated estimates
of his numerical strength. He may speak of his "puissant
legions whose exile Hath emptied Heaven" (I, 632, 633); he
may even boast that he

> "in one night freed
> From servitude inglorious well nigh half
> The Angelic Name;"   (IX, 140—142.)

but we are not to take him literally. For, repeatedly and
emphatically, in the course of the epic is the Traitor Angel
spoken of as having led away with him no more than the
"third part of Heaven's Sons" (see II, 692; V, 710; VI, 156).
Further, it would appear from what I have said already of
the three Miltonic hierarchs, Lucifer, Michael and Raphael,
that the one-third that hearkened to Lucifer belonged entirely

to his hierarchy. Indeed, this is the import of V, 683—710, where Beelzebub is commanded by his superior to assemble

"Of all those myriads which we lead the chief" (684)

and, accordingly, summons

"the regent Powers
Under him regent."　　　(697, 698)

At the same time, if we consider the titles, Thrones, Dominions, Princedoms, Virtues, Powers and the like, by which their Leader addresses the ruined angels, we must conclude that Milton shared the opinion of those Schoolmen who maintained that in the Fall every one of the Orders suffered depletion.[1]

Earlier writers did not always care to determine the exact proportion between the obedient and the disobedient angels; they often contented themselves with vaguely declaring — sometimes with merely suggesting — that very many suffered exile. Thus, Spenser, like the writer of the *Boke of St. Albans*[2]), thought it enough to say that

"The brightest Angell, even the Child of light,
Drew millions more against their God to fight."

(*Heavenly Love*, 83, 84),

and Langland would not commit himself to more than the bare suggestion that at Lucifer's fall there fell

"Mo þowsandes wiþ him þan man couthe noumbre."

(*Piers Pl.* B I, 115.)[3]

But there are others who hold more definite views on the matter. Nearest the apocalyptic and Miltonic conception comes that of the Cornish *Creation*, in which the Proud Archangel, flaunting his strength, boldly declares:

"Half of the angels with me
Have assented to shut up,
To maintain me, in spite to thee, as thou knowest."

(p. 21.)

---

[1] See Hagenbach, *Hist. of Doctrines*, I, p. 495.
[2] See *Lib. Armorum*, A, I a.
[3] Cf. also *Curs. Mundi*, 503 f.; *Cleanness* 220; *Minor Poems of W. Lauder*, p. 17, ll. 434 ff. On the other hand, in the Ethiopic *Enoch* VI, 5, the number of the renegades (though their sin consisted in lusting after the daughters of men) is given as two hundred only.

Moreover, here the insurgent angels are distinctly regarded as drawn from all the nine orders; for, God the Father threatens Lucifer with damnation, and

> "all that assented with thee,
> With them of the nine Orders." (p. 19.)

But the majority of medieval retailers of the legend maintained that not more than one-tenth of the entire heavenly host rebelled and was damned. I have so far encountered only one piece which, instead of speaking of the usual one-tenth, speaks of one-ninth. This is the *Myroure of Oure Ladye*, in which the author commenting on the hymn, *Celestis erat curia*, remarks:

> "The fyrste verse tellyth how by the malyce of lucyfer the nynte parte of aungels fell from heuven." (p. 189.)

As for those writers who speak of the defection of one-tenth of the heavenly host, there are nevertheless differences among them when it comes to determining the exact constitution of the one-tenth. We may set aside at once writings like the O. E. verse *Salomon and Saturn* (453), the Harl. MS *Fall and Passion* (30), and the alliterative *Cleanness* (216), in which no more is said than that a tenth of the angels fell. But others call for closer examination. There is the *York* cycle in which it is distinctly stated that it was of the nine created orders that one-tenth was tried and found wanting:

> "Neyne ordurs for to telle, þat tyde,
> Of Aungeles bryght he bad þer be,
> for pride;
> And sone þe tente part it was tried,
> And wente away, as was worthye,
> They heild to helle all þat meyne
> þer-in to bide." (VII, 16—22.)

On the other hand, the *Towneley* cycle leaves no room for doubt that the one-tenth of each of the ten originally created orders suffered damnation, so that only as many as would make up nine orders were left in Heaven. By themselves the following lines in the Creation play in the collection cannot, indeed, be understood to convey all this:

> "thou has maide ix, there was x,
> thou art foull comyn from thi kyn;
> thou art fallen, that was the teynd,
> ffrom an angell to a feynd." (I, 142—145.)

But they are to be interpreted in the light of these subsequent ones:

"x orders in heuen were
of angels, that had office sere,
Of ich order, in thare degre,
the x parte fell downe with me;

— — — — — — — — — — —

God has maide man with his hend,
to haue that blis withoutten end,
The ix order to fulfill,
that after vs left, sich is his will."   (I, 254—265).

But if ll. 143—145 of the *Towneley 'Creation'* are not to be taken as implying that the insubordinate angels belonged all to a distinct tenth order, certain other M. E. passages are doubtless to be so taken. Among these are *Curs. Mundi*, 514—516, *Adrian and Epotys* 103—106, *Piers Plow.*, B I, 105—111, and *Chester 'Lucifer'* (MS H), 197, 198. This belief, that the rebel spirits belonged to a distinct tenth order, had been endorsed by no less an authority than Gregory the Great and was at least as old as the Slavonic *Secrets*, in which we read how, after ten troops of angels had been created,

"one from out the order of angels, having turned away with the order that was under him, conceived an impossible thought, to place his throne higher than the clouds above the earth, that he might become equal in rank and power. And I threw him out from the height, with his angels, and he was flying in the air continuously above the bottomless." (XXIX, 4, 5.)

It will be observed that in this passage nothing is said of the rank of the tenth or unrighteous order. But it would appear from the first two of the four M. E. passages above indicated that the order that fell was the lowest, and from the other two that it was the highest. For, it is perhaps arguable that, if Man is to take the place of the fallen angels and is, at the same time, made (as the Psalmist says) a little lower than the angels, then the angels that fell ranked lowest in the celestial organization. But there can be little doubt that in *Piers Plow.* and the *Chester 'Lucifer'* the exiled order is regarded as having been higher than all the others.[1]

— — — — — — —

[1] See Skeat's Clarendon Press Edition of *Piers Plow.*, Vol. II, p. 25 and cf. *Gospel of Nicodemus*, IV 28, 44, 56. Note, however, that if in *Psalm* VIII, 6, Man is said to be lower than the angels, he is elsewhere

Finally, it is interesting to note that the early homilist had left the question of a separate insubordinate order or otherwise open, when he wrote:

"þat teonðe werod abreað and awende on yfele, oðer al swa fele þe me mihte þat tioðe hape fulfellen."   (*O. E. Hom.*, I, p. 219.)

(c) *The Date of the Fall.* — We may, to begin with, divide all references to the subject into those that suggest or state that the Fall occurred on the same day as the Creation of the Angels and those that do not.

To the first class belong the dramatizations of the legend in the *York, Chester, Towneley* and *Lud. Cov.* cycles in England and the *Viel Test.* in France. Now, it had been supposed by Augustine and maintained by Comestor that the reference in *Genesis*, I, 4 to the division of Light and Darkness on the first day of creation was really a reference to the separation of the Good Angels from the Bad:

"De duabus Angelorum societatibus diversis atque disparibus, quae non incongrue intelliguntur lucis et tenebrarum nominibus nuncupatae."
(*De Civ. Dei*, XI, c. 9.)

"Intelligitur etiam hic angelorum facta divisio; stantes lux, cadentes tenebrae, dicti sunt." (*Hist. School.*, III.)

Accordingly, except for the *Towneley* one, all the plays mentioned above assign both the birth of the heavenly host and the downfall of a portion of it to the first day of the creation of the World.[1] Indeed, they seem to go further and agree with the author of *Curs. Mundi*, who declares that Lucifer did not taste the joys of Heaven even for an hour:

"Þar he badd noght fullik an ure,
For, alsuiþe als he was made
he fell, was þar na langer bade."[2]   (488—490.).

In the *Towneley* play, too, Lucifer's archangelic glory is conceived of as extremely short-lived, but the play is unique in representing the sun of his glory as rising and setting, not on the first day, but on the fifth.[3] Similarly in *The Times' Whistle*, 877 ff., the angels appear to be made on a day sub-

---

considered their equal — "exactly like the angels" (Ethiopic *Enoch* LXIX, 11), "a second angel" (Slavonic *Secrets* XXX, 11).

[1] Cf. *Poems of Wm. of Shoreham*, VII, 403, 405.
[2] Cf. *Myroure of Oure Ladye*, p. 176.
[3] See p. 218 above.

sequent to the third, but it is distinctly stated that they fell on the day they were made. I may conclude my remarks on this class by adding that the Slavonic *Secrets*, XXIX, holds that both the creation and the expulsion happened on the second day, but I have still to discover the Early English author who subscribes to this view.

To the second class belong such references as those in the M. E. *Gen. & Exod.*, the prose *Lyff of Adam Eue* (and presumably also its metrical version, the *Cant. de Creat.*), the Cornish *Creation*, and *Par. Lost*. But having so much in common, these pieces have very little else. The author of *Gen. & Exod.* follows Hebrew tradition in speaking of Lucifer being created on Sunday, the first day of creation, and being expelled on Monday, the second:

> "He was mad on ðe sunedai,
> He fel out on ðe munendai;
> (ðis ik wort in ebrisse wen,
> He witen ðe soðe ðat is sen)." (71—74.)

Comestor in the fourth chapter of his widely read *Hist. Schol.*, thus discusses the grounds for this Hebrew belief and declares them unsound:

> "Illud primo die, istud secundo factum est; et cum hujus diei opus bonum fuerit, ut caeterorum, tamen non legitur de eo *vidit Deus quod esset bonum*. Tradunt enim Hebraei, quia hac die angelus factus est diabolus Satanael, id est Lucifer, quibus Hebraeis consentire videntur qui in secunda feria missam de Angelis cantare consueverunt, quasi in laudem stantium angelorum. Sed tradunt sancti, quia in signum factum est hoc, quia binarius infamis numerus est in theologia, quia primus ab unitate recedit. Deus autem unitas est, et sectionem et discordiam detestatur. (*Prov. VI.*)"[1]

In the *Lyff of Ad. & Eue*, though the Angels are created on the first day, they are regarded as falling on the sixth, after and (as we have seen) because of the creation of Man, but before his temptation and fall. We have already considered the authority there was for such a view; it only remains to point out that this view differs from that of

---

[1] Cf. Bede, *Hexameron*, Lib. I (*Patr. Lat.*, XCI, col. 19). The doctrine that the division of the waters by the firmament really means the separation of Good Angels from the Bad, which must therefore be regarded as happening on the second day of the Creation, is referred to by Augustine in *De Civ. Dei* XI, c. 34.

Tatian, who maintained that the fall of Satan occurred so late as after the fall of Man and as a punishment for his part in it, — a view which is, I believe, never countenanced in Early English literature.

As for the Cornish *Creation*, it leaves the impression that the author has slavishly followed a version of the angelic creation and defection in which, as in *Curs. Mundi*, the account of the revolt was, somehow, separated from that of their origin by an enumeration of the things made on the several days of creation. For, in this play, without any apparent reason Lucifer, who has been made on the first day, is shown suddenly bursting with pride and suffering the consequences of it, after the work of the fifth day of the making of the world has been recounted.

I would place the O. E. *Genesis* also within this class. For, though it does not define the interval between the birth of the Angels and their mutiny, it appears from the following lines that the interval was conceived of as a long one:

"Synna ne cuþon
firena fremman, ac hie on friðe lifdon
ece mid heora aldor; elles ne onʒunnon
ræran on roderum nymþe riht & soþ,
ær ðon enʒla weard for oferhyʒde
dæl on ʒedwilde." (18—23.)

If I am right in the interpretation I put on this passage, then in two interesting features of the question under consideration, Milton's epic (which also falls here) comes nearer O. E. *Genesis* than any of the other early writings here mentioned. For, in the first place, according to *Par. Lost*, V, 583, 585 ff., an entire *Annus Magnus* separated the birth of the Angels from the begetting of the Son of God, whose begetting it was that led immediately to their revolt and fall. And secondly, of all the writings discussed in this section, *Par. Lost* and the so-called Cædmonian *Genesis* alone conceive the entire creation of our World as subsequent to the fall of the disobedient Angels.[1] Nevertheless, it may be noted that while in the O. E. poem no indication is given of the time that lapsed between these two events, subtle time-indications scattered throughout *Par. Lost* enable us to determine the

---

[1] Cf. also *Christ. Doctr.*, VII (*P. W.* IV, p. 185).

number of "days" that are imagined by the poet as lapsing between them. "There are", says Masson, "*eighteen* days between the expulsion of the rebel Angels from Heaven and the completion of the new Universe by the creation of Man — the first *nine* of these being possibly metaphysical, but the second *nine* avowedly literal or human days."[1])

(d) *The Duration of the Fall.* — A question which seems to have been of peculiar interest to medieval minds was: How long did it take the expelled celestials to descend from Heaven to their "fit habitation"? We are familiar with Milton's finding: "Nine days they fell" (VI, 871).[2]) This answer had already been given in the fourteenth century by Langland:

> "But fellen out in fendes liknesse nyne dayes togideres."
> > (*Piers Plow.*, B. I, 119.)[3])

But there are other answers as well. It is, perhaps, not surprising that none of the Mysteries should seek to time the transit; their Lucifers, almost all in one breath boast in Heaven and lament in Hell. But narrative handlings of the legend frequently pause to measure the fall, and most often their verdicts differ. Thus, according to O. E. *Genesis*:

> "feollon þa ufon of heofnum
> þurh swa longe swa þreo niht and daȝas,
> þa enȝlas of heofnum on helle."[4]) (306—308.)

On the other hand, at least two accounts are agreed that the time taken by the fall was seven days and nights:

> "Seue daies and seue niȝt
> As ȝe seeþ þat falliþ snowe,
> Vte of heuen hi aliȝt
> And in to helle wer iþrow."
> > (*Fall and Passion*, 25—28.)

> "Seuen days and seuen niȝt
> Angels fellen adoun in to helle."
> > (*Cant de Creat.*, 44, 45.)

---

[1]) See *Milton's Poetical Works*, Vol. I, Introd., pp. 112—115.

[2]) Cf. Hesiod's *Theogony*, 722, where the fall of the Titans, too, lasts nine days.

[3]) Dr. Mabel Day, however, draws my attention to the possibility of *nine* being only a scribal emendation of an original *forty*.

[4]) It is surprising to find Hanford (*A Milton Handbook*, p. 198) saying that, in this poem, "Satan and his crew fall three days and three nights, as in Milton."

The author of *Cleanness* maintains it was forty days:

> "þikke þowsandeȝ þro þrwen þer-oute
> Fellen fro þe fyrmament, fendeȝ ful blake
> Weued at þe fyrst swap as þe snaw þikke,
> Hurled in-to helle-hole as þe hyue swarmeȝ;
> Fyltyr fenden folk forty dayeȝ leneþe
> Er þat styngande storme stynt ne myȝt;
> Bot as smylt mele vnder smal siue smokes for-þikke,
> So fro heuen to helle þat hatel schor laste,
> On vche syde of þe worlde aywhere ilyche."[1]   (220—228.)

But even this does not satisfy the author of *Curs. Mundi*,
who thinks the matter beyond human knowledge and, in any
case, one of thousands of years:

> "þe numbre þat out of heuen fell
> Þo can na tung in erth [noght] tell;
> Ne fra þe trone quar he can sitte,
> How farr es in to hell pitte;
> Bot bede sais fra erth to heuen
> es seuen thusand yeir and hundret seuen,
> Bi iornes qua þat gang it may,
> Fourti mile on ilk [a] day."[2]   (503—510.)

(e) *The New Abode.* — It will have been observed that
all the passages just quoted speak of the Angels falling from
Heaven to Hell. Two questions arise: Was Hell created
expressly for these ingrates? Have they all been confined
there ever since?

In *Matthew*, XXV, 41, we read of the everlasting fire
that it was "prepared for the Devil and his angels." Milton
keeps very close to both the thought and the language of the
Gospel and speaks of Hell as the wicked Angels' "prepared
ill mansion" (VI, 738), which opened wide to "receive their
fall" (VI, 54, 55), and as "their prison ordained in utter darkness" (I, 71, 72), which "Eternal justice had prepared For
those rebellious" (I, 70, 71). This Miltonic Hell not only is
specially prepared for the insurgent spirits of Heaven, but

---

[1] For the air being full of these Angels "as snow falling in the
skies" see Burton's *Anat. of Melancholy*, I 2, i 2.

[2] Cf. the calculation in Burton's *Anatomy*, I 2, i 2, of the 65 years
or more taken by a stone falling at the rate of a hundred miles an hour
to cover the "170 millions 803 miles" between the starry heaven or eighth
sphere and the earth. See also *The Myroure of Oure Ladye*, p. 304, and
Caxton's *Mirrour of the World*, XIX.

also necessarily exists prior to our later-created Heaven and Earth. That is why, in his Argument to the First Book, the poet, speaking of Hell, is obliged to add:

> "described here not in the centre (for heaven and earth may be supposed as yet not made, certainly not yet accursed) but in a place of utter darkness, fitliest called Chaos." [1]

The O. E. *Genesis* agrees with Milton in imagining Hell both as originally made for the rebels and as created before either our Heaven or Earth. When Lucifer boasts that he will establish his throne in the northern extremity of Heaven, God is angered:

> "sceop þam werloȝan
> wræclicne ham weorce to leane,
> helleheafas, hearde niðas;
> heht þaet witehus wraecna bidan
> deop, dreama leas drihten ure
> ȝasta weardas." (36—41.)

Early English writings, generally, have, however, little room in their versions of the Fall to indicate why or when Hell was created; in their work, most often, it simply exists. But the medieval playwrights, working on a larger stage, do sometimes pause to create their Hell. Thus, Jordan in his *Creation* — if indeed it be his — very distinctly retails the circumstances in which God was obliged to prepare Hell for the Devil and his Angels. Our Heaven and Earth have been created already, but evidently Hell as yet is not, when Lucifer begins to rebel. It is only when God the Father perceives how it stands with his Angels that He brings Hell into being:

> "Hell for thee shall be made,
> Qickly I command this,
> There thou shalt dwell,
> And all that assented with thee,
>   With them of the nine Orders." (p. 19.)

Similarly, in the English *Faust Book*, Mephistophiles, being asked when Hell was made, answers:

> "Faustus, thou shalt know that before the fall of my lord, Lucifer, there was no hell, but even then was hell ordained."
>
> (*Eng. Prose Romances*, III, p. 185.)

---

[1] Cf. *Christ. Doctr.*, XXXIII (*P. W.* IV, pp. 490, 491).

17*

But in the *Chester* and *York* Lucifer plays — ll. 50 f. and 25 ff. respectively — Hell is made along with our Heaven and Earth. Now, since all these are made on the first day and the Angels too are created and expelled on the same day, no great interval of time separates these events from one another; nevertheless, the point is that Hell is made in these plays without reference to the subsequent revolt and expulsion. Moreover, from the actual words put into the mouth of the Creator in the passages under consideration, it is to be inferred that in these plays Hell is conceived of as more or less a part of the Earth. For, the *Chester* Deus announces:

> "The worlde that is both voyde and vayne,
>   I forme in this formation,
> With a dungeon of darkenes that never shall
>   have endinge."

And his *York* equivalent proclaims:

> "Here vndernethe me nowe a nexile I neuen,
> Whilke Ile sall be erthe: now all be at ones
> Erthe haly and helle."[1]

Hell was, in fact, often located in the centre of the Earth; witness *The Myroure of Oure Ladye*: "Clerkes saye ... that helle ys in myddes of the erthe wythin as a core ys in myddes of an appel" (p. 305), and the similar statements in Hampole's *Pricke of Consc.*, 6441 ff., and the *Fragment on Popular Science* edited by Wright.[2]) Did the apparently indiscriminate use of the expressions "in terram" and "ad infernum" in the Scriptural texts which relate to the angelic expulsion foster this belief? For, if *Isai.*, XIV, 15, *2 Pet.*, II, 4, and *Apoc.*, XX, 2, 3, mention Hell and the bottomless pit — *infernum, tartarum, abyssum* — *Isai.*, XIV, 12, *Ezekiel*, XXVIII, 17, and *Apoc.*, XII, 9, indicate the earth or the ground, — *terram* — as the place of banishment of the degraded spirits.

However this may be, we are faced with the second question: If indeed the rebels were hurled down to Hell, have

---

[1]) In her Edition of the cycle Miss Toulmin Smith punctuates the second of these lines rather differently; but see my note in *Anglia*, XL, 27.

[2]) See Mätzner, *Wörterbuch*, s. v. Helle. Milton seems to adopt this view (which is also the view of Dante) in *Par. Lost*, XII, 42, though elsewhere — see p. 259 above — he argues that Hell is situated beyond the limits of the Universe.

they remained there ever since? Now, there is nothing in five of the six scriptural texts just mentioned to suggest that they have not been. In fact, one of them distinctly states — and so too does *Jude*, 6 — that, delivered unto chains of darkness, these damned spirits are to abide there till the Judgment. But the sixth text, *Apoc.*, XX, 2, 3, runs:

> "Et apprehendit draconem, serpentem antiquam, qui est diabolus et Satanas, et ligavit eum per annos mille; (3) Et misit eum iu abyssum, et clausit, et signavit super illum, ut non seducat amplius gentes donec consummentur mille anni; et post haec opertet illum solvi modico tempore."

We may wonder, with Marlowe's Faustus, how the Devil damned in Hell could issue out of Hell, but these verses mean that he did so issue bringing death into this world and all our woe. And the author of the Apocalypse is not alone in holding that Satan at least, if not also all his followers, roamed the world and beguiled the nations. St. Paul (*2 Corinth.* IV, 4) calls the Devil the god of the world, just as St. John names him its prince (*John* XII, 31). St. Paul even speaks of him in another place (*Ephesians* II, 2) as the prince of the powers of the air. This too is no personal fancy for the Slavonic *Secrets*, narrating the fall of the Traitor Angel, has the verse:

> "And I threw him out from the height with his angels, and he was flying in the air continuously above the bottomless." (XXIX, 5.)

And if we are to believe *Job*, I, 7, 8; II, 1, 2, and the Ethiopic *Enoch*, XL, 7, not only does Satan go to and fro in the earth and walk up and down in it, but also he dares to present himself before the Lord in Heaven.[1])

Further, according to early Hebrew demonology, not only Satan, but other spirits as well roamed the world and wrought evil. It is certainly not always clear that the spirits are those that fell with Lucifer for their pride; they are often those, or the evil offspring of those, who seeing the daughters of men descended to earth and thus lost heaven.[2]) Nevertheless, when it is remembered that the Neo-Platonists furnished

---

[1]) Cf. also *1 Kings* XXII, 21, and *Zech.* III, 1

[2]) See Ethiopic *Enoch*, IX, XVI, XL, LIII, LIV; *Bk. of Jubilees*, X, 8, 9; and Wace's *Apocrypha*, Vol. I, pp. 176—183. Cf. also Burton's *Anatomy*, I, 2, i, 2.

the elements, each with its peculiar class of demon — Salamanders of Fire, Sylphs of Air, Nymphs of Water and Gnomes of the Underworld — and that popular superstition peopled the regions of space with mysterious fairies and goblins, it becomes easy to understand how the few, fragmentary and not always consistent scriptural and rabbinical references to demoniac vagrancy come to be occasionally utilized to convey that of the Angels that fell with Lucifer some at least, if not all, were given to range the regions of Earth and Air. And we find no less a person than Gregory the Great lending his authority to such a belief:

> "Et scimus" (he says in his *Moral. Libri*, II, c. 47) "quod immundi spiritus, qui e caelo aethereo lapsi sunt, in hoc caeli terraeque medio vagantur."

Accordingly, in the cosmogony of the *Myroure of Oure Ladye*, the middle air is the home of fiends. After stating that the air round about our earth lies in three strata, of which that nearest the earth is the ordinary air which we go in and the birds fly in, the author continues:

> "The seconde parte of the ayre is darke & colde for the reflecyon of the sonne beames may not come so hye. And in this parte of the ayre dwelle fendes vnto the day of doume, and there are gendered tempestes of weder and hayle and snowe and thonder and lyghtnynge and suche other. And therfore in nyghtes tyme when the lower parte of the ayre ys darke by absence of the sonne, and in tempestes of weder, the fendes come downe to the erthe more homly then in other tymes." (p. 303.)

But more common is the belief that the fiends inhabit all the elements at once. Thus, in the early fifteenth century *Master of Oxford's Catechism*, we read:

> "*C.* Where be the anjelles that cod put out of heven, and bycam devilles?
>
> *M.* Som into hell, and som reyned in the skye, and som in the erth, and som in waters and in wodys."

And, likewise, in medieval versions of the Fall from Heaven, we encounter passages like these:

> "Þas oþer gastes þat fell him wiht
> Þe quilk for-sok godds grith,
> Efter þe will þai till him bare
> Þan fell þai depe, or lesse or mare;

Sum in þe air, sum in the lift,
Þar þai drei ful hard[e] schrift."
(*Curs. Mundi*, 491—496.)

"Þene fel he with his felawes and fendes bi-comen,
Out of heuene in-to helle hobleden faste,
Summe in þe Eir, end summe in þe Eorþe and summe
in helle deope."[1]
(*Piers Plow.*, A I, 112—14.)

"For pryde wrethe god can take,
That many arn fynndes now blake
And fellyn owte of heuyne, as I þe telle,
In to the netherest pytte of helle.
Summe arn yn erthe amo[n]ge man-kynd
That bring man-kynd yn de[d]ly synne."
(*Adr. & Epot.* 387—392.)

"And he and alle his feeren fullen out of heuene; heo fullen out
as þikke as þe drift of þe snouh. Summe astunte in þe eyr, and
summe in þe eorþe. Ȝif eny mon is elue Inome oþur elun Iblowe,
he hit haþ of þe angelus þat fellen out of heuene."
(*Lyff of Ad. & Eue*, p. 221.)

If there is little suggestion of Neo-Platonism in these
medieval pieces, there is a good deal in these words of the
Elizabethan divine, Hooker:

"The fall of the angels therefore was pride. Since their fall their
practices have been clean contrary unto those before-mentioned, for
being dispersed, some in the air, some in the earth, some in the
water, some among the minerals, dens and caves that are under
the earth, they have by all means laboured to effect an universal
rebellion against the laws, and as far as in them lieth, utter
destruction of the works of God."[2]
(*Ecclesiastical Polity*, I, c. iv, 3.)

None of the Mystery plays countenances the doctrine of
the demons of the elements in any form, but Milton, who as

---

[1] With these two passages we may compare Greene, *Friar Bacon*,
sc. IX, 59—68, and Burton's *Anatomy*, I, 2, i, 2:

"all that space between us and the moon for them that trans-
gressed least, and hell for the wickedest of them."

Cf. also *Deuelis Parlament*, 3: "Alle þe deuelis of þe eir, of erþe, &
of helle" and the *Boke of St. Albans* (*Lib. Arm.*), A i a.

[2] Cf. Burton's *Anatomy*, I, 2, i, 2:

"They are confined until the day of judgment to this sublunary
world, and can work no farther than the four elements, and as

Il Penseroso sought to unsphere the spirit of Plato to have him tell of

"those demons that are found
In fire, air, flood or underground",

is not without a belief in the demonic activities of the banished angels. He does not, indeed, believe, as do apparently the authors of *Curs. Mundi* and *Piers Plow.* that only the most sinful of the defiant spirits fell into Hell; yet, steeped as he is in the scriptures which term Satan prince of the air and god of the world, and the like, and learned as he is in rabbinical and classical demonology, he does not hesitate to affirm that the heathen deities are none other than the outcast angels:

"wandering o'er the earth,
Through God's high sufferance for the trial of man."[1)]
(I, 365, 366.)

It is true that at first Satan alone breaks the bounds of Hell, but his object in doing so is, as he tells Gabriel:

"to find
Better abode, and my afflicted Powers
To settle here on Earth or in mid Air."[2)] (IV, 939, 940.)

And he succeds. The air becomes "the realm itself of Satan" (X, 189), who rules it as "Prince of the Air" (X, 185). "God of the world invoked and worl. beneath" (*Par. Reg.* IV, 203), he comes to command universal allegiance; and, led out of their hated habitation, his followers, the demon spirits, roam the earth and are adored for deities:

"Regents and potentates and kings, yea gods,
Of many a pleasant realm and province wide."
(*P. R.* I, 117.)

They all have now their appointed realms over which they preside:

"Tetrarchs of fire, air, flood and on the earth" —
(*P. R.* IV, 201.)

God permits them. Wherefore of these sublunary devils, though others divide them otherwise according to their several places and offices, Psellus makes six kinds, fiery, aerial, terrestrial, watery, and subterranean devils, besides those fairies, satyrs, nymphs, etc."

[1)] Cf. *Christ. Doctr.* IX (*P. W.* IV, p. 218).
[2)] Cf. *Christ and Satan*, 112 ff.

so that from being at one time "Heaven's ancient sons, etherial Thrones" (*P. R.* II, 121), and, later, exiled spirits in bondage in the horrid pit, they become

> "Demonian Spirits, now, from the element
> Each of his reign alloted, rightlier called
> Powers of Fire, Air, Water, and Earth beneath."
>
> (*P. R.* II, 122—124.)

Are these condemned angels, then, no longer in Hell? This question was anticipated by the Fathers and answered by them in the paradox: "They are not and yet they are". Thus Bede clearly says that wander where these spirits will they carry their hell with them:

> "Ubicunque, vel in aere volitant, vel in terris, aut sub terris vagantur sive detinentur, suarum secum ferunt tormenta flammarum."
>
> (*Eccl. Hist.,* V, c. 15.)

And centuries later, Marlowe and Milton poetize this paradox. Consider the following dialogue in *Dr. Faustus,* sc. iii, 74—81:

> "*Faust.*   Where are you damned?
> *Meph.*   In hell.
> *Faust.*   How comes it then that thou art out of hell?
> *Meph.*   Why this is hell, nor am I out of it.
> Think'st thou that I, that saw the face of God,
> And tasted the eternal joys of heaven,
> Am not tormented with ten thousand hells,
> In being deprived of everlasting bliss?

And also this:

> "*Faust.*   First will I question thee about hell.
> Tell me, where is the place that men call hell?
> *Meph.*   Under the heavens.
> *Faust.*   Ay, but whereabout?
> *Meph.*   Within the bowels of these elements,
> Where we are tortur'd and remain for ever.
> Hell hath no limits, nor is circumscribed
> In one self-place; for where we are is hell;
> And where hell is, must we for ever be." (sc. v, 113—120).

Similarly, Milton says of his Satan escaped from hell, that he is still in hell, for hell is ever with him, nay, he is hell:

> "Horror and doubt distract
> His troubled thoughts, and from the bottom stir
> The hell within him; for within him Hell

> He brings, and round about him, nor from Hell
> One step, no more than from himself, can fly
> By change of place." (IV, 18—23.)

In this and with this everlasting inferno of his let us leave
Lucifer,

> "Fallen, fallen, fallen, fallen,
> Fallen from his high estate."

--- --- ---

Editions of Texts referred to.

Adrian and Epotys, ed. L. T. Smith in *A Common-Place Book of the Fifteenth Century.* London, 1886.

Aelfric, The Homilies of, ed. B. Thorpe. 2 Vols. London, 1843, 1846.

The Ancren Riwle, ed. J. Morton. London, 1853.

Ayenbite of Inwit, ed. R. Morris. E. E. T. S., O. S., 23.

Bacon's *Advancement of Learning,* ed. Spedding, Ellis and Heath, in Vol. 3 of *The Works of Francis Bacon.* London, 1870—1872.

The Boke of St. Albans, by Dame Juliana Berners, 1486. Facsimile produced by W. Blades. London, 1899.

Bokenam, *Lives of Saints,* ed. Horstmann. Heilbronn, 1883.

Browne, The Works of Sir Thomas, ed. C. Sayles. 3 Vols. Edinburgh, 1912.

Burton's *Anatomy of Melancholy,* 1621. Reprinted London, 1849.

Canticum de Creatione, ed. C. Horstmann in *Sammlung Altenglischer Legenden.* Heilbronn, 1878.

The Castell of Perseverance, ed. F. J. Furnivall in *The Macro Plays.* E. E. T. S., E. S., 91.

Caxton's *Golden Legend,* ed. F. S. Ellis. 7 Vols. London, 1900.

Caxton's *Mirrour of the World,* ed. O. H. Prior. E. E. T. S., E. S. 110.

Chaucer, Complete Works of, ed. W. Skeat. Oxford 1913.

The Chester Plays, ed. H. Deimling. E. E. T. S., E. S., 62, 115.

Christ and Satan, ed. R. P. Wülker in Vol. 2 of Grein-Wülker's *Bibliothek der Angelsächsischen Poesie.* Leipzig, 1883—1898.

Cleanness, ed. R. Morris in *Early English Alliterative Poems.* E. E. T. S., O. S., 1.

Cornish *Creation of the World* by William Jordan. Translated by J. Keigwin and edited by D. Gilbert. London, 1827.

Cornish *Origo Mundi,* ed. and translated by E. Norris in Vol. 1 of *The Ancient Cornish Drama.* 2 Vols. London, 1859.

Cornish *Passion,* ed. E. Norris: *Ibid.* Vol. 1.

Cornish *Resurrection,* ed. E. Norris: *Ibid.* Vol. 2.

Cursor Mundi, ed. R. Morris. E. E. T. S., O. S., 57, 59, 62, 66, 68, 99.

The Deuelis Perlament, ed. F. J. Furnivall. E. E. T. S., O. S., 24.

The Destruction of Troy, ed. D. Donaldson and G. A. Panton. E. E. T. S., O. S., 39.

The Fall and Passion, ed. F. J. Furnivall in *Early English Poems.* Berlin, 1862.

The Faust Book, ed. Thoms in *English Prose Romances,* Vol. 3.

A Fragment on Popular Science, ed. T. Wright in *Popular Treatises on Science.* London, 1841.

Genesis & Exodus, ed. R. Morris. E. E. T. S., O. S., 7.

Gesta Romanorum, ed. S. J. H. Herrtage. E. E. T. S., E. S., 33.

Gower's *Confessio Amantis,* ed. G. C. Macaulay. E. E. T. S., E. S., 81, 82.

Greban's *Le Mystère de la Passion,* ed. G. Paris and G. Raynaud. Paris, 1878.

Greene's *Friar Bacon and Friar Bungay,* ed. A. W. Ward in *Old English Drama.* Oxford, 1878.

Hali Meidenhad, ed. O. Cockayne. E. E. T. S., O. S., 18.

Hampole's *Pricke of Conscience,* ed. R. Morris. Berlin, 1863.

Heywood's *Hierarchie of the Blessed Angels.* 1635.

Hooker, *Works of Richard.* 2 Vols. Oxford, 1850.

Langland's *Vision of Piers Plowman,* ed. W. Skeat. E. E. T. S., O. S., 28. 38, 54, 67, 81.

Langland's *Vision of Piers Plowman,* ed. W. Skeat. 2 Vols. Oxford, 1886.

Ludus Coventriae, ed. K. S. Block. E. E. T. S., E. S., 120.

Lydgate's *Pilgrimage of the Life of Man,* ed. F. J. Furnivall. E. E. T. S., E. S., 77, 83.

The Lyff of Adam and Eue, ed. C. Horstmann in *Samml. Altengl. Legenden.* Heilbronn, 1878.

Lyndesay, Works of Sir David, ed. Small, Hall and Murray. E. E. T. S., O. S., 11, 19, 35, 37, 47.

Marlowe's *Dr. Faustus,* ed. A. W. Ward in *Old English Drama.* Oxford, 1878.

The Master of Oxford's Catechism, ed. T. Wright and J. O. Halliwell in *Reliquiae Antiquae.* 2 Vols. London, 1841, 1843.

Milton, Poetical Works of, ed. D. Masson. 3 Vols. London, 1874.

Milton, Prose Works of, ed. J. A. St. John and C. B. Summer. 5 Vols. London, 1848—1853.

Milton's Paradise Lost, ed. A. W. Verity. 2 Vols. Cambridge, 1929.

The Minor Poems of William Lauder, ed. F. J. Furnivall. E. E. T. S., O. S., 41.

The Mirror of the Periods of Man's Life, ed. F. J. Furnivall in *Hymns to the Virgin and Christ, etc.* E. E. T. S., O. S., 24.

Myrc's *Instructions for Parish Priests,* ed. E. Peacock. E. E. T. S., O. S., 31.

The Myroure of Oure Ladye, ed. J. H. Blunt. E. E. T. S., E. S., 19.

Old English *Genesis,* ed. R. P. Wülker in Vol. 2 of Grein-Wülker's *Angelsächsische Poesie.*

Old English Homilies (First Series), ed. R. Morris. E. E. T. S., O. S., 29, 34.

Ormulum, ed. R. Holt. 2. Vols. Oxford.

The Poems of William of Shoreham, ed. M. Konrath. E. E. T. S., E. S., 86.

Salomon and Saturn, ed. R. P. Wülker in Vol. 3 of Grein-Wülker's *Angelsächsische Poesie.*

Scot's *Discourse of Divels,* ed. Nicholson.

Spenser, The Poetical Works of, ed. J. C. Smith and E. de Sélincourt. Oxford, 1921.

The Times' Whistle, ed. J. M. Cowper, E. E. T. S., O. S., 48.

The Towneley Plays, ed. G. England and A. W. Pollard. E. E. T. S., E. S., 71.

268 P. E. DUSTOOR, LEGENDS OF LUCIFER.

Trevisa's *Bartholomæus de Proprietatibus Rerum*, printed by W. de Worde, 1491.
Viel Testament, Le Mystére du, ed. Baron J. de Rothschild. 5 Vols. Paris, 1878—1885.
Wycliff, Select Works of, ed. Arnold. 3 Vols. Oxford, 1869—1871.
York Mystery Plays, ed. Miss L. Toulmin Smith. Oxford, 1885.

———

Augustine, Bede, Comestor, etc., in Migne's *Patrologiae Cursus Completus.* 221 Vols. Paris, 1844 ff.
III Baruch, in R. H. Charles, *Apocrypha and Pseudepigrapha of the Old Testament*, Vol. 2. Oxford, 1913.
The Book of Jubilees: ibid.
The Ethiopic *Book of Enoch: ibid.*
The Gospel of Bartholomew, in: M. R. James, *The Apocryphal New Testament.* Oxford, 1924.
The Gospel of Nicodemus, in: Hone, *The Apocryphal New Testament.* London.
The Martyrdom of Isaiah, in: Charles, *op. cit.*, Vol. 2.
The Slavonic Secrets of Enoch: ibid.
Vita Adae et Evae: ibid.

UNIVERSITY OF ALLAHABAD. P. E. DUSTOOR.

———

224

THE METAMORPHOSES OF THE EDEN SERPENT DURING THE MIDDLE AGES AND RENAISSANCE

by Henry Ansgar Kelly

The varied appearances of the Eden serpent in medieval and renaissance literature, drama, and art have caused a good deal of interest among students of these periods; it is particularly mystifying to see the tempting reptile take on the head and other features of a woman. There has, however, been comparatively little formal study of these developments. The subject first received extended scholarly treatment in the early part of this century, from Hugo Schmerber and J. K. Bonnell,[1] but these pioneering works are frequently neglected, and their findings quite incomplete.

I. EASTERN TRADITIONS

Curiosity about the nature of the serpent who tempted the first parents of mankind developed early. That the serpent's curse entailed its crawling on its belly thenceforward suggested, of course, that it had previously had legs and feet, of which it was ever after deprived. Such was the rabbinic tradition, witnessed to by the Midrash and Targum,[2] as well as by Josephus, who adds that it also lost its voice.[3] It was said to look like a camel in its original state.[4]

As for the serpent's sex, apart from the fact that the Hebrew word for serpent (*nahash*) is in the masculine gender, the Eden serpent was thought

---

[1] Hugo Schmerber, *Die Schlange des Paradieses*, Zur Kunstgeschichte des Auslandes 31 (Strassburg 1905); J. K. Bonnell, "The Serpent with a Human Head in Art and in Mystery Play," *American Journal of Archaeology* 2.21 (1917) 255-291. See also Alice Kemp-Welch, "The Woman-headed Serpent in Art," *The Nineteenth Century and After* 52 (Dec. 1902) 983-991.

[2] *Bereshith Rabbah* 19.1: "Rabbi Hoshaya the Elder said: 'He stood out distinguished (erect) like a reed, and he had feet.'" —*Midrash Rabbah: Genesis*, trans. H. Freedman (London 1939, repr. 1951) 1.149. The Palestinian Targum expands God's curse to read, "Upon thy belly thou shalt go, and thy feet shall be cut off." —J. W. Etheridge, *The Targums of Onkelos and Jonathan ben Uzziel on the Pentateuch, with the Fragments of the Jerusalem Targum* (London 1862-1865) 1.166.

[3] Josephus, *Jewish Antiquities* 1.1.4, Loeb Library (London 1930) 22-24.

[4] *Bereshith Rabbah* 19.1. This opinion is ascribed to Rabbi Simeon ben Eleazar.

225

to have been very *male*, since it actually lusted after Eve,[5] thus maintaining (for us post-Freudians) its reputation as a phallic symbol.

As is well known, there is no devil or Satan figure in the Genesis account of the temptation of Eve, but Jewish as well as Christian tradition came to associate such a figure with the serpent. Most often the serpent was not taken to be a symbol of Satan, but an animal that was simply used by the devil to carry forward his determination to destroy mankind.

According to the ninth-century compiler of the *Chapters of Rabbi Eliezer the Great*, Sammael, the great prince in heaven, who had twelve wings to the seraphim's six, took his band and descended to earth and saw all the creatures that God had made; "and he found among them none so skilled to do evil as the serpent. . . . Its appearance was something like that of the camel, and he [Sammael] mounted and rode upon it. . . . Like . . . a man in whom there was an evil spirit, . . . all the deeds which it did, and all the words which it spake, it did not speak except by the intention of Sammael." After the sin of Adam and Eve was effected by this unholy teamwork, God "cast down Sammael and his troop from their holy place in heaven, and cut off the feet of the serpent."[6]

About the same time that Pseudo-Eliezer was at work with his *Chapters*, Pseudo-Ben Sirach came up with the story of Lilith as Adam's first wife,[7] but Bonnell rightly dismisses Lilith as a possible influence upon the feminized Eden serpent, since there is no evidence that she was ever regarded as serpentine in form in the Middle Ages.[8]

The tradition that the Eden serpent originally had feet that were cut off when it was cursed found its way into the Eastern tradition of the Christian church at an early date. A treatise on paradise among the spurious works of Saint Basil the Great assures us that in the beginning the serpent had nothing horrible about it, but was rather a mild and gentle creature that did not crawl on its belly in a wild and savage manner but carried itself high upon feet.[9] We see the tradition illustrated in the Byzantine Octateuchs

---

[5] *Ibid.* 18.6 (147): "Said R. Joshua ben Karhah: ' It teaches you through what sin that wicked creature inveigled them; viz., because he saw them engaged in their natural functions, he [the serpent] conceived a passion for her.'"

[6] *Pirḳê de Rabbi Eliezer*, trans. Gerald Friedlander (London 1916, repr. New York 1965) 92-93, 99.

[7] Israel Lévi, "Lilit et Lilin," *Revue des études juives* 68 (1914) 15-21, puts the *Sepher* or *Alphabet* of "Ben Sirach" in the ninth or tenth century, and believes that it comes from Persia.

[8] Bonnell (n. 1 above) 290 n. 2. Jeffrey M. Hoffeld, "Adam's Two Wives," *The Metropolitan Museum of Art Bulletin* 26 (June 1968) 430-440, asserts that Lilith is definitely the basis for the woman-headed Eden serpent, but he offers no proof.

[9] Pseudo-Basil, *De paradiso* 7 (PG 30.67-68).

of the twelfth century,[10] where in fact the serpent looks like a camel. The outline of the serpent's future shape can be seen in its neck, backbone, and tail, so that God had simply to curse away the camelian understructure, and the modern serpent was ready for action.

II. EARLY TRADITIONS IN THE WEST

In the West the Jewish traditions were preserved and enlarged by European rabbis; those who lived in northern France are particularly important. Rashi (Rabbi Solomon ben Isaac of Troyes, circa 1040-1105), for instance, repeated the Midrash interpretations of the serpent's passion for Eve and the idea that "it had feet but they were cut off."[11]

Andrew of Saint Victor (who died in 1175) was the first Christian exegete in the Middle Ages to draw systematically upon the works of the Jewish commentators. In his commentary on the Octateuch, which he finished by about 1147,[12] he seems to accept the reading that the serpent once had feet,[13] but not that it was inflamed with desire for Eve. Andrew acknowledges that the serpent was not speaking by itself but was possessed by the devil;[14] this was the traditional Western interpretation. Andrew takes it as a sign of Eve's great simplicity that she was not dumbfounded or startled when a hitherto mute brute started to speak to her.

Before the time of Andrew of Saint Victor, the usual iconographic representation of the Eden temptation featured an ordinary serpent twined about the fatal tree of knowledge, with Adam on one side and Eve on the other. At times, however, the devil was illustrated separately from the serpent, as in the Old English Junius manuscript (circa A.D. 1000). Here Satan himself is bound in hell, but he sends a subordinate to paradise who transforms

---

[10] T. Ouspensky, *L'octateuque de la bibliothèque du Sérail à Constantinople*, Bulletin de l'Institut archéologique russe à Constantinople 12 (Sofia 1907; pls., Munich 1907) 115, pl. 11 fig. 25 (f. 43v); D. C. Hesseling, *Miniatures de l'octateuque grec de Smyrne*, Codices graeci et latini, ed. Scatone de Vries, Supplement 6 (Leiden 1909) 6-7 figs. 19, 21. Cf. Sigrid Esche, *Adam und Eva; Sündenfall und Erlösung*, Lukas-Bücherei zur christlichen Ikonographie 8 (Düsseldorf 1957) 13-14, 28.

[11] See M. Rosenbaum et al., *Pentateuch with Targum Onkelos, Haphtaroth, and Rashi's Commentary: Genesis* (New York n.d.) 12, 15.

[12] Beryl Smalley, *The Study of the Bible in the Middle Ages*, ed. 2 (Oxford 1952, repr. Notre Dame 1964) 112.

[13] Andrew of Saint Victor, *Comm. in Gen.* 3, Bibl. Vat. Barb. lat. 693 fol. 109v: The curse is that only the serpent among the beasts of the earth goes upon its belly: "Maledicionem dicit serpenti & dampnacionis sentenciam inlligit inter cetera animancia & bestias terre que pedibus gradiuntur super terram; cum enim cetera pedibus gradiantur & tibiis & cruribus se subleuent a terra & terre graminibus uescantur, ipse solus uentre & pectore repperit [sic] & terram in cibum sumit."

[14] *Ibid.* 109: "Esto quod in serpente diabolus illum suo instinctu replens eique suum spiritum miscens eo more quo vates demoniorum inplere solet repleretur [sic] loqueretur."

himself into a serpent, shown in the branches of the tree. Later the demon appears as an angel of light and continues his temptation.[15]

Something similar happens in the mid-twelfth-century Anglo-Norman *Play of Adam*, though the sequence is reversed; the devil first appears in person —in what guise we are not told, except that he affects a friendly approach with a cheerful countenance in his attempt to persuade Eve. Later an artificially constructed serpent (supposedly a normally appearing one) ascends the tree and Eve pretends to be listening to it.[16] Though the devil does not now appear, it is understood that he is engineering the conversation.

In the *Saint Albans Psalter* (executed before the year 1123) the devil himself, in a typically horrible humanoid form, is in the tree, and the serpent issues from his mouth; in the serpent's own mouth is an apple, which Eve is taking.[17]

Eventually in Western art the Eden serpent appears with feet (and with wings). A striking example can be found in the *Huntingfield Psalter*, an English manuscript dated around 1170. Here, in the temptation scene, the serpent is twined around the tree as usual, but is equipped with a small pair of legs and a small set of wings, as well as doglike ears.[18] This development has nothing to do, it seems, with the tradition of the Eden serpent first having feet and then being cursed by their removal. Andrew of Saint Victor's lead in accepting this reading was not followed up. Rather it reflects a tendency in medieval iconography to represent all kinds of serpents as winged, footed, and dog-headed. Eden serpents with doglike heads appear in some of the earliest representations of the temptation.[19] This trait in medieval iconography may, however, be an independently developed tradition. The notion of flying serpents (and therefore, presumably, serpents with wings) was not a new one, but was known in antiquity. Isidore in his *Etymologies* has a nuber of them, including the dragon, which he defines as the largest of the ser-

---

[15] Oxford, Bodleian MS Junius 11, ed. Israel Gollancz, *The Caedmon Manuscript* (Oxford 1927).

[16] *Le mystère d'Adam* (*Ordo representacionis Ade*), ed. Paul Aebischer, Textes littéraires français (Geneva 1963) 44, 52: "Tunc tristis et vultu demisso recedet ab Adam et ibit usque ad portas inferni. . . . De hinc ex parte Evae accedet ad paradisum, et Evam laeto vultu blandiens sic alloquitur." "Tunc serpens artificiose compositus ascendit iuxta stipitem arboris vetitae. Cui Eva proprius adhibebit aurem, quasi ipsius auscultans consilium."

[17] Otto Pächt, C. R. Dodwell, and Francis Wormald, *The St. Albans Psalter*, Studies of the Warburg Institute 25 (London 1960) pl. 14.

[18] *Huntingfield Psalter*, Pierpont Morgan Library MS 43 fol. 8v, reproduced in Walter W. S. Cook, "The Earliest Painted Panels of Catalonia" 5, *Art Bulletin* 10 (1927-1928) 152-204 (p. 165 fig. 20).

[19] Three examples are given in Theodor Ehrenstein, *Das alte Testament im Bilde* (Vienna 1923) 37-38 figs. 5, 7, 16.

pents, if not of all land animals.[20] Although according to Isidore dragons and other serpents by definition do not have feet, they did come to acquire them in the course of time, as can be seen from the illuminated manuscripts of the *Physiologus*, or bestiary. In the oldest surviving illustrated bestiary, the ninth-century Bern manuscript, none of the serpents have appendages.[21] The vipers, which have arms in virtue of being half human in form, do not count (I shall deal with them later). In the only tenth-century illustrated bestiary that has come down to us, the Brussels manuscript, the serpents are footless.[22] No eleventh-century illustrated bestiaries are extant, but many survive from the twelfth century, and in them there is an abundance of footed and winged serpents of various kinds, including amphisbenas, asps, basilisks, dragons, and hydruses.

This is not the place to attempt to trace all the factors that contributed to this development, but as far as the devil in his role of serpent is concerned, the raw material for the transformation can be found in the *Stuttgart Psalter*, which is dated between 820 and 830.[23] The Eden serpent in this work is limbless (fols. 28v, 121v), as are the larger serpents or dragons, except that some have wings (fols. 69v, 107v). But we find a creature tormenting the damned in hell which has the head and forequarters, including the legs, of a dog, and a body that tapers into the tail of a serpent (fol. 10v). The whale that swallows Jonah is somewhat similar, except that its serpentine body ends in a fish's tail (fols. 79, 147v). The whale came to be identified with "Leviathan the twisting serpent" of Isaiah 27.1, and the whole verse was read as referring to the devil.

It is likely too that the dragon-devil of the Apocalypse would be influenced by his colleague, the beast from the sea, which shared with him the attributes of seven heads and ten horns, but which had in addition the feet of a bear. The ninth-century *Valenciennes Apocalypse* shows this creature to have only two feet, with the rest of its body being that of a sea serpent like the whale of the *Stuttgart Psalter*. The dragon, in contrast, is still limbless in this early work.[24]

When we come to the *Bamberg Apocalypse* at the beginning of the eleventh century, we see that a good deal of interchange has occurred among several

---

[20] Isidore, *Etymologiae, sive Origines* 12.4.4, ed. W. M. Lindsay (Oxford 1911). Other flying serpents are the jaculus and the siren serpent (12.4.29).

[21] *Physiologus bernensis* (Codex bongarsianus 318, Bern Burgerbibliothek), ed. Christoph von Steiger and Otto Homburger (Basel 1964). This manuscript represents the C tradition.

[22] *Physiologus* (A tradition), Brussels, Bibliothèque Royale 10074 fols. 141v, 143; given in Richard Stettiner, *Die illustrierten Prudentiushandschrifte* (Berlin 1905) pl. 177 figs. 2, 5.

[23] Wilhelm Hoffmann *et al.*, *Der stuttgarter Bilderpsalter* (Stuttgart 1965-1968).

[24] See Amédée Boinet, *La miniature carolingienne* (Paris 1913) pl. 159a. I wish to thank Ruth Mellinkoff and Barbara Abou-El-Haj for drawing my attention to these Carolingian whales and apocalyptic beasts, respectively.

of the evil monsters, including the beast from the earth and the red beast of Babylon. The dragon-devil now has a pair of wings and a pair of feet, and his "angels," when engaging in battle with Michael and his angels, resemble him, except that they have only one head apiece instead of seven.[25]

A serpent of this sort, that is, one having two wings and two feet, appears in the Eden scenes of the bronze doors of Saint Michael's Church, Hildesheim (A.D. 1015). In the panel portraying the temptation, this elaborate serpent, which obviously represents the devil or a delegated demon, looks on from one tree, while an ordinary limbless serpent with fruit in its mouth is coiled around the forbidden tree, tempting Eve. In the next panel it is the limbed serpent, now breathing fire, that Eve accuses when called to account by God, and the simple serpent has disappeared from the scene (or perhaps we are meant to think that the limbed serpent transformed itself into a limbless form, and then resumed its original shape.)[26] The next logical step would be to have a limbed serpent do the actual tempting, as in the *Huntingfield Psalter*.[27]

There was another traditional concept of the Eden serpent which I have not yet mentioned, namely, that before it was cursed it was able to hold itself erect, not by means of legs, but simply by standing on the tip of its tail. We see an example of this in the ninth-century *Grandval Bible*.[28]

Some scholars began to identify the Eden serpent as a particular species of serpent, especially the free-standing pareas, mentioned by Lucan in his *Pharsalia* and followed by Isidore. This tendency was objected to by Alexander Neckham, an Englishman (born at Saint Albans in 1157) who was a distinguished professor at Paris as early as 1180. In his *De naturis rerum* he says that he is not prepared to say whether the serpent used by Satan to deceive Eve was a viper. "Nor," he goes on, "will you wring from me the assertion that it was a pareas that appeared to the first parent, although some try to prove this to have been the case. Now they take their argument from what is said in Genesis::'Upon your belly shall you go.' For they conjecture from this that that serpent was erect, according to what Lucan says: 'And the pareas, tensed to plow his way with his tail.'"[29]

Neckham does not describe the viper. If, as seems likely, he was familiar only with Isidore or the most common form of medieval bestiary, which

[25] Heinrich Wölfflin, *Die bamberger Apokalypse* (Munich 1921) pl. 30.

[26] See Francis J. Tschan, *Saint Bernward of Hildesheim* 3, Publications in Mediaeval Studies 13 (Notre Dame 1952) pls. 118-119.

[27] Above, n. 18.

[28] Wilhelm Koehler, *Die karolingischen Miniaturen* 1.3 (Berlin 1930, repr. 1963) pl. 50.

[29] Alexander Neckham, *De naturis rerum* 2.105, ed. Thomas Wright, Rolls Series 34 (London 1863) 188. See Lucan, *Pharsalia* 9.721; Isidore 12.4.27.

simply repeated Isidore's entry,[30] he would have no definite picture in mind, since no description is given. If, however, he knew the definition of the Greek *Physiologus* in one of its Latin versions (the *Y*, *A*, and *C* traditions), he would have been thinking of a creature whose lower half was crocodilian and whose upper half was human in appearance, either male or female, depending on its own sex. The illustration in the Bern manuscript, however, provides the creatures with the lower extremities of a simple limbless serpent, and not those of a crocodile. The male has a triple fin at the end, like that of a fish.[31] This description of the viper may have been influential in the development of the tradition to which this essay is primarily directed.[32]

Those who believed the Eden serpent to be a particular kind of serpent that continued to exist after the fall did not regard God's curse as hereditary (at least not in all serpents), unlike those who held that the serpent had feet which were cut off. For they maintained that other serpents of the same kind remained erect after the curse, since a breed of this sort could be so described by Lucan and Isidore. Some authorities, by the way, following the lead of Saint Augustine, interpreted the curse as applying to the devil; and in the twelfth century Rupert of Deutz and Hugh of Saint Victor went further and exempted the serpent from it. Rupert was even able to prove from Genesis that the serpent had its legless nature and reptilian crawl from the beginning, before the fall.[33]

---

[30] Isidore, *Etymologiae* 12.4.10, and the various bestiaries in the expanded *B* tradition of the *Physiologus*; see Florence McCulloch, *Medieval Latin and French Bestiaries*, University of N. Carolina Studies in the Romance Languages and Literatures 33 (Chapel Hill 1960) 28ff. Neckham's initial characterization of the viper (p. 187) corresponds closely to Isidore's.

[31] *Physiologus bernensis* fol. 111. Francis J. Carmody gives what he takes to be the *Physiologus's* original description of the viper in his *Physiologus; the Very Ancient Book of Beasts, Plants, and Stones* (San Francisco 1953) chap. 13: "The Physiologus tells of the viper that the male has a man's face, the female a woman's face; from head to navel they have the form of men, thence to the tail the form of the crocodile." His edition of the *Y* text reads: "Physiologus dicit de vipera quoniam faciem habet hominis masculus, femina autem mulieris, usque ad umbilicum; ab umbilico autem usque ad caudam corcodrilli habet figuram." *Physiologus latinus versio Y* 12, University of California Publications in Classical Philology 12 (Berkeley 1941) 110.

[32] Schmerber (n. 1 above) 12-15 notes that in late Hellenistic times sarcophagi (especially Roman ones) showed Hercules fighting with a Hydra that was half woman and half serpent; he points out that Hydra here has the form of Echidna, her mother, who, according to Hesiod, "is half a nymph with glancing eyes and fair cheeks, and half again a huge snake, great and awful, with speckled skin" (*Theogony* 297-299, trans. H. G. Evelyn White, Loeb Classical Library). It was obviously this description that inspired the *Physiologus* notion of the viper, which in Greek is none other than *echidna*. The Latin form, *vipera*, is, like the Greek, in the feminine gender, and the female of the species therefore has denotative primacy over the male.

[33] Augustine, *De Genesi ad litteram* 11.36; Rupert of Deutz, *De Trinitate et operibus eius* in Gen. 3.18 (PL 167.303-304); Hugh of Saint Victor, *Adnotat. elucid. in Pent.* in Gen. (PL 174.42). I owe these references to an article on "The Lintel Fragment Representing Eve

III. Peter Comestor's Virginal Serpent

About the year 1170 a new tradition was born, that of the maiden-faced serpent in the Garden of Eden. It was fathered by the celebrated "Peter the Eater"—Petrus Comestor or Manducator (circa 1100-circa 1180), who was known as "the Master of the Histories," the histories being the chapters of his *Historia scholastica*, a paraphrase of the Bible, supplemented from various sacred and profane sources. He began this work around the time that he became a canon regular of Saint Victor in Paris.

In his "Story of the Book of Genesis," Peter speaks of the serpent as follows:

> "The serpent was more cunning than all other animals," both by nature and by accident—by accident, because it was filled with the demon. For when Lucifer had been cast out of the paradise of spirits, he envied man, because he was in the paradise of bodies. He knew that if he made him transgress he too would be cast out. Because he was afraid of being found out by the man, he approached the woman, who had less foresight and was "wax to be twisted into vice"[34] and this by means of the serpent; for the serpent at that time was erect like a man, since it was laid prostrate when it was cursed; and even now the pareas is said to be erect when it moves. He also chose a certain kind of serpent, as Bede says, which had the countenance of a virgin, because like favors like; and he moved its tongue to speak, though it knew nothing itself, just as he speaks through the frenzied and possessed.[35]

Peter does believe, however, that the serpent that Lucifer used had a voice of its own, since he says that part of the serpent's punishment was to have its voice taken away, and poison put in its mouth.[36]

Even though Peter's career began in Troyes, the chief center of rabbinical exegesis in the North, he does not follow the Jewish tradition of giving the

---

from Saint-Lazare at Autun," which Professor O. K. Werckmeister of UCLA is preparing for publication.

[34] Cf. Horace, *Ars poetica* 163.

[35] Peter Comestor, *Historia scholastica* 1.21, PL. 198.1072: "'Serpens erat callidior cunctis animantibus' et naturaliter et incidenter. Incidenter, quia plenus erat daemone. Lucifer enim delectus a paradiso spirituum invidit homini, quod esset in paradiso corporum, sciens si faceret eum transgredi, quod et ille eiceretur. Timens vero deprehendi a viro, mulierem minus providam et certam [*sic*; *lege* ceream] in vitium flecti aggressus est, et hoc per serpentem, quia tunc serpens erectus est ut homo, quia in maledictione prostratus est; et adhuc, ut tradunt, phareas erectus incedit. Elegit etiam quoddam genus serpentis, ut ait Beda, virgineum vultum habens, quia similia similibus applaudunt, et movit ad loquendum linguam eius, tamen nescientis, sicut et per fanaticos et energumenos loquitur."

[36] *Ibid.* 1.23 (PL 198.1074).

serpent feet in its pristine state, but apparently accepts the "upright but legless" tradition of the West. At any rate, when speaking of the serpent's fate, to go on its belly thenceforward, he does not speak of any loss of "footage."[37] But since he acknowledges that some serpents, like the pareas, remain in their upright position, he does not seem to think that God laid a curse upon all serpents, but only upon the individual one that was employed in Eden by the devil. If so, he presumably believed that there still existed venomless serpents with virginal faces and voices, which could move in an upright position.

Peter seems to cite the Venerable Bede as his source for the idea of a maiden-headed serpent, and his statement was interpreted in this way by many of his readers. An example is Stephen Langton, who glossed the *Historia* shortly after Peter's death.[38] But Bonnell appears to be correct when he says that the concept is foreign to Bede, and that perhaps Peter is attributing to Bede only what goes before "ut ait Beda," namely, "elegit etiam quoddam genus serpentis," and not what follows (virgineum vultum habens); but he also suggests a possible misreading of a phrase in a work attributed to Bede.[39]

IV. "A Certain Kind of Serpent"

Whether or not we are inclined to grant that a "misprint" may have led Peter to his conclusion that the serpent that deceived Eve had a virginal countenance, we must remain puzzled by the Master of the Histories' willingness to accept what should have struck him (I feel) as a most unlikely suggestion. What is the psychological explanation for his adoption of the idea?

We may be able to throw some light upon this problem by citing an earlier precedent of the very same notion; it is all the more remarkable in that it

---

[37] *Ibid.* For Peter's Jewish connections, see Esra Shereshevsky, "Hebrew traditions in Peter Comestor's *Historia scholastica*," *Jewish Quarterly Review* 59 (1969) 268-289.

[38] Stephen Langton, *Expositio litteralis in Hist. schol.*, Paris Bibliothèque Nationale MS lat. 14417 fol. 129v: "Dicit Beda uirgineum uultum habuisse." This gloss was written before 1187. In an *Expositio moralis*, composed in 1193 (MS 14414) Langton does not take up the subject of the maiden's head when speaking of the serpent (fol. 116v). Cf. F. Stegmüller, *Repertorium biblicum medii aevi* 5 (Madrid 1955) 235, 239. Nor does he refer to this interpretation in his own commentary on the Heptateuch (I have consulted only Cambridge Peterhouse MS 112 fols. 7v-8v), which was written also during his Paris period (i.e., before 1206); see Beryl Smalley, in G. Lacombe and B. Smalley, "Studies on the Commentaries of Cardinal Stephen Langton," *Archives d'histoire doctrinale et littéraire du moyen âge* 5 (1930) 5-220, esp. 163-169.

[39] Bonnell (n. 1 above) 257 n. 3. He quotes this sentence from the Pseudo-Bede *Quaestiones super Genesim*: "Serpens per se loqui non poterat . . . nisi nimirum illum diabolus utens, et velut organum per quod articulatum sonum emitteret" (PL 93.276), and asks if *velut organum* could have been corrupted into *vultum virgineum*.

seems highly unlikely for it to have influenced Comestor's work, for it appears only in an ancient Syrian biblical history called *The Cave of Treasures*.[40] This work, fictitiously ascribed to Ephraem the Syrian, says that Satan, filled with jealousy and wrath, "took up his abode in the serpent, and he raised him up and made him to fly through the air to the skirts of Mount (Eden), where-on was Paradise." Satan hid in the serpent because his own appearance was so foul that Eve would have fled from him if she had seen how he really looked; therefore just as a man who teaches a bird to speak Greek hides be-hind a mirror and makes the bird think that a fellow bird is speaking to it, Satan entered the serpent and called Eve by name. "And when she turned round towards him, she saw her own form [reflected] in him, and she talked to him; and Satan led her astray with his lying words, because the nature of woman is soft [or, yielding]."[41]

From this account I conclude either that Eve looked like a serpent or that the serpent looked like a woman! Budge's interpretation seems to be that Eve herself was somehow mirrored in the serpent. Luise Troje conjectures that the *Cave of Treasures* passage is a polemic against the Hellenistic goddess Isis-Thermutis, an erect serpent with the breasts and head of a woman.[42] The *Cave* serpent, however, seems to have been the usual legged masculine serpent of Eastern tradition; God says, "I have fettered his legs in his belly, and I have given him the dust of the earth for food."[43]

If we accept Mrs. Troje's reading of the motivation of the author of *The Cave of Treasures*, we should seek a similar movement in Peter Comestor's mind. We can hardly think of him as being exercised against a serpentine deity with a woman's face, nor are we able to see a polemic against Eve for any serpentine qualities she might have possessed; rather we must simply think that he accepted the idea of a woman-faced serpent because he knew

---

[40] E. A. Wallis Budge, *The Book of the Cave of Treasures* (London 1927) xi-xiv, puts the original work in the fourth century, but says that the form in which we have it is no older than the sixth century. Cf. Albrecht Götze, "Die Schatzhöhle," *Sitzungsberichte der Heidelberger Akademie der Wissenschaften*, philosophisch-historische Klasse 13 (1922) 4.38, who postulates a Syriac archetype of which two recensions survive: 1) a Nestorian Syriac edition, made after A. D. 500, and 2) a Monophysite Arabic translation, made circa 750-760. There is also an Ethiopic version, based on the Arabic.

[41] Budge 63-64.

[42] L. Troje, "*AΔAM* und *ZΩH*; eine Szene der altchristlichen Kunst in ihrem religions-geschichtlichen Zusammenhange," *Sitzungsberichte der Heidelberger Akademie der Wissenschaften*, philos.-hist. Klasse 7 (1916) 17.43 n. 3. Mrs. Troje also calls attention to a Gnostic principle, conceived of as a virgin above and serpent below. Alice Kemp-Welch (n. 1 above) 987-989 attempted, with no evidence, to bring the Gnostic Serpent-Sophia to bear upon the maiden-headed Eden serpent of the medieval West by way of the Albigensians.

[43] Budge 67.

that such serpents existed. I have mentioned the viper as one example. Were there others?

The siren is an obvious candidate. The classical form of this creature was half virginal, half birdlike.[44] Hyginus specifies that the upper part is that of a woman,[45] and no doubt the common view was that it had the head, arms, and torso of a woman, and the lower body, legs, and tail of a bird.

The *Physiologus*, in the chapter on the siren and onocentaur, says that the siren has the figure of a human being to the navel, and in the other half the figure of a bird.[46] Isidore follows this tradition in general, but adds that it has wings and talons.[47]

The *Physiologus* is commenting on the Septuagint version of Isaiah 13.21-22. Jerome, however, in his comentary on the same text says that the word that is translated by "sirens" he interpreted to mean either demons, or a kind of monster, or large flying dragons with crests.[48] Perhaps Isidore was inspired by Jerome when he included in his treatment of serpents the note that "in Arabia there are serpents with wings, which are called sirens; they run faster than horses, but they are also said to fly."[49]

Somewhat after Isidore's time, beginning with the *Liber monstrorum* (ascribed to Aldhelm, Bishop of Sherborne), the siren became half fish instead of half bird, and thus the mermaid was born.[50] But the tradition of the bird-siren lived on, and so apparently did that of the serpent-siren, for they are obviously combined in the scene of the siren and onocentaur sculpted on one of the capitals in the choir (right side) of the twelfth-century cathedral of Autun (fig. 1). Here the siren has only a woman's head, with a rather scaly body, a serpent's tail, and a bird's wings and feet.[51]

---

[44] See Edmond Faral, "La queue de poisson des sirènes," *Romania* 74 (1953) 433-506, esp. 439-440.

[45] Hyginus, *Fabulae* 125, ed. H. J. Rose (Leyden 1933, repr. 1963) 91.

[46] *Physiologus* Y 15 (113-114): "Dimidiam partem usque ad umbilicum hominis habent figuram, dimidio autem volatilis."

[47] Isidore, *Etym.* 11.3.30.

[48] Jerome, *Comm. on Is.* (PL 24.163): "Sirenae autem *thennim* vocantur, quas nos aut daemones, aut monstra quaedam, aut certe dracones magnos interpretabamur, qui cristati sunt et volantes."

[49] Isidore, *Etym.* 12.4.29.

[50] Faral (n. 42 above); see below, n. 51.

[51] There is a similar scene on a capital in the church at Vézelay, but the onocentaur (if such it be) is female, and there is a three-headed bird between it and the siren. Denis Grivot and George Zarnecki, *Gislebertus, Sculptor of Autun* (New York 1961) 66 (cf. pl. B 12-16), think that the three-headed bird belongs to the original scene. The coupling of onocentaur and siren by themselves, however, is obviously more primitive. Grivot and Zarnecki do not place the scene in the *Physiologus* tradition, perhaps because they consider the humanoid figure to be a faun. But as is pointed out by Richard Hamann, "Diana and the Snake-tongued Demon," *The Burlington Magazine for Connoisseurs* 61.2 (July-Dec. 1932) 207, centaurs and fauns are portrayed alike. Furthermore, the ordinary *Physiologus* description

Similar creatures can be found in another twelfth-century cathedral, that of Sens, not far from Peter's home city of Troyes; on one capital (in the left nave), there are two sirens of the Autun type; on another (in the right nave), one such siren is with a male of the species—he has the same attributes as his partner, except that he is endowed with a beard.

The maiden-faced scorpion is another medieval invention that antedates the *Historia scholastica*. Isidore, who wrote in the seventh century, says simply that the scorpion is a worm (that is, *vermis*, a word that he applies chiefly to insects and arachnids and not to serpents) with a sting in its tail.[52] He speaks of another kind of scorpion, however, which is a type of *virga*, that is, a "switch" or whip.[53] This coincidence may have inspired an etymological explanation of the Isidorean type, according to which the scorpion was characterized as a *virga* because it had the face of a *virgo*, as is implied in Holy Writ (though it is obvious that a *virga* was called a scorpion because of the scorpionlike wounds that it inflicted).

One of the scriptural bases for representing scorpions with female faces is the description of the hellish locusts in the Apocalypse; they had the power like that of the scorpions of the earth, and the torment they inflicted was like that of a scorpion; they looked like horses prepared for battle; they wore crowns on their heads, had faces like those of human beings and hair like that of women, and tails like those of scorpions, with stings in them. Furthermore, in the Greek text they are he-locusts, but they were transformed into she-locusts because of the gender of *locusta*.[54] We see an illustration of these creatures in the mid-eleventh-century Saint-Sever copy of Beatus of Liébana's *Commentary on the Apocalypse*, in which some have the bodies of lions and others the bodies of locusts, or grasshoppers.[55]

Another scriptural indication of the woman-headed scorpion occurs in the Book of Ecclesiasticus, where Jesus the son of Sirach warn that "a wicked woman is like a loose ox-yoke; a man who holds her is like one who grasps

of the onocentaur does not demand a complete ass's body; its lower part is simply said to "exceedingly wild," or, as the *Y* version says, "like an ass." See McCulloch (n. 30 above) 166.

[52] Isidore, *Etymologiae* 12.5.4: "Scorpio vermis terrenus, qui potius vermibus ascribitur, non serpentibus; animal armatum aculeo, et ex eo graece vocatum quod cauda figat et arcuato vulnere venena diffundat."

[53] *Ibid.* 5.27.18: "Virgae sunt summitates frondium arborumque, dictae quod virides sint, vel quod vim habeant arguendi; quae si lenis fuerit, virga est; si certe nodosa vel aculeata, scorpio rectissimo nomine vocatur, qui arcuato vulnere in corpus infigitur."

[54] Rev. 9.3, 5, 7-8, 10. In classical Greek locust (*akris*) is feminine but it is treated as masculine in this text of the New Testament.

[55] Paris Bib. Nat. MS lat. 8878 fol. 145; Jean Porcher, *Medieval French Miniatures* (New York [1960]) 27 (and pl. 18).

a scorpion."[56] The author of the *Ancrene Riwle*, who seems to have flourished somewhat later than Comestor,[57] applies the text to woman in general and attributes the sentiment to Solomon: "The man who grasps a woman is like one who grasps a scorpion." The scorpion is taken as a symbol of lechery in the *Ancrene Riwle*, and is described as "a type of worm that is said to have a head something like a woman's but behind this it is a serpent. It puts forth a fair countenance and flatters with its head but stings with its tail. Such then is lechery, the devil's beast."[58]

The *Ancrene Riwle* therefore describes a scorpion as a woman-headed serpent, a symbol of lechery, the animal used by the devil. If this work was written after Peter Comestor's *Historia*, it is barely possible that the latter work influenced this description. But it is obvious that the *Riwle* does not have the Eden serpent in mind at all, but is drawing on a tradition independent of it. The characterization of the scorpion as part serpent was obviously due to the fact that the Germanic cognate of *vermis* means not only "worm" but primarily "serpent" or "dragon" (that is, "large serpent").

V. THE SPHINX IN EDEN

One other fabulous monster from classical times must be mentioned as a possible influence on the womanized Eden serpent, and that is the Sphinx, who according to Hesiod is both daughter and granddaughter of Echidna. By Typhaon (another serpent-type) Echidna bore the hounds Orthus and Cerberus, as well as Hydra and Chimaera. Then she (Echidna, though Hesiod could possibly mean Chimaera) "was subject in love to Orthus and brought forth the deadly Sphinx which destroyed the Cadmeans."[59] Hesiod does not describe the Sphinx, but since she is found in such serpentine company, it is not surprising that she sometimes is thought to have something of the serpent about her. This characteristic, however, is mentioned, so far as I know, in only one classical literary source (which alludes to another written source), namely, a scholion on the *Phoenissae* of Euripides: "The Sphinx, as it is written, had the tail of a she-dragon" (δράκαινα).[60]

---

[56] Ecclus. 26.10: "Sicut boum iugum quod movetur, ita et mulier nequam; qui tenet illam quasi qui apprehendit scorpionem."

[57] C. H. Talbot, "Some Notes on the Dating of the *Ancrene Riwle*," *Neophilologus* 40 (1956) 38-50, suggests that the work may have been composed even in the first part of the thirteenth century.

[58] *The English Text of the Ancrene Riwle*, London British Museum Cotton MS Nero A XIV, ed. Mabel Day, Early English Text Society 225 (London 1952) 92.

[59] Hesiod, *Theogony* 306-327 (Loeb 100-103). Hesiod's word for Sphinx is Phix.

[60] W. Dindorf, *Scholia graeca in Euripidis tragoedias* (Oxford 1863) 3.407 (*Scholia in Phoenissas* 1760). Dindorf cites the twelfth-century San Marco manuscript and the fourteenth-century Munich manuscript as reading δράκαινα, whereas the thirteenth-century Paris manuscript and the Venice 1534 edition read the masculine form, δράκω. But ac-

The only ancient examples of the serpent-tailed sphinx that I have seen, however, have tails that end with a serpent's head.[61] This is a fashion popularized by the Chimaera,[62] and continued in the lion-headed, fire-breathing horses of the Apocalypse.[63] The ancient sphinxes of this sort could hardly have come to the attention of the people of the Middle Ages. But somehow or other the image made its appearance in the medieval West (whether or not it was identified as a sphinx), as in one of the capitals in the crypt of the Duomo of Modena (fig. 2). The work was done in the time of Wiligelmo (early twelfth century), and it shows a creature, repeated four times, with a woman's head covered by a flat hat; it has a heavy horse's body and hooves, the wings of a bird, and a (serpentine?) tail ending in a laughing head.[64]

From further south in Italy, in Terracina, comes a wooden chest tentatively dated in the eleventh century,[65] in which a sphinxlike creature is brought into conjunction with what is apparently a depiction of the fall of Adam and Eve (fig. 3). The serpent is erect between Adam and Eve where the tree is normally placed, and it seems to be speaking in Eve's ear, though Adam and Eve both hold foliage in front of them, which would indicate that they have already fallen. But this is the traditional stylized way of portraying the unfortunate couple. Above these three figures is what looks like a winged lion with a human face. Perhaps we are meant to think of the devil —we recall that in the eleventh-century door from Hildesheim a winged and footed serpent looked on as an ordinary serpent (or the same serpent simplified) did the actual tempting; and in the Junius manuscript and the

cording to the edition of Eduard Schwartz, *Scholia in Euripidem* (Berlin 1887) 1.414, not only the San Marco manuscript but the Paris manuscript as well (and a thirteenth-century Vatican manuscript) have δράκαινα.

[61] A. Dessenne, *Le sphinx: étude iconographique*: vol. 1, *Des origines a la fin du second millénaire*, Bibliothèque des écoles françaises d'Athènes et de Rome 186 (Paris 1957) 204-205, says that the serpent-headed tail is encountered among nearly all the neo-Hittite sphinxes of the ninth and eighth centuries before Christ; he shows a sample from Perachora, Corinth (pl. 38.6). An Etruscan example is in the museum at Palermo (coll. Casuccini no. 103), in Gustavo Körte, *I rilievi delle urne etrusche*, Imperiale istituto archeologico germanico (Berlin 1916) 3.222 pl. 150.15. An ancient Greek bronze statuette of a sphinx in the Berlin museum (no. 8266) has a tail that ends in a bearded serpent's head (*Archäologischer Anzeiger* 8 [1893] 96).

[62] According to the *Iliad* 6.181 the Chimaera is a lion in front, a goat in the middle, and a serpent behind. This description was also interpolated into Hesiod, after his statement that the Chimaera has three heads, a lion's, a goat's, and a snake's (*Theog.* 321-323).

[63] Rev. 9.17-19.

[64] Arturo Carlo Quintavalle, *Wiligelmo e la sua scuola*, I diamanti dell' arte 28 (Florence 1967) 37. Cf. the *Bamberger Apocalypse* (n. 25 above) p. 23, where similar creatures result from combining the locusts and serpent-tailed horses of Rev. 9.3-19.

[65] The chest is now in the Palazzo Venezia, Rome. See Federico Hermanin, *Il Palazzo di Venezia* (Bologna 1925) 28; *Roma e dintorni*, Touring club italiano (Milan 1965) 94.

Saint Albans Psalter the devil in human (angelic) form is pictured along-side the serpent or the same devil in his serpentine form. But it could also represent the cherub stationed before the garden of Eden,[66] or indeed the cherub (understood as Satan or one of the other sinful angels) who like Adam and Eve was cast out of Eden.[67] It is conceivable that the artist or his source would think of a cherub as a sphinx, from the various descriptions given in the Bible.[68]

It has sometimes been doubted, however, whether the scene deals with the garden of Eden at all, since it is difficult to recognize any other biblical or Christian motif on the chest. But we may point to the scene of the eagle fighting the serpent immediately above the scene that I have been discussing. This struggle was taken as an allegory of Christ's defeat of Satan, and it be-comes very common in Italy from the eleventh century on.[69] Most of the other panels also represent scenes of struggle, and it seems that serpents are the chief enemies of the men, centaurs, birds, and other beasts. Perhaps the scenes are illustrations of the consequences of original sin.

An unequivocal designation of the Eden serpent as a sphinx comes in the *Chester Plays*, which could not have been composed in English before the last quarter of the fourteenth century.[70] The play of the Fall, however, may have been based on an earlier Latin play, since fragments of Latin dialogue appear in the best manuscript.[71] At the place where the devil disguises him-self as a serpent there occurs this marginal notation:

Versus: Sphinx: volucris penna, serpens pede, fronte puella.

The devil's account of the serpent in the play corresponds to this descrip-tion:

> A manner of an adder is in this place,
> That wings like a bird she has,
> Feet as an adder, a maiden's face;
> Her kind I will take.[72]

---

[66] Gen. 3.24; the Latin reads *cherubim*, which was often understood as singular in the Middle Ages.

[67] Ezek. 28.12-19 (Vulgate).

[68] Ex. 25.19-20; Ezek. 41.18-19; cf. Ezek. 1.5-11.

[69] Rudolf Wittkower, "Eagle and Serpent; a Study in the Migration of Symbols," *Journal of the Warburg Institute* 2 (1938-1939) 293-325 esp. 318.

[70] F. M. Salter, *Medieval Drama in Chester* (Toronto 1955) 33-42; Glynne Wickham, *Early English Stages* 1 (London 1959, repr. 1966) 133-137.

[71] *The Chester Plays* 1, ed. Hermann Deimling, Early English Text Society extra series 62 (London 1892, repr. 1959) 30: At the point where Eve takes the apple: "Vah! Quam dulcis est! Impertiendum est marito." When she suggests that Adam eat, and he agrees: "Quando ita vis, faciam." —B. M. Harl. 2124, A. D. 1607.

[72] *Ibid.* 28. The variants in the Latin verse in the four less authentic manuscripts are proved false by their lack of agreement with Ausonius.

The Latin hexameter is based upon a line in the *Riddle of the Number Three* of the fourth-century poet Ausonius of Bordeaux, who follows a common Greco-Latin tradition characterizing the Sphinx as having the wings of a bird, the body of a lioness, and the face of a girl:

Sphinx: volucris pennis, pedibus fera, fronte puella.[73]

The author of the *Chester Plays* or the author of his source cleverly substituted serpent's feet for those of the lioness; he kept the meter by availing himself of the poetic option of using the singular for the plural—necessarily, for the feet, but for good measure for the wings. The questions arise (and I must leave them unanswered for the present): How did the author of this verse know Ausonius? And how did he know (if he did not simply improvise it) that the Sphinx was sometimes characterized as partly serpentine?

VI. Species of Womanized Serpents

We cannot tell with certainty how the author of the *Chester Plays* envisaged his adder, nor specify the kind of costume used by the actor who played the devil when he assumed the adder's form. Presumably the devil's ordinary (that is, nonserpentine) costume included feathers, since the banns for the play of the temptation of Jesus promise the customary appearance of "the devil in his feathers, all ragger [*lege* ragged] and rent."[74] The author of the *Chester Plays*, however, may have been inspired by another, more common way of portraying the Eden serpent, that is, as a traditional winged and footed serpent like the one in the *Huntingfield Psalter*, but with a woman's head. Winged serpents of this kind were not given reptilian or batlike wings, such as demons in their humanoid forms usually possess, but rather feathered, birdlike ones.

The earliest instance of a woman-headed Eden serpent of this kind that has come to my attention occurs in a copy made in 1220 of Beatus's *Commentary on the Apocalypse*, which is now in the Pierpont Morgan Library.[75]

---

[73] Ausonius, *Griphus ternarii numeri* 41, ed. Rudolf Peiper, *Decimi Magni Ausonii Burdigalensis Opuscula* (Leipzig 1886) 202.

[74] *Chester Plays* 6. M. D. Anderson, *Drama and Imagery in English Medieval Churches* (Cambridge 1963) 169-170 (and pl. 24a), suggests that a feathered fiend that appears on a misericord in the church at Gayton in Northamptonshire could have been inspired by a play. It could conceivably double as the Chester serpent without further transformation, although we might object that the feet of this creature have talons like those of a bird of prey; but since it was anyone's guess what the feet of a serpent looked like, such ones as these might have been considered perfectly satisfactory.

[75] Morgan MS 429 fol. 6. The colophon is dated 1258 of the Spanish era, which is the equivalent of A. D. 1220. It is interesting to see that in the same manuscript there is another depiction of the Eden temptation (a detail of the *Mappa mundi* page, fol. 32), where the tempter is just an ordinary serpent twined around the tree. See Cook (n. 18 above) 165 fig. 19.

The serpent in the temptation scene (fol. 6v) has only the tail of a serpent, with the body and wings of a bird and a vulturelike (or, if one insists, serpentine) neck topped by the tiny head of a woman (fig. 4).[76]

A slightly different version of the woman-headed serpent appeared a short time after the Beatus version. On a pillar of the Virgin portal of the Cathedral of Notre Dame in Amiens there is a statue of the Virgin (dating from circa 1230) crushing a sphinxlike serpent under her feet in fulfillment of the prophecy made in the curse of the Eden serpent (fig. 5). It is wingless, however, and has only one pair of legs (with paws), in front, and a serpentine tail in back; and the beast has what looks like a wimpled woman's head. In the panel below, where the temptation of Eve is depicted, the serpent is of the same type, except that it has no headcovering, and the hair is visible (fig. 6).[77]

These species of serpent tended toward extinction after the fourteenth century. It is evident that some modifications would have had to be made in these types before an actor could easily assume their form. Another, more adaptable, kind of serpent, which would better allow for stage use, is suggested in William Langland's *Piers the Plowman*. He has it that Satan disguised himself "ylyke a lusarde with a lady visage."[78] If a lizard is to be considered a serpent, then there is a precedent in nature for the serpent's feet. The celebrated picture of the fifteenth-century Dutch painter Hugo van der Goes

---

[76] Another early example of this kind of illustrated serpent-lady appears in *Queen Blanche's Psalter*, which was executed about 1230. See Porcher (n. 55 above) pl. 42. Another instance can be seen in the *Holkham Bible*, an English work with a French text, which seems to have been produced in the London area about 1330; see W. O. Hassall, *The Holkham Bible Picture Book* (London 1954) 65. Another example is the *Bible historiale* in the Geneva library (MS fr. 2 fol. 7), which dates from the second half of the fourteenth century; see Hippolyte Aubert, "Les principaux manuscrits à peintures de la bibliothèque publique et universitaire de Genève," *Bulletin de la Société française de reproductions de manuscrits à peintures* 2 (1912) 61-62 (pl. 31). But here the serpent is given two pairs of feet.

[77] Somewhat similar Eden serpents appear in two Jewish manuscripts executed at the end of the thirteenth century (thereby showing that, even though the tradition of the lady serpent did not originate with the Jews, it eventually found its way to them). One is in a Cologne manuscript discussed by Elisabeth Moses, "Über eine kölner Handschrift der Mischneh Thora des Maimonides," *Zeitschrift für bildenden Kunst* 60 (1926-1927) 71-76, fig. on p. 74. The other is in the British Museum (Add. 11,639 fol. 520v) and is available on postcard; it is likewise in the style of northern France. The *Queen Mary's Psalter*, ed. George Warner (London 1912) pl. 5, has a similar serpent; this work is dated in the beginning of the fourteenth century. All three of these serpents have an enlarged body, between the woman's head and the serpent's tail, where the legs issue on each side much like a mammal's hind limbs. The *Queen Mary's Psalter* miniature is also noteworthy in showing conventional demons nearby aiding in the temptation.

[78] *Piers the Plowman* B 18.335, ed. W. W. Skeat (London 1869) 338. Cf. the four-footed winged serpent of the *Bible historiale* (n. 76 above) and the figure on the Terracina chest (fig. 3).

in Vienna has a serpent that looks like a child dressed in a salamander suit;[79] all four of her limbs are reptilian. In another Dutch picture, painted around the turn of the sixteenth century, that in the *Breviarium Grimani*, van der Goes's example has inspired a similar depiction, except that here the upper limbs and torso are human (the sex, however, is obscured).[80]

Arnoul Gréban no doubt had a lizardlike serpent in mind, for the devil in his biblical play (written around 1452) says that he will take on a virginal face and the feet and body of a serpent; and the stage direction says that he goes on four feet, like a serpent.[81] The sixteenth-century Lucerne plays are similar, and Bonnell attempts to deduce the same for other plays.[82]

Other portrayals of the Eden serpent have no problem with serpents' feet at all, since they use realistic legless snakes, and simply cap them with tiny human heads. An early example of this type occurs in the *Peterborough Psalter*, dated about 1250 (fig. 7).[83] In the fourteenth century a similar serpent was fashioned in the temptation fresco of the Upper Church of the Basilica of Saint Francis at Assisi.[84] Perhaps the most famous instance of this kind occurs in the temptation scene by Masolino in the Brancacci Chapel of the Chiesa del Carmine at Florence (circa 1428). Other examples are numerous.[85]

---

[79] Cf. Anderson (n. 74 above) 144.

[80] Both the van der Goes painting and the Breviary picture (fol. 286v) are reproduced in Ehrenstein (n. 19 above) 58 fig. 89-90, and in Robert A. Koch, "The Salamander in van der Goes' Garden of Eden," *Journal of the Warburg and Courtauld Institutes* 28 (1965) 323-326 pls. 47a and 48c. Herbert Leon Kessler in an appendix to Koch's note ("The Solitary Bird in van der Goes' *Garden of Eden*," 326-229) gives two more examples of Eden serpents influenced by van der Goes: in one, formerly in the Hirsch collection (pl. 49c), the salamander-serpent has been given female breasts; in the other, a *Garden of Paradise* by a follower of Bosch, now in the Chicago Art Institute (pl. 50ab), the serpent seems to be completely human, except that a serpentine tail descends from its back.

[81] Arnoul Gréban, *Le mystère de la passion*, ed. Omer Jodogne, Académie royale de Belgique, classe des lettres, mémoires 10.12.3 (Brussels 1965) 1.18.

[82] Bonnell (n. 1 above) 281-288. We may add to his list the *Passion of Semur*, which survives in a manuscript dated 1488; it has a serpent with the breast of a woman and the feet and tail of a serpent, and it goes upright. See the ed. of mile ÉRoy, *Le mystère de la Passion en France du XIVᵉ au XVIᵉ siècle*, Revue bourguignonne 13.3-4 (Dijon 1903) 13: "Habeat pectus feminae, pedes et caudam serpentis, et vadat totus directus, et habeat pellem de quodam penno [*lege* panno] rubro." Cf. Grace Frank, *The Medieval French Drama*, ed. 2 (Oxford 1960) 176.

[83] *Le psautier de Peterborough*, ed. J. van den Gheyn (Haarlem [1906]) pl. 15 (Bibl. royale de Belgique MS 9961-62 fol. 25).

[84] Beda Kleinschmidt, *Die Wandmalereien der Basilika San Francisco in Assisi* (Berlin 1930) pl. 7a.

[85] See, for instance, Ehrenstein (n. 19 above) 18 fig. 57 (Ghiberti), 54 fig. 75 (della Quercia), 56 fig. 81 (Lippi), 60 fig. 90 (School of Raphael). There is a crowned serpent-lady of this type on the enameled altar of the Stiftskirche in Klosterneuberg, which Ehrenstein dates as 1186 (46 fig. 46), but according to Schmerber (n. 1 above) 8 this part is a fourteenth-century restoration. Bonnell (n. 1 above) 266 fig. 1 shows Didron's sketch of a double-

The Eden serpent was also often adorned with more features of a woman than just her face or head. A very early example (circa 1220) occurs in the base of the statue of the Virgin in the door decoration in the cathedral of Notre Dame in Paris, where the serpent has not only the head but the breasts, shoulders, and arms of a woman, above a serpentine body that tapers so severely that the creature looks like a mermaid. The arms, however, end in clawlike hands, and there is a pair of wings issuing from her back (fig. 8).

Another serpent with the upper part of a woman's torso (but without claws or wings) occurs in a Paris psalter of the middle of the thirteenth century.[86] Later examples of the type can be seen in Bosch's *Haycart* triptych and in Raphael's Vatican Stanze. Michelangelo's celebrated representation in the Sistine Chapel goes much further, so that even the upper legs of a woman appear, both of which turn into serpentine bodies that twine around the tree; the end of one of them is visible, and presumably the end of the other is hidden behind the tree. As Bonnell suggests,[87] it seems clear that Michelangelo was primarily influenced by the classical giant, with its human body and serpentine legs. Titian's painting of the temptation, now in the Prado, has an infant version of the same type, that is, a serpent that has two distinct tails, while the upper part is a torso of a very young child—and therefore one of indeterminable sex.

VII. THE REACTION OF THE LEARNED

What effect did Comestor's novel conception of the Eden serpent have upon the scholarly and literary world? Not much, it seems. But in the realm of theology, Saint Bonaventure, writing at the middle of the thirteenth century, accepts the notion as a solution to a problem raised in his commentary on the *Sentences* of Peter Lombard. He admits that if the devil had appeared in human form it would have been easier for him to have engaged Eve in conversation; but divine providence was unwilling to permit him so advantageous a strategy, and he had to be content with a compromise, namely, the body of a serpent, which nevertheless had a virgin's face, as the Venerable Bede asserts. As a result he could be concealed from one end, but was left open to discovery from the other.[88]

Later in the century (1287) the concept was introduced into a literary history by Guido delle Colonne. In his prosaic retelling of Benoît de Sainte-Maure's *Roman de Troie*, he inserts a long explanation of the beginnings of

---

headed serpent, and is no doubt correct in his surmise that the head is repeated to indicate motion, or rather progressive action.

[86] Paris Bib. Nat. MS lat. 10.434 fol. 10; Porcher (n. 55 above) pl. 44.

[87] Bonnell (n. 1 above) 275.

[88] Bonaventure, *In 2 Sent.* 21.1.2 ad 2, *Opera omnia* 2 (Quaracchi 1885) 495.

idolatry. From the time that Lucifer fell, he says, "God changed him into a brute animal, that is, a twisting serpent, and since he is of a huge size he is called a dragon." Guido goes on to indicate, however, that this description is purely allegorical:

> For he is said to be twisting and to be in this sea [the ocean, where he was seen by Saint Brendan] because the devil acts with shifty cunning in the sea of this world in his effort to deceive the souls of wretched men. He is that Leviathan who from the very outset of his fall became a serpent, and, envying the glory of our first parents, had the daring to enter into the paradise of delights; and going erect like a man, he infected them with the vice of prevarication by means of his blind temptations, so that they lost their fear of God's commandment, and by their transgression deserved to be cast down from the glory of that paradise, just as he had deserved by his own fault to be cast down from the glory of heaven.
>
> In spite of what we read in the beginning of the Book of Genesis, according to the Mosaic tradition (where it is said: "But the serpent was more cunning than all the animals that God had made, and he said to the woman, 'Why did God command you?'" and so on), nevertheless according to the tradition of the sacred writings of the catholic and universal Church it is confirmed that, as Bede has written, the devil at that time chose a certain serpent from a certain type of serpents, one that had a virgin's face, and moved its tongue to say what it did, though with no knowledge on its part, just every day the devil still speaks through unknowing fanatics and energumens, that is, through men whose bodies are possessed by these demons; this is discussed in the book *Scholastic Histories*, near the beginning, where the author sets out a history and explanation of the Book of Genesis. Therefore, whatever we Catholics know through these writings, it is certain that that Leviathan, that is, the prince of devils, once cast down from the heavenly heights, either transformed himself into a material serpent or entered into a real one and by his cunning temptations brought about the fall of our wretched parents and their descendants into everlasting ruin.[89]

Peter's theory also appeared in the encyclopedias of natural history—for instance, in Vincent of Beauvais's great *Mirror of Nature*, the final form of which appeared just after the midpoint of the thirteenth century. But in addition to quoting Peter's comments directly,[90] Vincent also records

---

[89] Guido de Columnis, *Historia destructionis Troiae* 10, ed. Nathaniel Edward Griffin, Mediaeval Academy of America Publications 26 (Cambridge, Mass. 1936) 96-97.

[90] Vincent of Beauvais, *Speculum naturale* 30.68, in *Speculum quadruplex* (Douai 1624) 2265-2266.

the modification of the theory produced by Thomas of Cantimpré (or of Brabant) in his *De natura rerum*,[91] a work composed during the 1220s and 1230s,[92] the time in which the first iconographic representations of maiden-headed Eden serpents began to appear.

In his discussion of serpents Thomas comes to one called dracontopod, which is described in the *Book of Monsters*, a work that he ascribes (perhaps accurately) to Aldhelm, the English bishop (d. 709).[93] Aldhelm (if we may, for the moment, accept his authorship of the book as established), in turn, draws on the Pseudo-Clementine *Recognitions* in Rufinus's Latin translation. The author of the *Recognitions* simply mentions the dracontopods of Greek legend to deny that they were the giants mentioned in the sixth chapter of Genesis.[94] Aldhelm improvises a description from the etymology of the word and says: "Greek fables tell of men with enormous bodies, who in spite of such great size were similar to the human race, except that they had tails of dragons, so that they were called dracontopods in Greek."[95] This description occurs in the part of his work dedicated to monstrous types of men, and not in his section on serpents; but he does regard the viper as a

---

[91] *Ibid.* 20.33 (1478). Vincent does not cite Thomas by name but by his work: *Ex libro de natura rerum* or *Ex libro de naturis rerum.*

[92] Cf. C. Ferckel, *Die Gynäkologie des Thomas von Brabant, ausgewählte Kapitel aus Buch I de naturis rerum, beendet um 1240*, Alte Meister der Medizin und Naturkunde 5, ed. G. Klein (Munich 1912) 3; and Lynn Thorndike, *A History of Magic and Experimental Science During the First Thirteen Centuries of Our Era* 2 (New York 1923, repr. 1947) 373.

[93] Beowulf scholars have assigned the *Liber monstrorum* to England; see Dorothy Whitelock, *The Audience of Beowulf* (Oxford 1951, repr. 1958) 47-53; Kenneth Sisam, *Studies in the History of Old English Literature* (Oxford 1953, repr. 1962) 75-77, 288-290. Edmond Faral, "La queue de poisson des sirènes," *Romania* 74 (1953) 433-506 esp. 441-470, discusses the possibility of Aldhelm's authorship, on the basis of Thomas's ascription.

[94] *Recog.* 1.29.3, ed. Bernhard Rehm and Franz Paschke, *Rekognitionen in Rufins Übersetzung*, Die Pseudoklementinen 2, Griechischen christlichen Schriftsteller 51 (Berlin 1965) 25: "Exin nona generatione nascuntur gigantes illi qui a saeculo nominantur, non dracontopedes, ut Graecorum fabulae ferunt, sed immensis corporibus editi, quorum adhuc ad indicium in nonnullis locis ossa immensae magnitudinis ostenduntur." This passage may also have been the source for Aldhelm's description of Hygelac's bones, or at least it may have influenced his expressions. He says: "Et fiunt monstra mirae magnitudinis, ut rex Hugilaicus, qui imperavit Getis et a Francis occisus est, quem equus a duodecimo aetatis anno portare non potuit. Cuius ossa in Rheni fluminis insula, ubi in Oceanum prorumpit, reservata sunt et de longinquo venientibus pro miraculo ostenduntur." *Liber monstrorum* 1.3, ed. Moritz Haupt in his *Opuscula* 2 (Leipzig 1876) 218-252 (Index lectionum aestivarum 1863) 223.

[95] *Liber monstrorum* 1.49 (234-235): "Ferunt fabulae Graecorum homines immensis corporibus fuisse et in tanta mole tamen humano generi similes, nisi quod draconum caudas habuerunt, unde et graece dracontopedes dicebantur." Haupt emends *dracontopedes* to *dracontopodes.*

serpent, in spite of the fact that its upper part is very human in appearance.[96]

As we saw, however, Thomas of Cantimpré considers the dracontopod to be a serpent; it has, according to him, not only a dragon's tail but a dragon's body, and apparently only its face has a human appearance. He believes it likely that it was this breed of serpent that the devil used in deceiving Eve, even though he himself describes two other possible candidates for the role, namely, the viper with its half-human, half-crocodilian appearance,[97] and the scorpion, a serpent (and not a worm) with a flattering and virginlike countenance and a poisoned sting in its knotty tail.[98]

Thomas's entry on dracontopods can be translated as follows:

> Dracontopods are serpents, and the Greeks say, according to Aldhelm, that they are large and powerful. They have virginal faces like those of human beings, but they end in the body of dragons. It can be believed that the serpent by which Eve was deceived was from this class of serpents. For Bede says that that serpent had a virginal countenance, so that the devil allured her with a form similar to hers, for every animal loves what is similar to it. But he hid the remaining serpentlike part in the fruits of the trees. But we do not see how the devil could bring it about that the serpent could form articulated words, unless perhaps we should wish to say that, as the serpent has a human countenance, it also had the windpipe and organs arranged for uttering human sounds, just as we see birds imitating human sounds in speaking.[99]

[96] *Ibid.* 3.18 (250-251): "Vipera autem eo quod vi pariat ita nuncupatur. De qua scribunt physici quod ignotum genus quoddam humanae formae simillimum usque ad umbilicum habeat et semen ore concipiat, et fracto latere moriens pariat." If one did not know of the *Physiologus* specification that it was like a crocodile below, one would gather that it was serpentine, since it is after all a serpent. We have already noted that in spite of the *Physiologus* account, the ninth-century Bern manuscript illustrates vipers with serpentine lower extremities.

[97] Thomas, *De natura rerum* (British Museum MS Egerton 1984) 96v: "Dicit philo*sophus* [*sic*] quod ulpera faciem habet humanum usque ad umbilicum; ab umbilico uero usque ad caudam figuram cocodrilli." Royal 12 E XVII (a copy of the anonymous expanded version) reads correctly "Physiologus" (fol. 129). But Konrad von Megenberg, in his German adaptation of Thomas's work, obviously followed a manuscript with the reading of "Philosophus," since he attributes the statement to Aristotle. —*Das Buch der Natur* 3 E 37, ed. Franz Pfeiffer (Stuttgart 1861, repr. Hildesheim 1962) 285. For a modern German translation of Konrad, see the edition of Hugo Schulz (Greifswald 1897).

[98] Thomas, *De natura rerum* (Egerton 1984) 95v: "Scorpio serpens est, ut dicit Solinus, qui blandum et quasi virgineum wltum habere dicitur, sed habet utique in cauda nodosa aculeum venenatum quo pungit et inficit proximantem."

[99] *Ibid.* 93rv: "De drantopedibus [*sic*]. Drrantopedes [*sic*] serpentes sunt, et referente Adelino Greci dicunt, magni et potentes. Hii facies habent virgineas, faciebus humanis similes, sed in draconum corpus desinunt. De hoc genere serpencium credi potest fuisse ser-

If we are mystified at how Thomas was able to create this kind of a creature out of Aldhelm's description, we need only glance at some of his other entries, and we will realize that he had "more than Circean powers of transformation."[100]

It is not altogether clear that Thomas means his dracontopod to be girl-like only in its "face," in the narrow sense of that word, since he speaks of the viper as having "a human face down to the navel." But he was later understood to be speaking restrictively because of a misreading of the name of the serpent as *draconcopes* instead of *dracontopes*. This mistake appears already in Albert the Great[101] and Vincent of Beauvais,[102] and was the reading of the manuscript used by Konrad von Megenberg in the middle of the fourteenth century for his German adaptation of Thomas's work; he accordingly etymologizes the word, which really means "dragon-foot," as *Drachenkopf*, "dragon-head,"[103] that is, "dragon with a human head."

Albert the Great does not suggest that this serpent, which had "the virginal face of a beardless human being," was the kind used by the devil in Eden, but he does say that he has heard from reliable witnesses that such a serpent had been killed in a German forest, and its body could be seen by whoever wanted to do so for a long time, until it finally decayed.[104] He strongly denies, however, that the viper is like a man in its foreparts,[105] and he does not even mention the tradition that the scorpion had a virginal face; furthermore, he classifies it among the worms.[106]

It seems to have been Thomas of Cantimpré's dracontopod, probably in its mutated draconcopedal form, that inspired the first illustrator of the

---

pentem quo Eua decepta est. Dicit enim Beda quod serpens ille wltum virginalem habuit, ut forma consimili dyabolus eam alliceret. Omne enim diligit simile sibi. Partem uero reliquam serpenti similem arborum fructibus occultauit. Quomodo autem dyabolus potuerit efficere ut serpens articulata uerba formaret non videmus, nisi forte uelimus dicere quod sicut serpens habebat wltum humanum, ita et arterias et officia disposita habuerit ad proferendum uoces humanas, sicut aues uidemus voces humanas loquendo imitari." The Royal manuscript gets the name correctly: "Dracontopedes" (fol. 125).

[100] See Pauline Aiken, "The Animal History of Albertus Magnus and Thomas of Cantimpré," *Speculum* 22 (1947) 205-225, esp. 209.

[101] Albertus Magnus, *De animalibus* 25.29, ed. Hermann Stadler from the Cologne autograph; Beiträge zur Geschichte der Philosophie des Mittelalters 15-16 (Münster 1916-1920) 1567.

[102] Vincent of Beauvais, *Speculum naturale* 20.33 (n. 90 above) 1478. I have checked only this printed text.

[103] Konrad von Megenberg, *Buch von Natur* 3 E 11 (Pfeiffer 270, Schulz 228).

[104] Albertus Magnus (n. 101 above): "Draconcopodes dicunt Graeci serpentem magnum de ordine tertio et genere draconum, quem dicunt vultum virgineum imberbis hominis habere: et talem serpentem a fide dignis audivi interfectum esse in silva Germaniae et diu monstratum nostris temporibus omnibus volentibus eum videre donec computruit."

[105] *Ibid.* 25.61 (1577).

[106] *Ibid.* 26.39 (1595-1596).

Speculum humanae salvationis, since his serpent is a huge two-legged dragon, with wings, whose womanlike head towers above Eve; and we may note that it does not have its body hidden in foliage (fig. 9).[107] The text of the *Speculum* itself, however, which was composed around 1324, reflects only Peter Comestor's account.[108]

VIII. Masculinization and Extinction

The serpent in the text of the *Speculum humanae salvationis* retains its masculine gender in spite of its virginal face. Such was not the case in the *Chester Plays*, where Eve tells God, "This adder, Lord, she was my foe."[109] The serpent in William Jordan's Cornish play, *The Creation of the World*, written in 1611, is also feminine. The English stage direction reads: "A fine serpent with a virgin face and yellow hair upon her head."[110]

In other English plays it is not so, however. In the York pageant of the fall "the worme" whose likeness Satan takes upon himself is not described, but he is definitely masculine. Eve says of him, "With tales untrue he me betrayed."[111]

In the Lincoln (N. Town) play, the *Serpens* is described as "a fair angel," "the false angel," and "a worm with an angel's face." Eve says of him, "He hight us to be full of grace the fruit if that we eat. I did his bidding, alas, alas! . . . I suppose it was Sathanas."[112]

In the 1565 text of the Norwich play, the serpent appears and says, "Angel of light I show myself to be," and alludes to "my voice so small." Eve later tells Adam, "The heavenly king most strong to eat of this apple his angel

---

[107] MS of Selestat, now at Munich, Staatsbibliothek lat. 146 fol. 4v. Cf. the similar serpent in the version of the *Speculum* in Brussels Bibl. Roy. MS 281-283 fol. 5 (circa 1350), in Cook (n. 18 above) 163 fig. 21. Cf. also the woodcut in the Dutch 1483 edition, ed. Ernst Kloss (Munich 1925).

[108] *Speculum humanae salvationis* 1.11-16, ed. J. Lutz and P. Perdrizet (Mulhouse 1907-1909) 1.4:

> Quapropter diabolus, homini invidens, sibi insidiabatur
> Et ad praecepti transgressionem ipsum inducere nitebatur.
> Quoddam ergo genus serpentis sibi diabolus eligebat,
> Qui tunc erectus gradiebatur et caput virgineum habebat.
> In hunc fraudulosus deceptor mille artifex intrabat,
> Et per os eius loquens, verba deceptoria mulieri enarrabat.

[109] *Chester Plays* 32.

[110] William Jordan, *Gwreans an Bys; the Creation of the World*, ed. Whitley Stokes, in *Transactions of Philological Society* (1863), cited in E. K. Chambers, *The Medieval Stage* (Oxford 1903, repr. 1963) 2.142, 435.

[111] *York Plays* 5.12.122-123, ed. Lucy Toulmin Smith (Oxford 1885, repr. New York 1963) 26.

[112] *Ludus Coventriae, or the Plaie Called Corpus Christi*, ed. K. S. Block, Early English Text Society extra series 120 (London 1922, repr. 1960) 23-25, cf. 182.

hath prepare," and she confesses to God, "The serpent deceived me with that his fair face."[113]

According to the inventory of the players, the actor who plays the serpent was to wear a white wig and colored tights and tail.[114] It seems, then, that his legs would be showing as such. It is not clear whether the white hair that he puts on is meant to make him look like a woman; it would not seem so, to judge from Eve's mention of "his fair face." It is true that "his" can be neuter as well as masculine, but it cannot be feminine.

M. D. Anderson suggests that the bosses in the Norwich Cathedral, which were made early in the sixteenth century, were influenced by earlier portrayals of the biblical plays. The Temptation boss shows a serpent with the upper torso of a young man or boy; of course, it could also be that of a very young girl. The point is that there has been no attempt to emphasize its femininity by giving it a woman's breasts, such as Eve has.[115] We may recall that Titian's cherubic serpent was also too young for its sex to be determined. The serpent of the *Breviarium Grimani* was also of indistinct sexuality.

Miss Anderson also draws attention to the Creation scene in the stained glass in the church of Saint Neot in Cornwall (it was worked on from 1400 to 1532, and is partially restored), where the serpent has the face of a man with a bulging body—which looks as if an actor has slipped on a sacklike disguise.[116] His hair is somewhat like that of the serpent of the Norwich boss.

Another definitely masculine portrayal of the human-headed serpent can be seen in the painting of the German artist Georg Penz (1500-1550), now in the Ferdinandeum at Innsbruck. Here the serpent has the upper torso, arms, and bearded and horned head of a satyr![117] Finally, in the church of Santa Maria della Pace in Rome, the fresco by Girolamo Siciolante da Sermoneta portraying the sin of Adam and Eve (circa 1560-1565) has a male version of the two-legged variety of serpent immortalized by Michelangelo and Titian (fig. 10).

The reasoning of Peter Comestor which demanded a woman's head, was obviously lost upon such artists. And in fact, the need for any kind of human head disappeared among the artists of the seventeenth century and later, though no doubt one can find a number of revivals of the old tradition of the lady serpent.

---

[113] *The Creation of Eve, with the Expelling of Adam and Eve out of Paradise,* acted by the Grocers of Norwich; ed. Joseph Quincy Adams, *Chief Pre-Shakespearean Dramas* (Boston 1924) 90-91.

[114] *Ibid.* 89 n. 1: "A coat with hosen and tail for the serpent, stained, with a white hair."

[115] M. D. Anderson (n. 74 above) 87, 143 (and pl. 13b).

[116] *Ibid.* 144 (and pl. 15b). *Blue Guide to England,* ed. L. Russell Muirhead and Stuart Rossiter (London 1965) 194.

[117] Ehrenstein (n. 19 above) 67 fig. 117.

Peter's bizarre notion of a lady-faced Eden serpent did not find widespread support among scripture scholars and theologians, and it appears to have been abandoned by them much earlier than by the iconographers. It is instructive to read what Nicholas of Lyre had to say upon the subject early in the fourteenth century in his postill on Genesis 3:

> The demon's entering into the serpent for this purpose was not a thing chosen by him, but rather was arranged by God, who did not allow man to be tempted by the devil in a pleasing and noble appearance, through which he could be more easily deceived, but rather in a horrible appearance, in which the demon's fallaciousness could be more quickly perceived. Nevertheless some say that that serpent had a pleasing and virginal face; but this has no scriptural authority, and therefore the first interpretation seems better.[118]

Three hundred years later the same conclusion was reached by painters, sculptors, and playwrights.

IX. Conclusion

The Jewish and Byzantine tradition of the Eden serpent was, as we have seen, fairly straightforward. The serpent had feet to begin with, since he could walk, and they were cut off from him and from all his race as a punishment for tempting Eve. In the West, serpents had no feet to begin with, but by a miraculous iconographic mutation some of them acquired feet in the course of time, and the Eden serpent was at times included among their number.

A further complication was introduced in the West, this time perhaps because of a simple graphic mutation (like the one that transformed Thomas of Cantimpré's *dracontopes* into a *Drachenkopf*); according to Peter Comestor the devil used a serpent with a woman's face in order to gain Eve's confidence more easily. Peter may have honestly thought that the venerable Bede supported this view, but he was no doubt also more easily inclined to accept the view because he was familiar with some variety or varieties of serpent-woman combination; I suggested as possibilities the viper of *Physiologus*, the sphinx, the siren, and the scorpion, and I stated that the author of *The Cave of Treasures* before Peter's time may have been influenced in a similar way in creating an Evelike serpent.

---

[118] Nicholas de Lira, *Postilla*, in *Biblia sacra cum glossa ordinaria* (Douai 1617) 90: "Quod autem ad hoc serpentem intravit, non fuit ex electione, sed magis ex divina dispensatione, quae non permisit hominem tentari per diabolum in specie gratiosa et nobili, per quam posset facilius decipi, sed magis in specie horribili, in qua fallacia daemonis citius poterat deprehendi. Aliqui tamen dicunt quod ille serpens habebat faciem gratiosam et virgineam, sed hoc de scriptura nullam habet auctoritatem, et ideo primum melius videtur."

It might be thought that Peter had a deeply misogynic view of woman to have postulated a serpent with a woman's countenance in the Garden of Eden. It is true that he had a low opinion of woman, but he was not saying that the first woman was like a snake, but rather that the snake was like a woman. It is doubtless true that some of the serpent-ladies of the past were thought of as *femmes fatales*—the siren and the scorpion are obvious examples. But Peter gives as the reason for the woman-headed serpent's appearance in the garden the simple consideration that since one approves of what is similar to oneself the devil sought to win Eve's confidence in this way. He approached her because she was weaker and more suggestive than Adam. Far from considering Eve serpentine herself, Peter specifies that women in such situations are weak, and they are baleful only because of their malleability, and not because they are actively dangerous. There is nothing reptilian about Eve's successful efforts to convince Adam to follow her course.

Though relatively few scholars of the Middle Ages were ready to accept Peter's new serpent, it made a decided impact upon the visual and dramatic arts, beginning, in the former, about fifty years after Peter introduced the idea. It opened up for the artists intriguing new possibilities in an old scene, and they rose to the challenge with great inventiveness. Yet they did not simply visualize the monster with the abandon of the grotesque-drawers and misericord-makers, for they were not dealing with a whimsical creature of the imagination, but with a very real and painfully authentic beast. They therefore combined the features of a woman with the characteristics of real serpents. The fact that serpents had attained many forms accounts for the variegated results of their efforts. The dramatists were able to choose from among these offerings the types that were most suited for representation upon the stage. The solutions that were arrived at in all the media assured for Peter's odd notion an important and lasting place in the monuments of medieval and renaissance culture, before the fundamental absurdity of the concept could raze the strong walls of tradition that had been erected around it.

Department of English
University of California
Los Angeles, California, 90024, U.S.A.

Fig. 1. Onocentaur and siren. Capital of the arch in front of the south apse, Cathedral of Autun. Early twelfth century

Fig. 2. Capital in the crypt of the Duomo of Modena. Early twelfth century

Fig. 3. Terracina chest, Palazzo Venezia. Eleventh century?

252

Fɪɢ. 4. Beatus of Liébana's *Commentary on the Apocalypse,* Pierpont Morgan Library MS 429, fol. 6v. ᴀ.ᴅ. 1220

FIG. 5a. Portal of the Virgin, Cathedral of Notre Dame, Amiens. Circa 1230

FIG. 6. Panel in the base of the middle pillar of the door of the Virgin, Cathedral of Notre Dame, Amiens. Circa 1230

FIG. 7. Peterborough Psalter, Brussels (Bibl. Roy. MS 9961–9962, fol. 25). Circa 1250

Fig. 8. Base of pillar, Virgin's door. Cathedral of Notre Dame, Paris. Circa 1220

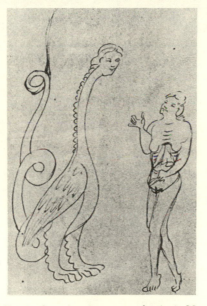

Fig. 9. *Speculum humanae salvationis.* Munich (Bayerische Staatsbibliothek MS lat. 146 fol. 4v). Middle of fourteenth century

FIG. 10. "Peccato originale" by Girolamo Siciolante da Sermoneta, in the church of Santa Maria della Pace, Rome. Circa 1560–1565

THE WITCHCRAFT BASIS IN MARLOWE'S
FAUSTUS

PAUL H. KOCHER

THE tendency of present-day scholarship is to view the character of Faustus as the product of Marlowe's creative genius working upon the materials afforded him by the English translation of the *Faustbuch*. This is only part of the truth. An equally essential part, as I shall show, is that Faustus is also in important respects the product of Marlowe's own wide familiarity with Renaissance, medieval, and classical ideas about witchcraft. An examination of the play will reveal that, since Faustus is a witch, Marlowe has endowed him with much of the motive and behavior commonly believed to be typical of those who had signed the compact with Hell. Not that Faustus is merely a conventional portrait of a witch, of course. So high, imperious, and passionate a figure does not abide final classification. But many of his thoughts and actions are unmistakably those of the witch of European tradition; and they are not to be found in the *English Faust book*. The demonstration of this fact in the following pages will put us in possession of information both as to Marlowe's learning and as to the right interpretation of what is perhaps his greatest dramatic achievement.

It should be stressed, in this connection, that the intention of this paper is never to point to any one work as the specific source of any given idea of Marlowe's, and that every work cited is offered merely to illustrate the broad background of superstition with which Marlowe is acquainted.

In an interesting recent article, "Marlowe, Faustus, and Simon Magus,"[1] Beatrice Daw Brown maintains a thesis different from that just set forth. Her contention is that the prototype of Marlowe's Faustus, in so far as he departs from the hero of the *English Faust book*,[2]

[1] *PMLA*, LIV (1939), 82–121.

[2] Hereafter referred to as "*EFB*." References are to the later edition printed by W. J. Thoms in *Early English prose romances* (2d ed.; London, 1858), Vol. III. It varies from the edition of 1592 only in minor details, none of them significant for our purpose.

[MODERN PHILOLOGY, August, 1940] 9

is the magician Simon Magus. This contention is, in the main, reconcilable with the view which I propose to establish, since Marlowe may be thought to have been influenced both by the legend of Simon Magus in particular and by witchcraft tradition in general, the former being but a crystallization of many elements present in the latter. Such a reconciliation, however, seems a little artificial, and I find it necessary to express the conviction, on the one hand, that general witchcraft tradition of itself sufficiently explains those traits in Faustus which are not drawn from the *EFB* or attributable to Marlowe's poetic invention, and, on the other hand, that the opposing view falls short of establishing any direct use by Marlowe of the Simon Magus story. It will be best to postpone general comment on the latter point until after the evidence for the dramatist's resort to general witch lore has been presented.

The term "witch" is used throughout this paper in a broad sense to include anyone who performs supernatural acts by demonic agency. No attempt is made to distinguish it from such other terms as "conjurer," "black magician," or "enchanter." In using all these terms as loosely synonymous I am following the usual Renaissance practice, as exemplified in the definition given by William Perkins: "A Witch is a Magician, who either by open or secret league, wittingly and willingly consenteth to use the aide and assistance of the Deuill, in the working of wonders."[3] Faustus comes clearly within the definition.

I. THE GIFTS OF MAGIC

We have first to consider the motives which impel Faustus to enter upon the crime of sorcery. One of the chief of these is the desire for power to control the grand forces of Nature. And here the witch basis of his characterization is seen to be clearly and importantly operative. For although we must rule out of consideration some of the desired powers, like that of producing winds, tempests, lightning, which are mentioned specifically in the *EFB* and hence can show nothing as to Marlowe's own familiarity with witchcraft-learning, Faustus covets other powers not there mentioned which were widely believed to be possessed by witches.

[3] *A discourse of the damned art of witchcraft* (Cambridge, 1608), p. 167. Thomas Cooper, *The mystery of witchcraft* (London, 1617), p. 177, adopts this phrasing.

Such, for instance, is the power ".... to make the Moone drop from her spheare" (l. 273).[4] As A. W. Ward has pointed out,[5] in Roman literature enchanters were credited with the skill to draw the moon from heaven. There are examples in Virgil (*Eclogues* viii. 69), Horace (*Epodes* v. 45–46), Apuleius, Ovid, Lucan, Tibullus, and others. I should like to add that the same thought is very frequently repeated in Renaissance works. Reginald Scot declares: "And concerning this matter Cardanus saith, that at everie eclipse they were woont to thinke, that witches pulled downe the sunne and moone from heaven."[6] Bodin says: "... Hippocrate au liure de morbo sacro, deteste les Sorciers, qui se vantoyent de son temps d'attirer la Lune ... ."[7] In Lyly's *Endimion* (Act I, scene iv) we find the witch Dipsas boasting "I can darken the Sunne by my skil, and remooue the Moone out of her course; ....." It is scarcely possible, however, that Marlowe, with his thoroughgoing knowledge of the original classical sources, did not get the idea straight from them.

From the classics likewise seems to come inspiration for others of Faustus' ambitions to change the face of nature—to "make swift Rhine circle faire Wertenberge" (l. 117), "make .... the ocean to ouerwhelme the world" (l. 274), "drie the sea" (l. 173). These are characteristic Marlovian enthusiasms whose real originality everyone will wish to defend. It does no wrong to his genius, nevertheless, to say that his conception of what a witch may do through demons takes its temper from beliefs already existing. The might of the classical sorceress is well described in the words of Medea in Seneca's *Medea:*

I have driven the seas back to their lowest depths, and the Ocean, his tides outdone, has sent his crushing waves farther into the land. .... Phasis has turned his swift waters backward to their source, and Hister, divided into many mouths, has checked his boisterous streams and flowed sluggishly in all

---

[4] The text used is that of Tucker Brooke in *The works of Christopher Marlowe* (Oxford, 1910).

[5] In a note in his edition of *Faustus* (Oxford, 1878), p. 149. I shall take pleasure in citing Ward's excellent notes from time to time. He is, I believe, the only scholar who has made any detailed observations upon my subject.

[6] *The discoverie of witchcraft* (repr. of 1584 ed.; B. Nicholson, 1886), Book XII, chap. xv, p. 203. Scot reverts to the idea twice more: Book I, chap. iv, p. 8, and Book XII, chap. iv, p. 177.

[7] "Refutation des opinions de Iean Wier," p. 409 (bound in with his *De la demonomanie des sorciers* [Anvers, 1593]).

his beds. The waves have roared, the mad sea swelled, though the winds were still . . . . [trans. F. Miller ("Loeb Library"), ll. 755–66].

Similar powers are given by Ovid to Medea in the *Metamorphoses* (vii. 199–207), a work intimately known and greatly loved by Marlowe, as hundreds of footnotes to his plays and poems testify:

. . . . when I have willed it, the streams have run back to their fountain-heads, while the banks wondered; I lay the swollen, and stir up the calm seas by my spell. . . . . Thee also, Luna, do I draw from the sky . . . . [trans. F. Miller ("Loeb")].

Lucan's *Pharsalia* (vi. 469–80), a poem which Marlowe in part translated, thus enumerates the deeds of the Thessalian witches:

Though the winds are still, the sea rises high; or again it is forbidden to be affected by storms, and is silent while the South wind blusters . . . . the waterfall is arrested on the steep face of the cliff; and the running river forsakes its downward channel. The Nile fails to rise in summer; the Meander straightens its course; the Arar hurries on the sluggish Rhone; the mountains lower their tops and level their ridges. . . . . When the tide is driven on by the moon, the spells of Thessalian witches drive it back and defend the shore [trans. J. Duff ("Loeb")].

These passages and others like them from the Roman writers are referred to, sometimes at great length, by many Renaissance witch treatises;[8] but it is impossible to doubt that Marlowe, if he used them at all, went direct to the originals. That he did use them seems quite probable. Faustus' grandiose schemes for manipulating rivers, seas, and hills savor strongly of these classical texts, and Marlowe is, beyond all question, deeply read in the works from which these texts come. Moreover, as in the quotation from Ovid just given, they appear in the originals side by side with that other dream of drawing the moon from its sphere, which Marlowe pretty certainly got from the classics. A conclusion of general indebtedness naturally follows. It must be emphasized, of course, that the indebtedness is no more than general. Marlowe gives the older ideas new poetic value, as well as a modern geographical application.

Faustus wishes to dry the sea in order to extract treasure from the

---

[8] See H. Boguet, *An examen of witches* (trans. of the *Discours des sorciers*, ed. M. Summers [London, 1929]), chap. xxvi, pp. 77 ff.; M. del Rio, *Disquisitionum magicarum libri sex* (Venetiis, 1640), Book II, Ques. 9; J. Bodin, *De la demonomanie des sorciers* (1593), Book I, chap. v, p. 92. Ward has mentioned some of the classical passages but has not developed the comparison here intended.

wrecked ships at its bottom. This seems to be not an altogether new piece of imagination. Del Rio writes: "Melidenses Indos inuenio solitos merces, quarum iactum fecerunt, conari incantationib. e pelagi fundo extrahere, quo eventu nescio. Lege Castannedam, lib. 1 Histor. Indica c. 30."[9] Eight of the forms for conjuration set forth in the *Verus Jesuitarum libellus*[10] call for the bringing of gold "ex abysso maris" by a demon. The following is one example:

> Ego N. servus Dei, voco, cito, exorcizo te, o Spiritus! per sanctos apostolos et discipulos Dei . . . . et per sanctissima et terribilissima verba: Aphriel, Diefriel . . . . compare coram me in pulcra, affabili, et humana forma, et affer mihi (ex abysso maris) N. milliones optimi auri et expensibilis ubique monetae Hispanicae sine ullo tumultu, damno corporis et animae. . . . .

Also quite pertinent is Boccaccio's account[11] of a sorcerer named Theban who invokes a god "that hast also giuen power to my verses to drie up the seas, that I at my plesure might search the botome therof. . . . ."

Furthermore, the magical power "to slay mine enemies and ayde my friends" (l. 332), asked of Mephistophilis by Faustus, is quite ordinarily offered by the Devil to the witch initiate. We have the testimony of Remy that Satan allures the prospective witch "by providing drugs to poison those upon whom a man wishes to be avenged, or to heal those to whom a man owes a debt of gratitude."[12] Bartolommeo della Spina says likewise that the Tempter promises witches "quod vindicari & in hostes suos retorquere possent iniurias, quas alio modo repellere non valent. . . . ."[13]

According to popular belief, a witch had power not only to slay his enemies, God permitting, but to practice against the life of kings. This idea is probably embodied in Faustus' lines:

> The Emprour shal not liue but by my leaue,
> Nor any Potentate of Germany [ll. 346–47].

[9] Book II. Ques. 12, p. 113.

[10] Reproduced in *Das Kloster*, ed. J. Scheible (Stuttgart, 1846), II, 836 ff. The *Libellus* was published in Paris in 1508.

[11] Fol. Dvʳ. Ques. IV, of *Thirteene most pleasaunt and delectable questions* (London, 1587).

[12] N. Remy, *Demonolatry* (Lyons, 1595; Eng. trans. ed. M. Summers, London, 1930), Book I, chap. i, p. 1.

[13] *De strigibus* (Coloniae: Apud M. Cholinum, 1581), chap. xxv, p. 160. A. Roberts, *A treatise of witchcraft* (London, 1616), p. 27, says that witches stipulate for means to "helpe and hurt at their pleasure, and others like unto these."

One has only to turn over the pages of Kittredge and Notestein to encounter many instances of the Elizabethan belief that kings were vulnerable to magic. The safety of Elizabeth herself was much feared for. Notestein relates the great precautions taken by her councilors to protect her, and details several trials of conjurors suspected of attempting her life.[14] In particular there was the affair at Abingdon in 1578–79, in which four women, accused of making waxen images against the queen and two of her councilors, were hanged amid great public excitement.[15] The discovery of the images caused, as Reginald Scot says, "the terror & astonishment of manie thousands."[16] Conceivably, Marlowe may have heard of it. Deriding the vulgar credulity on this point, Scot remarks that, if witches had such powers,

No prince should be able to reigne or live in the land. For (as Danoeus saith) that one Martine a witch killed the emperour of Germanie with witchcraft: so would our witches (if they could) destroie all our magistrates.[17]

As to things military, Faustus will have his spirits invent "stranger engines for the brunt of war" and bring him coin with which to levy soldiers to drive out the Prince of Parma (ll. 120–25). Ward notes many legends of the exploits of wizards in war.[18] A passage from Del Rio is also worth recording:

Mihi dubium non est posse magicē per Daemones . . . . praestigijs, & industria varia, qua (ut & robore) plus cunctis mortalibus pollent, & urbes ob-

---

[14] W. Notestein, *A history of witchcraft in England from 1558 to 1718* (Washington, 1911), pp. 24–28. At p. 24: "Elizabeth had hardly mounted her throne when her councilors began to suspect the use of sorcery and conjuration against her life. As a result they instituted the most painstaking inquiries into all reported cases of the sort, especially in and about London and the neighboring counties. Every Catholic was suspected." A poem by J. Aske, *Elizabetha triumphans* (1588; repr. J. Nichols' *Elizabeth*, II, 555), shows the current popular distrust of Catholic magic: "This Pope doth send Magitians to her land./To seeke her death, by that their devillish arte." Statements constantly turn up in the chronicles and witch treatises that other sovereigns were attacked by sorcerers: Edward II and III, Henry V and VI, Richard III, and Queen Mary of England, King Duffus of Scotland, Charles IX of France. It was commonly rumored that the death of Ferdinand, Earl of Derby, in 1594 was due to witchcraft.

[15] G. L. Kittredge, *Witchcraft in Old and New England* (Cambridge, Mass., 1929), pp. 87–88, relates the incident and quotes a statement by Ben Jonson (*The masque of queens*) that he remembered its happening in his youth.

[16] Cited by Kittredge, *ibid.*, p. 88. There were a number of other supposed attempts against Elizabeth, among them one made by Nicholas Johnson in 1580.

[17] Book III, chap. xiv, p. 49.

[18] P. 134. See also F. Hutchinson, *An historical essay concerning witchcraft* (London, 1720), chap. ii, p. 34: "1563. The King of Sweden carried four Witches with him in his Wars against the Danes. Scot l. 3 c. 15." The *Malleus maleficarum* gravely inquires ". . . . if a prince . . . . employ such a wizard as we have described for the destruction of some castle in a just war . . . . is his whole army to be considered as protectors and patrons of that wizard?" (Part II, Ques. 1, chap. xvi, p. 152).

sidione liberare . . . . & expugnandas praebere, & in praelijs victoriae causam esse, nō desunt exempla, nec ratio expugnat. . . . .[19]

He argues, however, that God rarely permits Satan to give money to his devotees: "Impijs etiam hac ratione diabolus pecuniam, belli neruum, suppeditaret, quare facile pios opprimerent, nisi Deus miraculo nouo subueniret."[20] In chapter vi of the prose *Historie of Fryer Bacon*,[21] Bacon does indeed invent some extraordinary instruments for capturing a town in France, and imagines many more.

Where knowledge is concerned, Faustus will require his demons to "reade mee straunge philosophie,/And tell the secrets of all forraine kings" (ll. 114–15), and later asks a book "wherein I might see al plants, hearbes and trees that grow upon the earth" (ll. 607–8). This sort of information is exactly what is possessed by many of the demon princes whom Reginald Scot, drawing upon Wier's *Pseudomonarchia daemonum*, and through him upon the fable world of medieval demonology, is able to characterize with a quite domestic intimacy. "Astaroth . . . . answereth trulie to matters present, past, and to come, and also of all secrets. . . . . He maketh a man woonderfull learned in the liberall sciences. . . . ." "Buer . . . . absolutelie teacheth philosophie morall and naturall, and also logicke, and the vertue of herbes. . . . ."[22] Again, we read in the *Daemonologie* of James I that Satan

. . . . will oblish himselfe to teach them artes and sciences, which he may easelie doe, being so learned a knaue as he is: To carrie them newes from anie parte of the worlde . . . . to reueale to them the secretes of anie persons, so being they bee once spoken, for the thought none knowes but God . . . . [Book I, chap. vi, p. 21; ed. G. B. Harrison].

In the last chapter of the prose *Historie of Fryer Bacon* Bacon says: "I likewise have found out the secrets of trees, plants and stones, with their several uses."[23]

Some additional and more particular texts can be brought to show

[19] Book II, Ques. 12, p. 107.

[20] *Ibid.*, p. 112.

[21] Reprinted in Thoms's *Early English prose romances*. It is in chap. v of this work that Bacon proposes to wall England about with brass, an idea adapted by Marlowe (l. 116). He must have been acquainted with the tradition on which the story rests, possibly with the prose work itself. Indebtedness to Greene's play on this theme seems unlikely.

[22] These descriptions occur in Scot at Book XV, chap. ii, p. 319, and chap. i, p. 315, respectively.

[23] Thomas Cooper (p. 129) states that Satan is "exquisitely skilfull in the knowledge of naturall things, as of . . . . vertues of plants, rootes, hearbs, etc. . . . ."

that English writers believed a witch could ascertain through her familiars the secret counsel of kings. Thus William Perkins:

.... some deuills are present at all assemblies and meetings, and thereby are acquainted with the consultations and conferences both of Princes & people. .... And hence it is apparent, how Witches may know what is done in other countries. .... .[24]

Similarly, Thomas Cooper:

The presence of Sathan and the euill Angels, in most places, and communicating their knowledge together, where-through they are acquainted with the secret consultations of Princes, may giue also furtherance to this knowledge of things to come. .... .[25]

When Valdes is picturing to Faustus the delights of magic, he promises that they shall be attended by spirits in the shapes of lions, Almaine rutters, Lapland giants, and beautiful women (ll. 153–58). The lion forms may have been inspired by parts of the *EFB* wherein devils appear as various kinds of beasts, although not lions specifically; but, if not, there is abundant precedent for the idea: some of Reginald Scot's demon potentates, for instance, rise up in that form.[26] The giants are probably Laplanders because, as Ward notes,[27] Lapland was commonly regarded as the home of witches. Some lines from the play *Look about you* bear out the point:

> Then nyne times like the northern Laplanders,
> He backward circled the sacred Font,
>
> . . . .
>
> And so turn'd witch, for Gloster is a witch
>   [Scene 14, ll. 2125–30].

The advantages of assuming the bodies of lovely women were well known to malign spirits. The Tempter, says Remy, "fabricates some fair and delectable body and offers it for a man's enjoyment."[28] Lavater, extracting the essence of many a medieval legend, gives authority for three of the different forms imagined by Marlowe:

[24] Pp. 59–60.

[25] P. 130. Also J. Cotta, *The triall of witch-craft* (London, 1616), p. 117. Cotta explains it as Satan's imitation of the prophet Elisha, who divined the hidden plans of the king of Syria (II Kings 6:12).

[26] "Marbas, alias Barbas is a great president and appeareth in the forme of a mightie lion . . . . " (Book XV, chap. ii, p. 314). Roberts, p. 31: ". . . . sometime he [Satan] sheweth himselfe in the forme of foure-footed beastes, foules, creeping things, roaring as a Lyon, skipping like a Goat. . . . ."

[27] P. 137. Roberts, p. 20, refers to the magicians of Lapland and other northern countries. See also M. Summers, *The geography of witchcraft* (London, 1927), chap. i, p. 8.

[28] Book I, chap. i, p. 1.

We read that many spirites haue appeared unto certaine Hermites and Monkes in the shape of a woman, alluring and intising them to filthie lust. They appeare also in the fourme of brute beastes. . . . . At one time some hath beene seene riding on horsebacke, or going on foote. . . . .[29]

In the background of this part of our subject lies the wild region of tales of the succubi and incubi, demons taking on sex in order to have intercourse with men and women.

Thus far we have spoken of specific powers envisioned or bargained for by Faustus, and have traced their origins to the witchcraft tradition. It remains to suggest that not merely in these particulars but in the whole general conception of Faustus' motives Marlowe is vitally influenced by witch lore. Faustus is animated by longing for wealth, honor, knowledge of hidden things, pleasure, imperial sway, godhead. So, according to prevalent belief, were the men and women who turned witch. Since the point is of great importance both for the interpretation of the drama and for the understanding of Marlowe's methods of composition, I shall ask leave to cite as many as four or five representative texts. Bodin:

Les autres pour trouuer des tresors: qui pour guerir de sa maladie: qui pour iouir de ses plaisirs, les uns pour paruenir aux honneurs & dignitez, les autres pour sçauoir les choses futures ou absentes, & les plus meschans pour se vanger de leurs ennemis appellent aussi le Diable ... .[30]

Boguet:

Furthermore, he [Satan] makes fair promises. For to some he offers riches, assuring them that they will never lack for anything: to the vengeful he suggests the means to avenge themselves on their enemies: others he persuades that he will advance them in honour and rank. . . . .[31]

Del Rio:

Velle in illis prodigiosis effectibus imitari, est animi prorsus superbi, & stulti, & violentis, ambientisque Dei similitudinem in omnipotentia, aut omni scientia. tales imitantur Diabolum, qui similis esse voluit altissimo.[32]

Cooper declares that Satan works by "Puffing them [witches] up with conceit of extraordinary skill in Natures secrets, & so with a vain imaginatiō to be as gods, through such rare knowledge and great power. . . . ."[33]

[29] L. Lavater, *Of ghostes and spirites* (London, 1572; reprinted Oxford University Press, 1929), Part I, chap. xix, p. 92.
[30] Book I, chap. vi, p. 99.   [32] Book II, Ques. 4, p. 77.
[31] Chap. viii, p. 22.   [33] P. 9

Danaeus has this apposite description:

Other some there be, who being borne away w̃ fonde vanitie of a proude mynde, whyle they are not able to containe themselues within the compas of mans understanding & capacitie, doo yeelde themselues vassals to Satan, being desierous to know thinges to come, & to foretel them to other: or els ambitiously desiering easely and with smal trauayle to dooe those thinges which other cannot. By which meanes, many both of the honourable, and learned sorte, are seduced by satan, as certen noble men & women of worship & honour, and many schollars. . . . .[34]

Renaissance treatises on witchcraft are abundantly sown with similar expressions. I have not space for a detailed comparison of the *EFB* with Marlowe's play on this question of Faustus' motives, but I think it is a fair summary to say that the *EFB*'s treatment is quite bare and that Marlowe has enormously amplified the whole subject. What Marlowe adds is very much closer to the content of the excerpts from Danaeus, Cooper, and Del Rio just given than to anything in the *EFB*. In fact, it is sufficiently close, as it seems to me, to justify the conclusion that Marlowe was genuinely influenced by the custom of the witch tractates. The existence of this influence should not be stated categorically, since there is no denying the fact that aspirations to power, wealth, and knowledge are the very stuff of Marlowe's personality, voiced by all of his great characters. But if there is a general correspondence between Faustus' hopes and those by which Satan is usually thought to beguile wizards; if, in addition, there is a correspondence between these temptations in some particulars; and if, finally, Marlowe uses witch lore (not drawn from the *EFB*) in other parts of his play, there would seem to be good reason for thinking that the shape Marlowe gives to the character of Faustus in the scenes of his exultant anticipation owes something to the psychological analysis made by writers on witchcraft. Probably the most satisfactory view is that the characterization of Faustus is due exclusively neither to Marlowe's witch-learning nor to his projection of his own traits into the drama. The two currents flow together and reinforce each other.

[34] *A dialogue of witches* (London, 1587), Eiiᵛ, chap. ii. See also Institor and Sprenger. *Malleus maleficarum*, trans. M. Summers (London, 1928), introduction to Part III, p. 203; T. Potts, *The wonderfull discouerie of witches* (London, 1613, reprinted by G. B. Harrison [London, 1929]), p. 22.

II. THE INCANTATION

As Faustus is largely a witch in motive, so is he in conduct. Thus his *modus operandi* when he first conjures up Mephistophilis has abundant precedent in treatises on and popular superstitions about black magic. Here, as elsewhere, Marlowe can be shown to display considerable acquaintance with Renaissance, and possibly classical, learning. It will be the easier to do so because the *EFB* (chap. ii) contains very little that could possibly be held to have served as Marlowe's original.

One who would practice magic, Cornelius tells Faustus, must be "grounded in Astrologie,/Inricht with tongues, well seene in minerals" (ll. 167–68).[35] These are no mere haphazard pronouncements. "Of all operations in occult science there is not one that is not rooted in astrology"—so runs Morley's paraphrase of a portion of chapter liii of Book II of Agrippa's *De occulta philosophia*.[36] The reason is that the wizard operates by drawing down the powers of the heavenly bodies and using them to compel the rising of spirits. This he does by inscribing in his circle the proper symbols ("Figures of euery adiunct to the heauens,/And characters of signes and erring starres" [ll. 245–46], as Faustus calls them) which represent the various heavenly objects and incorporate their virtue. He must know the symbols, which ones to use, and the proper time and manner of their use—all depending upon the science of astrology. The theory is thus explained by Bodin in an attack on the Florentine Academy:

... les nouueaux Academiques ont posé ceste maxime, qu'il faut coupler & lier le ciel & la terre, les puissances celestes & terrestres, & conioindre les uns auec les autres, pour attirer la puissance diuine, par les moyens elementaires, & celestes. Voila l'hypothese de Procle, Iamblique, Porphyre, & autres Academiques. Sur laquelle hypothese on peut dire que le maistre en l'art Diabolique ... [Pico della Mirandola] a fondé toutes les sorceleries & inuocations des Diables ... . Car il compose de caracteres, qu'il dict propres aux Demons de chacune planette, lesquels characteres il veut estre grauez au metal propre à chacune planette, à l'heure qu'elles sont en leur exaltation ou maison auec une

---

[35] As possible sources must be noticed passages in the *EFB*, chap. i, saying that Faustus "accompanied himself with divers that were seen in those devilish arts, and that had the Chaldean, Persian, Hebrew, Arabian, and Greek Tongues" and that he "named himself an astrologian." Remark, however, that Marlowe goes farther, making languages and astrology *prerequisites* for magic.

[36] H. Morley, *The life of Henry Cornelius Agrippa* (London, 1856), I, 184.

conioinction amiable, & veut alors qu'on ayt aussi la plante, la pierre, & l'animal propre à chacune planette, & de tout cela qu'ō face un sacrifice à la Planette, & quelquesfois l'image de la Planette ... [Book I, chap. iii, p. 60].[37]

Furthermore, he must be "Inricht with tongues" because spirits are invoked not only in Latin but also in Greek and Hebrew. Thus Greek and Hebrew letters are written within the magical circle, especially the Hebrew,[38] which are used to spell out one or more of the seventy-two different forms of the mystic name Jehovah (Faustus writes "Iehouahs name,/Forward and backward anagrammatiz'd"), possessed of extraordinary potency over demons. The necessity that the magician be "well seene in minerals" is recognized by Boissard: ". . . . metallorum naturas, loca, & nomina: in quibus oportet multùm versatum esse. . . . ."[39] But the reason for this requirement is rather hard to fix. Perhaps it is that the magician needs this knowledge in his alchemical experiments, alchemy being considered as closely related to magic.[40] Perhaps it is that the efficacy of charms often depends on their being engraved on the right sort of substance, as in the quotation from Bodin just given.

For the actual process of conjuring Faustus is advised to carry with him "wise Bacons and Albanus workes,/The Hebrew Psalter and new Testament." Bacon and Abano, reputed magicians, will supply the formulas for incantation, which will include recitations from the Psalter and New Testament. Ward's note[41] citing Reginald Scot and Mor-

[37] See likewise L. Thorndike, *A history of magic and experimental science* (New York, 1923), II, 258.

[38] A look at the diagrams culled from ancient books of magic by Scheible (*Das Kloster*, III, esp. pp. 288, 330) will convince anyone. Agrippa, *De occulta philosophia* (*Opera*, Vol. I [Lugduni, n.d.]), Book I, chap. lxxiv, p. 117: "Hebraeas literas compertum à sapientibus omnûm esse efficacissimus, quia habent similitudinem maximam cum coelestibus, & mundo. Caeterarum verò linguarum literas tantam efficaciam non habere, quia ab illis remotius distant." M. Conway, *Demonology and devil-lore* (New York, 1879), II, 334, summarizes the contents of the early Raven book printed at Dresden in 1501, saying that the magician must "mark a circle on parchment with a dove's blood; within this circle write in Latin the names of the four quarters of the heaven; write around it the Hebrew letters of God's name, and beneath it write Sadan; and standing in this circle he must repeat the ninety-first Psalm. In addition there are seals in red and black, various Hebrew, Greek, and Latin words, chiefly such as contain the letters Q, W, X, Y, Z. . . . ."

[39] J. Boissard, *De magia*, in the *Tractatus posthumus* (Oppenheimii Typis Hieronymi Galleri [n.d.]), p. 27.

[40] P. Binsfeldio, *Commentarius in titulum codicis lib. ix de maleficis et mathematicis* (bound in the same volume with his *De confessionibus* [H. Bock, 1605]), Ques. v, concl. 9, p. 479: "Alchimistae ut plurimum etiam sunt inuocatores Daemonum, ut plurimum Alchimia saepè sit coniuncta cum magia."

[41] P. 141.

ley's Agrippa upon the use of the Psalms and the Gospel of John for invoking devils can be supplemented by statements in Bodin and others.[42]

Before Faustus begins to summon the fiends, he has "prayde and sacrific'd to them" (l. 241). Their appetite for such acts of homage was often mentioned in the Renaissance. Binsfeld explains it as Satan's desire to ape God: "Hinc summoperè desiderat adorari, quod diuinae maiestati competit. . . . . Ex eadē caussa Daemones sacrificia expetunt."[43] James I on incantation: "Two principall thinges cannot well in that errand be wanted: holie-water (whereby the Deuill mockes the Papistes) and some present of a liuing thing unto him" (Book I, chap. v, p. 17). Francis Coxe:

. . . . whē the spirite is once come before the circle, he forthe with demaundeth the exsorciste a sacrifice, whiche moste commenlye is a pece of waxe cōsecrated, or hallowed after their owne order (For they haue certayn bokes, called bokes of consecration) or els it is a chickē, a lapwing, or some liuinge creatur, whiche when he hath receyued: then doeth he fulfill the mynd of the exsorcist, for oneles he hath it, he will neither doe, neither speake any thinge. Of this testifieth bacon in his boke of Necromancie. . . . .[44]

After the circle has been drawn, the divine Name, the appropriate astrological symbols, and the "breuiated names of holy Saints" are

[42] Bodin, Book I, chap. iii, p. 56: "Et le protecteur des Sorciers, apres auoir mis les cercles & caracteres detestables (que le ne mettray point) por trouuer les tresors, il escript qu'il faut en foissoiant dire les Psalmes, De profundis, Deus misereatur nostri etc. ... & lire la Messe ... . Et pour faire autres meschancetez, que le n'escriray point, ils disent le Psalme cent & huictièsme." G. Gifford, *A dialogue concerning witches* (London, 1593; repr. Shak. Assn. Fac., Oxford University Press, 1931), sig. F2ᵛ: "Such an one is haunted with a fayrie, or a spirit: he must learne a charme compounded of some straunge speaches, and the names of God intermingled, or weare some part of S. Johns Gospell or such like. . . . ." The spurious fourth book of Agrippa's *De occulta philosophia* (p. 440) recommends the use in magic of "versiculus in Psalmis vel aliqua parte Sacrarum literarum." See also Thorndike, II, 858; Perkins, p. 146. These ideas are ubiquitous.

[43] *Tractatus de confessionibus maleficorum et sagarum* (H. Bock, 1605), Dubium IV, 16, Praeludium, p. 178. Sacrifice could mean simply worship, but in Marlowe's phrase "prayde and sacrific'd" it seems to imply something other than prayer: to wit, a blood sacrifice.

[44] *A short treatise declaringe the detestable wickednesse of magicall sciences* . . . . (London, 1561), sig. B1ᵛ. The allusion to Bacon will be noticed. See likewise Bodin, Book II, chap. iii, p. 162: "Nous auons dict de ceux qui inuoquent les malins esprits à leur ayde ... & qui font les inuocations par ceremonies, sacrifices, & paroles propres à cela ... ." Kittredge, p. 94, gathers some English cases, especially one in 1590 in which a dead cock was seized with other paraphernalia for conjuring in a field near London. Seymour, p. 27, narrates the Irish case (in the year 1324) of Dame Alice Kyteler and others who were accused of offering living animals in sacrifice to demons. J. Nyder's *Formicarius*, Book V, chap. iv, has a like case. See also Thorndike, II, 320. M. Murray, *The witch-cult in western Europe* (Oxford 1921), gives a full discussion.

written in. Agrippa tells us why Jehovah's names are of supreme virtue in magic:

Deus ipse licet sit unitissimus, sortitur tamen diversa nomina, non quae diversas ejus essentias aut deitates exponant, sed quasdam proprietates ab eo emanantes, per quae nomina, in nos, & ea quae creata sunt, multa beneficia, & diversa munera, velut per carnales quasdam distillant [Book III, chap. xi, p. 272].

Marlowe need not have known this cabalistic doctrine, however; the writing of the divine names is called for by almost every recipe in magic. Scot speaks of "the holy Names of God written all about"the circle (Book XV, chap. i, p. 473). Del Rio (Book II, Ques. 5, p. 80) condemns sorcerers for employing "aliqua nomina Dei incognitae significationis. . . . ." The spurious Book IV of the *De occulta philosophia*, a conventional treatise on black magic, says: "In circulo autem ipso inscribenda sunt divina nomina generalia, & quae nobis defensionem praestant: & cum iis nomina divina, quae praesunt huic planetae, atque oficiis ipsius spiritus. . . . ." (p. 450). In *Faustus* Jehovah's name is said to be anagrammatized because all of the seventy-two names of God are variations (i.e., anagrams) of one mystic Name, formed by the transpositions of its component letters.[45]

Saints' names were apparently not so generally used as the other methods of command, possibly ˌecause Protestant sorcerers loyally scorned them. But there are instances. Consider, for example, the terrible compulsion suffered by any unlucky demon invoked like this:

Ego N. servus Dei, voco, cito, exorcizo te, o Spiritus! per sanctos apostolos et discipulos Dei, per sanctos Evangelistas, sanctum Matthaeum, sanctum Marcum, sanctum Lucam, sanctum Johannem, et per tres sanctos viros: Sadrach, Mesach et Abednego, et per omnes sanctos Patriarchas, Prophetas, et Confessores Sacerdotes, et Levitas, et per castitatem omnium virginum sanctarum, et per sancta et terribilissima verba: Aphriel, Diefriel . . . . compare coram me. . . . .[46]

[44] Ward, p. 145, quotes as to the seventy-two names that "denotant semper Nomen Dei sive legantur a principio, fine, vel a dextris aut sinistris, suntque ingentis virtutis."

[46] From the *Verus Jesuitarum libellus*, p. 837, previously cited. Most of the other formulas for incantation there offered similarly invoke the saints. Ward, p. 146, notes that the elect souls of the blest formed part of one of the hierarchies of the heavenly system to which appeal was made in magic. Petri de Abano's *Elementa magica* (bound in Pars I of the *Opera* of Cornelius Agrippa, pp. 455–77) has a complete recital for conjuring, which runs, in part ". . . . & per hagios & sedem Adonay, & per ô Theos, iscyros athanatos, paracletus: & per haec tria secreta nomina, Agla, On, Tetragrammaton, adjuro contestor . . . ." (p. 461). See also Kittredge, p. 199, and Del Rio, Book I, chap. iv, Ques. 1, p. 29.

I have not been able to find, however, that these saints' names were ever abbreviated, if that is what Marlowe means by the word "breuiated"; and it may well be, as I have seen it suggested, that Marlowe is rather thinking of the names of the saints as they appear in a Catholic breviary or some epitome of their lives. (See *OED*, "breviate," "breviary.")

The first part of the Latin invocation spoken by Faustus seems to be largely of Marlowe's invention. It bears no particular resemblance to the invocations of the classical hags Medea (Ovid *Met.* vii. 192–219) and Erictho (Lucan *Pharsalia* vi. 695–749) except in the fact that it is a frank salutation and appeal to the infernal powers. This, however, is worth remarking. Erictho calls upon the Furies, Hell and its rulers, Chaos, Hecate, the Fates; on the other hand, Renaissance magical books like the *Elementa magica* of Petri de Abano and Book IV of the *De occulta philosophia* try to make the whole process of conjuring seem a rite of holiness. As Bodin (Book I, p. 56) puts it, "la plus forte sorcelerie prend un beau voile de pieté." The magician cleanses himself by fasting and prayer to God for nine days before the act of magic. When the time for conjuration arrives, he consecrates the circle and all his instruments (see the quotation from Francis Coxe, above). If he prays, it is to God, and he never salutes the fiends but wields against them the adverse power of holy names. Theoretically, the wizard is still on the side of the angels. Marlowe casts aside this pretense and makes the ceremony a dedication to Satan from the beginning. He is thus falling in—whether designedly or not it is hard to say—with the classical tradition and with that faction of Renaissance conjurers whose outright worship of the Devil is exemplified in the quotations under my earlier discussion of Faustus' sacrifice to the powers of Hell. We may note in this connection that Faustus addresses the spirits of fire, air, and water because they are fiends, inhabiting these elements after their fall from Heaven.[47]

The phrase "quid tumeraris?" of the quartos, emended by textual critics to "quid tu moraris?" (correctly, as the subsequent quotations will show), is usually believed to have sprung from the *EFB:* "Faustus

[47] The usual classification of evil spirits is sixfold: (genus) igneum, aereum, terrestre, aquaticum, subterraneum, lucifugum. Guazzo, Book I, chap. xix, p. 129; Del Rio, Book II, Ques. 27, sec. 2, pp. 213–18. Some writers like Agrippa, Book III, chap. xvi, p. 288, accept Marlowe's fourfold division.

vexed at his spirit's so long tarrying, used his charms, with full purpose not to depart before he had his intent . . . ." (chap. ii). It can be proved, however, that magicians expected trouble with recalcitrant spirits and customarily incorporated in their spells a phrase similar to this.

Cito, cito, cito, non morare: sed perfice meum postulatum! Veni, veni, veni! Quid tardaris tamdiu? Festina adventare: nam jubet te Adonai+ Schadai+Rex regum+El+Ali. . . . .[48]

Venite ergo in nomine Adonay Zebaoth, Adonay Amioram, venite venite quid tardatis: festinate, imperat vobis Adonay Rex regum, El, Aty, Titiep. . . . .[49]

Et tunc paulisper quiescat, respiciendo circum circa, si spiritus aliquis compareat. Qui si tardaverit, reiteret invocationem, ut supra, usque tres vices. Et si pertinax non comparuerit incipiat conjurare potestate divina, ... reiterando per tres vices, de fortioribus in fortiores, objurgationibus, contumeliis. . . . .[50]

Because they represent general counsel and general formulas for all magicians, these quotations are the more adequate to show how widespread is the belief in the probable delay of the demon summoned. One should also notice that in the first two of the quotations the point about the delay is cast in the form of a question (quid tardaris?) as it is in *Faustus*, a form not at all necessarily intimated by the *EFB*.

In all the quotations the enchanter overrides the reluctance of the spirit by managing against him the names and power of God. Faustus does somewhat the same thing in citing Mephistophilis by Jehovah, Gehenna, the sign of the cross, and holy water. He is resorting to what Agrippa calls the third and most potent means to bind spirits to obedience:

Tertium vinculum ipsum est ex mundo intellectuali atq; divino, quod Religione perficitur: ut puta cum adjuramus per Sacramenta, per miracula, per divina nomina, per sacra signacula, & caetera religionis mysteria: quare hoc vinculum omnium supremum est [Book III, chap. xxiii].

---

[48] From the *Verus Jesuitarum libellus*, p. 845.   [49] Petri de Abano, p. 461.

[50] From the directions to conjurors given in *De occulta philosophia*, Book IV, p. 451. In the play called *John of Bordeaux* (*ca.* 1590-94; Malone reprints), Bacon asks the trembling spirit Astro, who is hesitating to appear, "quid moraris?" (l. 657). Medea in Greene's *Alphonsus of Aragon* calls the ghost of Calchas: "I charge thee come; all lingring set aside" (III, ii, 863). H. Logeman, *Faustus-notes* (University of Ghent, 1898), p. 32, remarks that Schröer cites from Scheible's *Kloster*, V, 1157, the formula; "Cito, cito, cito veni nec morare velis."

Specifically, the use of holy water and the sign of the cross in conjuration has excellent authority. So Bodin: "... en toutes Sorcelleries, & communications detestables des Sorciers, à chacun mot il y a une croix, & à tous propos Iesus Christ, & la Trinité & l'eau beniste."[51] Reginald Scot:

> The reason that Magitians give for Circles and their Institution, is, That so much ground being blessed and consecrated by holy Words, hath a secret force to expel all evil Spirits from the bounds thereof; and being sprinkled with holy water, which hath been blessed by the Master, the ground is purified from all uncleanness . . . . [Book XV, chap. i, p. 472].

Del Rio declares it vicious magic "si adhibeantur certi characteres, aut figurae aliae, praeter signum crucis, ..."[52] A quotation from James I last given above also mentions holy water as essential in the ritual. It would seem, however, that the cross and blessed water were more normally employed in the preparation of the circle than in the actual invocation, contrary to Marlowe's usage.

We come now to one of the most interesting and persuasive evidences of Marlowe's debt to witchcraft theory. The debt in this case is not to any of the vagaries of popular fancy but to the views of theologians. Faustus learns from Mephistophilis that the latter was not compelled to appear by Faustus' conjuring speeches: he came of his own free will because, hearing these blasphemies, he had good hope to get Faustus' soul (ll. 280–89). The *EFB* has absolutely nothing on this point. But the better treatises on witchcraft are full of it. Guazzo: "Et sciendum est doemones non coactè, sed spontè accurrere ad hoc faciendum [making a pact], quia graui odio hominem prosequuntur. . . . ." (*Compendium maleficarum* (Book I, chap. vii, p. 33); Del Rio: ". . . . demones ab hominibus cogi nequeunt, ut id faciant: sponte ergo daemones accurrunt: Demones autem graui hominem odio prosequuntur, quare nec putandi gratis accurrere, sed vicissim aliquod operae suae precium stipulari" (Book II, Ques. 4, p. 72); James I:

> . . . . it is no power inherent in the circles, or in the holiness of the names of God blasphemouslie used: nor in whatsoeuer rites or ceremonies at that time used, that either can raise any infernall spirit, nor yet limitat him perforce within or without these circles. For it is he onelie, the father of all lyes, who hauing first of all prescribed that forme of doing, feining himselfe to be com-

---

[51] "Refutation des opinions de Iean Wier," p. 459 (bound with the *De la demonomanie*).
[52] Book II, Ques. 5, p. 80. See Del Rio also at Book I, chap. iv, Ques. 1, p. 29.

manded and restreined thereby, wil be loath to passe the boundes of these injunctiones; . . . . that he may haue the better commoditie thereafter, to deceive them in the end with a trick once for all; I meane the euerlasting perdition of their soul & body [Book I, chap. v, pp. 16–17].[53]

The doctrine of voluntary ascent, then, is well established in witchcraft theory. The remainder of the *Faustus* passage seems to be Marlowe's own elaboration of it. Fundamentally, of course, these authorities contradict those (I have cited some of them above in the discussion of Faustus' black rites) who hold that there is a real, effective force in magical words and symbols. The difference marks a split in Renaissance (and medieval) opinion. Marlowe lays both parties under contribution.

III. THE WITCH COMPACT

Since the terms of the written covenant come almost verbatim from the *EFB*, only some supporting lines need be noticed under this head.

Besides denying the Christian religion, Faustus affirmatively dedicates himself to Beelzebub as his sole God (ll. 292–93). The Devil often makes this requirement of witches. Danaeus says:

Wherefore he [Satan] cōmaundeth them to forswere God theyr creator & al his power, promising perpetually to obey and worship him, ... that they shall acknowledge him for their god, cal upō him, pray to him, & trust in him. Then biddeth he thē that they fall down & worship him. . . . ."[54]

And Boguet: ". . . . he makes them abandon their share in Paradise and promise that they will, on the contrary, for ever hold him as their sole master and be always faithful to him" (chap. xxi, p. 59). Similarly, Fairfax writes of the temptation of a young girl by Satan: "After these words she named God; whereunto he answered, there was no God but he. She asked what he was god of? He answered, 'God of Faith.' "[55] The citations given above as to Faustus' prayer to devils before his incantation are also applicable here.

At another time Faustus promises to build to Beelzebub "an altare and a church,/And offer luke warme blood of new borne babes" (ll. 445–46). This is a queer mingling of classical or Hebrew methods of sacrifice with the widely circulated Renaissance superstition that

---

[53] The same doctrine is announced in Gifford, sig. F4ʳ; Binsfeld, *Tractatus de confessionibus maleficorum*, sec. 9; Remy, Book II, chap. ix, p. 128. Thorndike, II, 849, calls it a "familiar theological conclusion."

[54] Sig. Eiᵛ (chap. ii).

[55] E. Fairfax, *Daemonologia*, ed. W. Grainge (1882), p. 41. Perkins, p. 184: ". . . . they giue themselues unto Satan as their god . . . ."; Cooper, p. 68.

witches were especially eager to kill unbaptized infants.[56] Renaissance witches do not erect altars and churches to the Devil: they worship him by night in the wilder fastnesses of the open country. On the other hand, they specialize in slaying babies. Binsfeld:

. . . . pro certo habendum est, quod Dęmones feruntur delectari sanguine humano. 26q. 5. c. Nec mirum. Sic omni tempore suos cultores solicitauerunt ad effundendum sanguinem, & ad immolandum homines. Psal. 105 [p. 642].

. . . . Quod autem Daemon maximè insidietur infantibus necdum baptizatis, id accidit ex inuidia maxima. Inuidet enim illis aeternam foelicitatem, quam ipse amisit: & infantes, si Baptismo abluerentur, consequerentur [p. 645] [*Comment.*, Lex VI, Ques. 2].

Bodin:

... le plus meschant meurtre entre les animaulx c'est de l'homme, & entre les hommes d'un enfant innocent, & les plus aggreable à satan, comme celuy que nous auons dict des sorcieres, qui reçoiuent les enfans, & les offrent au Diable, & soudain les font mourir, au parauant qu'on les ait presentez à Dieu ... [Book II, chap. viii, p. 222].

Bartolommeo della Spina:

Quod vero diabolus exigat à strigis ut strigēt omni tanto tēpore puerum unū, siue puellā, idipsumq́; pro voto illius perficiant: & si flebile sit, non tamen incredible: tum ex parte daemonis, qui maximo odio persequitur nomē Christi: quod praecipuè relucet in effectu in pueris baptizatis: unde persequitur eos, ac si Christum persequeretur. Prohibet etiam quantū sibi possibile est baptismū: & hoc propter inuidiā, qua humanae saluti semper insidiatur [chap. xxxiii, p. 195].[57]

The probability, therefore, is that when Faustus speaks of sacrificing newborn babes he means to kill unbaptized children as the offering most acceptable to Lucifer.

Later, after he has offended Lucifer by wishing to repent, he vows:

> Neuer to name God, or to pray to him,
> To burne his Scriptures, slay his Ministers
> And make my spirites pull his churches downe [ll. 709–11].

---

[56] Of the witch Erictho, Lucan writes (*Pharsalia* vi. 557–58) ". . . . she pierces the pregnant womb and delivers the child by an unnatural birth, in order to place it on the fiery altar. . . . ." Horace's sorceress Canidia (*Epode* v) starves a young boy to death—not an infant. But these are isolated texts, and in view of the much more highly developed form taken by the doctrine in the Renaissance, Marlowe is probably relying on contemporary theories.

[57] Equally pointed statements will be found in Guazzo, Book II, chap. iii, p. 152; Nyder, *Formicarius*, Book V, chap. iii; Boguet, chap. xxxi, p. 89; Remy, Book II, chap. iii; *Malleus malef.*, Part II, Ques. I, chap. xiii, p. 141; Jonson's *Masque of queens* and his notes thereto; H. Holland, *A treatise against witchcraft* (Cambridge, 1590), sig. F2r.

There is much testimony that foul spirits abhor the name of God. Boguet declares:

> He [Satan] makes these wretched creatures [witches at the Sabbat] repeat their renunciation of God, Chrism, and Baptism, and renew the solemn oath they have taken never to speak of God, the Virgin Mary, or the Saints except in the way of mockery and derision . . . . [chap. xxi, p. 59].

Bodin: "Ie ne doubte point, que les malins esprits n'ayent en horreur ce sacré nom, & qu'ils ne fuyent soudain quand ils oyent prononcer Iehouah" (Book II, chap. ii, p. 134). According to Fairfax, Helen Fairfax saw Satan in the shape of a young man, and asked him: " 'In the name of God, what are you?' He presently did forbid her to name God, to which she replied, 'You are no man if you cannot abide the name of God. . . . . ' "[58]

I am not able to produce strong cases on all fours for the burning of Scripture, slaying of ministers, and leveling of churches. The Devil's hatred for the things of religion, however, was a normal enough part of witch tradition. Guazzo, citing Grillandus, says that when one becomes a witch

> . . . . oportuit primo abnegare baptismum, & omnia Christianae fidei documenta relinquere. . . . . Deinde Ecclesiastica Sacramenta cuncta proijcere, pedibusquè propriis conculcare crucem, & imagines B. Mariae Virg. & aliorum sanctorum . . . . [Book I, chap. vii, p. 35].

Del Rio remarks:

> . . . . docet enim Diuus Antonius, apud Athanasiũ, cunctis Daemonib. hostile odium in homines esse grauius in Christianos, atrocissimum in religiosos, & virgines Deodicatas: singulos tamen, non nisi, quãtum Deus permittit, nocere [Book II, Ques. 27, sec. 2, p. 223].

There are, of course, all sorts of tales in the *Malleus*, Bodin, Nyder, and others of how evil spirits vex the monasteries, but their assaults seldom kill the monks and nuns.

[58] P. 38. The witchcraft manuals are thick with stories of travelers who stumble by chance upon the Sabbat orgies of the witches and disperse them by pronouncing the name of God (e.g., Bodin, Book II, chap. iv, p. 167). In the play *The birth of Merlin* the Devil warns Joan: "Thcu must not speak of goodness nor of heaven, /If I confer with thee" (Act III, scene i, ll. 206–7). H. L. Stephen, *State trials* (London, 1899), I, 222, records the testimony of the father of two bewitched children at the trial of the Suffolk witches in 1665: ". . . . this deponent hath demanded of them, what is the cause they cannot pronounce those words [Lord or Jesus]: they reply and say, that Amy Duny [one of the accused] saith, I must not use that name."

For the pulling down of churches we have Macbeth's injunction to the witches:

> answer me:
> Though you untie the winds and let them fight
> Against the churches [*Macbeth*, IV, i, 51–53].

Kittredge has several instances of Elizabethan popular belief in the idea. Particularly, the destruction of St. Paul's steeple by lightning in 1561 was sometimes explained in this way.[59] Remy likewise says:

> More than once we have seen the images of Saints broken and cast down in their shrines by lightning, believed to have been directed against them by some Demon. For nowhere do the Demons more love to perpetrate their iniquities than where their hideousness is enhanced and intensified by contempt [Book III, chap. iii, p. 145].[60]

In their extreme statement, nevertheless, Faustus' promises are greater than the conventional witch can perform. Marlowe is standing upon accepted folk notions, but reaching higher.

As his share in the agreement, Lucifer is to receive Faustus' soul wherewith to "Inlarge his kingdome" (l. 472). Satan always has this aim in increasing the number of witches, we are told by many writers. James I says:

> For as the meanes are diuerse, which allures them to these unlawfull artes of seruing of the Deuill; so by diverse waies use they their practises, answering to these meanes, which first the Deuill used as instrumentes in them; though al tending to one end: To wit, the enlargeing of Sathans tyrannie, and crossing of the propagation of the Kingdome of Christ . . . . [Book II, chap. iii, p. 34].

Mason says that Satan pretends to be controlled by magicians, "but it is onely to this end, that he may thereby the more strengthen them and enlarge his owne kingdome, by bringing into, & detaining men in this wicked errour. . . . . "[61] The idea, in this very phrasing, is quite common.

---

[59] Kittredge, pp. 155 ff. He says: "It is only natural that the Prince of the Powers of the Air should manifest his hatred of God by attacking churches" (p. 155). Cotta, p. 29: "Speede in his Chronicle . . . . within the time of Henry the 4. doth make mention of the apparition of the Divell in the habite of a Minorite Fryer at Danbury Church in Essex, with such thundring, lightning, tempests, & fire-bals, that the vault of the Church brake, and halfe the Chancell was carried away."

[60] According to Bodin, some witches "avoient paction expresse avec Satan de rompre les bras & les cuisses des Crucifix . . . ." (*Refutation*, p. 456).

[61] J. Mason, *The anatomie of sorcerie* (London, 1612), p. 44.

IV. THE CONSEQUENCES

Most of the incidents of Faustus' twenty-four years of questionable "voluptuousness"—dealings with the Pope, the Emperor, the horse-courser, the Duke of Vanholt and Helen of Troy—need not detain us. They contain witchcraft material plentifully, but it is all imported without change from the *EFB*. The same is true, for the most part, of Faustus' several efforts to repent, frustrated by the threats of the devils. Marlowe's fiends, however, are somewhat more resourceful than those of the *EFB:* they entice Faustus to suicide when he shows a disposition to repent (ll. 630–36 and 1287–90). The books on witchcraft teach that Satan habitually thus tempts witches, particularly when he fears to lose them, since their self-slaughter damns them irrevocably. Remy writes:

That as an End to a Life of every Crime and Impiety, the Demon insistently urges and impels his Subjects to kill themselves with their own Hand, especially when he sees that there is imminent Danger of their being Suspected. But God in his Goodness and Mercy often thwarts this cruel Scheme . . . . [Book III, the heading of chap. vi].

Guazzo says: "Post multas impietates à Maleficis patratas, Daemon tandem conatur eos ad interitum per ipsorummet manus inducere" (the heading of Book II, chap. xix). The *Malleus maleficarum:*

. . . . after they [witches] have confessed their crimes under torture they always try to hang themselves; and this we know for a fact. . . . . For, as we have said, the devil causes this, lest they should obtain pardon through contrition or sacramental confession . . . . [Part II, Ques. 1, chap. ii, p. 102].[62]

Faustus' tormentors are only following a customary technique.

Turning now to the last scene, we meet with one or two very interesting possible reminiscences of Marlowe's reading. Faustus in despair says to the students, "The Serpent that tempted Eue may be sau'd, but not Faustus . . . ." (ll. 1371–72). The *EFB* has merely: ". . . . but even as Cain, he also said, that his sins were greater than God was able to forgive . . . ." (chap. lxii, p. 298). But the *Malleus maleficarum* (Part I, Ques. 17, p. 82) comes considerably nearer Marlowe in this statement, which it makes the subject of a full chapter of discussion: "So heinous are the crimes of witches that they exceed even the sins and the fall of the bad Angels; and if this be true of their

<hr />

[62] Other authorities: Boguet, chap. xlv; Bodin, Book III, chap. vi, p. 311; Roberts, p. 15; James I, Book II, chap. vi, p. 51.

guilt, how should it not also be true of their punishments in hell?"
Reginald Scot (Book III, chap. xviii, p. 55) repeats the statement:
"Yea, M. Mal. writeth, that A witches sinne is the sinne against the
Holie-ghost; to wit, irremissible: yea further, that it is greater than
the sinne of the angels that fell." He proceeds with his characteristic
humor to make fun of it.

Farther on in the same scene, Faustus cries: ". . . . I woulde weepe,
but the divel drawes in my teares. . . . . Oh he stayes my tong, I would
lift up my hands, but see, they hold them, they hold them" (ll. 1386–
90). It is not sacrilege against these moving lines to point out that certain widely circulated superstitions are here embodied and trans-
figured.

An unrepentant witch cannot weep; no tenet of the witchcraft
creed is more universal than this. So strong was this belief that inability to shed tears was often held to create a presumption that an accused person was a witch. The *Malleus maleficarum* recommends that
a judge

. . . . take note whether she is able to shed tears when standing in his presence,
or when being tortured. For we are taught both by the words of worthy men
of old and by our own experience that this is a most certain sign, and it has
been found that even if she be urged and exhorted by solemn conjurations to
shed tears, if she be a witch she will not be able to weep: although she will assume a tearful aspect and smear her cheeks and eyes with spittle to make it
appear that she is weeping; wherefore she must be closely watched by the attendants [Part III, Ques. 15, p. 227].

James I: "No not so much as their eyes are able to shed teares (thret-
ten and torture them as ye please) while first they repent (God not
permitting them to dissemble their obstinacie in so horrible a crime)
. . . ." (Book III, chap. vi, p. 81). Boguet interprets the cause of this
phenomenon as does Faustus:

In conclusion, it is probable that the reason for the inability of witches to
shed tears is that tears are chiefly proper to penitents for washing and cleans-
ing their sins . . . . and therefore they cannot be welcome to the Enemy of our
salvation, who consequently prevents them as much as he can [chap. xl, p.
122].

The binding of Faustus' tongue and hands by devils invisibly present certainly owes something to Renaissance and earlier demon lore.
Some typical quotations will be of interest. Guazzo says that Satan

"Potest impedire multum linguae, manuum, crurium, retinendo in venis spiritus vitales" (Book I, chap. iv, p. 19). Binsfeld thus describes Satan's method of keeping an arrested witch from confessing: "Tertium modum taciturnitatem inducendi considerare possumus, per assistentiam demonis interius in faucibus & ore malefici, & eum impedientis ne possit loqui" (*Comment.*, Lex VII, Ques. 1, p. 676). Here is an account from the *Sadducismus debellatus* of the behavior of a possessed woman: "And when any desired her to cry to the Lord Jesus for help, her Teeth were instantly set closs, her Eyes twisted almost round, and she was thrown upon the Floor. . . . ."[63] Similarly, from Boguet:

. . . . if they tried to get her to kiss the Cross, she held her hands out to prevent anyone from approaching her . . . . and if they tried to get her to take the Cross in her hands to sign herself with it, she was at once deprived of all use in her arms and hands, so that she could not even take hold of it [chap. liii, p. 175].

Several of these quotations match the situation in *Faustus* in that they illustrate the Enemy's efforts to retain those who are trying to slip from his grasp.

The burning of magical books (*Faustus*, l. 1477: "Ile burne my bookes") was the usual way of renouncing the black art. The heading of the last chapter of the prose *Historie of Fryer Bacon* runs: "Howe Fryer Bacon burnt his books of Magick, and gave himselfe to the study of Divinity only." Kittredge[64] quotes from a confession by one Hugh Draper accused of sorcery in 1561, "y^t longe since he so misliked his science that he burned all his bookes." These are but a few of many citable loci.

The Epilogue charges Faustus with an unlawful curiosity to know secrets intended by God to remain hidden. This condemnation of those engaged in any species of occult searching is very frequent, of course, and is quite ordinarily applied to witches. Binsfeld: "Quarta caussa dispositiua ad maleficia est Curiositas, quae his portentis illuditur per Daemonum fallacias, quando id imprudenter appetit scire, quod ei nulla ratione competit inuestigare . . . ." (*De confessionibus,*

---

[63] (London, 1698), p. 20.

[64] N. 86 to chap. xvi (p. 555). Consult also Bodin, Book IV, chap. v, p. 387; Guazzo, Book III, p. 379.

Dubium IV, p. 165). Remy: "Some of these [witches] owe their fall to their persistent and over-curious temerity in inquiring into and weighing with their native reason those things which necessarily transcend the understanding of all the senses" (p. v of the Dedication).[65]

The proofs of Marlowe's reliance upon general witch lore have now been offered, and we may turn to the question, raised by Beatrice Daw Brown, of the bearing of the Simon Magus legend upon Marlowe's play. Mrs. Brown very ably shows in the first division of her paper that this legend had an important formative influence upon the Faust story and that its chief constituents were incorporated in the *Faustbuch*, whence Marlowe drew them; to that I gladly agree, although one should note that it does not follow that Marlowe recognized the relationship of his materials to the Simon story. But Mrs. Brown proceeds also to argue that Marlowe had additional separate and independent recourse to the Simon story[66] as told in the *Acts of Peter* and the Clementine *Recognitions*, and to that I see no reason to agree. She relies upon certain views of Marlowe's methods, upon certain general resemblances between the characters of Simon and Faustus, and upon certain specific parallels in thought and language between Marlowe's play and the Simon sources designated.

As to the first, her belief seems to be that the Faustus of the *EFB* was an uninspiring figure who would not be likely to capture Marlowe's imagination and that the dramatist may well have looked elsewhere for some grander prototype. Everyone will have his own opinion on these points, but the hero of the *EFB* seems to me to be by no means lacking in power and to be neither more nor less suggestive to the imagination than the originals of such other vigorously conceived characters as the early Barabas, Gaveston, Young Mortimer, the Guise. The probable stimulative effect of the witch tractates is likewise an important factor to be weighed.

In the last analysis the case for Simon Magus must rest, as Mrs.

[65] See excellent statements by Perkins, p. 11, and Cooper, p. 49. The latter says that the sin of curiositie which causes "search after knowledge and hidden Mysteries" is itself caused by "selfe conceit" (cf. *Faustus*, opening chorus, 1. 20, describing Faustus as "swolne with cunning, of a selfe conceit").

[66] For a valuable summary of the Simon Magus legend see P. M. Palmer and R. P. More, *The sources of the Faust tradition from Simon Magus to Leessing* (New York: Oxford University Press, 1936).

Brown recognizes, upon the demonstration of close resemblances to Marlowe's hero, both general and particular. She points out general similarities between Simon and Marlowe's Faustus, such as the fact that they both are large in imagination, restless in spirit, incisive in logic directed against Christian dogma, hungry for truth, superbly self-confident, and desirous of being held to be a god. The existence of this broad similarity may willingly be granted, but it is not enough. Simon Magus is far from being the only man, real or fictitious, who possessed these qualities in the centuries before Marlowe; and, more important, Faustus is by no means the only one of Marlowe's great protagonists who displays them. In short, every one of the traits mentioned is traceable clearly either to Marlowe's own temperament, or to witch tradition in the mass, or to the *EFB*, or to all together. The large, trampling spirit and anti-Christian logic are the poet's own; the desire for godhead may be found in witch lore (as shown above under the discussion of Faustus' motives); the scholarship of the man may result from passages in the *EFB* or from the same curiosity, "still climbing after knowledge infinite," which Marlowe gives to Tamburlaine; and so on.

For these reasons the general resemblances noted by Mrs. Brown bear little weight as proof of her theory, and most of the burden must be carried by specific parallels which she adduces. These seem to me, after careful consideration, ineffectual for various causes. Some of the passages in *Faustus*, like those about the magician's power over kings and the burning of his books, to which Simon Magus passages are compared, embody common witch superstitions which could be found in dozens of sources, as indicated in the appropriate places in the discussion above. In other comparisons, I cannot help feeling that too much is made of the use of conventional images, as in the Actaeon and Icarus cases, or of normal theological language, as in lines declaring that heaven was made for man and those describing Faustus' wish to leap up to God. Moreover, in speaking of the influence of the *Acts of Peter* on the Benvolio scenes (Act IV, scene 2B), Mrs. Brown goes much farther than the great majority of students of Marlowe would go when she assigns these scenes to Marlowe, rather than to Rowley or Birde. If she should be wrong in this ascription of authorship, her argument as to the parallels recoils embarrassingly. Elsewhere it would appear that she does not allow enough weight to suggestions from the *EFB*, as when she declares both Simon and Marlowe's Faustus to be logicians but does not cite *EFB*,[67] or when she remarks that both Simon and the Faustus of the drama temporarily repent but the Faustus of the *EFB* does not. Other parallels cited, like those to Faustus' questioning of Mephistophilis about the structure of the universe, may be judged to be only such distant resemblances as might easily occur when two works discuss the same subject.

Regrettably, Mrs. Brown's argument cannot receive here the extended examination which it undoubtedly deserves. The following conclusions may be stated. While it is not altogether inconceivable that Marlowe thought of some one magician as the exemplar for Faustus, filling out the portrait with details supplied by his knowledge of witchcraft, there is as yet no adequate proof that this was his method. In the absence of more specific evidence, Simon Magus remains no more likely a candidate than such other reputed magicians as Roger Bacon or Henry Cornelius Agrippa, both of whom, incidentally, are mentioned in Marlowe's play, whereas Simon Magus is not. It must be emphasized, finally, that all the main component qualities in the characterization of Faustus may be satisfactorily accounted for, without resort to the theory of a specific exemplar, by the nature of Marlowe's personal ethos and his poetic genius, by his knowledge of witchcraft, and by his study of the *EFB*.

To return now to some conclusions from the witchcraft material presented in the main body of my own paper. The total pressure of this evidence is such as to require the conclusion that Marlowe's knowledge of witch tradition was one of the decisive factors in the shaping of the play. Taking the Faustus of the prose history, who is a witch, Marlowe has infused the reach and lift characteristic of his own great spirit but has worked fairly consistently within the outline supplied him by prevalent witch theory. Neither the dramatist's basic conception of his hero's character, therefore, nor his intention in many

---

[67] Chap. i: "Faustus continued at study in the Uniuersity, & was by the Rectors and sixteen Masters afterwards examined howe he had profited in his studies; and being found by them, that none for his time were able to argue with him in Diuinity, or for the excelency of his wisedome to compare with him, with one consent they made him Doctor of Diuinitie."

particular passages can be rightly understood save with reference to that body of belief.

Marlowe's familiarity with the subject was, one judges, extensive although not necessarily profound. What he knows seems to consist of that sediment—part inchoate impression, part precise recollection —which remains in the mind after ample reading in a congenial field. That books and not oral transmission are the main channel of his information is indicated by the presence of many learned elements too complex and dignified for the common tradition of the tongue. No specific witchcraft texts can be pointed to as Marlowe's sources. We can decide with assurance, however, that he got the bulk of his materials rather from classical and Continental originals (either directly through writers like Bodin or indirectly through those English authors, like Scot, who are really commentators on the witch lore of the Continent) than from the native English superstition. All records prove that, where witchcraft is concerned, the domestic product is, fortunately for England, a meager and unimaginative thing beside the deadly luxuriance of the foreign growth. Only from abroad could Marlowe have received inspiration for Faustus' dreams of the miracles of magic and for the incantation scene. It goes without saying that he uses his originals not in the manner of a dusty scholarship but with the bold and sovereign hand of the poet.

The significance of these observations for an interpretation of the nature of Marlowe's mind and art is considerable. More and more, as we come to know Marlowe better, we must conceive of him as a dramatist who combines, translates, intensifies the common materials of his age, less and less as a poet-god creating his flaming worlds out of nothing. Examine the constitutent elements of *Faustus*. If the witchcraft influences, the all-pervading debt to the English *Faust book*, multitudinous echoes of biblical texts, and reminiscences of the early play *The conflict of conscience* are all laid together, the residue of unsupported invention is amazingly small. One is reminded of Milton and discerns something of the same power of gathering and assimilation at the basis of Marlowe's genius.

UNIVERSITY OF WASHINGTON

ESSAY REVIEW

SALEM WITCHCRAFT IN RECENT FICTION
AND DRAMA

DAVID LEVIN

Peace, My Daughters. By Shirley Barker. (New York: Crown. 1949. Pp. ix, 13, 248. $3.50.)

A Mirror for Witches. By Esther Forbes. (Boston: Houghton Mifflin Co. 1954. Reissue. $3.00.)

The Crucible. By Arthur Miller. (New York: Viking. 1953. Pp. 145. $2.75.)

The Gospel Witch. By Lyon Phelps. (Cambridge: Harvard University Press. 1955. Pp. 92. $2.75.)

In the last six years American publishers have issued one history, an anthology of trial documents, two novels, and two plays about the Salem witchcraft trials. The subject is especially interesting today because of a few parallels to McCarthyism and because of our interest in abnormal psychology, which has drawn some writers to study the adolescent girls whose fits and accusations led twenty people to the gallows. Since the Salem episode has become a symbol of the bigot's tyranny—a symbol so completely accepted that a prominent Washington correspondent of the New York *Times* and a comic-strip writer for the San Francisco *Chronicle* can both refer, without being corrected, to the witches whom Cotton Mather burned in Salem—the four recent novels and plays raise some interesting questions about the aims and techniques of historical fiction and drama.

None of these books is merely a story set against the background of the period; three of them concentrate on real historical characters, and all four pretend to portray history, give or take a few facts. All try to explain the outbreak of accusations and the curious testimony against the defendants. All but one begin with the first accusations and end with the last executions. All have something to say of the connection between Puritan theology and the injustice done at Salem.

537

Arthur Miller makes the most ambitious historical claims, and for that reason among others his play *The Crucible* deserves a more thorough discussion than I have space for here. Although confessing, perhaps patronizingly, that his play is not history in the "academic historian's" sense, he declares that it reveals "the essential nature of one of the strangest and most awful episodes in human history." *The Crucible*, although it set few records on Broadway, has been steadily popular elsewhere. Produced simultaneously by amateur theater groups in San Francisco and San Mateo, California, it attracted such large audiences over a period of several months last year that the San Francisco company turned professional and continued for some time to produce the same play as its first professional offering. In France, too, the play has been popular. Besides Mr. Miller's dramatic skill, there are several reasons for this popularity.

The subject, of course, is adaptable to the stage, and Arthur Miller has taken advantage of its dramatic opportunities. One could transcribe verbatim the examination of any of a dozen defendants, and if played with moderate skill the scene would amuse, anger, and terrify an audience. The magistrates' persistent cross-examination, the afflicted girls' screams and fits (which Mr. Miller certainly underplays), the defendant's helplessness in the face of what seems to us a ludicrously closed logical system (*Examiner:* Why do you hurt these girls? *Defendant:* I don't. *Judge:* If you don't, who does?), the appearance of her "specter" on the beam or in the magistrate's lap at the very time when she is declaring her innocence, her evasive answers, her contradictions, and her collapse into confession—these are almost unbearable to watch.

The Crucible dramatizes brilliantly the dilemma of an innocent man who must confess falsely if he wants to live and who finally gains the courage to insist on his innocence—and hang. To increase the impact of this final choice, Mr. Miller has filled his play with ironies. John Proctor, the fated hero, has been guilty of adultery but is too proud to confess or entirely to repent. In order to save his wife from execution by showing that her leading accuser is "a whore," he has at last brought himself to confess his adultery before the Deputy-Governor of Massachusetts Bay; but his wife, who "has never told a lie" and who has punished him severely for his infidelity, now lies to protect his name. Denying that he had been unfaithful, she convinces the court that he has lied to save her life. In the end, Proctor, reconciled with his wife and determined to live, can have his freedom if he will confess to witchcraft, a crime he has not committed.

This battery of ironies is directed against the basic objective of the play: absolute morality. In the twentieth century as well as the seventeenth, Mr. Miller insists in his preface, this construction of human pride makes devils of the opponents of orthodoxy and destroys individual freedom. Using the Salem episode to show that it also blinds people to truth, he has his characters turn the truth upside down. At the beginning of the play, the Reverend John Hale announces fatuously that he can distinguish precisely between diabolical and merely sinful actions; in the last act the remorseful Hale is trying desperately to persuade innocent convicts to confess falsely in order to avoid execution. The orthodox court, moreover, will not believe that Abigail Williams, who has falsely confessed to witchcraft, falsely denied adultery, and falsely cried out upon "witches," is "a whore"; but it is convinced that Proctor, who has told the truth about both his adultery and his innocence of witchcraft, is a witch.

What Mr. Miller considers the essential nature of the episode appears quite clearly in his play. The helplessness of an innocent defendant, the court's insistence on leaping to dubious conclusions, the jeopardy of any ordinary person who presumes to question the court's methods, the heroism of a defendant who cleaves to truth at the cost of his life, the ease with which vengeful motives can be served by a government's attempt to fight the Devil, and the disastrous aid which a self-serving confession gives injustice by encouraging the court's belief in the genuineness of the conspiracy— all this makes the play almost oppressively instructive, especially when one is watching rather than reading it. When one remembers the "invisible" nature of the crimes charged, the use of confessed conspirators against defendants who refuse to confess, the punishment of those only who insist on their innocence, then the analogy to McCarthyism seems quite valid.

But Mr. Miller's pedagogical intention leads him into historical and, I believe, aesthetic error. Representative of the historical distortion is his decision to have the Deputy-Governor declare the court in session in a waiting room in order to force a petitioner to implicate an innocent man or be held in contempt of court. Obviously suggested by the techniques of Senator McCarthy, this action is unfair to the Puritan Judge. And it is only the least of a number of such libels. In the Salem of 1692 there were indictments and juries; in *The Crucible* there are none. Mr. Miller's audience sees in detail the small mind and grandiose vanity of Samuel Parris, the selfish motives of the afflicted girls, the greed of Thomas Putnam; but it does not learn that a doubtful judge left the court after the first verdict, that there was a recess of nearly three weeks during which the government anxiously sought procedural advice from the colony's leading ministers, or that the ministers' "Return," though equivocal, hit squarely on the very logical fallacies in the court's procedure which *The Crucible* so clearly reveals. In 1692 there was a three-month delay between the first accusations and the first trial. Each defendant was examined first, later indicted, and then tried. In *The Crucible* the first "witch" is condemned to death just eight days after the first accusations, when only fourteen people are in jail. Whatever its eventual justice, a government which adheres to trial by jury and delays three months while 150 people are in jail is quite different from a government which allows four judges to condemn a woman to death within a week of her accusation.

Since Mr. Miller calls his play an attack on black-or-white thinking, it is unfortunate that the play itself aligns a group of heroes against a group of villains. In his "Note on Historical Accuracy," Mr. Miller remarks scrupulously that he has changed the age of Abigail Williams from eleven to seventeen in order to make her eligible for adultery. But this apparently minor change alters the entire historical situation. For Mr. Miller's Abigail is a vicious wench who not only exploits her chance to supplant Elizabeth Proctor when the time comes, nor only maintains a tyrannical discipline among the afflicted girls, but also sets the entire cycle of accusations in motion for selfish reasons. Although Mr. Miller's preface to the book suggests other psychological and historical reasons for the "delusion" and even admits that there were some witches in Salem Village, his portrayal of Parris, Abigail, and the Putnams tells his theater audience that a vain minister, a vicious girl, and an arrogant landgrabber deliberately encouraged judicial murder and that a declining "theocracy" supported the scheme in order to remain in power. One might fairly infer from the play it-self that if Abigail had never lain with Proctor nobody would have been executed.

There can be no doubt that "vengeance" was, as Mr. Miller's Proctor says, "walking Salem," but it is equally certain that many honest people were confused and terrified. Underplaying this kind of evidence, Mr. Miller consistently develops historically documented selfish motives and logical errors to grotesque extremes. Every character who confesses in *The Crucible* does so only to save his skin. Every accuser is motivated by envy or vengeance, or is prompted by some other selfishly motivated person. And the sole example of ordinary trial procedure is an examination in which the judges condemn a woman because they regard her inability to recite her commandments as "hard proof" of her guilt.

The skeptical defendant's plight is naturally moving, but making the "witch-hunters" convincing is not so simple a task. Mr. Miller fails to do them justice, and this failure not only violates the "essential nature" of the episode but weakens the impact of his lesson on the audience. The witch-hunters of *The Crucible* are so foolish, their logic so extremely burlesqued, their motives so badly temporal, that one may easily underestimate the terrible implications of their mistakes. Stupid or vicious men's errors can be appalling; but the lesson would be even more appalling if one realized that intelligent men, who tried to be fair and saw the dangers in some of their methods, reached the same conclusions and enforced the same penalties.

The central fault is Mr. Miller's failure to present an intelligent minister who recognizes at once the obvious questions which troubled real Puritan ministers from the time the court was appointed. Cocksure in the first act and morally befuddled in the last, Mr. Miller's John Hale is in both these attitudes a sorry representative of the Puritan ministry. "Specter evidence," the major issue of 1692, is neither mentioned nor debated in *The Crucible*. Preferring to use Hale as a caricature of orthodoxy in his first act, Mr. Miller does not answer the question which a dramatist might devote his skills to answering: What made a minister who saw the dangers, who wanted to protect the innocent and convict the guilty, side with the court?

Even though the dramatist must oversimplify history, the fact that dramatic exposition may be tedious does not excuse *The Crucible*'s inadequacies; Mr. Miller finds plenty of time for exposition in the first act and in the later speeches of Hale and the Deputy-Governor. The fault lies in Mr. Miller's understanding of the period; its consequences damage his play as "essential" history, as moral instruction, and as art.

Certainly the accurate portrayal of a non-villainous Puritan minister would be difficult. The easiest course is to concentrate on the innocent defendant—an intelligent character who deplores the court's folly and dies in defense of reason and truth. To oppose such a character, moreover, the author can exploit the villainous traits of Parris and the afflicted girls' flirtation with sorcery, if not with actual witchcraft. Three of the four recent novels and plays arrange this alignment.

Lyon Phelps's poetic drama *The Gospel Witch*, "written in the spirit rather than in the fact of history," concentrates on Martha Corey, a reasonable, pious woman, and her husband Giles, a garrulous old man. Both of them talk too much, the wife too intelligently and wittily and the husband too foolishly; the husband is too simply credulous, and the wife has too much faith in reason. Brought under suspicion partly because of Giles's unintentionally lethal gossip about her, Martha satirically anticipates her examiners' questions and the evidence against her; confident that she can show them the gaps in their reasoning, she thus incriminates herself. Given to cryptically wise statements, to saying

> . . . each thing a thousand times
> in a thousand different ways,

she fails at first to take her danger seriously enough; and her answers to the authorities show that she characterized herself accurately when she told her husband that "wisdom's a limited virtue." Enraged by the injustice to his wife and grieving over his folly, Giles resolves to say nothing after he himself is arrested, and he dies without breaking his vow.

Mr. Phelps avoids Mr. Miller's fatal polarization. He refrains from telling his actors that John Hathorne is *"a bitter, remorseless Salem judge"*; his afflicted girls, though two of them practice witchcraft, are not so coolly vicious as Mr. Miller's Abigail; his Thomas Putnam is motivated not so much by greed as by anxiety for his afflicted daughter's safety. But Mr. Phelps's most important improvement on *The Crucible* is his presentation of the orthodox point of view. Instead of having a minister test a defendant's innocence, as Mr. Miller's Hale does, by asking him to recite the Ten Commandments, Mr. Phelps writes two crucial scenes during which a cautious, fair officer of the court is slowly forced to suspect that Martha Corey is guilty. Here, too, the controversy over specter evidence is underemphasized, and Mr. Phelps relies on extreme coincidence when he has Martha dress in a romantic costume just before two elders come to interview her. But the persuasion of Ezekiel Cheever is entirely convincing to the reader.

Although he has rebuked Putnam for forgetting the Puritan's obligation to fight the Devil even when God's immediate purposes seem least clear, Cheever refuses to consider Martha Corey guilty when Putnam's tortured daughter accuses her. Asking for proof, he remains unconvinced even when Putnam, in anguish, holds out the "proof": his daughter's unconscious body. At the Coreys' house he restrains Putnam again in the name of decency and fairness. But as Martha seems to reveal uncanny prescience about several different subjects; as she promises, in fatal imagery, that unless the government stops turning "over souls for lice as you'd leaf a cabbage" it will get more "devils" than it bargained for and God "will forsake far more than the earth you walk"; then he can do nothing but pray that God will help her if she is innocent. By the end of the play, moreover, both he and Putnam have begun to suspect that they have abetted a terrible injustice, that they "have built a gallows where the heart cracks," that this "chaos" was not "a public test" but "a personal trial."

The difference between *The Crucible* and *The Gospel Witch*, then, is not only that the latter portrays the Puritans more accurately. Although Mr. Miller's introduction (without noting the coincidence) echoes Increase Mather's injunction to "pity rather than censure" the judges, his play presents too many orthodox characters whom one can only condemn; Lyon Phelps has portrayed some witch-hunters whom one must pity.

Both Shirley Barker and Esther Forbes bring the Devil into their novels. In Miss Barker's *Peace, My Daughters* the afflicted girls are again the real witches, but Miss Barker does not stop here. The Devil, in the form of a shoemaker named John Horne, persuades the reverend Samuel Parris to sign his book! Arguing simply that the *ministers* need the Devil in order to maintain their authority and that of God's laws, he wins the allegiance of several of the colony's leading men. Here, as late in 1692 the Mathers actually began to suspect he had done, the Devil uses the witch-hunt to confuse God's people. He promises Parris that he will bring exactly twenty people to execution before leaving the area; he provides spectral evidence against innocent people; he encourages vigorous prosecution of the defendants.

Although this fantastic device is interesting, it is finally ineffective. The alignment of characters, of course, is even more extreme than in *The Crucible,* and the unfairness of representative trial evidence is accordingly exaggerated. Even more damaging, however, is the confusion of purpose caused by the Devil's relationship with Miss Barker's heroine. A passionate woman, frustrated by the death of her fiancé and by her marriage to an old man who is past love-making, Remember Winster is powerfully attracted to Horne, who falls in love with her. Out of fidelity to her husband and moral reluctance to go to bed with the Devil, she manages on several occasions (but only after the reader has been titillated by descriptions of her powerful desire to yield) to restrain herself in time. This courtship threatens to become the central plot of the novel. For her scruples and her knowledge of the conspirators' secret she must suffer imprisonment as a witch; she is rescued from the water during an extra-legal ducking only when the Devil himself uses his supernatural power to intervene. He gains her bed at last, but only at the cost of his pride; since she will not have him as himself, even after he has struck her husband with lightning, he is forced to appear as her lost fiancé, the miraculous survivor of a shipwreck.

Around this story of seduction Miss Barker places accounts of the real people who were tried and executed. But despite her efforts to put the two stories together, the connection between the problems of the real people and the struggle of Remember Winster seems tenuous. The Devil offers at first to abandon his assault on the village if Remember will yield to him, but the symbolic connection between this fantasy and an average citizen's responsibility for what happened is not clearly suggested. Finally, there is too little uncertainty among the characters; Remember knows positively that the trials are a diabolical conspiracy, and the genuine issues are deprived of reality for want of genuinely bewildered people.

The greatest virtue in Miss Barker's approach to the subject is her willingness to look at the supernatural through seventeenth-century eyes. In an excellent scene during which the Devil conjures up specters to worship him at a Black Sabbath, and then disperses them in an instant, she approaches the effect of Hawthorne's "Young Goodman Brown," and her heroine, like Goodman Brown, doubts momentarily that a human being can distinguish at all between the real and the unreal. For this kind of imaginative insight Miss Barker had the example not only of Hawthorne, but of Esther Forbes.

First published in 1928, and recently reissued, Miss Forbes's *A Mirror for Witches* is the best of these four works on witchcraft. It is a little masterpiece—as faithful as "Young Goodman Brown" to the seventeenth-century's view of demonology, yet more refined in technique than Hawthorne's story. Instead of choosing an innocent defendant for her protagonist, Miss Forbes portrays a guilty one. Written as though by an anonymous Puritan in the last years of the century, this is the story of Doll Bilby, a fictitious young witch who is executed in Cowan Corners (Salem Village) a few years before 1692. From the prose style, which suggests that of the Puritans without exact imitation, to psychology and the evidence, the point of view is consistently that of the late seventeenth century. Miss Forbes's technical achievement is prodigious. Her narrator never forgets his conviction that Doll Bilby was guilty, and yet the irony in this situation is consistently gentle. Miss Forbes does not burlesque him; her evidence, chosen with great care, is beautifully ambiguous: convincing evidence of witchcraft for any seventeenth-century observer, yet having quite another meaning for us. The author never has to intrude on the story, for the "true," scientific hypotheses or interpretations are made by a minister, Mr. Zelley, who later comes to deny that there are any witches and to die on the gallows at Salem. During Doll's life, however, even he must finally recognize that she is a witch, for she herself confesses the fact.

A Mirror for Witches is the story of how a witch is convicted in advance, for it reports carefully all the events which add to her notoriety long before she is officially accused. Doll is the orphan of witches who have been burned in France. Adopted by an English sea captain named Bilby, she is eventually brought to New England. From the moment when Mrs. Bilby, apparently pregnant after years of marriage, believes her "child" blasted by Doll's first look, a natural enmity exists between foster-mother and child, and Captain Bilby's partiality for his Doll aggravates his wife's hostility to her. More and more isolated by this hatred and her own perversity, the child is desolate when Captain Bilby dies, and she even comes to believe that she has caused his death. In her lonely, loveless despair she calls out to the Devil in the "wilderness"; God's grace has not come to her, and she is convinced that the Devil must be her god. She takes a lover whom she believes to be a devil but who is really the pirate son of a reputed witch, and she "marries" him according to the rites of hell. At the end she is accused of bewitching the sickly sisters of a rejected suitor, and she dies in childbirth in prison, deprived of all help because everybody, including herself, believes that she will bring forth a fiend.

But no outline of the plot can do justice to this beautiful novel. Miss Forbes's fidelity to the lore of demonology, her fairness (despite a minor injustice to Increase Mather) to the trial judges and to Puritan beliefs, and her skillful presentation of Doll's essential goodness make the book more moving than any of the others. The reader is forced to recognize not only this goodness in Doll, but also the overwhelming evidence of her guilt. The cruelty and injustice in this book are the more terrifying because the cruel and unjust people are not vicious or stupid; they are predestined to cruelty and injustice by all the circumstances of their intellectual environment. The novel does not lack vindictive people, nor does Miss Forbes fail to suggest that witchcraft trials served such people's ends; but she has made Arthur Miller's point more emphatically than he by presenting the Puritan's attitude with the greatest sympathy and skill.

NEW ENGLAND WITCHCRAFT IN FICTION

G. HARRISON ORIANS

Marion, Ohio

I

S A. DRAKE, writing of Salem Witchcraft in 1884, declared that
. until the appearance of Longfellow's *New England Tragedies*[1]
"there had been no serious attempt to make use of this sinister chapter for any other purpose than that of impartial history."[2] This is a
statement which research will scarcely justify. In fact, fictional accounts of the witchcraft delusion are much more numerous than the
relative insignificance of the outbreak in New England would lead
one to expect. These I propose to examine with a view to showing
something of their character and perhaps of their extent. Contemporary accounts of witchcraft were written as defenses of advocates or
as counterblasts.[3] Fictional accounts, on the other hand, were the
result of historical ambitions or *cacoethes scribendi,* and did not appear until the awakening of American literary aspirations following
the War of 1812. With the advent of the Era of Good Feeling there
came a critical insistence in America for literary productions, rivaling
political outpourings, which would express native sentiment and celebrate American life.[4] But not until Cooper's success in *The Spy,* in
adapting the formula of the historical romance to American subject matter, was there received the sort of impetus needed. Young
writers soon panted for such distinction as was coming to this able
romancer. But where should they turn, what materials should they
employ? While they were stirred with such queries, they found direction and encouragement from W. H. Gardiner, who in 1821
pointed out three periods of American history ready for the novelist's

---

[1] Boston, 1868.

[2] *New England Legends* (Boston, 1884), p. 194.

[3] For these, turn to Burr's *Narratives of the Witchcraft Cases, 1648-1708* (New York.
1914).

[4] Representative patriotic outbursts may be found in: Solyman Brown's *American Poetry*
(New Haven, 1817). Introduction and notes; J. K. Paulding, "National Literature," in
Salmagundi Second Series, August 19, 1820; William E. Channing, "Remarks on National
Literature," apropos of an Oration delivered before the American Philosophical Society, Oct.
18, 1823, by C. J. Ingersoll. Printed in *Works* (Boston, 1880).

purpose.[5] Fertilest of these were the colonial days of New England, and so optimistic was he as to the romantic possibilities of this period that in the decade following his utterance many phases of Puritan life were poured into fiction. Witchcraft, as one of the colorful though minor incidents of that life, was soon appropriated.[6] Five volumes in the twenties were devoted to the theme, two of them full-length.

II

The turning to the witch theme for works of imagination began with Jonathan Scott's *The Sorceress* in 1817, a poem of superstition after the manner of *The Lady of the Lake*.[7] The earliest prose tale I have encountered is *Salem, an Eastern Tale*,[8] contributed in three instalments to *The New York Literary Journal and Belles-Lettres Repository* in the fall of 1820.[9] It is a story of the strange wooing of Faithful Handy, and of jealous rage venting its spleen in charges of witchcraft against Patience Peabody. Release from the law came after external pressure brought about a recantation. Several of the surnames in this tale will look familiar to the student of Salem history, but only Abigail Williams, who as one of the accusers bore testimony in many trials, can be pronounced authentic in character. Other names were loosely handled. Deliverance Hobbes, committed for witchcraft in 1692, appeared in the narrative as an abettor of charges. To induce belief in the background of superstition, the author assigned conversations on witchcraft to Increase and Cotton Mather[10] and represented them in joint attendance at the examination of the accused. The Mathers, because of their tomes on strange providences,

[5] *The North American Review*, XV, 250.

[6] Optimism about witchcraft as a theme for imaginative works was voiced by Whittier in the Preface to his *Legends of New England* (Hartford, 1831) and in his Introduction to the *Remains* of J. H. C. Brainard (Boston, 1832). This sentiment was not universal. Witness the protest in *The Atlantic Magazine* (May 1824) I, 21: "The belief in witchcraft . . . was but local and temporary, and with its best appliances, would furnish but a poor substitute for the widely-spread submission of the soul of man to the empire of judicial astrology." For lingering optimism, see the introduction to *Delusion* (Boston, 1840).

[7] The use of the compact with infernal powers, which constituted so basic an idea in New England witchcraft, was popularized through other traditions. See Byron's *Deformed Transformed* or its American imitation in Sands' *Bridal of Vaumond* (1817).

[8] This tale was offered under the sort of fictional device popularized by Irving. The only initials affixed are R. N. T., which may point to either the author or the editor.

[9] III, 329 ff. Instalments ran from September to November, 1820.

[10] Specific reference was made in appended notes to *The Wonders of the Invisible World*.

were undoubtedly figures of importance in the witching times; and they frequently appeared in witchcraft novel, often in contradiction, as in *Salem,* to the known facts of their biographies.

The second fictional treatment was by James McHenry, an Irishman who came to Baltimore in 1818 only to launch two years later upon a novelistic career. His second purely American production was *The Spectre of the Forest,*[11] titled after Goffe the regicide, a Scott-like novel copiously supplied with the American ingredients then so zealously sought for. The action took place in the region of the Housatonic River, Connecticut, and the time was somewhere between 1723 and 1725. In the second volume the author introduced the trial of a reputed witch, the mother of Amos Settle, who through malice and superstition was committed and brought to trial. Condemnation having been pronounced, the stage was set for the execution. An attempted rescue by Goffe was thwarted; but there was last minute aid through the young hero, who had just returned from England as the King's special emissary, and was instrumental as his agent in the suppression of the persecution. The author found, he acknowledged, no evidence of the hanging of witches in Connecticut,[12] but fabricated his tale from a hint given in Trumbull[13] and from his own belief that records may have wilfully been destroyed.

The *Witch of New England,*[14] which appeared the next year, was based on a similar set of facts. This novel was doubtless the product of a double interest, the unusual vogue of the Waverleys and the reissue, in 1823, of Calef's *More Wonders.* The novel itself I have

[11] In two volumes. New York: Bliss and White, 1823.

[12] For the study of Connecticut cases see Charles H. Levermore, "Witchcraft in Connecticut," in *The New England Magazine,* new series, VI (1892), 636-644. The first case in Connecticut unidentified by early writers was that of Achsah Young, "one of Windsor," executed in 1647. See H. R. Stiles, *The History and Genealogies of Ancient Windsor* (Hartford, 1891), I. 147 (quoted by Wertenbaker).

[13] *History of Connecticut* (2 vols. Hartford, 1797). Trumbull wrote in his Preface: "It may possibly be thought a great neglect, or matter of partiality, that no account is given of witchcraft in Connecticut. The only reason is, that after the most careful researches, no indictment of any person for that crime, nor any process relative to that affair can be found. The minute in Goffe's Journals, published by Governor Hutchinson, relative to the execution of Anne Coles, and an obscure tradition that one or two persons were executed at Stratford, is all the information to be found relative to that unhappy affair."

[14] Philadelphia: Carey and Lea, 1824. 12 mo.

not seen, but *The Christian Spectator* pronounced the author humorously ignorant of the scenery and manners he sought to describe.[15] Jared Sparks, who scored its violations of good sense, was equally severe in advancing charges of plagiarism:

> The principal character in the story is an old woman who pretends to witchcraft, commits certain horrid crimes and is executed accordingly. The other characters are few and the time occupied is short. . . . The author has not meddled much with history, except in his introduction, and the interweaving with his narrative a number of facts which he has collected and used without ceremony, borrowing occasionally the very language of the works from which his selections are made.[16]

If the author of *The Witch of New England* had difficulty in supplying authentic New England characters, no such embarrassment was felt by Lydia Maria Child in her *The Rebels; or Boston Before the Revolution*,[17] which not only abounds in political figures—Otis, Warren, Adams, Hutchinson, Byles—but is liberally supplied with romantic ingredients: an incognito heiress, a halted bridal, buried treasure. Not the least of these is the conception of Molly Bradstreet, witch, a Meg Merrilies creature with powers of clairvoyance. Molly, who learned her lore from a Scotch woman, was versed in the art of getting money left in the grip of Satan, but her real power was only that wielded by a strong mind over the vulgar and the superstitious. She is so conventionally drawn, however, as to impart little added interest to the novel.

John Neal's *Rachel Dyer* (1828) makes a definite attempt to describe the Salem excitement in 1692, and opens with fifty pages of history and apologetics. And though Neal did not freight his novel with passages from old records, yet he relied firmly on fact as in the description of the trials and in the biographical sketch of his central character, George Burroughs, Harvard graduate of the class of 1670.[18] Burroughs, the most important of all the Salem victims, became in Neal's hands, as he was in life, a kind yet intrepid spirit who boldly opposed himself to deluded authorities.

The chief inspiration of the novel seems to have been Neal's twofold objection to the court procedure of the time. First, it allowed the accused no trained defense. Thus the fate of old ladies like Sarah

[15] *Monthly Christian Spectator*, VII, 79.   [16] *North American Review*, XXV, 84.
[17] Boston: Cummings, Hilliard and Company, 1825.
[18] Sibley, *Biographical Sketches of the Graduates of Harvard University*, II, 323-334.

Good, enfeebled, scarcely aware of the crime imputed, was almost immediately sealed. Second, it admitted spectral testimony as valid in determining guilt.[19] Neal was particularly impressed with the mockery of the trials, declaring of the Court: "None but a witch could escape your toils." Of this spirit of protest George Burroughs became the author's mouthpiece: he harangued the judges for hours on end, he met the accusers face to face and ridiculed their beliefs, and in strained rhetoric condemned the perjurous testimony permitted at the trials. The terror he struck in court and his reproof of superstitious belief eventually proved his own undoing, for such was the popular frenzy that marked disbelief in witchcraft was cause for prosecution.

Rachel Dyer is important in the tradition not only because of its moderation and restraint but as the sole unrelieved tragedy among the tales examined. From the standpoint of the twenties it is also significant as calling attention to what was distinctive in the early history of New England. In his "Unpublished Preface"[20] Neal avowed among other motives that of showing to native novelists "that there are abundant and hidden sources of fertility in their own beautiful earth, waiting only to be broken up. . . ." In its treatment of witchcraft *Rachel Dyer* is thus a protest against the neglect of native materials.

III

Neal's optimism about American materials was seconded by Whittier, though the latter turned chiefly to the poetical possibilities of the witchcraft theme.[21] His sole prose treatment is a brief legend called "The Haunted House."[22] The tale, which belongs to the *poltergeist* tradition, was founded on the incidents of a diabolical possession at the house of William Morse of Newbury, which led his wife

[19] Such *prima facie* evidence had been inveighed against by Samuel Willard, but his words were tardily received. See his spirited dialogue, published anonymously: *Some Miscellany Observations on Our Present Debates Respecting Witchcrafts in a Dialogue Between S. and B. by P. E. and J. A.* (Philadelphia, 1692). Ascribed authorship and place of publication were fictitious. See also the *Congregational Quarterly*, XI, 400 ff. On spectral testimony, turn to Increase Mather's *Cases of Conscience Concerning Evil Spirits Personating Men* (Boston, 1693).

[20] Written for the projected *Blackwood's* series in 1825 but unprinted until *Rachel Dyer* in 1828 when it appeared with the new preface.

[21] Whittier's poems on this theme are: "The Weird Gathering," "Moll Pitcher," "Mabel Martin," "The Prophecy of Samuel Sewall," "The Witch of Wenham," and "Calef in Boston."

[22] This and the tale which follows, "The Pow-waw," formed a part of his *Legends of New England* (Hartford, 1831).

and Caleb Powell to be accused of witchcraft.[23] Briefly, it is the story of an alleged witch who, because her son was rejected by the fair Mary McOrne (recoiling from the infernal reputation of her prospective mother-in-law), haunted her dwelling by a succession of strange sounds, preternatural visitations, and unseemly visions. As a story of witchcraft, it is particularly interesting as demonstrating how fully a belief in witchcraft was dependent upon neighborhood gossip, and how, in a credulous age, witchcraft provided a ready interpretation for every strange and unintelligible occurrence. Alice Knight may almost stand representative of the race of witches: an ancient beldame, sharp-tongued, pretending to extraordinary powers, "her hand was against every man and every man's hand was against her."

Another of Whittier's tales, "The Pow-waw," might be mentioned in this connection. It is a story of incantations by a band of Indians and the activities of a New York clergyman who exorcised the pow-waw by a polyglot Bible. As far as the Puritans of New England were concerned, the Indian wizards were cousins germane to the witches, for both indulged in fiendish practices. Devil-worshiping Indians were thus readily suspected of witchcraft, as in C. M. Sedgwick's *Hope Leslie* (1827),[24] in which an old Indian hag was sentenced to death for hellish incantations over a dominie suffering from a rattlesnake bite. And though the dominie speedily recovered, the wretch was saved, not by gratitude or a relaxation of discipline, but by midnight aid of the courageous heroine.

Occasionally in the thirties other old crones and sibyls were introduced without being charged with heinous sins. These are numerous,[25] but let *Blackbeard*[26] stand representative of the lot. One of

[23] Increase Mather, *An Essay for the Recording of Illustrious Providences* (1684), Chap. V, printed in *Narratives of the Witchcraft Cases*, pp. 23-31; W. E. Woodward, *Records of Salem Witchcraft* (Boston, 1864), II, 251-261; S. G. Drake, *Annals of Witchcraft* (Boston, 1869), pp. 141-150. For another case of diabolical tricks, see Richard Chamberlain, *Lithobolia*, in *Narratives of Witchcraft Cases*, pp. 58-77.

[24] For another fictional treatment of an old Indian woman reputed to be a witch, see "Boyuca" by Robt. C. Sands, contributed to *Tales of the Glauber Spa* (N. Y., 1832).

[25] See, to name only a couple, [J. C. Hart's] *Miriam Coffin, or the Whale Fisherman, a Tale of Nantucket* (New York: Carvills, 1834); also, *The Swiss Heiress, or the Bride of Destiny, An American Novel* (N. Y., 1836). In *Miriam Coffin* one of the important characters is an old Indian sorceress of the order of Whittier's Moll Pitcher.

[26] In two volumes. New York: Harpers, 1835. Though the novel was published anonymously, the enthusiasm evinced for Philadelphia marks the author a native of that city. It may be safely ascribed to Lemuel Sawyer, reputed author of *Printz Hall* (1838) on the strength of a title-page reference of the later novel.

the minor characters was an old granny, who because she was sufficiently ugly was believed a witch, and because pirates, unknown to
the populace, used her log-house for midnight celebrations, was
thought to hold nocturnal resort for "witches out of Salem and other
parts."

Two slender one-volume tales take up the theme in the late
thirties. The first of these, *The Witches; a Tale of New England*,[27]
describes the witchcraft excitement in Fairfield, Connecticut, thus
recalling to mind that the craze of 1692 spread far beyond Salem.
It is the story of two women committed by the authorities: Goodwife
Clason, "a poor, decrepit woman bending under accumulated troubles," and the beautiful Mercy Disborough beloved by a douce David
and less truly by Deacon Goodspeed, whose unctuous addresses she
rejected. During the excitement the hypocritical Deacon was most
active in setting on foot the persecution, and it was his jealous rage,
as Mercy charged, that brought her to the scaffold.[28]

In *The Witches*[29] I find the sole fictional treatment of the water
ordeal,[30] a test employed on the theory that the pure element of
water would reject a satanist. Both victims were ducked as witches:
the old lady was drowned, thus mutely vindicating her innocence.[31]
Mercy floated, and thus convicted was on her way to the scaffold
when there was heard the warwhoop of savages. In the onset, under
the leadership of the Mohegan Onico, Mercy was rescued, and the

---

[27] Bath, 1837. Noted in the list of new Publications in *The North American Review*.

[28] Portions of this tale rest definitely on history. Mercy Disborough and Goody Clausson
were reputed witches tried in Fairfield in 1692, but the former, so far from being an un-
attached young lady, was the dutiful wife of one Thomas Disborough of Cambridge.

[29] It is true that both women were subjected to the water-test, in sixteenth-century fashion, as Judd explains: "Mercy Disborough and Elizabeth Clausson were bound, hand and
foot, and put into the water. Witnesses testified that they 'swam like cork,' yet Elizabeth
was acquitted and Mercy was not condemned." (*History of Hadley*, new edition [Spring-
field, 1905], p. 234.)

[30] I find this ordeal used but five times in America. See Increase Mather, *Remarkable
Providences*, Chapter V, wherein he condemns the water test severely, but records that a
man and a woman, probably Mr. and Mrs. Ayres, submitted to it in 1662. This action was
illegal, and the couple soon fled from such excited neighbors. The second was the Fairfield case. The experiment was tried a third time at Hartford, Connecticut, in August,
1697. Mistress Benom, who was so tried, was subsequently acquitted at her trial. The
fourth was Grace Sherwood, the *one* Virginia Witch, who was ducked at John Harper's
plantation at Lynhaven Bay, Virginia. She began to swim despite her bonds, and was
returned to jail and "held for future trial but seems to have eventually come off free"
(J. E. Cooke, *Harper's Monthly*, July, 1884; Burr, *op. cit.*, pp. 438-442). Fifth, there was a
reported New Jersey case noted by Kittredge, *Witchcraft Old and New* (Cambridge, 1929).
Chapter XV, note 69.

[31] For a brief history of the water test see H. C. Lea, *Superstition and Force* (4th Ed.,
Phila., 1892), p. 325 ff.

villainous Deacon tomahawked. The delusion slowly wore away and in time most of the so-called supernatural phenomena were explained, including the mystery of a haunted house, where the regicides, Edward Whalley and William Goffe, had been in hiding.[32]

Delusion; or the Witch of New England,[33] which followed two years later, had no factual basis and was descriptive of scenes and characters wholly fictitious. The author did attempt, from a reading of Upham,[34] to impart the furor of the mental epidemic in 1692, though the tragic interest of that year was "considerably softened in the narrative." The story itself followed closely the general outlines of its predecessor. In both tales there is a pair of accused persons, the one young and fair, the other old and withered. In both there are heroines about to be sacrificed to the ignorance of the time yet steadfast in faith. Both have youthful lovers preferred to officious deacons. But there is a difference of stress. *Delusion* is, in fact, the *ordeal* of Ellen Grafton, as the author avows:

The object of the author has not been to write a tale of witchcraft, but to show how circumstances may unfold the inward strength of a timid woman, so that she may at last be willing to die rather than yield to the delusion that would have preserved her life.

Thus he subjected her to perjured charges, sent her before a host of accusers and finally before the jury where sat her quondam lover, who with the rest voted her guilty. Even so, reduced as she was, to the dreadful alternative of life or gallows, she went unflinchingly to prison with steadfast faith in heaven triumphing over the fear of death.

Two years later a third of the series in which a youthful heroine occupies the center of the stage appeared.[35] This was *The Salem Belle, a Tale of Love and Witchcraft in 1692* (1842),[36] a story beautifully told of Mary Lyford, granddaughter of General Goffe, who

[32] Goffe and Whalley (joined in 1655 by Col. John Dixwell) lived for a while at Hadley, Connecticut, where they effectively eluded the King's officers. See Stiles' *History of the Three Judges* (Hartford, 1794).

[33] *Delusion, or the Witch of New England* (Boston, 1840). Entered 1839. 12 mo. pp. 160.

[34] See the Introduction, page xvi. The author may have consulted James Thacker's *Essay on Demonology* (Boston, 1831).

[35] In the Preface to *Delusion* it is stated: "If it is objected that the young and lovely are seldom accused of any witchcraft except that of bewitching hearts, we answer that of those that were actually accused, many were young; and those who maintained a firm integrity against the overwhelming power of the delusion of the period must have possessed an intellectual beauty which it would be vain to endeavor to portray."

[36] Boston, 1842. 12 mo. In neither the first nor second edition was there any hint of the authorship.

was condemned for witchcraft at Salem.[37] She escaped by ship through the aid of her lover, who confronted the superstitious jailor with an apparition of the Devil properly befiended with smoking mouth and cloven foot. Brief as it is, this story does contribute a fairly accurate picture of the public malady at Salem and the terrible engine of power, which the general belief in supernatural agencies put into the hands of "designing men to punish private wrongs." This last is illustrated in the plot of Trellison, the rejected suitor, who, "mistaking the bitter passion of revenge for zeal in the service," brought down with his own hand the threatened ruin upon the innocent victim. *The Salem Belle* was sufficiently popular to call for reissue in 1847.

Of similar pattern but more seriously historical in its major characters was *The Fair Puritan*[38] of W. H. Herbert. Though the novel under this title was not published until 1875,[39] the first eleven chapters, a mere fragment, were issued in paper-back form in 1845 under the title of *Ruth Whalley: or the Fair Puritan,* and thus may be considered at this point. Witchcraft, in *The Fair Puritan,* is a very minor theme, simply a trumped up charge against Ruth Whalley by the governor Edmund Andros, who held her prisoner in his own home as a hostage for the appearance of her rebellious father, Merciful. Effectively frustrated in shaping her will to his purpose, he attempted to bring fear of death as a witch upon her head. He was unsuccessful in consequence of her firm determination and the downfall of his government. The historical portions of the novel describe the activities of Merciful Whalley and his associates, revolutionary spirits who presented the first organized resistance to the authority of the crown

[37] There is no reason to believe that either the ascribed relationships or the action are historical.

[38] This was ready for the press in 1856 and was stereotyped at that time. Commercial disaster halted publication, however, and the plates were misplaced. The novel was not issued until after their rediscovery in 1875. (*Life and Writings of Frank Forester,* Edited by David W. Judd, London, n.d. [1884], p. 50.)

[39] If we can believe the assurance of Herbert's biographer, the completed novel in thirty chapters was published in periodical form in 1853 under the title of *The Puritans of New England; a Historical Romance of the Days of Witchcraft.* The later publisher was seemingly unaware of this prior venture, or at least of the issue by a Philadelphia house under the title of *The Puritan's Daughter* [1854?], "the publisher laboring under the impression that it was an original production from the fact of the purchase of the manuscript which Herbert had retained while correcting the proofs of the previous issue, a habit in which he indulged to a vexatious extent." (Judd, *op. cit.,* pp. 50, 86).

in the colonies and were successful, in 1688, in cashiering the tyrannous Andros.[39ᵃ]

Conventional plot situations reappeared in *The Puritan and His Daughter*,[40] the last and favorite novel of James Kirke Paulding. The novel, which diffusely records the antagonism of two bigoted fathers, shows their eventual inability to thwart the romance of young souls on sectarian or political grounds. Witchcraft climaxed in the final chapter was only one of a succession of barriers to matrimony—the last, in fact, after parental objections, physical separation, shipwreck, and Indian captivity have been hurdled. Paulding's account of the superstition prevalent in a nameless frontier village was drawn from Salem accounts. It sprang up by the removal from Naumkeag of a pastor and flock, devout believers, all, in witchcraft, "coming as they did from the very focus of witchendom." Thus Paulding was true to the spirit if not to the history of New England obsessions. The charge of witchcraft, as in *The Salem Belle,* was brought by a rejected suitor, and salvation came through a similar medium, the remorse of the depraved wretch forcing him to cry out in time to stay execution. In conformity to Paulding's contempt for the blood-pudding romance, however, we are spared the highly melodramatic scenes with which other romances had been seasoned.

IV

Nathaniel Hawthorne is perhaps the most revered name that appears in our survey. In the subject of witchcraft, Salem-born as he

[39ᵃ] In the discussion of the witchcraft theme in the forties, I cannot forego mention of *Naomi, or Two Hundred Years Ago* (1848), by Eliza B. Lee. Although this is primarily a novel of the Quaker intruders in New England, of Mary Dyer and Wenlock Christison and the Quaker-baiting divine, John Norton, the stern justice and the unrelenting spirit of persecution then abroad were equally illustrated in the witchcraft passages which the author offered to heighten her picture of Puritan life. *Naomi* is supplied with two kinds of witches (to employ the classification of Gaule): the fortune-telling witch, and the speculative, sciential, or arted witch. Of the first class is Mother Bunyan, a quack reputed to know the secrets of futurity and described by the author as "the Mrs. Turner of New England, ready for any nefarious and dirty work." Of the second type is a nameless old lady, full of loneliness, who was banished to the forest wilderness for alleged witchcraft. At worst it appears she was nothing more than an irregular practitioner who, already under suspicion for the mystery of her circumstances, became known as a witch because of her intimate knowledge of winds and diseases and healing lore. Her story bulks three chapters, but may be summed up almost in the words of one burned for sorcery, Mareschale D'Ancre:

"I was tried and condemned as a witch, and was only saved from hanging, and condemned to banishment, by the clemency of the judge [*vide* the case of Katherine Harrison, of Westmoreland]. I was a witch, a declared witch by the highest tribunal of this land: I, whose only art was the gift of observation, whose only sorcery was a retentive memory."   [40] New York: Baker and Scribner, 1849.

was, he naturally became interested in the legendizing twenties, an interest he turned to fictional account as early as 1825 in his unpublished "Seven Tales of My Native Land."[41] We cannot be certain, of course, of the contents of this projected volume but we are fairly sure there were tales of witchcraft and piracy.[42] Hawthorne had shown the tales to his sister, Elizabeth, in the summer of 1825, and though her recollection of them was vague, she recalled the names of two, "Susan Grey" and "Alice Doane," the last "a tale of witchcraft."[43] These may have been the two tales which Hawthorne acknowledged were in "kinder custody" at the time he made a bonfire of his college series.[44]

Of "Alice Doane" we are fairly certain. It appeared retailored in *Tales and Sketches* under the title, "Alice Doane's Appeal." The actual narrative is so meager as to be almost confusing, but it is set in a discursive framework of the historic memories of Gallows Hill. The author as cicerone read his story of witchcraft to two young ladies who with him had climbed the eminence, but who were more stirred by the thoughts of the past woes which the hill summoned to mind than they were by his Gothic tale.

The central character in the tale itself is an old wizard, probably "that conception," as Hawthorne says, in which he "endeavored to embody the character of a fiend, as represented in our traditions and the written records of witchcraft." The theme is stated in the author's own words which are summary themselves:

> In the course of the tale, the reader had been permitted to discover that all the incidents were the results of the machinations of the wizard, who had cunningly devised that Walter Brome should tempt his unknown sister to guilt and shame, and himself perish by the hand of his twin brother. I described the glee of the fiends at this hideous conception, and their eagerness to know if it were consummated. The story concluded with the appeal of Alice to the spectre of Walter Brome; his reply absolv-

---

[41] For these he sought a bookseller in vain. Andrews, a Salem printer, saw merit in them but was forced to forego publication until he had ready money, and he delayed so long that Hawthorne again secured the copy. In a state of deep depression he burned the manuscript in his own fireplace. Out of its ashes there burst "The Devil in Manuscript" (pub. Dec. 1834) who symbolized the fiendish practices which the author had recorded.

[42] James T. Fields spoke, in 1871, of an anonymous informant, an early and intimate friend of Hawthorne's who read the tales in manuscript and pronounced them striking, "particularly one or two witch stories." "Hawthorne," in *Yesterdays with Authors* (Boston, 1871), p. 65.

[43] Julian Hawthorne, *Nathaniel Hawthorne and His Wife* (Boston, 1874), p. 124; G. P. Lathrop, *A Study of Hawthorne* (Boston, 1876), p. 134.

[44] See the autobiographical paragraphs in his "Alice Doane's Appeal."

ing her from every stain; and the trembling awe with which ghost and devil fled, as from the sinless presence of an angel.

The story was supposed to have been enacted about one hundred and forty years before, which places the action in the period of the Salem mania.

A second tale, "The Hollow of the Three Hills," which appeared in *The Salem Gazette* in November, 1830, was possibly also one of the "Seven." Like "Alice Doane's Appeal," it is sketchy in character. The author chronicled the spectral revelations of a withered old crone to a lady who had come to consult her in the Hollow, a one-time witches' rendezvous. The Sibylline disclosures, audibly presented, were the revolting sins of the supplicant and the deep woes which she brought upon all who cherished her.

The most familiar of Hawthorne's tales of witchcraft is "Young Goodman Brown," of which the scene is laid in witch-haunted Salem. It is chiefly interesting as presenting a full-length description of a Witches' Sabbath.[45] The meeting depicted was a kind of cursed sacrament, an infernal service profaning that of the church, with diabolical hymns and orgiastic rites and blasphemous sermons by the Black Man. The witches were summoned to a night service by long blasts, and made their way on broomsticks or the magic rod of the devil. With the proselytes who had come to ratify the foul compact, there were assembled several of the reputed witches of 1692: Goody Clouse, who was cried out upon and condemned, but who was still awaiting execution when the Governor ended the proceedings in 1693; Goody Carrier, of whom Cotton Mather remarked, "this rampant hag was promised by the devil that she should be 'Queen of Hell' "; Indian pow-waws in damnable league with Satan; the devil, dressed in black, with his bloody seal for the initiates; and all of Salem village who had sold their souls to him, the deacons and many so-called good men of the town. The story is typical of Hawthorne's attitude toward witchcraft material. He accepted for fictional purposes the theological sin of witchcraft, of a signed compact whereby one transferred allegiance and worship from God to the Devil. He then elaborated his characters, real and imaginary, under this conception until they embodied all the reputed characteristics, drawing from the resulting fabric the threads of his allegory.

[45] Such meetings were frequently described in the records to which Hawthorne had access in the Essex County Court. See also C. W. Upham, *Lectures on Witchcraft* (Boston, 1831), pp. 46-48; Cotton Mather, *Wonders of the Invisible World*, Chapter I, Section i, "Trial of G. B." II; Hale, *A Modest Inquiry*, Chapter II, Sections vii-ix.

This is equally true of his treatment of the Governor's sister in *The Scarlet Letter*. She was put to death on a charge of witchcraft in 1655, as has been said, for her splenetic disposition and for "having more wit than her neighbors." While Mistress Hibbens's rank and final fate are hinted in the novel, she became in the author's hands a shadowy creation, a mere symbol. Dimmesdale, who wore his own invisible veil, was also representative. In him one beholds the secrecy and concealment of mankind, through its essential falsity finally resulting in disintegration of the moral sense. After the forest meeting with Hester, he became perplexed as to the real substance of his character, and only with difficulty restrained wicked impulses. Thus bewildered, he was confronted by Mistress Hibbens, who may be said to represent the power of guilt to penetrate the secret of fiend-haunted bosoms. She greeted him as one ready to sign a compact, and proffered her services in forwarding a midnight parley with the devil. As witch, open in her infernal dealings, she became a challenge to the minister's inconsistency, in yielding himself to "what he knew was deadly sin." Again, as in "Young Goodman Brown," it is the theological conception which dominates the incidental and the historical which is submerged.

In 1851 Hawthorne made slight use of witchcraft history in the construction of his *House of the Seven Gables*, in the first chapter of which he referred to Mathew Maule as one of the martyrs of the terrible delusion of 1692. The story is a legendary one and spans the time from the Salem Witchcraft, "now gray in the distance, down into our own broad daylight." The organic bond for such scattered characters of past and present is an inherited tragedy, first signalized by a scaffold malediction, which through many years taught the infallible lesson that "the wrong-doing of one generation lives into successive ones, and . . . becomes a pure and uncontrollable mischief." This curse had its origin in the death of old wizard Maule, a victim of the rapaciousness of Colonel Pyncheon, an unprincipled fanatic too severely tempted by the pride of estate. Maule, who "declared himself hunted to death for his spoil" by the persecution of Pyncheon, did not hesitate to expose this personal enmity:

With the halter about his neck, and while Colonel Pyncheon sat on horseback, grimly gazing at the scene, Maule addressed him from the scaffold and uttered a prophecy of which history as well as fireside tradition has preserved the very words. "God," said the dying man, pointing his finger with a ghastly look at the undismayed countenance of his enemy —"God will give him blood to drink."

308

The same malediction,[46] though with variations, had been previously employed by Neal in *Rachel Dyer,* there offered as a transcript from the death scene of Sarah Good. He spared the unhappy elder, however, against whom the words were actually uttered, and had her curse fall on the head of Micajah Noyes, a character of the author's own making. Neal gave the prophecy an almost immediate fulfilment at the hands of the Mohawk Indians. Hawthorne, it will be remembered, sent his Colonel to death by a hemorrhage which stained his ruff and beard.

For the conception of an inherited curse, as his biographers suggest, Hawthorne had far more sources of inspiration in his own family history than in tradition or trial records. The fact that his great grandfather, John Hathorne, who was doubtless cursed a score of times, had committed sins in the name of justice and had zealously persecuted guiltless old crones and poor unfortunates with stern and unyielding severity, left its impress upon Hawthorne's sensitive nature. At last, in the preface of *The Scarlet Letter* he made the following vow: "I, the present writer, as their representative, hereby take shame upon myself for their sakes, and pray that any curse incurred by them—as I have heard, and as the dreary and unprosperous condition of the race for many a long year back, would argue to exist—may be now and henceforth removed." Thus out of history and family tradition Hawthorne was led to give fictional treatment to the theme of generations damned by unrighted wrongs.

V

By far the fullest treatment of Salem witchcraft appeared in 1857 by John W. DeForest, an American realist of the Balzac school. *Witching Times,* the name of DeForest's historical romance, appeared serially in *Putnam's Magazine,*[47] and is the only fictional treatment which covers the entire period of the Salem distresses, and provides a comprehensible and psychological account of actors, scenes, and motives in that mad delusion. The narrative begins with September 1691, and continues down to the Spring of 1693 when the general reprieve was issued by Governor Phips.

[46] This malediction is preserved in Calef, *More Wonders,* Part V, under date of June 30, 1692. The words were directed by Sarah Good against the Rev. Mr. Noyes, the junior Elder at Salem town, who at the execution urged her to confess, denouncing her as a witch. See also Upham, *op. cit.,* p. 100.

[47] VIII, 570-594; IX, 11-28, 188-207, 297-317, 394-413, 515-524, 621-630; X, 62-74, 218-231, 393-404.

In its central episodes the story was a domestic one, chronicling the fortunes of Henry More, middle-aged, and Rachel, his daughter, who had just returned from England. They were received into the home of his married sister and her husband Bowson. During the mania, the Uncle, who was never tough-minded, became almost idiotic with superstitious terror and finally verged into mild insanity, believing himself befiended. He was so obviously *non compos mentis* that he was not arraigned. More,[48] who was the leader of the opposition—what little became articulate,—disputed "boldly and obstinately" with the advocates of the Delusion. Finally, incurring the enmity of the authorities, he was denounced by the canting Rev. Samuel Parris as a Sadducee. To the end, however, he retained the friendship of Elder John Higginson, who preached the mild gospel of faith, hope and charity, but whose non-subscription to the fury of the time made him unpopular. More was in time brought to the scaffold. Rachel, through the jealous rage of Elder Noyes, a rejected suitor for her hand, was cried out upon and condemned at the January session, 1693. Mark Stanton, her young and daring husband, through the aid of a grateful Indian was successful in a jail delivery and escaped with her to Virginia. They returned in safety after the insane craze was over. Such are the central episodes of the story, but it is even more truly a history of the major events, the examinations, commitments, trials, and hangings which took place in Salem village. One finds included dramatic accounts of most of the victims who paid the penalty of the law, Bridget Bishop, Martha Carrier, Goody Nurse, George Burroughs, etc., not even excepting the revolting case of Giles Cory, pressed to death under rule of *peine forte et dure*.

It is easily established that there was historical warrant for most of the materials incorporated in the novel. If the reader of DeForest will turn first to Calef and Upham, he will see how closely the novelist followed them even in minor details. It is of interest, moreover, to note the use to which he put some of his sources. To his fictitious hero, Henry More, he transferred the reputation and indictments of George Burroughs, especially his reputed feats of strength.[49] To the

---

[48] The selection of the name of Henry More as the mouthpiece for the moderns is a strange one in the light of the Cambridge Platonist's publication (with additions) of Glanvill's *Sadducismus Triumphatus* (1681), a defense of the belief in witches and supernatural appearances.

[49] For the reputed deeds of George Burroughs, see Upham, *Salem Witchcraft*, II, 296-304; Cotton Mather, *The Wonders of the Invisible World* (Boston, 1693), Chapter I, Sec. I,

romantic story of Mark and Rachel is added the poignant trial scene from the records of Martha Cory; and the second charge to the jury, after a verdict of *not guilty* had been returned, had historical origin in the trial of Rebecca Nurse.[50] The episode which he related of a two-hour sermon of Parris' interrupted by comment occurred in reality to Rev. Lawton, back on a visit. In the midst of the discourse Miss Pope spoke up and said, "Come, now, enough of that."[51] Other interruptions followed.

It is my opinion that the author sought to show in the character of More the effect of witchcraft upon the mind of a man with a broad, unprovincial education. He early counseled: "Let us be cautious how we peril our neighbors' necks, because there happen to be such things as . . . disturbed nerves and hysteria." He circulated, with warm sympathy, a petition to the Governor, praying him to check the persecutions. All to no avail. Henry More had resided in England for twenty-five years, but his neighbors in Salem meanwhile had been sinking into depression among the gloomy forests of New England, where savages lurked; and their conquest of nature afforded scant opportunity for broadening views. Their libraries, moreover, were limited and contained such volumes as would heighten credulity. In consequence, when the terror of the incredible witch descent upon Massachusetts broke out, they had not the mental vigor to withstand it; they lacked the background of a transatlantic outlook which the first generation and DeForest's hero possessed. Thus More's voice was unheeded and only drew opposition to himself. He was a nineteenth-century spirit (the author's own voice) swallowed up in the babble of seventeenth-century persecution.

VI

Thus I have examined the stories of witchcraft with a view to showing the use of the theme prior to Longfellow. I have not sought to bring the record down to the present, though I may strain my imposed limits long enough to mention Caroline Derby's *Salem* (1874),[52] a novel indicative of the later interest in the fate of Rebecca Nurse,[53] who in this tale is paired with Goody Campbell, a fictional

---

"The Tryal of G. B."; see also W. E. Woodward for the transcript of the Essex Court Record in the case of G. B.

[50] See Calef, *More Wonders*, Part V, under date of June 30, 1692.

[51] *Ibid.*, March 24, 1692.

[52] Published under the pseudonym of D. R. Castleton. The full title is *Salem; a Tale of the Seventeenth Century* (New York, 1874).

[53] See the poems on her sad fate by David Foster and Rose Terry Cooke.

creation. Other phases of witchcraft were poured into fiction during the revival of romance in the late nineties, but though the last word has undoubtedly not been uttered, witchcraft has been frequently enough handled in fiction to render unlikely the appearance of new and uncharted treatment.[54]

The theme was sometimes interestingly handled but most of the earlier attempts were very brief or tended to verge upon absurdity. Even in the work of abler literary men, Paulding, Hawthorne, and DeForest, the possibilities of the theme seem to have been rapidly exhausted. At best they could but rely upon the accounts of Calef, Mather, Hutchinson, Upham, and the Essex County Records. These were of themselves compounded of highly credulous materials, and where was the temerity to superadd imaginative construction? Then, too, each novelist was under the iron necessity of creating a picture of the delusion, if the obsessions of the actors were to be readily believed, and here history carefully drew the limits.

Almost all the longer tales were cast in the mould of the historical romance. The earliest attempts were naturally patterned after the Waverley novels, but no imitativeness can be charged against such

[54] Later novels of witchcraft, without reference to merit, are: Pauline B. Mackie, *Ye lyttle Salem Maide: Story of Witchcraft* (Boston, 1898); Amelia E. Barr, *The Black Shilling* (N. Y., 1903); Marvin Dana, *A Puritan Witch* (N. Y., 1903); L. F. Madison, *Maid of Salem Towne* (Philadelphia, 1906); W. M. Martin, *Shoes of Iron* (Boston, 1907); Henry Peterson, *Dulcibel: a tale of old Salem* (N. Y., 1907); Herbert Gorman, *The Place Called Dagon* (N. Y., 1927); Esther Forbes, *Mirror for Witches* (Boston, 1928); Durward Grinstead, *Elva* (New York, 1929).

Elva is probably the best novel of Salem witchcraft that has appeared. It is more faithful to the real facts of the Delusion than any of the prior accounts, but it does not secure accuracy at the expense of fictional interest. There are no lengthy transcripts from trial records as in Neal or even in DeForest; the narrative is not buttressed with footnotes, and yet the touch of authenticity is always felt, whether in the description of individuals, of religious excitation, or of examinations, trials, and hangings. Historical materials, when introduced, are so skillfully blended with fictional elements that recognition comes as a surprise.

The whole book is skillfully composed. What can be done in the matter of supplying motives for the accusers and of tracing the stages in the fearful hysteria which upset the reason of Salem village, Grinstead has done. As a student of the mania of witchcraft there was danger that he might approach his material as a series of case studies, but he successfully blended the psychological phenomena, which he studies as a modern, with the theological conception of a compact with the Devil, which is seventeenth century in outlook. No other novel of the Salem witchcraft has provided this unity of outlook, this close-knit character of the events, this psychological insight and rationalistic interpretation.

The result is convincing. The outstanding historical figure, as in *Rachel Dyer*, is George Burroughs, and he is an impressive creation. Certain puzzling queries Grinstead grappled with: what brought the charges of witchcraft upon this minister, and why did he not escape the snares set for him? There is convincingly presented, in answer, the story of the old parish feud, the desire of the Circle girls for a victim of sufficient weight to interest Cotton Mather in their antics, and finally the perverted passion of the neurotic Elva Pope and the heated fancies of the epileptic Anne Putnam.

independent workmen as Neal and Paulding, or Hawthorne.[55] And yet all clung to romantic treatment. Even the *Witching Times* of DeForest, who was soon to write high realism, is a tale of other days with romance, satire, and realism well blended.

But this romantic glow was not easily attained. To anyone not familiar with the wearisome repetition of charges with which the afflicted assailed the accused, it might appear the simplest thing to construct out of the episodes of that time a romance neither harsh nor revolting to refined taste. But the motives of the actors and the sources of enmity were so thoroughly obscured, and the interrelation of accusations so befogged, that it was difficult indeed to weave them into a narrative. Thus beset with confusion, the novelist had to resort to fairly simple patterns of malice or jealousy, patterns which sooner or later suggested other tales, even when the authors were innocent of indebtedness. It was this inherent plot weakness that accounts for the constant recurrence of fair Puritans charged with witchcraft. The earliest victims of the witchcraft delusion were old and decrepit, women sunk in the economic and social scales, but the novelists preferred making their heroines young and beautiful, a practice which, though stimulative of interest in the novel, was scarcely one which imparted a correct historical view.

Witchcraft, it needs to be said in extenuation of the cumulative effect of the record, was not the sole fictional theme treated by the romantic novelists of the nineteenth century. Piracy, Revolutionary warfare, the waning Indian, the Regicides, Theological pietism, Western humor, the Frontier, Spanish American conquest,—all held a prominent place in romantic literature. And yet as a theme witchcraft was more frequently employed than has been hitherto suspected, more frequently, in fact, than its relative unimportance in the annals of America really warranted. It is true, as Kittredge maintains, that New England witchcraft was after all a "very small incident in the history of a terrible superstition." But this is not the impression which would be conveyed by the quantity of the fiction examined. The necessity of finding a colorful subject for historical romance, and at the same time the relative poverty of America in the counterparts of European romance, served to heighten the interest in the Witch Invasion of New England.

[55] For Paulding's insistence upon native models, see note 4 above; as for Neal, he declared in his Preface to *Rachel Dyer* his intention of imitating no one, and indeed of resembling no other.

THE CONCEPT OF THE DEVIL AND THE MYTH OF THE PACT IN LITERATURE PRIOR TO GOETHE

WOLFGANG S. SEIFERTH

Howard University

> "Mephisto leers at us with a thousand grimaces." Albert Schweitzer

I

The meteoric rise of Satan on our literary horizon is a striking and signal experience. The acclaim given to Thomas Mann's *Doktor Faustus* in 1949 was the public recognition of this experience; it had been preceded and accompanied by smaller signs of similar importance. Only a few can be mentioned here;[1] their number could easily be tripled in the less conspicuous ranks of literature. These instances, different as they may be in other respects, seem to suggest a growing disposition of modern man to return to medieval preoccupations, concepts and moods. In our generation we have experienced such tremendous forces of perversion and evil that the concepts of progress and the promise of the rational mastery of life which inspired preceding ages have been riddled and undermined.[2]

The great school of Realism, expanding from France over western Europe, had also dealt abundantly with the darkest sides of human existence, but it had defined the evil in man in terms of his environment. The rationalistic hope was not abandoned that human science and skill would gradually transform man's environment, bringing forth finally an age of peace and plenty. The devil cannot be expected to make more than a rare appearance among these writers for the same reason that forbade Courbet to paint an angel: he never had seen one. Such rare appearance, when it does occur, rather suggests traditions prior to and outside Realism, like Balzac's character of Vautrin, and, as late as 1903, Shaw's *Don Juan in Hell*, the authors in both instances performing a respectful bow to Goethe's Mephistopheles.

In contrast to this psycho-sociological concept of evil and to the expectation of its final conquest within a rationalistic world, there had always been a powerful undercurrent of thought flowing from the reservoir of Romantic philosophy and its vast medieval sources, insisting on

[1] Dorothy Sayers, *The Devil to Pay* (1939); George Bernanos, *Sous le soleil de Satan* (1940); Denis de Rougemont, *The Devil's Share* (1944); John Masefield, *The Witch*; Leo Feuchtwanger, *Wahn oder der Teufel in Boston*; Karl Zuckmayer, *Des Teufels General* (1946); Elisabeth Langgässer, *Das Tryptichon des Teufels* (1949) and *Das unauslösliche Siegel* (1950). The more popular stratum is aptly represented by C. H. Lewis, *The Screwtape Letters* (1944).

[2] Cf. the theological conclusions on the problem of evil in man's rational world in the neo-orthodox teachings of Karl Barth and Reinhold Niebuhr; also, on a more general plane, Erich Kahler, "Säkularisierung des Teufels," *Die Verantwortung des Geists* (Frankfurt am Main: S. Fischer, 1952); A. R. King, "The Christian Devil," *Religion in Life*, XX, 1 (1950); D. M. Key, "The Life and Death of the Devil," *Religion in Life*, XXI, 1 (1951); W. von Einsiedel, "Der Böse und das Böse," *Merkur*, V, 5 (Stuttgart, 1951).

the metaphysical nature of evil, and issuing finally in Schopenhauer's pessimism. Whenever this undercurrent broke forth into the realm of creative literature, suggesting suprahuman manifestation of evil, it could scarcely shake the authority of the acknowledged writers of the day, as is proved for England by the complete oblivion of James Hogg's *The Confessions of a Sinner* since its first and only publication in 1824,[3] and for America by the isolated career of Herman Melville, who has only recently experienced a veritable renascence.

This suprahuman manifestation of evil is the most impressive characteristic of Russian literature in the nineteenth century, especially in the works of Gogol and of Dostoevski. A fundamental difference unfolds here, above the common ground of realism, between the sociological interpretation of life on the one hand and the depth experience of the Russian writers on the other. When Zola began *Les Rougon-Macquart*, Dostoevski was pondering his own cycle of novels under the title *The Life of a Great Sinner*, from which project the important figures of his novels are derived. Here man was to become the arena where Satan and God strive for mastery; where personified evil would appear to Ivan Karamasov in the flesh, Ivan's own distorted self; where the Grand Inquisitor would admit that he is no longer in league with the Savior, but with his antagonist. Dostoevski locates the devil in the intellectual regions, as the Middle Ages did; the great temptations are questions, temptations of an intellect which tries to fathom the mystery of human existence and finds itself confronted with the alternative of faith and nonfaith. Dostoevski's work stands out prophetically: it traces back to concepts and poetic figures of the Middle Ages, and likewise it points forward to Thomas Mann, de Rougemont, and their companions.[4] It cancelled the proud self-sufficiency of man, and reintroduced the medieval suspicion of the intellect, just when Europe was paying tribute to the spirit of unending progress and to hope of cultural perfection of man.

The footprints of the devil in modern literature thus trace back to the great Russians and to their understanding of man's nature. This heritage is still accumulating: on the one hand it fans the despair of Existentialism, on the other it helps to rediscover essentials of religion.

Medieval tendencies in a different field are certainly expressed by the growing interest in Dante's *Divine Comedy*. Within the last thirty years three major efforts have been made to render this work into Eng-

[3] James Hogg's *The Confessions of a Sinner* was not reprinted until very recently and unavailable even in larger libraries in England. For its sudden rise to continental acknowledgement, precipitated by André Gide's interest, cf. *Merkur*, V, 5 and the publication of a German translation under the title *Vertrauliche Aufzeichnungen und Bekenntnisse eines gerechtfertigten Sünders* (Stuttgart, 1951).

[4] The prophetic quality of Dostoevski's work has been defined more recently by René Fueloep-Miller, *Fyodor Dostoevsky, Insight, Faith, and Prophecy* (New York, 1950), and William Hubben, *Four Prophets of our Destiny, Kierkegaard, Dostoevsky, Nietzsche, Kafka* (New York, 1952).

lish, with the utmost metrical faithfulness,[5] thus raising this representative medieval poem from obscurity to spiritual appreciation and importance outside of scholarly circles.

Having thus identified a medieval disposition in the contemporary mind, in various fields and forms, we are able once more to appreciate the figure of the devil in older literature, in the centuries of his unquestioned and legitimate existence. From this vantage point we shall throw a searching light on him and on the myth of the pact in the literature of the Middle Ages and of the Renaissance.

II

The footprints of the devil on the highways and byways of literature are legion. Folklore, fairy tales, popular and local traditions must consequently remain beyond the scope of this study, as must also manifestations of superstition such as witchcraft. We shall consider only documents in which the concept of the devil and the myth of the pact have reached a certain maturity of form and thought. Foremost among such sources are the legends of the saints. Finality of thought, based on the moral teachings of the church, joins here with forms and figures of archetypical quality. Most representative within this group is the *Legenda Aurea* of Jacob de Voragine, archbishop of Genoa. This remarkable collection was compiled just at the time when the Middle Ages reached their cultural and spiritual peak. It spread over all of Europe; it was translated into various languages and became influential in the national literatures. It proved to be a treasure chest of themes, motives, and inspirations. Its sphere of influence reaches up to the highest planes of European literature, including Dante and the Italian *novella*, Marlowe, Milton, Calderon, Flaubert, and Dostoevski. The ties with German literature are numerous. The Faust tradition drew nourishment from this source. But even some motives of Schiller's ballads are contained as modest variants in the *Legenda Aurea*. Gottfried Keller's *Sieben Legenden* were inspired by it, and recently Thomas Mann has drawn upon similar sources.

The entire lore of the devil can be reconstructed from the *Legenda Aurea* [6] and related sources. Using the simple literary form of the legend as the point of departure, this paper will also include representative examples of higher literary forms.[7] Pertinent passages gathered from these materials amount to a systematic and complete presentation of the con-

[5] Melville Best Anderson (1921); Laurence Binyon (1947); Dorothy Sayers, *Inferno* (1949).

[6] This paper is based on Jacobus de Voragine, *Legenda Aurea. Deutsch von Richard Benz*, 2 vols. (Jena, 1917-1921). This German translation is a complete and accurate rendering of early text manuscripts of the thirteenth century. Quotations (translated by the present writer) and pertinent passages are given by volumn and column, for instance (I 66).

[7] Cf. André Jolles, *Einfache Formen* (Halle, 1930), pp. 23-61; and Heinrich Günter, *Die christliche Legende des Abendlandes* (Heidelberg, 1910).

cept of the devil and what this concept meant to man's life. Within this concept several groups of activities of the devil can be distinguished.

The Devil as Accuser on the Day of Judgment

There was once a sinful man who was transported in a vision before God's tribunal. Satan was there and said to the Lord, "Thou hast no title to this soul, it is mine; I have good testimony as to that." Said the Lord, "Where is the testimony?" Satan replied, "The testimony has come from thine own mouth and will be valid in eternity. For thou didst say 'In the hour that thou eatest thereof, thou shalt surely die.' This man here is of the race of those who like to eat forbidden fruits; thus he is sentenced by that covenant and must perish with me in the judgment." And again Satan spoke and said, "I have also a title on him by prescription of Common Law, for I have owned him for thirty years and he has obeyed me as a serf. He is mine also because the good that he perhaps has done is outweighed infinitely by the bad."

The Lord does not render judgment at once but gives the man eight days to prepare his defense. On his way home in great distress the man is met by Truth and Justice. Truth interprets the Genesis passage that had been quoted so readily by the devil as referring to bodily death only, death being the fate of creaturely life ever since the Fall. Justice proves that this man's reasoning powers "had always fought against that serfdom and grumbled against this ruthless master." When the good and the bad deeds are finally put on the scales, Saint Mary, in the character of Mercy, tips the scales in favor of the good. Here the vision ends; the man wakes up and resolves to change his life (II 16-18).

Next in importance to the divine tribunal is the contest of angels and demons for the soul of man. The bishop Forseus witnesses such a contest shortly before his death. The demons know the divine law point by point and insist that he has not lived up to it. They accuse, the angels defend; in the ensuing combat Forseus is injured for certain transgressions but saved in the end (II 208).

It is not only because of the magnitude of Dante's poetic conceptions that the *Divine Comedy* must remain outside of this study, except for a few confirming glances. Dante uses demons almost exclusively as agents of torment in *Inferno*. But in two instances the contest of angels and demons for the soul of man is found in the great poem; here Dante follows faithfully the pattern set forth in the *Legenda Aurea*.

The reader is told that Saint Francis claimed the soul of Guido da Montrefeltro at the latter's death but that he was opposed victoriously by "un de' neri Cherubini" (*Inf.* XXVII 113), "one of the black Cherubim," who reproached Francis for doing injustice to him since Guido had been in his bondage for some time past. The same contest and argument, but with different outcome, takes place in *Purgatorio:* Buonconte da Montefeltro, Guido's son, sees "l'angel di Dio... e quel d'inferno" contesting for his soul, The angel remains victorious "per una lacrimetta" (V 107), "for one little tear."[8]

These examples may stand for many. In all these instances the literary motive is the dream, a vision, a visit of mortal man to the beyond. The pattern of the morality play of some centuries later emerges from these examples as far as Marlowe's *Faustus:* " Hell strives with grace for conquest in my breast" (scene 13).

The concept of the devil prevailing here derives, at least partly, from the Greek *diabolos,* the slanderer. "The devil will be present at the tribunal and will repeat the words of our confession of sin; he will remind man of everything he has done, of place and hour, and he will call to man's mind the good that he might have done instead" (1 15). The demons know man's mind, the obvious and the hidden; they know the divine law, which fact suggests their angelic pre-existence; they search for companions to share their eternal pain; they plead with their opponents for what they consider their lawful property. The demons' success may ultimately amount to a proof of their superiority over God's purposes and justify thereby their revolt.

But this concept does not constitute a dualism of hostile powers. The demons remain a part of the divine order; they exist and function with God's approval. The basic monotheism is maintained; its unity of purpose and its emphasis on man is only strengthened by the efforts of the demons, which will be outweighed by the works of the saints and the mercy of God.

The Devil as Tempter

In contrast to the metaphysical nature of the devil's role in the Last Judgment, this second group of demonic activities is part of the life in the flesh and of decisions daily to be made. Temptation is the ever present threat to man's integrity: "For the devil tempts adult man in cunningly entrapping his reasoning power; in provoking his will power by allurements; in oppressing man's virtue by violence" (II 223). Thereby the moral order of life is perverted and the divine purpose defeated. This concept of the devil is rich in psychological truth and consequence: man's power of judgment, his freedom of choice, the very core of his nature, lie exposed to attack and may eventually be perverted. The pattern of this attack is the serpent's stratagem in the garden of Eden: "Ye shall be as gods knowing good and evil." This pattern extends roughly from the twelfth century Anglo-Norman *Adam,* has a full share in the *Legenda Aurea,* and leads up to Milton's *Paradise Lost.* The variety of tactical approach and of psychological refinement in this pattern is striking whenever an effort is made to overwhelm a man of character and intelligence. But the pattern is just as visible in the demonic dealings with

[8] Cf. *La Divina Commedia,* ed. C. H. Grandgent, revised edition (D. C. Heath, 1933), where on page 363 the contest between angel and demon for the soul of man is traced back as far as to Etruscan art.

the common lot of people, laymen and monks alike, as is evident in the legend of Saint Dominic, who once meets the evil spirit sneaking about in the monastery disguised as a friar. Dominic compels the devil to reveal to him the tricks by which he tempts the friars at prayer, at dinner, at the monastic meetings; even ascetic discipline may prove to be fatal. The devil will lose his gains in the end, he admits, when the uneasy minds of the friars involved would be relieved in confession and they would be penalized in the chapter hall which he could not invade at all (1 719).

A refined strategy of temptation is shown in a story with three riddles that occurs twice in the *Legenda Aurea* (I 28-32 and II 63-64). A cleric is about to fall into the toils of a fascinating woman, his confessant, and is saved from this fatal involvement only by the intervention of Saint Andrew (or Saint Bartholomey), to whom he is especially devoted. The saint, in the garb of a pilgrim, solves the three riddles posed by the temptress; with the last answer he identifies her as what she really is: the devil. In the other version it is the saint who poses the questions and forces the temptress to reveal her identity. Here the myth of the Sphinx has found one of its medieval variants.

Again a side glance at the *Divine Comedy* helps to bring peculiar qualities of the legend into focus. In the many instances of temptation, as related in *Inferno* and in *Purgatorio*, Dante does not employ a tempter in person who would subject his victim to his tricks and trials. The temptation is completely implicit in the human situation as such. This situation is portrayed with utmost accuracy: passion, disdain, envy, wrath, pride, and so on, are at work in man's mind. The promptings of a tempter in person are not needed. The downfall is accomplished by a perversion of the will. Thus in Dante's own case:

> ... With perverted steps on ways untrue
> He sought false images of good, that ne'er
> Perform entire the promise that was due. (*Purg.* XXX, 130-132)

Consequently it is not the serpent who is responsible for the fall of man but "il trapassar di segno" - "the ordered limit overpast" (*Par.* XXVI, 117), in this instance disobedience caused by pride.[9]

Dante, whose poetic sublimity is matched only by his intellectual power, goes far beyond the allegoric devices as employed in the *Legenda Aurea*. He intends to trace the basic concepts of vice and virtue to their origins. His pen swiftly moves back and forth between abstract categories of human behavior and most concrete human situations. The abstractions spring to pulsating life in the tales of torment and of repentance. It is the art of counterpoint; while the legends of the saints, monophonic in middle key, employ allegories as real, and evolve the perversion of the will in a persuasive dialogue between tempter and man.

In some legends the strategy of temptation seems to be planned in

[9] Quotations from Laurence Binyon's verse translation (New York: Viking Press, 1947).

advance in a council of the demons. Here the devils boast of their accomplishments, concoct new plots, and suggest new techniques; gradually their activities assume the proportion of a major conspiracy. Among the legends of the holy cross the story of a Jew is told (II 159-162) who, unable to find night quarters in Rome, spends the night in the ancient temple of Apollo and there witnesses a midnight council of the devils. Their superior seats himself amidst them and inquires about their dealings with men to find out what evil each of them has done. One devil has caused war and social commotion, and much blood has been shed; another caused storms and shipwrecks and drowned many people; a third devil incited quarrels and jealousy at a wedding where the bridegroom was slain. Finally, a fourth devil admits that he needed forty years to seduce a monk to a sin of the flesh. Satan acknowledges him to be the master of them all for having employed temptation so successfully, and makes him sit at his right side: a moral disaster, in his judgment, infinitely outweighs physical catastrophes or mere violence. Such boastful reports, or plans, are made competitively, each demon trying to outdo the preceding one, so that gradually bigger and better catastrophes may be brought about and man's virtue drowned in despair.

The council of the demons and the competitive reports have become consequential. The council forms an important part of the Low German *Redentin Easter Play*, [10] where it is motivated by Christ's harrowing of hell. In Milton's *Paradise Lost* the council is convened to recover the former rank of the demons in the universe, and finally it aims at "pursuing vain war with Heaven" (Book II). An assault on man, who has just been created, appears as the most appropriate way to humiliate God, "which, if not victory, is yet revenge." Thereby the council of the demons becomes part of a major theme of Milton's epic: the revolt of the fallen angels, the self-assertion of the God-forsaken creatures who, seized by a passion for the extreme, embark upon ever grander projects. This theme gives Milton's seventeenth century epic its importance for modern man, who finds himself portrayed and profoundly analyzed in the demons of hell. The despair of Existentialism is fully anticipated here.

In the later *Faust* tradition both the council and the competitive reports are manifest. The performance of a *Faust* drama in the city of Danzig in 1668 is recorded.[11] Here the competition takes place before Faustus himself and becomes a contest of efficiency. "Hierauf begibt es sich, daß Doktor Faustus, mit gemeiner Wissenschaft nicht befriediget, sich um magische Bücher bewirbet und die Teufel zu seinem Dienste beschwöret, wobei er ihre Geschwindigkeit explorieret und den geschwindesten erwählen will: es ist ihm nicht genug, daß sie so geschwinde seien wie Hirsche, wie die Wolken, wie der Wind, sondern er will einen, der so geschwinde [ist] wie des Menschen seine Gedanken." The most

[10] Translated and edited by A. E. Zucker (New York, 1941).
[11] In the diary of a councilman, quoted in H. W. Geissler, *Gestaltungen des Faust* (Munich, 1927) I, 220.

obvious temptation of modern man, the compulsion toward ever increased efficiency, speed, and power is anticipated here and warningly
identified as a demonic gift. On the other hand, the whole wide range of
temptation in the daily lives of common people is reflected in a passage
of the puppet play tradition, which at the same time achieves supreme
blasphemy in paraphrasing Christ (Math. xxviii. 19-20): "darum so ver-
nehmet meinen Befehl und fahret in alle Welt, und lehret sie alles
Übles tun: die Sekten untereinander falsch disputieren, das Vorderste
zum Hintern kehren; die Kaufleute falsch Gewicht, falsche Ellen führen;
die Frauenzimmer hoffärtig sein, Unkeuschheit treiben; auf den Univer-
sitäten, wo die Studenten zusammen kommen, lehret sie fressen, saufen,
schwören, zaubern, zanken und schlagen, daß sie mit ihren Seelen zu
unserer Höllen fahren."[12]

Even Lessing, at the height of the Enlightenment, contemplated using
the contest of efficiency and the council of demons in his Faust drama.
"Der Übergang vom Guten zum Bösen" appeals to his Faust as the un-
excelled example of speed: "Ja, der ist schnell; schneller ist nichts als der,"
and Faust chooses the demon offering such speed. Lessing's council of
demons is a noble piece of prose; it consummates all the inherent qualities
and suggestions of the theme and concentrates — as the foremost objective of demonic efforts — on the moral disaster to be invited through
man's unending quest for understanding and truth.

In spite of the medieval legacy of black magic, pact, and demonic
tricks, Lessing intended to lead Faust to salvation. Here, only a few years
prior to Goethe's work on the *Urfaust*, the decisive departure from the
medieval suspicion of the intellect is made.

The Contrite Devil

From this group of demonic activities a particular phenomenon
evolves: the fallen angel recalls the blessedness of his former fellowship
with God in which he has been superseded by man; longing for the
heavenly regions seizes him; he contemplates ways to recover his former
state. For a brief moment there is the suggestion of a moral evolution,
of self-mastery and contrition in the fallen angel. There is a brilliant
flash of such light, signaling poetic potentialities, in the legend of Saint
Martinus (II 374), "who was of great mercy towards the sinners and
embraced gladly all those who would repent. The devil once quarreled
with him just for that reason, and Martinus said: 'If thou, o miserable one,
wouldst only cease to tempt man and wouldst feel contrition for what
thou hast done, I would assure thee of Christ's mercy, so great is my
trust in the Lord.' "

Caesarius von Heisterbach, an early thirteenth century writer, produced a didactical tale on the same theme with the ring of authenticity

---

[12] *Das Puppenspiel vom Doktor Faust*, ed. C. Höfer (Leipzig: Inselverlag, n. d.),
page 6.

and finality.[13] A priest, listening to the confessions of his parishioners and absolving them, noticed among them a young stranger. The stranger bent his knees to confess and related the most monstrous crimes, so that the priest angrily said, "if thou werest a thousand years old, even then all these sins were too many and too difficult for thee to commit." "I am more than a thousand years old," replied the stranger. "Who art thou, then?" "I am one of those who fell with Lucifer. I have confessed only a small fraction of my sins; if thou carest to hear the rest — they are innumerable — I am ready to confess." The priest, like Saint Martin, now assured the demon of mercy if he would accept penance. "Throw thyself three times a day upon the ground and say, 'Lord God, my creator, I have sinned against thee, have mercy upon me.' Let that be thy penance." The stranger said, "That I cannot do; it is much too hard... I cannot humiliate myself before him; lay anything else upon me and I will gladly accept it." The priest concluded the session indignantly: "Since thy pride is so great that thou art unable to humiliate thyself before thy creator, leave me alone. Neither now nor in future wilt thou share in God's mercy."

In the *Volksbuch von Dr. Johann Fausten* [14] the motive of the contrite devil is bound up with Faust's own recurring moods of contrition. Remorsefully Faust inquires into the nature of hell and the lives of its inhabitants, forbidden questions indeed, that the evil spirit must not answer. But contrition is contagious to the devil: for a short moment the fallen angel abandons his part and takes over that of the guardian angel, a potentially great passage that the obscure author of the *Volksbuch* fails to realize.

> Fragte Faust also: "Wenn du wie ich, ein Mensch, von Gott geschaffen, wärest, was würdest du tun, um Gott und den Menschen zu gefallen?" Darüber lächelte der Geist und sagte: "Wäre ich ein Mensch wie du, wollte ich mich beugen vor Gott, solange ich Athem hätte, mich hüten, seinen Zorn zu wecken, und seine Lehre, Gesetze und Gebote treulich halten, ihn anrufen, loben, ehren und preisen." — "Wolltest du, Mephostophiles, ein Mensch sein statt meiner?" — "Ja," sagte der Geist seufzend," ... denn obgleich ich gegen Gott gesündigt habe, wollte ich doch wieder in seine Gnade kommen" (p. 565).

Marlowe's *Faustus* compresses this motive into a few powerful lines

[13] Caesarii Heisterbacensis monachi *Dialogus Miraculorum*, Dist. III, cap. 26, repr. in Johannes Bühler, *Das deutsche Geistesleben im Mittelalter* (Leipzig, 1927), pp. 418-420. The quotation is translated by the present writer. Cf. also the middle high German metrical treatment of Caesarius' tale *Von Des Dufels Bihte*, Germanische Bibliothek, Untersuchungen und Texte, vol. 37 (Heidelberg, 1934), ed. A. Closs; also A. Closs in *Modern Language Review*, London, vol. XXVII, 3, p. 297 ff.

[14] *Faust. Das Volksbuch nebst einer Einleitung über den Ursprung der Faustsage*, ed. Karl Simrock (Basel, 1903³). Cf. also *Deutsche Volksbücher*, ed. Severin Rüttgers (Leipzig: Inselverlag, n. d.), "Doktor Faustus," pp. 551-605. Quotations from this edition.

which drown the philistine tone of the *Volksbuch* in waves of wrath,
irony, and warning:

> Why, this is hell, nor am I out of it.
> Think'st thou that I, who saw the face of God,
> And tasted the eternal joys of heaven,
> Am not tormented with ten thousand hells,
> In being depriv'd of everlasting bliss?
> O Faustus, leave these frivolous demands,
> Which strike a terror to my fainting soul![15]

Milton's Satan in *Paradise Lost* is the most majestic representative of
the contrite devil; the forces that rule out contrition are profoundly realized. He possesses the fullest self-knowledge; he knows his character and
the workings of his mind; he knows that pride, envy, and ambition have
motivated his choice. Intellectually he comes closer to contrition than
any of his demons. Ultimately it is a morbid sense of duty, as in Marlowe's *Faustus*, a conspirator's responsibility, that binds him to those that
followed him:

> Is there no place
> Left for repentance, none for pardon left?
> None left but by submission; and that word
> Disdain forbids me, and my dread of shame
> Among the spirits beneath whom I seduced. (Book IV)

His intelligence tells him that reconciliation can never be sincere on his
part, that even if accomplished it must end only in new revolt since his
self-chosen destiny drives him to rule, and rule he can only through evil:

> So farewell hope, and, with hope, farewell fear.
> Farewell remorse. All good to me is lost.
> Evil, be thou my God. By thee at least
> Divided Empire with Heaven's king I hold,
> By thee, and more than half perhaps will reign. (Book IV)

The Manichaean concept of the "Divided Empire" springs to life again
with its insistence on the eternity of evil, and turns the contrite devil to be
the tempter again.

In the puppet plays that carry on the Faust tradition in the seventeenth and eighteenth centuries, the contrite devil has become sentimen-
tal and didactic: he would undergo the most torturing punishment,
carried to unimaginable extremes, for half of eternity, only in order to
have one last glance at the glory of God for his comfort.[16]

Nowhere outside of Dante is the dualism of good and evil so manifest as in the figure of the contrite devil. All avenues of redemption are
closed to him; pride robs him of the tears of repentance; free will that
would raise him at once to the human level is lacking. His only passion
is envy of man's blessedness that he has lost (I 606). He is singled out

[15] *Plays by Christopher Marlowe*, ed. Edward Thomas (New York: E. P. Dut-
ton, 1950), Everyman's Library, p. 158.
[16] *Das Puppenspiel vom Doktor Faust*, p. 54.

for an unrelenting revenge. The contrite devil forms an alarming commentary upon the easy and tacit acceptance by medieval Christianity of the eternity of hell, implying eternal revenge and hatred.

When all the world dissolves,

. . . .

　　　All places shall be hell that are not heaven.[17]

The forbidding contrast of this concept to God's universal love goes almost unnoticed. The contrite devil seems to be motivated primarily by recollections of his former fellowship with God. But the frequency with which he appears, the insistence with which he mingles with the saints and the people, suggest a deeper plane of significance, a genuinely religious source that had been covered up under the sway of the Church Triumphant. Origen's genial concept of *apocatastasis*, the "restitution of all things" (according to Acts iii.21), would acknowledge only temporary existence to hell since only God is eternal. To Origen the ultimate eternity of hell appeared to be a triumph of Satan, a metaphysical dualism which he was not willing to admit. The created spirit, after apostasy, error, and sin, will always return to its origin in God. A thousand years before Dante had conceived the fateful inscription over the gate of Inferno: "Lasciate ogni speranza, voi ch'entrate!" ("Relinquish all hope, ye who enter here!" *Inf.* III, 9) Origen had forcefully denied eternity to hell. For three hundred years, his "restitution of all things" was allowed to contribute to the formation of Christian conscience and to the light illuminating the mystery of God's love. In the sixth century his doctrine was declared heretical, but it was taken up brilliantly around the middle of the ninth century in the first great system of medieval thought, *De Divisione Naturae* by Johannes Scotus Erigena, whose teaching becomes most consequential for both scholasticism and mysticism. To Erigena evil is merely a negation of good, sin is misdirected will, hell is the inner state of the sinful will; its punishment will result in final purification and the redemption of all, even of animals and devils. Since Erigena's fundamental identity of philosophy and religion could be construed as pantheism and since he held the Eucharist to be merely symbolical or commemorative and the Mosaic account to be allegorical, the main body of his writings was banned from the University of Paris in 1210 and condemned repeatedly. But from this underground existence there rose the contrite devil, a legendary and literary figure, a powerful reflection of these fruitful heresies, reminding the medieval world time and again of the saying that one "rather ought to be in the wrong with Origen than in the right with the others."[18]

---

[17] Marlowe, p. 165.

[18] Attributed to Vincent of Lerins, fifth century apologist. As to Origen, cf. the article in the *Encycl. Brit.*, vol. XVI (1951); Walter Nigg, *Das Buch der Ketzer* (Zürich, 1949), pp. 47-61; H. U. von Balthasar, *Origenes, Geist und Feuer* (1938). The reference to Erigena I owe to my colleague Professor William A. Banner of Howard University School of Religion. Cf. the article in the *Encycl. Brit.*, vol. VIII (1951). The extraordinary longevity of the "restitution of all things" is

Under the perspective of the "restitution of all things" that an early Christian thinker had opened up and that literary imagery had transformed into the figure of the contrite devil, Klopstock's *Messias* regains part of the importance that it once held as the heralding voice of new literature in Germany. The first three cantos of the *Messias* were among the most widely read literary products of midcentury, largely because of the figure of Abbadona, the contrite demon, whom Klopstock introduces so conspicuously (Canto 2) and whose final destiny is one of the unifying principles of the epic (Cantos 5, 9, 19). Here the leading German poet before Goethe ennobles the obscure existence of the contrite demon and makes the latter's quest for salvation legitimate. The perennial speculation about the otherwise unavoidable dualism of good and evil comes here to its conclusion; the medieval dogmatic concept of the devil is dissolved and refuted, and superseded by the brotherly and compassionate sentiments of protestant Pietism. The line of demarcation between demon and man is erased *sub specie aeternitatis*; the former appears equipped with the power to will and to choose like man, and is admitted into fellowship with man and nature in the worship of the creator of the universe.

Klopstock's concept of the contrite demon is an essential part of the spiritual ferment of midcentury to which Goethe owes an important part of his development. In a letter dated November 1768 addressed to E. Th. Langer, Goethe explains his own place in the Frankfurt *Brüdergemeinde* with a symbolic reference to Klopstock's ninth canto: "Von Seiten der Gemeinde läßt man mich denn in den Circkel, so mit einer stillen Connivenz, wie die Engel den Abbadona in ihren Kreis um Golgotha ließen." [19] This *Connivenz* bore lasting fruits for Goethe in a deeper understanding of Jesus and of the humaneness of his teachings, which experience was to crystallize later in *Iphigenie, Bekenntnisse einer schönen Seele*, and *Faust II*. If, on behalf of the contrite devil, we here transgress the period of this paper, it is only to quote Goethe once more, who in 1816, the year in which details and plot of *Faust II* assumed a more concrete shape in his mind, is reported to have spoken to J. D. Falk as follows: "Ich habe es ihnen [den Deutschen] nie recht zu Danke gemacht! Vollends, wenn ... sie in der Fortsetzung von *Faust* etwa zufällig an die Stelle kämen, wo der Teufel selbst Gnad' und Erbarmen vor Gott findet, das, denke ich doch, vergeben sie mir sobald nicht! ... Nahm doch selbst die geistreiche Frau von Stael es übel, daß ich in dem Engelgesang Gott-Vater gegenüber den Teufel so gutmütig gehalten hätte! sie wollte ihn durchaus grimmiger. Was soll es nun werden, wenn sie ihm auf einer noch höheren Staffel und vielleicht gar einmal im Himmel wieder begegnet?" [20] Making allowances for the occasional unreliability of Falk's proved as late as 1880 by Dostoevski, who uses a legendary variant of it in the opening phase of his tale *The Grand Inquisitor: The Wanderings of Our Lady through Hell*, culminating in Mary's prayer for "mercy on all without distinction" (The Novels of Fyodor Dostoevsky, vol. I, book 5, chap. 5; New York: Macmillan).

[19] Goethe, *Gedenkausgabe* (Zürich: Artemis Verlag, 1949), XVIII, 108.
[20] Goethe, *Gedenkausgabe*, XXIII, 822; also V, 640.

recollections and for the playful mood of the remark, made at the expense of the reading public, it yet is a flicker of the once brilliant concept of the "restitution of all things."

The Pact with the Devil

Of the pact with the devil and of its consequences the *Legenda Aurea* contains various notable examples. They are epitomized in the legend of Saint Anthony, whom the devil approached "in a giant's shape. He dared to say, 'Anthony, behold, I am the power and the wisdom of God. What dost thou want me to give to thee?'" (I 160). The four instances to be discussed here belong to the best known and most important of the whole legendary tradition.

(1) The story of Eradius' daughter (from the Basilius legend, I 186-90), a love story, involves realistic elements of ageless quality that are merely disguised in the costume of the pact. Eradius' servant plans to win the favor of his master's daughter through a pact with the devil. "This accomplished, the devil incited the maiden's heart with an overpowering love for the young man. She fell sick, threw herself to the ground, and pleaded tearfully with her father to marry her to this servant." In spite of his laments and in spite of social considerations, the father finally gives in, has the young people married, and endows them generously. Loyal to the pact, the young husband separates himself from the company of Christians, and soon is suspected of his sinful partnership; his wife is greatly alarmed by his apparent indifference towards this suspicion. When she finally urges him to accompany her to church, he confesses to her the way he had won her. But she, in return, does not give him up as lost; she turns for advice to the saintly bishop, who wins the young man back and forces the devil to surrender the agreement: "Thou dost me wrong, Basil," the devil says, "I did not approach him; he approached me and renounced Christ and gave himself into my power. Behold, here is his signature." Basil tears the agreement to pieces and brings the young man back into the fold of the church and into the arms of his loving wife.

(2) The story of Cyprianus (in the Justina legend, II 198-203) is staged against the background of the early church. Cyprianus, a pagan scholar and magician, falls in love with Justina, a Christian. He employs several devils to obtain her favor. But their schemes fail. The sign of the cross puts them easily to shame. The devils must confess to Cyprianus that "the crucified one is stronger than we are, he will deliver to eternal fire and endless torment us and all those who deceive man." The scholar Cyprianus shuns loyalty to any secondary authority, and now self-preservation teaches him: "Then I must become a friend of the crucified one, lest I should suffer that pain." He becomes a Christian, excels in wisdom and good works, and becomes bishop. Later he and Justina die as martyrs.[21]

[21] Calderon's play (1637) is based on this legend.

(3) Theophilus (from the legends of the Virgin, II 137-8) is a bishop's deputy and modestly lets the occasion pass to become bishop himself. Soon afterwards he finds himself ousted by the new bishop. To recover his lost status, he signs a deed with the devil who promises to restore him to his rank and to the friendship of the bishop. After this has been achieved, Theophilus recovers his senses and his judgment and takes refuge with the Holy Virgin. She appears to him twice and reproaches him for his disloyalty, but finally she accepts his repentance and brings the deed back to him. Theophilus now makes his experience public and dies in peace.

The Theophilus story is the best known of this group and had been treated poetically prior to the *Legenda Aurea*. Its attraction for German authors is demonstrated by Hrothswith's treatment (tenth century) and by the Low German *Theophilus drama* of the sixteenth century;[22] by its very nature, it also played its part in the discussion of the origins of the Faust tradition.

(4) The fourth instance is found, like the preceding one, among the legends of the Holy Virgin (II 14-16). A knight known for his generosity pawns his wife to the devil in return for the recovery of his riches. But the wife is protected by the Virgin, who assumes her shape for the encounter with the devil and subdues him. The knight, bewildered and overwhelmed, resorts to prayer and penitence and, by virtue of contrition, is finally assured of his salvation.

The revival of this legend by Gottfried Keller in his *Sieben Legenden* in 1873 under the title *Die Jungfrau und der Teufel* should be noted here. Keller does not accept the effectiveness of medieval repentance; he makes the knight die an unrepentant sinner. This is characteristic not only of Keller, who, of Protestant descent and far from any dogma, had grown up in the humanism of the Goethe epoch, but it is also in a larger sense characteristic of modern man's inability to comprehend fully, as medieval man did, the possibilities of conversion, which fact in itself is a secret token of pride, an insistence on personality and character foreign to the medieval legend.

In all these instances the modesty of the goal is noteworthy: to win a maiden, to recover a lost status, or to pursue vanity (as in *Päpstin Johanna*). There is no trace yet of Faustus' restless curiosity, of his reckless desire to live the fullest life, or of his dreams of power and beauty. Accordingly, the conflict of loyalties implied in the pact is quickly resolved by repentance, by entrusting oneself to the Saints or to the Virgin, and pleading for intercession. It is a routine procedure and the solution seems to come too rapidly: a *deus ex machina* (or *dea*) snatches the hero away from the certain doom that would result from apostasy. Thus the ultimate power of God is recognized as being greater than that of demons or men. The monotheistic unity is preserved. The tempter, even

[22] *Theophilus*, ed. R. Petsch (Heidelberg, 1908).

while he springs his trap on man, is still an agent of a greater power. Accordingly, the devil in his dealings with men always has reason to expect foul play and in most instances he says so; neither deed nor signature can protect his claims.

The pact with the devil can be illumined clearly by its counterpart: the pact with the angels that is ever present in the lives of the saints and projects itself irresistibly even into the pact with the devil, in that the tempter at times warns his partner of the consequences of his choice, as in Marlowe's thirteenth scene. In most instances, the pact with the devil is blasphemously patterned after the angelic speech. " I am the angel of the Lord; the Lord sends me to thee to be thy guardian angel. Whatever thou ask from me, will be given to thee by God" (Gregorius legend, I 295). Eusebius is assisted by angels in the holy office (I 682). These instances, so frequent in the legends of the saints and of the martyrs (II 179), trace directly back to similar suggestions in the Acts of the Apostles (Acts v and xii) where angels render comfort and help; and finally to the Gospel record of the temptation of Christ (Mark i and Math. iv). Here the pact with the devil is offered and rejected, and superseded by the pact with the angels "who administered unto him." Here the pattern of the pact originates, as far as this paper intends to go.[23] The underlying experience of Jesus is clearly described. The word temptation denotes a real experience, such as pain, sorrow, disappointment, solicitation to sin, conflict of duties. Jesus is assailed by doubts as to his ministry, and doubt opens the mind to temptation. Jesus masters the doubts and the angels serve him.

III

The experience of doubt, well known to the Gospel writers and to the Fathers of the Church, has no legitimate place in the medieval legends. The *Legenda Aurea* was compiled under the sway of the Catholic dogma; the dogma meant to speak with authority and to eliminate doubt. In the legends the pact with the devil is not motivated by doubt, most certainly not by doubt of God's existence, universality, and mercy. But with the advent of the Reformation, when the existence of two hostile dogmas undermined the certainty of either one, doubt as the motivation of the pact emerges with fullest force. If not God, his Gospel, and his saints (as proclaimed in the legends), then man himself is the center of the universe, and his ambitious dreams, his earthly satisfaction, constitute the only meaning of life. "Ye shall be as gods" is the naturally

[23] For the demonology of the intertestamental period, in the *Books of Enoch* and the *Testament of the twelve Patriarchs*, cf. the article on "Intertestamental Religion" in *Abingdon Cokesbury Bible Commentary* (New York, 1929). It will be noticed that the functions of these demons — to tempt, to accuse the fallen, to torment the condemned — have outlasted the religious and dogmatic evolutions of more than fifteen centuries and are consequently almost identical with the categories of demonic activity as drawn from thirteenth century sources and presented in this paper. For the Old Testament period cf. Riwkah Schärf, *The Figure of Satan in the Old Testament* (diss. Zürich, 1947).

and psychologically true response to the experience of doubt, to the
cravings of self-assertion, and also to the noble dreams of the Renaissance and of the age of exploration. Consequently the demonic pact now
aims at objectives far more fateful and far higher than winning the
favor of a woman or regaining lost goods. Only now the monotheistic
unity is challenged increasingly by a genuine dualism of eternally hostile forces. The Manichaeism of early Christianity converges upon
Christianity once more. In the myth of the pact, as it now develops,
the devil rises in open revolt and tries to draw man into his conspiracy,
promising him whatsoever he wants. Without faith to sustain him, man
stands alone between the contending parties and is forced to make his
choice. The characters of *Doctor Faustus* and of *Paradise Lost* are the
poetic expressions of this choice to be made amidst doubt, promises, and
aspirations; they are both actors and victims of the conspiracy against
God that is described from now on in the myth of the pact.

Doubt as a most compelling force is a distinct feature of the *Volksbuch von Doktor Johann Fausten*. His contempt for theology is both
often and crudely expressed; he questions the immortality of the soul and
at the same time he despairs of God's mercy to him. His efforts to
repent are not sustained. His final outcry, "Ich sterbe als ein böser und ein
guter Christ," [24] is the accurate formula of doubt. Likewise in Marlowe's
Faustus, "My heart's so harden'd, I cannot repent" (p. 168), and later,
"the serpent that tempted Eve may be saved, but not Faustus" (p. 192).
Only doubt makes the demonic pact acceptable; at the same time, it
takes away some of its severity, since Marlowe's Faustus doubts even
hell; and that in spite of Mephistopheles' insistence that hell is right
here. Milton's Eve opens her mind to doubt under the impact of the
questions raised by the serpent:

> . . . and wherein lies
> Th' offense, that Man should thus attain to know?
> What can your knowledge hurt him, or his tree
> Impart against his will, if all be his?
> Or is it envy? and can envy dwell
> In heavenly breasts? (Book IX)

Here the classical paradigm of temptation is spelled out, and certainly
within the limits of Genesis iii: first doubt is cast on God, jealousy is
insinuated, finally impunity suggested. These main features of temptation are portrayed here with extraordinary psychological fidelity and
carry over into the pact between devil and man as it will prevail from
now on.

As the certainty of faith fades away in doubt, man's aspirations and
dreams, ennobled by the reasoning power of humanism, become asso-

---

[24] Cf. footnote 14: *Deutsche Volksbücher*, p. 603. Thomas Mann makes this
same word the central theme in Adrian Leverkühn's last musical efforts, in a situation identical with that in the *Volksbuch*. Cf. Thomas Mann, *Doktor Faustus*
(Stockholm, 1947), p. 739.

ciated with the pact; they shimmer sometimes like gold under the trash of the cheap imagery of the *Volksbuch:* ". . . darnach trachtete er Tag und Nacht, daß er Adlers Flügel an sich nahm und alle Gründe des Himmels und der Erde erforschen wollte."[25] Among the conditions of the pact this noble agreement occurs: ". . . daß er [der Geist] ihm auf alle Fragen nur wahrhafte Antworten gäbe." [26] This Faust gropes in the darkness with problems of the physical universe, of space, time, and speed. To be sure, he does so in terms of popular superstitions, yet also with a sense of awe for the unorthodox quality of these questions, the mere posing of which strengthens his doubt and intensifies his quest. Marlowe's Faustus is even more the Renaissance man. The poet sympathizes with these aspirations and expresses them fervently. Speaking of medicine, Faustus' judgment is:

> Couldst thou make men to live eternally,
> Or, being dead, raise them to life again,
> Then this profession were to be esteem'd. (p. 150)

The most striking passage visualizes technological opportunities offered in the pact, carried by Marlowe far above and beyond the pranks and tricks of the *Volksbuch:*

> I'll have them [the spirits] fly to India for gold,
> Ransack the ocean for orient pearl,
> And search all corners of the new-found world
> For pleasant fruits and princely delicates;
> I'll have them read me strange philosophy,
> And tell the secrets of all foreign kings;
> I'll have them wall all Germany with brass
> And make swift Rhine circle fair Wertenberg [sic];
> . . . .
> Yea, stranger engines for the brunt of war,
> Than was the fiery keel at Antwerp's bridge,
> I'll make my servile spirits to invent.

Dominion over the world, possession of its riches, all knowledge of antiquity and of the secrets of hostile princes, conquest and victory with the help of new, unheard-of weapons—these are now the aspirations of the pact. The passion for the extreme [27] overwhelms man who is about to replace God's word with his own, exactly as the myth of the fallen angels had once suggested: man is the fallen angel from now on. The devil, once a modest and servile agent, has outgrown all restrictions of dogma and pious tradition. His metaphysical function on judgment day,

[25] Cf. footnote 14: *Deutsche Volksbücher*, p. 551.

[26] *Ibidem*, p. 553.

[27] This passion for the extreme is the major theme of Adrian Leverkühn's life and art in Thomas Mann's *Doktor Faustus:* "Wir liefern das Äußerste in dieser Richtung" (p. 357); "die prangende Unbedenklichkeit" (p. 367); "Das Extreme daran muß dir gefallen" (p. 381). About the kinship of Thomas Mann's novel with medieval patterns and concepts, particularly of the *Volksbuch*, cf. this writer's article "Das deutsche Schicksal in Thomas Manns *Doktor Faustus*," *Monatshefte*, XLI (1949), pp. 187-202.

his psychological significance as the tempter have been superseded and are overshadowed by his new opportunity: to supply men with the technological means to conquer, to rule, to enjoy the physical and the social realms, since the spiritual destiny of man is shrouded in doubt and in uncertainties. The "Divided Empire" prevails.

As the early phase of the pact with the devil could be illumined by its counterpart, the pact with the angels, this final phase, as manifest in Marlowe's *Faustus*, finds its counterpart in Shakespeare's *Tempest*. Conceived about twenty years after Marlowe's *Faustus*, it displays the popular concepts of white magic just as accurately as Marlowe's tragedy does those of black magic; the mellow wisdom of Shakespeare's older age contrasts beautifully with Marlowe's passion and impetuosity. Prospero shies away from the passion for the extreme, and he surrenders his unlimited powers in order to live in peace with those whom he subdued. Ariel proves to be the spirit of true humanity and reconciliation:

> Hast thou, which art but air, a touch, a feeling
> Of their afflictions, and shall not myself [Prospero]
> One of their kind, that relish all as sharply,
> Passion as they, be kindlier mov'd than thou art? (V.i)

Thus it is the inspiration coming from the world of the spirits that moves man either to extremes and to despair or to peace with himself and with others.

IV

The technological aspect of the pact with the devil affords a perspective of early Christian concepts as well as of our own dilemmas. In the earliest lore of the devil and in the legends of the high Middle Ages, the devil often appears equipped with scientific apparatus, and his partners, the magicians, know how to handle this machinery (I 557-568). Marlowe's *Faustus* and Milton's *Mammon* have technological ambitions; their respective authors approve of them with a secret sense of pride, very contrary to the authors of the legends. In modern times, these objectives have been more than matched, to such a degree, in fact, that they have become an end and purpose in themselves, have invaded all forms of human existence, even the most private and spiritual, and have turned against man himself, their creator. In spite of all triumphs over the physical world, we have a keen apprehension of insecurity — or is that just on account of these triumphs? After man has pushed himself into the very center of creation, and, for centuries, has been creating like a god, he is losing control of his man-made world: his machinery assumes self-motion and defies him.

The medieval fascination with the sciences, as manifest in the legendary association of devil and science, was perhaps not so much a dogmatic phenomenon or a phase of evolution, but rather, by inference from our own experience, it suggests a similar apprehension. The fear is expressed here that the unalterable and predestined facts of the physical world, if given priority, would outweigh and destroy the concept of the Creator and of the ordered universe (I 169), just as astrology would paralyze the free will (II 424-431): both the concept of the Creator and that of free will being cornerstones of medieval Christianity. It is the determinism in the exact sciences that was suspected of demonic potentialities, amounting eventually to a denial of God and of man if allowed to establish itself as the only truth. And to worship only the devil, we remember, had been the main condition of the pact.

Here, in the confusion of means and ends of which we are apprehensive, the myth of the pact proves to be truly prophetic; as Albert Schweitzer expressed it in 1932 on the occasion of the centenary of Goethe's death: "Mephistopheles leers at us with a thousand grimaces."

La Croyance au Merveilleux
à l'Époque classique

par Emile BOUVIER

J'ai contracté envers M. Daniel Mornet une dette intellectuelle que je n'espère plus pouvoir acquitter. Il avait bien voulu accepter de diriger la préparation d'une thèse en vue du doctorat ès-lettres qui n'a jamais été soutenue, et ne le sera jamais, du moins par l'auteur de ces lignes. La modeste contribution que j'apporte à ce volume de « Mélanges » constitue donc l'aveu d'une faillite. Mais, si peu que ce soit, ce sera toujours mieux que rien, et, comme dans les liquidations judiciaires, la preuve de la bonne foi du débiteur. Peut-être aussi la relation de cette entreprise et le bilan de ce qui en reste (un énorme manuscrit inachevé, et qu'il faudrait mettre à jour, les parties les plus anciennes datant de 1930) serviront-ils à des chercheurs mieux doués ou plus heureux. Je suis à leur disposition pour partager avec eux les fruits amers de mon expérience.

*

A l'origine, j'avais simplement songé à écrire l'histoire d'un genre, celui des contes de fées, tel qu'il s'est développé en France aux XVII et XVIII° siècles. Il s'agissait d'une étude d'histoire littéraire pure, destinée à préciser les notions un peu confuses de « Genre », d' « Evolution des Genres », et de corriger, si j'ose dire, Brunetière par Lanson. Je croyais avoir rencontré un échantillon typique de « mutation brusque » dans la génétique des espèces littéraires, et il me plaisait de savoir dans quelles circonstances précises cette nouvelle espèce était apparue, ce qu'elle était devenue sous l'influence du milieu et comment elle s'y était progressivement adaptée.

Je dis que ce phénomène est typique, parce qu'il se présente sous un aspect beaucoup plus net, plus tranché, plus pédagogique, si l'on veut, que les vicissitudes de la poésie, du drame et autres genres plus imposants. D'abord, l'emploi du merveilleux féerique nous fournit un critérium de classement extérieur irrécusable. Ensuite, le point de départ du conte merveilleux classique peut être daté avec une rare précision bibliographique : 1696 ; et l'on attribue communément à un homme de lettres, Charles Perrault, le mérite de cette « invention ».

335

Le succès immédiat des « Contes de ma mère l'Oye », les si nombreuses imitations qu'ils suscitèrent, nous permettent d'assister, dans les cinq ou six années qui suivent, à la naissance d'une « mode » littéraire. Elle aurait pu être éphémère, comme le fut celle des « ana », comme le seront plus tard celle des « Héroïdes » ou celle des « Haï-kaï ». Mais il se trouve (et nous passons ici de la définition d'une « mode » à celle d'un « genre ») que le conte merveilleux fleurit encore cinquante ans plus tard, qu'il pousse ses ramifications tout au long du XVIIIᵉ siècle, qu'il engendre le conte fantastique du romantisme..., bref, que cette espèce devient l'une des plus vigoureuses de la flore littéraire. Ceci suppose des adaptations successives aux transformations du goût public. Et de fait, si la forme et les conventions caractéristiques du conte de fées à la Perrault se perpétuent, sa substance se transforme : exotique, romanesque, précieux, humoristique, grivois, satirique, philosophique, moral, tous les dix ans environ, le genre en question se renouvelle ; chaque génération y mire ses curiosités et y insère ses revendications. On peut ainsi doser la proportion des structures stables et des éléments mouvants que désigne cette expression ambiguë, « évolution du genre », ce qui demeure et ce qui change.

En dépit de la frivolité de l'exemple choisi, je persiste à croire que cette étude eût été instructive. Elle n'est pas encore faite en tant qu'ouvrage d'ensemble. Mais elle a été esquissée par M. Mornet lui-même dès 1925 dans l'introduction de son édition de la « Nouvelle Héloïse » ; et elle existe en « pièces détachées », sous forme de monographies, éditions critiques, études particulières, etc. C'est justement la publication, en 1928, d'une de ces études, à vrai dire fort importante, savoir la thèse présentée par Mlle Storer à l'Université de Paris sur « La mode des contes de fées (1685-1700) » qui m'a obligé à modifier mon dessein primitif, à laisser tomber la première partie de mon travail, et à creuser, au contraire, les autres.

⁂

Au fond, je n'en fus pas autrement fâché. L'ouvrage de Mlle Storer, irréprochable du point de vue de l'érudition pure et de la critique historique, passait un peu rapidement sur un problème qui irritait, au contraire, de plus en plus ma curiosité. C'est ce que j'appellerai le paradoxe de l'apparition du conte merveilleux au beau milieu du rationalisme classique. Nous parlions tout à l'heure de « mutation brusque », mais il ne faut pas nous payer de métaphores ! Tout livre est écrit, en principe, volontairement, par un homme, à l'usage d'autres hommes, et, tout au moins au XVIIᵉ siècle, destiné à plaire au public qui le lira. Or, l'emploi du merveilleux féerique, c'est-à-dire la trouvaille essentielle de Perrault, semble en opposition flagrante avec ce que l'on nomme ordinairement le goût classique. Ce démenti que l'histoire donne à la théorie nous oblige, soit à limiter chronologiquement la définition traditionnelle du classicisme, soit à rectifier cette définition, soit à expliquer par la persistance d'un goût « pré-classique », « anti-classique », l'accueil enthousiaste fait par les contemporains de Boileau aux extravagances des nouveaux conteurs.

J'avais d'abord vérifié la troisième de ces hypothèses sous son aspect technique, celui des « sources » possibles du merveilleux féerique. On les repère aisément dans la « Bibliothèque bleue », dans les romans chevaleresques ou pastoraux, chez certains conteurs du xvi⁰ siècle et les compilateurs d' « Histoires prodigieuses » ; et aussi, plus rapprochées, dans les genres précieux (poésie, romans héroïques, allégories, voyages imaginaires), surtout au théâtre (opéras et ballets). On devine également l'existence d'une copieuse littérature orale, de contes « parlés », fortement teintés de merveilleux folklorique. Ces précédents rendaient moins étonnante la vogue des contes de fées, et il fallait bien reconnaître qu'il ne s'agissait pas d'un cas de génération spontanée.

M. Mornet a depuis lors magistralement démontré dans son « Histoire de la Littérature française, classique » (1940) que bien des genres se sont, en effet, développés à cette époque « sans que jamais la raison et les réguliers aient pu leur imposer véritablement leur joug » ; que le théâtre classique, c'est aussi bien que « Bérénice » et « Le Misanthrope », « la variété, la fantaisie, le spectacle... la surprise et l'inattendu » ; que l'on écrit, « pour piquer la curiosité », des romans qui nous conduisent « hors de la nature, dans des pays impossibles ». Il est certain que dans le climat analysé par M. Mornet, mes propres constatations prennent une tout autre valeur. Pratiquement, elles seraient à reprendre en fonction des conclusions de cette vaste enquête, dans laquelle elles s'insèrent parfaitement.

*
* *

J'emploie ce dernier mot dans son sens strictement historique. Car une difficulté subsiste, qui est plutôt de l'ordre psychologique. M. Mornet reconnaît lui-même que la littérature classique reste une littérature raisonnable et tend vers l'universel. Qu'est-ce à dire, sinon que l'esprit humain incline à cette époque dans un certain sens ? que le mouvement des idées s'effectue, en général, dans une direction jalonnée par les deux mots-clefs : nature, raison ?

Ceci m'est apparu particulièrement vrai en ce qui concerne, non seulement les théories et les lois du genre romanesque, mais l'évolution concrète de ce genre. Malgré tout ce que l'on peut dire sur les « exceptions », l'apparition du conte merveilleux constitue une anomalie qui rompt la continuité d'une courbe ascendante, laquelle commence avec la « nouvelle », vers 1665, et au sommet de laquelle apparaîtra le roman réaliste de mœurs contemporaines, c'est-à-dire, en apparence, le récit le plus éloigné de la féerie. D'où un nouveau point d'interrogation : ces deux pôles sont-ils aussi éloignés que nous le croyons aujourd'hui ? Cette anomalie ne s'expliquerait-elle pas par une illusion d'optique ?

D'autre part, une analyse des arguments échangés au cours des nombreuses polémiques que suscita, au XVIIᵉ siècle, en général, l'emploi du merveilleux dans les ouvrages d'imagination m'avait amené à cette proposition inattendue : théoriciens et praticiens, réalistes et fantaisistes, Anciens et Modernes, considèrent qu'à côté de l' « extraordinaire réel », dont l'histoire nous offre des exemples, mais dont il ne faut user qu'avec discrétion, il existe un « Merveilleux vraisemblable », dont l'usage est tout indiqué dans les fictions. « Vraisemblable » désigne ici — soulignons cette définition capitale — *l'adéquation des événements et de leur interprétation aux croyances du public auquel on s'adresse*. Autrement dit, les dieux d'Homère sont vraisemblables au temps d'Homère, les Génies en Orient, etc. Le romancier a donc à choisir entre des faits-vrais, ou des faits fictifs, mais vraisemblables. Or, à supposer que les fées soient invraisemblables, leurs prodiges peuvent être « vrais » ; et il n'est peut-être pas impossible, par l'intermédiaire de certaines croyances encore vivaces, de les rendre « vraisemblables ». Hypothèse dont l'énormité m'a fait longtemps hésiter ! Paradoxe logique plus déconcertant encore que le paradoxe historique d'où nous étions partis ! Ce que nous jugeons aujourd'hui absurde, impossible, fabuleux ou mensonger, pouvait-il, à cette époque, correspondre aux croyances d'un lecteur français, non pas rustique et ignorant, mais cultivé et délicat ? La réponse à cette question supposait une nouvelle enquête, non plus sur le merveilleux *dans la littérature*, mais sur la croyance au merveilleux *hors de la littérature*. Il s'agissait, en effet, de savoir quels aspects du surnaturel étaient pris au sérieux, à quel degré, dans quelle mesure. Nous sortions de l'histoire des lettres pour entrer dans celle des idées.

Quelques années plus tard, j'y aurais rencontré Paul Hazard. Sa « Crise de la conscience européenne » (1935) embrasse justement tout le mouvement de pensée dont je ne prétendais suivre qu'un des courants. Faute de cette puissante synthèse, je dûs commencer à poser le problème en fonction de mes propres préoccupations. Et j'aperçus aussitôt une distinction fondamentale : toute croyance au merveilleux suppose d'abord l'affirmation de faits « *contra ordinem naturae* », puis aussi, et parallèlement, un système d'hypothèses explicatives. Ces hypothèses peuvent se succéder, se détruire, sans que soit mise en cause l'authenticité du prodige qu'elles expliquent. Il y avait donc une issue au dilemme. Soit un prodige comme celui de la fille qui, dans « Les Fées » de Perrault, vomit deux crapauds et deux vipères. Si on l'explique par le sort jeté par une fée, il sera « invraisemblable » pour qui ne croit pas à l'existence des fées. Mais il peut demeurer « vrai » en tant que prodige et devenir « vraisemblable » si on le rapporte à l'action d'un être surnaturel dont l'existence est admise et dont les pouvoirs surnaturels sont reconnus, en l'espèce le Diable.

Mon premier soin fut donc de dresser la liste des prodiges réputés authentiques au xviiᵉ siècle et le répertoire le plus complet, le plus vénérable, me fut fourni par la Mystique, science qui traite des pouvoirs surnaturels des anges et des saints. Toutes les merveilles décrites par mes conteurs, des plus sublimes aux plus triviales, y figurent. Le merveilleux chrétien aurait donc amplement suffi à combler les vœux des imaginations les plus dévergondées si son usage n'avait été interdit aux littérateurs. Force était donc à ceux-ci de se rabattre sur d'autres systèmes d'explication pour présenter ces faits « vrais ». Ces systèmes sont essentiellement des « mythologies ». Laissant de côté la mythologie païenne, à propos de laquelle tout avait été dit (en particulier par le P. Delaporte), à laquelle personne ne croyait plus et qui ne fournissait plus guère que des figures de style, je distinguai et décrivis, d'après les documents contemporains : une mythologie empirique (celle du peuple, avec ses fées, ses farfadets, ses lutins, etc.), une mythologie philosophique (celle des penseurs de la Renaissance, cabalistes, mages, occultistes, etc., avec ses génies élémentaires ou sidéraux, ses sylphes, ses salamandres, etc.), une mythologie spiritualiste (celle des spirites modernes, avec ses fantômes, revenants, etc.). En somme, trois catégories de « puissances » que l'on avait longtemps révérées ou redoutées.

Au xviiᵉ siècle leur prestige a sensiblement diminué. Dans les milieux éclairés, on ne croit plus du tout au pouvoir des lutins et des fées, fort peu à celui des génies et des magiciens, de moins en moins à celui des revenants. Mais le gain n'est pas grand, car il existe une autre « puissance » qui a recueilli l'héritage de toutes ces surhumanités détrônées et qui peut même « singer » les miracles divins : c'est le Diable, escorté de ses délégués, démons, sorciers, sorcières, et de ses esclaves, les possédés. La mythologie diabolique, ou démonologie, codifiée au xviᵉ siècle, toujours en vigueur au xviiᵉ siècle, authentifie et explique en même temps tous les phénomènes surnaturels. Bien mieux que l'angelographie ou l'hagiographie, elle les vulgarise et les situe au cœur même de l'existence quotidienne. Et j'ai pu conclure que la seule forme de merveilleux romanesque sérieusement accréditée chez les « honnêtes gens » du siècle de Louis XIV est le merveilleux diabolique.

On voit dès lors comment se présente le succès paradoxal de nos conteurs : par une transposition, un changement de plan. Les prodiges qu'ils évoquent sont « vrais », pour ne pas dire familiers, en tant que manifestations du pouvoir satanique. Ils seraient à la fois « vrais » et « vraisemblables » si on les présentait comme tels : il est normal qu'une fille possédée vomisse des crapauds et des serpents ; des autorités dignes de foi l'attestent. Mais, ainsi présenté, *ce ne serait plus de la littérature* ; car ces récits ne sauraient « plaire ». Nous resterions dans le domaine scientifique, et toute littérature comporte une part de jeu. Le jeu consistera à attribuer aux fées ce qui revient au démon. Le merveilleux chrétien, proscrit, s'est camouflé dans les petits genres,

et ces productions frivoles sont une façon déguisée d'exploiter un
fonds de croyances dont on entrevoit la solidité et la richesse. Abstraction faite de leur déguisement féerique, ces fictions sont adéquates aux
croyances du public auquel on les destine ; elles répondent aux
exigences de la théorie classique, elles décrivent un aspect important
des mœurs contemporaines, elles comportent à la fois vérité et
agrément.

*
* *

Il aurait été sans doute préférable de s'en tenir là.

Mais, d'une part, l'histoire littéraire nous montre que le ton de
nos conteurs se modifie progressivement au cours du siècle : une ironie,
déjà perceptible chez Perrault, se glisse dans la narration des merveilles qu'ils rapportent. Peu à peu, on sent qu'ils se détachent de la
matière merveilleuse qu'ils utilisent, un peu comme leurs devanciers
avaient fait du merveilleux païen, convention romanesque, allégorie
commode, ornement verbal. Leur scepticisme s'étend de la mythologie
au prodige lui-même. Ils en viendront à badiner avec Satan, alors
qu'ils n'osaient même pas le nommer. Ce qui signifie qu'ils ne croient
plus et qu'ils invitent leurs lecteurs à ne pas croire à son intervention
dans les choses de ce monde. Le renouveau du conte fantastique au
début du XIXe siècle inaugure le renversement de cette tendance : il est
en relations étroites avec les sources occultes du romantisme, telles que
M. Viatte les a décrites. Dans l'intervalle, c'est-à-dire de 1680 à 1780
environ, le pouvoir émotif du merveilleux n'a cessé de se dégrader.

Par ailleurs, l'histoire des idées nous révèle que le problème du
merveilleux, sous son aspect sérieux, autrement dit la réflexion sur
l'existence de phénomènes surnaturels, oriente toutes les recherches de
l'ère classique, est à l'origine de ses découvertes. Le mot de « rationalisme » domine toute l'époque qui s'étend de Descartes à Lavoisier.
Certes, nous n'irons pas jusqu'à prétendre que tout l'irrationnel se
réduit à la mystique divine ou diabolique, ni que la seule ambition des
« rationaux » (comme dit Paul Hazard) fut de réintégrer la démonologie dans l'ordre des lois naturelles. Mais nous sommes bien obligés
de constater que les discussions de cet ordre, les mots de sorciers,
devins, possédés, charmes, maléfices, âmes damnées, incubes, vampires,
ou inversement miracles, prophéties, secours céleste, présages, extases,
etc., figurent, ne fût-ce qu'à titre de corollaires, dans tous les systèmes
de l'univers proposés par les penseurs, les savants, les historiens clas-
siques, depuis Gassendi et Malebranche, en passant par Spinoza ou
Locke, jusqu'à Montesquieu et à l'Encyclopédie. Or, l'apparition du
conte merveilleux se produit juste au moment, à la fin du XVIIe siècle,
où la balance, longtemps indécise, penche du côté de la « nouvelle
philosophie », au point culminant de cette crise de conscience diagnos-
tiquée par Paul Hazard. On conçoit qu'il y ait encore là matière à

réflexions, plus sérieuses, évidemment, que les aventures de Peau d'Ane ou les Mille et une Nuits, mais invinciblement attirées par elles.

Et c'est pourquoi, en 1934, le sujet de mon hypothétique et de plus en plus volumineuse thèse était devenu : « La croyance au merveilleux à l'époque classique (1660-1700) », et aux chapitres qui traitent de la crédulité des sujets de Louis XIV (1re et 2e parties), d'autres étaient venus s'ajouter qui retracent les progrès de l'incrédulité. Ils anticipaient, pour tout ce qui concerne la première moitié du XVIIe siècle, qu'il m'avait fallu au moins évoquer, sur les travaux autrement importants et nourris de MM. Busson, Adam, Pintard, etc., publiés à partir de 1933, sans parler de force études sur l'histoire des sciences (Mouy, Humbert, etc.), de la philosophie (Carré), ou du milieu social. Une mise à jour s'impose, que des événements indépendants de ma volonté m'ont empêché d'entreprendre à partir de 1939. Je ne puis que décrire sommairement le système d'idées, de faits et de textes que j'avais tant bien que mal édifié à cette date et qui est resté à peu près tel quel, c'est-à-dire inachevé et incomplet.

*
**

III. — A première vue, on s'expliquerait mieux que le conte merveilleux soit apparu au moment où le système démonologique, héritier des diverses mythologies, était le seul qui permit d'expliquer les phénomènes « *supra ordinem naturae* », où son autorité n'était pas contestée. Mais il était depuis longtemps battu en brèche par un nouveau mode d'explication et un nombre croissant d'esprits cultivés, dédaignant l'interprétation mythologique (volonté d'un être doué de pouvoirs surhumains) se ralliaient à la conception de l'univers dans laquelle le merveilleux apparent se ramène à un mécanisme matériel.

Les démonologues avaient triomphé des cabalistes avec l'aide d'alliés fort dangereux, les physiciens. Le rôle de ceux-ci avait d'abord été de substituer à l'art de capter la bienveillance des génies une « magie naturelle », fondée sur la connaissance des propriétés occultes des choses, sur la sympathie des diverses parties de l'univers, sur les influences secrètes et le pouvoir de l'imagination. Il y avait en un sens progrès, mais le mystère continuait à planer sur l'étendue des pouvoirs de cette « Nature » et, en fait, tout était « possible ». Soit un phénomène insolite, comme l'envoûtement, mort d'une personne dont on perce l'image d'une épingle : le cabaliste dira : « C'est la volonté d'un génie dont nous nous sommes assuré le concours qui la tue » ; le démonologue dira : « C'est le démon » ; « C'est, dira l'occultiste, la vertu occulte d'un astre, ou d'un objet, ou d'une idée homicide. » Ces trois explications n'ont pas besoin d'établir un rapport de contiguïté matérielle entre l'aiguille et le corps du patient. Mais il y en a une quatrième qui consiste à affirmer que ce rapport existe, *quoique invisible*, et que tout se justifie, y compris l'inexpliqué, par des contiguïtés matérielles.

9

Or, cette interprétation est commune, à des degrés divers, à trois philosophies : l'une, l'aristotélisme, ou, du moins, une certaine variété d'aristotélisme, joue au xviiᵉ siècle un rôle de plus en plus effacé ; les deux autres sont l'atomisme épicurien, restauré et réhabilité par Gassendi, et le dualisme cartésien. Des notions comme celles de corpuscules, émanations, pores, matière subtile, que l'on retrouve dans ces deux physiques, permettent d'imaginer un mécanisme reliant l'aiguille de l'envoûteur à la personne de l'envoûté. L'explication vague des occultistes est périmée, celle du pouvoir démoniaque superflue.

Mais cette physique corpusculaire ne nous fournit que des schémas hypothétiques : le développement de l'esprit expérimental va procurer aux savants les moyens de vérifier ces mécanismes secrets. Il débute par la simple « curiosité », devient systématique avec les méthodes baconiennes de la recherche scientifique, vulgarise ses résultats avec les Académies, les journaux, les démonstrations publiques et exerce, par l'invention d'instruments sensationnels, une influence profonde sur l'opinion. Les phénomènes dits merveilleux sont naturellement les premiers auxquels s'applique la « nouvelle physique ». J'en ai trouvé force exemples, dont le plus célèbre est l'histoire, en 1692, de la baguette divinatoire de Jacques Eymar. Par ailleurs, les études sur les « possessions », entre autres, attestent l'extension des théories corpusculaires dans le domaine de la pathologie. Le mystérieux « pouvoir de l'imagination », si controversé, se ramène à l'action des « humeurs » et le démon n'intervient plus dans ce que l'on commence à appeler des « maladies » mentales.

IV. — Toutefois, la physique mécaniste n'exclut pas la crédulité. Elles font, en réalité, fort bon ménage, les physiciens eux-mêmes admettant l'existence de manifestations surnaturelles autorisées par la Providence, œuvre des Saints ou des Démons. Il n'y a pas conflit entre science et religion, mais un choix à faire, dans chaque cas particulier, entre deux explications également satisfaisantes : naturelle ou surnaturelle, matérialiste ou mythologique.

A priori, les sceptiques et libertins, toujours actifs, inclinent vers la première. Leur opposition est particulièrement vive en ce qui concerne la sorcellerie et les possessions, leurs grands chevaux de bataille. Mais ils ne nous apportent guère que des motifs de suspicion, nous invitent à douter, à suspendre notre jugement. Il en sera autrement lorsque la « nouvelle logique », l'art de bien conduire son esprit dans la recherche de la vérité, aura établi les règles qui permettent de distinguer avec assurance le vrai et le faux. Ce critérium de l'évidence rationnelle s'appliquera aussi bien dans les polémiques confessionnelles entre catholiques et réformés que dans les discussions entre clercs et laïques. Toute religion se piquera d'être « éclairée » et ses propres ministres s'attacheront à la séparer de la « superstition ». Ce souci est déjà très apparent au milieu du xviiᵉ siècle et l'on peut, dès 1670, parler d'un « rationalisme ecclésiastique », dont Malebranche posera les fondements dogmatiques. Ses premières victimes seront les légendes hagiographiques d'une part, les histoires de sorciers et de revenants, de l'autre. On se persuade de plus en plus qu'avant d'attribuer à Dieu ou au Diable la responsabilité d'un prodige, il faut prouver que ce prodige est conforme à une définition, répond à certaines conditions. Personne n'osait affirmer de tel miracle qu'il fut impossible ; désormais on pourra dire que ceux du Saint-Nombril de Chalons ou du Chevalier de Saint-Hubert n'existent pas, car ils sont incompatibles avec les caractères évidents d'une intervention surnaturelle.

V. — Pourtant, un fait est un fait. Sur un récit cohérent, conforme à l'idée que l'Eglise nous propose de la « sur-nature » et appuyé sur des témoignages, le rationalisme n'a plus prise. Après criblage, il reste une foule de merveilles historiquement authentifiées, dont le « *Sadducismus triumphatus* » de Glanvill, entre autres, dresse la longue liste.

C'est ici que va commencer le travail de la critique (Bayle et consorts), qui exténuera progressivement l'autorité du témoignage. Les fameuses controverses qui occupent le dernier tiers du XVIIᵉ siècle, sur l'origine des fables, sur les comètes, sur les oracles des anciens, sur les devins, prophètes et inspirés, m'ont permis de mettre en lumière cette démarche particulière de l'esprit d'incrédulité, qu'il ne faut pas confondre avec le « scientisme » et le « rationalisme ». Mais elle aussi s'arrête devant un obstacle en apparence infranchissable, une autorité sacrée, celle de l'Ecriture. Les pouvoirs des Anges et des Démons sont articles de foi, illustrés par la Bible et l'Evangile. Les règles de la critique du témoignage, valables contre des témoins humains, ne s'appliquent pas à la révélation.

VI. — Qu'à cela ne tienne ! Cet obstacle, on le tournera ; on élaguera et l'on interprètera la révélation ; la critique biblique des Richard Simon, des Spinoza, des Van Dale, met à rude épreuve les prodiges de l'Ancien Testament. Un protestant de Hollande, Balthazar Bekker, s'en prend directement à Satan et dans un gros livre qui constitue la Somme du merveilleux démonologique, « Le monde enchanté », en vient à douter, sinon de son existence, du moins de son intervention dans les affaires de ce monde. Nous touchons avec Tolland, Collins, Shaftesbury, au seuil de la religion « naturelle », qui ravalera la mythologie chrétienne au rang des « fables », produit de l'esprit humain. En attendant, on discute ferme sur les magiciens de Pharaon, le passage de la Mer Rouge, l'histoire de Tobie et la baleine de Jonas... le Parlement continue à juger les sorciers... Thomasius à les défendre... Et nous voici au terme de la « Sixième partie » du manuscrit que j'ai sous les yeux, dont les trois derniers chapitres restaient à rédiger lorsque, en 1939, je fus appelé à d'autres occupations.

*
**

Cette « rallonge » démesurée (800 pages !), indépendamment de l'intérêt qu'elle peut présenter pour les amateurs de perspectives idéologiques, prouve au moins aux historiens de la littérature que le merveilleux est, à l'époque classique, quelque chose d'actuel, d'une actualité comparable à celle que revêt, par exemple, de nos jours, la question sociale, ou celle de la valeur du progrès technique. On le retrouve partout, dans les domaines de l'activité intellectuelle en apparence les plus éloignés. Des associations d'idées invincibles rattachent l'histoire de Cendrillon aux faits-divers relatés par le Mercure, aux comptes rendus du Journal des Savants, aux dissertations des gazettes de Hollande, à des centaines de lourds in-quarto. Une matière très grave alimente ces contes frivoles, qui reposent sur des substructures sociales massives.

Mais leur légèreté trahit l'effritement de ces fondations. Lorsque les hommes de lettres commencent à jouer avec des croyances, c'est qu'elles ont cessé d'être « tabou ». Les jeux de Perrault avec ses fées, ogres et chats bottés, coïncidant avec les progrès de l'incrédulité, avec l'indécision d'une opinion publique partagée, annoncent l'irrévérence de la société voltairienne. Le conte merveilleux classique, feu follet dansant à la surface d'une civilisation officiellement catholique, apostolique et romaine, est comme l'émanation littéraire de la décomposition qui s'opère dans les couches profondes d'une idéologie.

Acknowledgments

Hoak, Dale. "Art, Culture, and Mentality in Renaissance Society: The Meaning of Hans Baldung Grien's *Bewitched Groom* (1544)." *Renaissance Quarterly* 38 (1985): 488–510. Reprinted with the permission of The Renaissance Society of America. Courtesy of Yale University Sterling Memorial Library.

Bazin, Germain. "The Devil in Art." In Père Bruno de Jesus-Marie, ed., *Satan* (London: Sheed and Ward, 1951): 351–67. Courtesy of Yale University Medical Library.

Davidson, Jane P. "Great Black Goats and Evil Little Women: The Image of the Witch in Sixteenth-Century German Art." *Journal of the Rocky Mountain Medieval and Renaissance Society* 6 (1985): 141–57. Reprinted with the permission of the Rocky Mountain Medieval and Renaissance Society. Courtesy of Brian P. Levack.

Hoak, Dale. "Witch-Hunting and Women in the Art of the Renaissance." *History Today* 31 (1981): 22–6. Reprinted with the permission of History Today Ltd. Courtesy of *History Today*.

Bekker, Hugo. "The Lucifer Motif in the German Drama of the Sixteenth Century." *Monatshefte* 51 (1959): 237–47. Reprinted with the permission of the University of Wisconsin Press. Copyright 1959. Courtesy of Yale University Sterling Memorial Library.

DuBruck, Edelgard. "The Devil and Hell in Medieval French Drama: Prolegomena." *Romania* 100 (1979): 165–79. Reprinted with the permission of the Société des Amis de la Romania. Courtesy of Yale University Sterling Memorial Library.

Boatright, Mody C. "Witchcraft in the Novels of Sir Walter Scott." In *The University of Texas Bulletin No. 3326, Studies in English 13* (1933): 95–112. Courtesy of Yale University Sterling Memorial Library.

Bonnell, John K. "The Serpent with a Human Head in Art and in Mystery Play." *American Journal of Archaeology* 21 (1917): 255–91. Courtesy of Yale University Sterling Memorial Library.

Comensoli, Viviana. "Witchcraft and Domestic Tragedy in *The Witch of Edmonton.*" In Jean R. Brink, Allison P. Coudert and Maryanne C. Horowitz, eds., *The Politics of Gender in Early Modern Europe*, *Sixteenth Century Essays & Studies* 12 (1989): 43–59. Reprinted with the permission of Sixteenth Century Journal Publishers, Inc. Courtesy of Yale University Law Library.

Dustoor, P.E. "Legends of Lucifer in Early English and in Milton." *Anglia* 54 (1930): 213–68. Courtesy of Yale University Sterling Memorial Library.

Kelly, Henry Ansgar. "The Metamorphoses of the Eden Serpent during the Middle Ages and Renaissance." *Viator* 2 (1971): 301–27. Reprinted with the permission of the University of California Press. Copyright 1972 by the Regents of the University of California. Courtesy of Yale University Sterling Memorial Library.

Kocher, Paul H. "The Witchcraft Basis in Marlowe's *Faustus.*" *Modern Philology* 38 (1940): 9–36. Courtesy of Yale University Sterling Memorial Library.

Levin, David. "Salem Witchcraft in Recent Fiction and Drama." *New England Quarterly* 28 (1955): 537–46. Reprinted with the permission of the New England Quarterly Inc. Courtesy of Yale University Sterling Memorial Library.

Orians, G. Harrison. "New England Witchcraft in Fiction." *American Literature* 2 (1930): 54–71. Courtesy of Yale University Sterling Memorial Library.

Seiferth, Wolfgang S. "The Concept of the Devil and the Myth of the Pact in Literature Prior to Goethe." *Monatshefte* 44 (1952): 271–89. Reprinted with the permission of the University of Wisconsin Press. Copyright 1952. Courtesy of Yale University Sterling Memorial Library.

Bouvier, Emile. "La Croyance au Merveilleux à l'Époque Classique." In Daniel Mornet, ed., *Mélanges d'Histoire Littéraire* (Paris: Nizet, 1951): 99–108. Reprinted with the permission of Nizet. Courtesy of Nizet.